# Secure XML

# Secure XML

## The New Syntax for Signatures and Encryption

Donald E. Eastlake III

Kitty Niles

**♦♦ Addison-Wesley**

Boston • San Francisco • New York • Toronto • Montreal
London • Munich • Paris • Madrid
Capetown • Sydney • Tokyo • Singapore • Mexico City

Many of the designations used by manufacturers and sellers to distinguish their products are claimed as trademarks. Where those designations appear in this book, and Addison-Wesley was aware of a trademark claim, the designations have been printed with initial capital letters or in all capitals.

The authors and publisher have taken care in the preparation of this book, but make no expressed or implied warranty of any kind and assume no responsibility for errors or omissions. No liability is assumed for incidental or consequential damages in connection with or arising out of the use of the information or programs contained herein.

The publisher offers discounts on this book when ordered in quantity for bulk purchases and special sales. For more information, please contact:

U.S. Corporate and Government Sales
(800) 382-3419
corpsales@pearsontechgroup.com

For sales outside of the U.S., please contact:
International Sales
(317) 581-3793
international@pearsontechgroup.com

Visit Addison-Wesley on the Web: www.awprofessional.com

Library of Congress Cataloging-in-Publication Data

Eastlake, Donald.
    Secure XML : the new syntax for signatures and encryption / Donald E. Eastlake III, Kitty Niles.
          p.   cm.
    Includes bibliographical references and index.
    ISBN 0-201-75605-6
    1. XML (Document markup language)   2. Computer security.   3. Computer networks—Security measures.   4. Data encryption (Computer science)   I. Niles, Kitty.   II. Title.

QA76.9.A25 E32 2002
005.8—dc21

                                                                                2002066531

ISBN 0-201-75605-6
Text printed on recycled paper
1 2 3 4 5 6 7 8 9 10—MA—0605040302
First printing, July 2002

# Contents

# Detailed Contents

# Preface

This book explains the guts of XML Digital Signatures and XML Encryption. Along the way, it describes how you, as a designer, implementer, or evaluator of an XML application, can make use of these technologies. Using this book, a skilled reader can design and implement interoperable XML-based authentication and/or confidentiality mechanisms for his or her particular applications.

The Extensible Markup Language (XML) is rapidly becoming the new standard in application-level computer communications. As its use spreads, mechanisms to assure the authenticity and confidential communication of XML documents and messages become essential.

Material provided in this book minimizes needed prerequisite knowledge, although it requires general familiarity with computer concepts. For the reader not familiar with digital security or cryptology concepts, Part I includes a chapter covering these topics in the depth needed to understand the remainder of the book. For the reader not familiar with XML, Part II provides in-depth coverage of XML and related standards. This material provides not just the background needed for the rest of this book, but also enough general coverage that it should be helpful in understanding most XML applications and systems. Readers with sufficient knowledge in the areas covered can skip or skim this background material.

After providing the introductory and background material in Parts I and II, the book covers the topics of XML digital signatures, XML encryption, and XML canonicalization in depth. This discussion includes specific formats and examples and covers keying material, combined use of signatures and encryption, algorithms, and profiling of signature use for particular applications. If your interest lies only in XML digital signatures or XML encryption, you can skip the chapters associated with the other topic. Any nontrivial use of XML Security, however, will require some familiarity with XML canonicalization, keying information, and the relevant algorithms.

This book is firmly based on the official, adopted standards of the World Wide Web Consortium, Internet Engineering Task Force, and other relevant standards bodies when available. Additional material is based on the most recent drafts or informational documents available at the time of writing and the authors' personal knowledge and experiences.

In general, we present areas of XML Security by giving an informal syntax with a skeletal example, followed by the formal syntax and then by a number of more complete examples. The material is organized so that the formal syntax and complete examples can be read in either order.

Throughout the book, we include notes that might be of interest to the reader, where the authors either have some particular knowledge of the history involved or have some heretical opinion.

## Notations

This book uses some special typographical notations to represent, present, and set off special kinds of information. These notations are described below.

### Boxes

Throughout this book, you will find short sections of text set off in boxes. These come in three varieties: Note, History, and Soapbox.

#### Note

Items of particular **importance** are set off in Note boxes. Pay particularly close attention to such boxes when you encounter them.

#### History

The **historical** background and evolution of particular design decisions, terms, organizations, or policies are described in History boxes. Skipping them won't cause you to miss any technical content but you may find them illuminating.

#### Soapbox

Scattered throughout the book, these boxes consist of personal opinions and **heretical** comments. You can ignore them or, if you want, you can ignore the rest of the book and just read the Soapboxes.

The name "soapbox" for heretical ravings comes from the use of actual wooden crates that had previously been used to ship soap as makeshift platforms by street-corner speakers.

## Character Sequences and Code

Much of the discussion in this book needs to clearly specify character sequences and source code.

In cases where a character sequence is relatively short (sometimes only one character) and confusion seems unlikely, the sequence appears intermixed with normal text but surrounded with double curly quotes. For example, "foo" is the three-character sequence of an "f" followed by two "o" characters [RFC 3092]. In some cases, the name of the character is followed by the quoted character in parentheses. For example, this sentence contains a comma (",") and ends in a period ("."). For longer character sequences or in cases where clarity is particularly important, the characters are set off on a separate line or lines in a fixed-width font and highlighted:

```
foo
```

The only exceptions involve tabular contexts or a series of lines or paragraphs, each of which starts with a special character sequence. In those cases, the character sequence just appears in bold face.

Code is generally a larger character sequence intended for automated processing or a version of such a character sequence simplified for expository purposes, as in the skeletal XML given below. Code appears in the same way as longer character sequences but usually consists of multiple lines and may start with a one-line description followed by a blank line.

```
Code example:

Sections of code appear like this in a fixed-width font
so exact spacing and line breaks can be indicated.
   This line starts with three spaces.
```

In some cases, code has line numbers so that detailed comments in the text can be associated with particular lines. In such cases, "[Lnn] " has been added to the beginning of each line. The space after the closing bracket is part of the line numbering.

```
Line Numbered Code example:

[L30] <Line>
[L31] <Another>Line</Another>
```

```
      An unnumbered line within numbered lines.
[L32] </Line>
```

## References

In some cases, you may want to look up authoritative sources or more detailed explanations. These resources are indicated by a short label in square brackets ("[ ]"). For example, the reference to IETF Request for Comments number 3092 appeared earlier as [RFC 3092]. The References and Acronyms section lists these labels in alphabetic order and gives further information on the material.

## Skeletal XML

XML can quickly become quite complex, voluminous, and deeply nested, making the parts of importance to a discussion difficult to see because they are scattered like trees in a very large forest. In such cases, skeletal XML is used to give an abstracted overview. A statement in main text is used to indicate skeletal XML. In skeletal XML, the following rules apply:

1. A cardinality indicator character can suffix elements. (These suffixes are similar to those used in DTD, as described in Chapter 3.) In particular,

   ? means the preceding item appears 0 or 1 times.

   + means the preceding item appears 1 or more times.

   * means the preceding item appears 0 or more times.

2. Attributes may be completely omitted or appear with no value:

```
attribute=
```

   Attributes may also be followed by the cardinality indicator ("?") to indicate that they are optional.

3. The appearance of an element enclosed in parentheses instead of angle brackets, such as

```
(foo id=/)
```

   instead of

```
<foo id=value>content</foo>
```

indicates that the element's content has been omitted for the sake of simplicity.

4. Ellipses ("...") can appear where elements or levels of structure are omitted.

## Byte Objects

Character coding issues, octet sequence padding, and other issues related to byte objects are discussed in this book. To refer to specific eight-bit bytes by their binary values, such octets are written as two hexadecimal digits, preceded by the lowercase letter "x", and with all three characters underlined. For example, a zero byte is <u>x00</u>; a byte whose value is 87 decimal, which is the ASCII code for a capital "W", is <u>x57</u>; and a maximum-value byte (255 decimal) is <u>xFF</u>.

## Italics

*Italics* indicate variable descriptive terms that can be replaced by fixed real data values.

## Bold Face

**Bold face** indicates important text or code. It is also sometimes used for character objects that appear in tables or at the beginnings of a sequence of lines or paragraphs, as in the description of the cardinality characters in skeletal XML, and the names of functions when functions are being described.

## Acknowledgments

The authors would like to acknowledge the helpful comments and encouragement from the following: Mark Baker, Elaine Brennan, Jill Eastlake, Emily Frey, Karen Gettman, Ravi Gudiparti, Jill Hobbs, Hilarie Orman, Radia Perlman, Joseph Reagle, and Michael Rys.

We would also like to acknowledge the many persons to whose work, work in progress, or personal conversations we directly or indirectly referenced during the development of this book, particularly including the following: Mark Bartel, Ronald Bourret, John Boyer, Juan Carlos Cruellas, Blair Dillaway, Barbara Fox, Christian Geuer-Pollmann, Elliotte Harold, Paul Hoffman, Merlin Hughes, Takeshi Imamura, Gregor Karlinger, Charlie Kaufman, Brian LaMachia, Hiroshi Maruyama, Denis Pinkas, John Ross, Jim Schaad, Jeff Schiller, Bruce Schneier, Ed Simon, David Solo, Mike Speciner, and Kent Tamura. Marshall Rose is specially acknowledged for the term "Soapbox" as we use it in this book.

Finally, we want to acknowledge all the hard work of the many other members of the working groups and leadership involved in XML Security and this book at the IETF, the W3C, and Addison-Wesley Professional.

# Part I | Introduction

Part I of this book consists of two introductory chapters. Chapter 1 provides a high-level introduction to XML and the standards specifying it, and explains why someone would want to "secure" XML. Chapter 2 provides a general introduction to digital cryptography. If you are generally familiar with both XML and digital cryptography, you can skim these two chapters.

Part II covers XML basics in great depth but has very little discussion of XML Security.

Building on the earlier chapters, Part III covers authentication, including digital signatures, message authentication codes, and canonicalization.

Part IV discusses keying and the format of keying information for both XML authentication and confidentiality.

Part V goes into XML encryption, which is the way to obtain confidentiality, and considers issues that arise in combining authentication and confidentiality.

Finally, Part VI describes all of the algorithms, both cryptographic and non-cryptographic, that can be invoked by well-known names that are specified in the XML Security standards and related documents.

# 1 | XML and Security

The Extensible Markup Language (XML) is rapidly gaining ground in application-level network communications. As it becomes used for a wider range of purposes, the need to authenticate and maintain the confidentiality of XML grows ever stronger.

Chapter 1 provides a brief overview of XML, the security needs of XML, the current status of XML Security standardization, and ongoing work in XML Security.

## 1.1   XML

XML is an open-specification, platform-independent, extensible, and increasingly successful profile of the Standard Generalized Markup Language (SGML) [ISO 8879].

The World Wide Web Hypertext Markup Language (HTML) is also a profile of SGML. HTML markup is primarily concerned with the appearance of the material. In addition, HTML can translate some standard types of information into a specific format (appearance) by a particular browser [HTML]. In contrast, XML markup is primarily concerned with the user-extensible structure of the data [XML].

Among the basic goals of XML was to enable the serving, receiving, and processing of general information in a simplified manner on the Web in the same way that has been possible with HTML for display information. XML design goals include ease of implementation and the ability to use SGML tools with XML. The uses of XML go well beyond Web pages, however—to not just static documents, but general protocol messages between computer processes and general data storage within computers.

In many of its newly emerging roles, XML needs security. That is, it must be able to authenticate information and/or keep it confidential.

**History**

> The term "markup" has its origins in the publishing industry. In traditional publishing, markup happens after the writing is complete but before the book goes to typesetting. An editor annotates the text with handwritten instructions for the typesetter. These instructions, which specify the layout, are known as markup. Many contemporary word processing programs insert electronic markup automatically as the user creates the text.

### 1.1.1    Origins of XML

The World Wide Web Consortium [W3C] established the XML Working Group in 1996. The W3C is the lead organization for the development and maintenance of interoperable specifications for the content of the World Wide Web. Its membership includes representatives from universities, technical organizations, and industry. The consortium is responsible for the development of the XML 1.0 W3C Recommendation [XML] and has change control over XML. The XML working group was initially known as the SGML Editorial Review Board.

The Web originated as a way to publish scientific documents with HTML as its markup language. At that time, HTML had only a few dozen tags. Today, most of the billions of Web pages in existence continue to use HTML, but the Web has grown into a full-fledged interactive medium supporting such diverse applications as e-mail, electronic banking and commerce, sophisticated search engines, streaming video, voice interaction, and multicasting.

**Note**

> Because of its publishing and "markup language" background, XML uses the term "document" very liberally. Do not be surprised to see the term "document" when, in other computer contexts, you might see "message," "object," "PDU" (Protocol Data Unit), or the like.

HTML has grown, along with the expanding Web uses, to well beyond its initial design. The current version of HTML, version 4.1, is a complex language containing approximately 100 tags, and there has been pressure to add more. Additionally, the browser wars between Netscape Navigator and Microsoft Internet Explorer and side skirmishes with other browsers have littered the battlefield with inconsistencies and quirks.

Despite its phenomenal success, HTML has a number of shortcomings:

- HTML generally assumes that any additional tags will be standard and universally known, at least to browsers supporting that version or feature. No standard mechanism provides for private tag use between consenting parties.

- It takes many tags to format a page supporting current Web technologies. Downloading and displaying such a page can be time-consuming.

- Devices such as a Palm Pilot or smart phone are not as powerful as a modern PC. They can generally process standardized, well-formed HTML. Unfortunately, these devices cannot adequately process extended and malformed HTML or HTML with the embedded scripting languages that are in frequent use today. (Because it was a competitive advantage in the browser wars to try to do something reasonable with syntactically incorrect HTML, most browsers have such a "feature.")

- Adding more universal tags to an already burdened language might have less than satisfactory results. Some applications would benefit from having to know about fewer tags.

You can use XML to express a diverse range of information—for example, the contents of a letter or Web page or a generic piece of information such as a remote procedure call. The W3C Extensible Hypertext Markup Language (XHTML) Recommendation [XHTML] is an XML version of HTML. XHTML is a language for content that both conforms to XML and, by following some simple guidelines, operates in HTML 4-conforming user agents. XML addresses some of the shortcomings of HTML that were exposed by HTML's success. XML incorporates many features of HTML and introduces new possibilities. XML, however, does not attempt to replace HTML. The two will coexist for a long time.

## 1.1.2   XML Goals

The XML Recommendation [XML] specifies the following goals:

- XML should be usable over the Internet.

- XML should support a variety of applications—for example, authoring tools, filters, and translators.

- XML and SGML should be compatible. For example, SGML tools should be able to read and write XML data.

- Programs to process XML documents should be easy to write. Specifically, the committee wanted to make it possible for developers to create useful XML programs that did not depend on reading a Document Type Definition (DTD). (A DTD is an SGML standard way of profiling XML by syntax specification, which we discuss extensively in Chapter 4.)

- For compatibility between XML documents, optional features in XML are to be kept to a minimum, ideally zero.

- An XML document should be human-legible and clear. For example, an XML document should have a textual format rather than a binary format.

- The XML design should be ready quickly to provide open, nonproprietary, textual data formats to meet the Web's obvious need for extensibility [XML A].

- The design of XML should be formal and concise.

- XML documents should be easy to create.

- Terseness in XML markup is of minimal importance.

**Soapbox**

What is missing from this list? These goals never mention security! Security is best and most simply done when it is part of the original design, not when it is a later add-on. Thus it is not surprising that we will find difficulties and complexities in securing XML, particularly in the area of canonicalization (see Chapter 9).

Many of these goals have been achieved, to a greater or less degree. Some would say XML was particularly successful in not achieving terseness.

---

### 1.1.3   Advantages and Disadvantages of XML

XML, like most languages, has both advantages and disadvantages.

XML allows the creation of individual markup tags that you can tailor to describe the specific structure of one or more documents. There is no need to rely on a generic set of tags or to wait for standards organizations to adapt tags appropriate to specific applications, as with HTML. With XML, the needs of a specific industry can be met without imposing multiple industry-specific tags on everyone's browsers. In this area, XML offers greater flexibility than ASN.1 DER, for example, which typically requires precise and complete predefinition of a binary format. ([ASN.1] and [DER] provide a standard syntax and binary encoding intended for specifying protocols.)

XML tags can represent formatting rules, as is true with HTML. In addition, XML tags can represent data descriptions, data relationships, or even business rules.

Browser-oriented XML abstracts the presentation rules into separate documents, whereas HTML embeds much of the appearance within the data. For example, you might present information as a list or as a table. A decision to change the display later requires recoding documents in HTML; in XML, however, you could accomplish this goal by creating a different extensible style sheet. ASN.1 provides no such style sheet support. XML can carry arbitrary information, including structural and display information.

XML tags can be chosen to be self-describing, which makes messages and documents more readable. This technique can be used in only the most limited way with HTML and not at all in binary-encoded ASN.1. The text basis for XML and HTML also means that, while customized tools work better, you can manipulate these languages with any general text tools. By comparison, binary formats such as ASN.1 are painful to deal with and require special tools.

The major disadvantages of XML relate to its relative lack of automated processing libraries and its verbosity. However, code libraries and tools continue to improve in quality and availability and, for many applications, terseness is not important.

See Table 1-1 for a comparison of XML, HTML, and ASN.1.

**Table 1-1** | XML, HTML, and ASN.1

| Property | XML | HTML | ASN.1 |
|---|---|---|---|
| **Flexibility** | High | Low | Medium |
| **Human Readability** | High | Medium | Low |
| **Verbosity** | High | Medium-High | Low |
| **Presentation Support** | High | Medium | Low |

### 1.1.4　Uses of XML

XML is spreading rapidly. Some of its uses now include the following:

- Electronic commerce and banking, including business-to-consumer and business-to-business dealings
- Creation of new languages—for example, Voice Extensible Markup Language [VXML]
- Communications with handheld devices and smart phones
- Sharing and storing of data and information exchange between incompatible systems
- Inter- and intra-organization exchange of information
- Integration of data from multiple sources in a single display and rearrangement of data on the fly
- News or press releases where the content is available to multiple Web sites
- Development of scientific applications and profession-specific markup languages, such as music notation, chemical symbols and formulae, and mathematical notation
- Loading and unloading of databases
- Maintenance of large Web sites so that XML tools can be used to convert the data to the most appropriate format for the client, including formats adapted to disabled users
- Preservation of data in a human readable format
- Court filings [Georgia, New Mexico]
- Electronic books

## 1.2　The Need for Secure XML

Many XML uses today need security, particularly in terms of authentication and confidentiality. Consider commercial transactions. It should be clear why purchase orders, payments, delivery receipts, contracts, and the like need authentication. In many cases, particularly when the transaction involves multiple parties, different parts of a message need different kinds of authentication for different recipients. For example, the payment portion of an order from a customer to a merchant could be extracted and sent to a payment clearing system and then to the customer's bank. Likewise, court filings, press releases, and even personal messages need authentication as a protection against forgery.

Confidentiality is also important for many applications. Consider medical records. As with authentication, granularity below the document level is often required. For example, a company personnel record might include data, such as a phone number or address, which are generally available within the company, as well as performance or salary information, which is more highly restricted. In another example, a customer record might include a credit card number that is more sensitive than other data. By encrypting different fields with different keys, the fields can be secured to different classes of recipients.

Non-XML mechanisms can provide security. For example, you can obtain confidentiality and authentication by using Pretty Good Privacy (PGP) [RFC 2440] or Secure Multipurpose Internet Mail Extensions (S/MIME) [RFC 2633] binary formats. Their use, however, requires the addition of non-XML mechanisms that may have different concepts of user identity or otherwise clash with XML systems.

For point-to-point security between a sender and receiver, you can use mechanisms such as a Transport Layer Security (TLS) [RFC 2246], Secure Sockets Layer (SSL), or IP Security (IPSEC) [RFC 2401] secure channels. Unfortunately, they can provide only one level of confidentiality for all material sent through that channel and have limited authentication provisions. After data that pass through such a secure channel are stored, the data typically

- Are not associated with any authentication from that channel that could be forwarded to or recognized by a third party,

- Have no integrity protection, and

- Have no confidentiality because it was all decrypted as it exited the tunnel.

Increasingly, for simplicity and flexibility reasons, users desire to work with all-XML systems using XML security mechanisms. Such security mechanisms can support the authentication and confidentiality of documents and portions of documents in a general and powerful way.

## 1.3    Status of XML Security Standardization

As this book goes to print, various components of XML Security are at various stages in the standardization process.

Canonical XML [Canon] (see Chapter 9) became a full World Wide Web Consortium Recommendation in 2001 and has been published by the Internet Engineering Task Force (IETF) as an Informational RFC. XML Digital Signature [XMLDSIG], which provides authentication (see Chapter 10), is a full Recommendation in the W3C and a Draft Standard in the IETF. These rungs on the standardization ladder indicate that the standard has reached a level of stability for which implementation and operational deployment are reasonable.

XML Encryption [XMLENC], which provides confidentiality, and Exclusive XML Canonicalization [Exclusive] are W3C Candidate Recommendations. The probability of major or incompatible changes with these recommendations is not high. See Chapters 9 and 15.

## 1.4    Work in Progress

Work has been done and continues to progress on higher-level structures built on XML Security. The following efforts are covered in this book:

- The XML Key Management Specification [XKMS] is the focus of a W3C working group [XKMS WG]. An overview of version 1.0 appears in Chapter 14.

- "Advanced" XML Signatures [XAdES], which meet certain government directives for trust, are under development in [ETSI]. An overview of a draft appears in Chapter 12.

- The Decryption Transform for XML Signature [Decrypt] is currently a W3C Working Draft in the XML Encryption Working Group [XMLENC WG]; it is covered in Chapter 16. (It is designed to help a signature verifier figure out which parts of the signed data were encrypted before and after signature creation.)

- Although not directly related to XML Security, work continues in the W3C on the refinement of SOAP. See Chapter 8.

In addition, some higher-level trust work is not covered in this book:

- XACML, eXtensible Access Control Markup Language, under development by the Organization for the Advancement of Structured Information Standards (OASIS) consortium [OASIS]

- SAML, Security Assertion Markup Language, under development by the OASIS consortium [OASIS, Vtrust], which combines previous S2ML and AuthXML efforts

- XTASS, XML Trust Assertion Service Specification, which was merged in S2ML

**Soapbox**

Some of the earlier higher-level trust-related XML proposals were released early to block "boxing" patents. Because it is so simple to obtain patents on obvious and trivial extensions to published ideas, it is frequently a good idea to put out documentation on extensions to such ideas. Otherwise, you can find yourself boxed in by some company with more legal clout than technical expertise.

# 2 | Digital Cryptography Basics

This chapter introduces the basic building blocks of modern digital cryptography, describes what they can do for you, and explains how to compose them to produce useful and practical secure services.

If you are familiar with these basics, you can probably skip this chapter. Good general references in this area are [NetSec] and [Schneier]. This chapter—and indeed this book—do not generally get down to the details of bit-level formats or algorithms. That is, they do not provide enough information for you to implement the cryptographic algorithms mentioned. Nevertheless, this chapter should provide a foundation of knowledge about modern digital cryptography that will make later chapters more comprehensible.

Sections 2.1, 2.2, and 2.3 generally discuss "symmetric" functions where the originator and receiver compute the same quantity or use the same secret key. Sections 2.4, 2.5, and 2.6 focus on "asymmetric" functions involving a public-private key pair. The remaining sections (2.7–2.11) discuss a variety of other important aspects of basic digital cryptography.

## 2.1 Message Digests

Message digest functions convert sequences of bits, possibly quite long, called messages, into fixed-length binary "fingerprints" or message digests of the original sequences. See Figure 2-1. A message digest function has two goals:

- It should be computationally infeasible to find another message whose digest is the same as the digest of a given message.

- It should be computationally infeasible to find two arbitrary messages whose digests are the same.

In the common case where an authentication method takes a large amount of computational effort and that effort is proportional to the number of bits

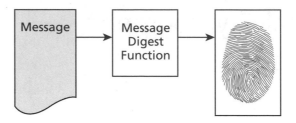

**Figure 2-1** | Message digest function

being authenticated, you can secure a large document by authenticating its much smaller fixed-size message digest.

A message digest function is not identical to a checksum. A checksum is usually quite simple and is designed to detect transmission errors or accidental changes. An adversary can deliberately circumvent the testing of a checksum by adjusting the message to leave the checksum unchanged. By comparison, a message digest is complex and is designed to defeat attempts by an adversary to change the message.

First, consider a checksum calculated by simply adding all octets in a message and discarding the bits of the sum above the least significant eight bits. In most cases, an adversary could easily modify the message to become a different message with the same checksum. For example, inserting an octet with value V into the message will have no effect on the checksum if you can also insert a second octet with value $(256 - V)$ anywhere in the message.

Next, consider a more complex function in which you take the product of the octets in the message, adding to each octet its position in the message, and the check octet is the middle eight bits of this product. For example, if the message consists of bytes with values

$$V_1, V_2, V_3, \ldots$$

then the check octet is the middle eight bits of

$$(V_1 + 1) * (V_2 + 2) * (V_3 + 3) \ldots$$

With this level of complexity, it is no longer quite so trivial for an adversary to figure out how to change the message without changing the check byte, although it can still be done. Cryptographically or computationally secure message digest functions are substantially more complex than this example, producing check quantities of at least 128 bits or 16 eight-bit bytes. They largely meet the following goals.

Expressing the goals of message digests more formally, if the message digest is N bits, then

1. To find a second message with the same message digest as a given message, no method should require an expected effort significantly less than trying $2^{N-1}$ possible other messages;

2. To find two arbitrary messages with the same message digest, no method should require an expected effort significantly less than trying $2^{N/2}$ messages, remembering all their digests, and looking for a match.

Like other modern digital cryptographic functions, message digest functions are typically used and sometimes defined only for integer numbers of octets, rather than arbitrary numbers of bits.

## 2.2    Message Authentication Codes

A message authentication code (MAC) function computes a MAC from a message and a secret key. If the originator and the receiver share knowledge of that secret key, the receiver can calculate the same function of the message and secret key and see if it matches the MAC accompanying the message. See Figure 2-2. If the MAC matches, then you know, within the strength of the MAC function and key, that some program with possession of the secret produced the MAC. Of course, every program that can verify the MAC needs to know this secret. Thus all of them can create valid MACs even if they should only receive and verify these codes.

A simple MAC function might append the secret to the message, then calculate a message digest of the result and use it as the MAC. The message (without the secret) and MAC could then be sent to the recipient. The recipient would also append the secret (which the receiver needs to know as well) to the message and calculate the same message digest function. If the resulting digest matches the MAC, it validates the message.

MACs are normally based on a message digest code; however, the simple technique suggested previously has subtle weaknesses that are beyond the scope of this book. Better, stronger MAC functions exist. All of the MAC functions discussed in this book (see Chapter 18) are based on the provable "security" HMAC [RFC 2104] method of combining a message, secret quantity, and message digest function to produce a MAC. [Schneier] documents other strong MAC functions as well.

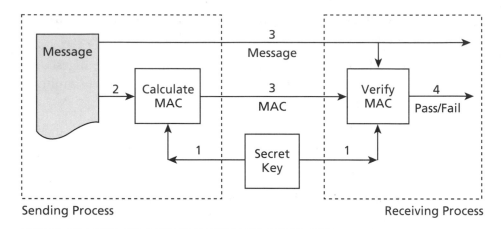

1. Distribute the secret key. Done in advance by secure channels.
2. Sender calculates the MAC of the message and the key.
3. Transmit the message and MAC to the receiver.
4. Receiver calculates the MAC using the message and key, compares it with the transmitted MAC, and judges the integrity of the transmission.

**Figure 2-2** │ Message authentication codes

A difficulty with MAC authentication in a system with multiple originators and receivers is that you must choose between two strategies, both of which have problems:

1. Have a different secret for every pair of entities. This method is logistically difficult because the number of keys increases with the square of the number of entities and the keys must be securely distributed. If the system includes E number of entities, you have $E*(E - 1)/2$ pairs. For example, for 100 entities, you have 4950 pairs. For 1000 entities, you have 499,500 pairs.

2. Share one secret among all the entities. This technique is relatively insecure. The more entities that have a secret, the more likely the secret is to be compromised due to loss, subversion, or betrayal. This technique also means the same secret will be used many times; the more exposures of the uses of a secret, the easier an adversary may find it to break that secret analytically. In addition, with this strategy any of the entities can forge messages from any of the other entities and a recipient will be unable to detect this fraud based on the MAC.

Digital signatures, as described in Section 2.6, are an operationally superior method of authentication in many circumstances.

As with message digest functions, if a strong MAC is N bits long, the difficulty of finding two messages with the same MAC is proportional to $2^{N/2}$. You should pick N large enough for your application and then, to avoid the secret quantity being the weak point, use a secret quantity that is random (see Section 2.10) and at least N/2 bits long. For example, if you need a 160-bit MAC, the secret key should be at least 80 random bits.

## 2.3    Secret or Symmetric Key Ciphers

Secret key ciphers have been known for centuries, although the oldest were weak and had no key. Today's modern ciphers involve a reversible data scrambling system such that it is computationally infeasible to recover the unscrambled data without knowledge of the secret key used to scramble that data. See Figure 2-3. The original version is called the plain text; the scrambled version is called the cipher text.

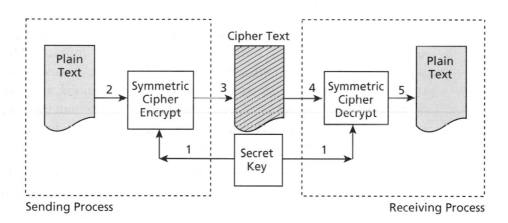

1. Distribute the secret key. Done in advance by secure channels.
2. Feed plain text into the symmetric cipher to encrypt it under the key.
3. Store or transmit the cipher text.
4. Retrieve or receive the cipher text, and feed it into the symmetric cipher algorithm to decrypt it under the key.
5. The result should be the original plain text.

**Figure 2-3**  |  Secret key encryption

Perhaps the best-known symmetric cipher is the Data Encryption Standard (DES [FIPS 186-2]). With 56 bits of actual key and a number of weaknesses, DES is not considered strong by current standards. In addition, it was designed for hardware efficiency, not software efficiency. Triple DES is a popular stronger symmetric cipher consisting of three applications of DES with different keys. Of course, it is also three times slower than DES.

Recently, NIST (see Appendix D) ran an extensive public process to select a successor to DES. They eventually chose the submission called Rijndael, now known as the Advanced Encryption Standard (AES [FIPS 197]). This encryption method has three variations with different key sizes and strengths. AES is generally believed, even in its weakest variation, to be stronger than Triple DES and faster in software than DES.

For an ideal symmetric cipher with an N-bit key, no method should be able to find the plain text with an expected effort significantly less than trying $2^{N-1}$ key values. In reality, symmetric ciphers often fall short of this ideal. That is, although they have an N-bit key, due to some systematic weakness, there is some technique to crack the code with less expected effort than trying $2^{N-1}$ key values. As long as the weaknesses are known and the cipher remains strong enough, this shortcoming is acceptable.

Symmetric ciphers among multiple entities have the same security problems as message authentication codes. It may be logistically impractical to have a separate secret key pair between all pairs of entities and insecure for all of them to share the same secret key. "Enveloped encryption," as discussed in Section 2.8, may represent a superior alternative. If the system includes a centralized trusted server, it is also possible to use a secret key distribution system such as [Kerberos]. Kerberos is not covered in this book.

In real systems, further complexities arise. Many symmetric ciphers are "block ciphers" that work on blocks of data significantly larger than an eight-bit byte or octet. Thus they commonly require a "padding" method to match the data to an exact multiple of the block size before encryption and a corresponding unpadding after decryption. In addition, algorithms can be used in a variety of "modes," such as "electronic codebook mode," "cipher feedback chaining mode," and "output feedback chaining mode." See [Schneier], [FIPS 46-3, FIPS 81], or similar references for information on these topics. For the particular block cipher algorithms described in Chapter 18, the chaining and padding methods are described or referenced there.

## 2.4   Public or Asymmetric Key Ciphers

"Public" key ciphers rely on the recent (a few decades old) discovery of encryption functions with the following characteristics:

1. A different key is needed to decrypt information than the key used to encrypt it. See Figure 2-4.

2. It is computationally infeasible to determine the decryption key from the encryption key.

3. Knowing the encryption key offers no help in decryption. Knowing the decryption key offers no help in encryption.

This set of characteristics dramatically changes the security model in comparison with secret key ciphers. Some application that wants to receive confidential messages could advertise a "public" encryption key to the world,

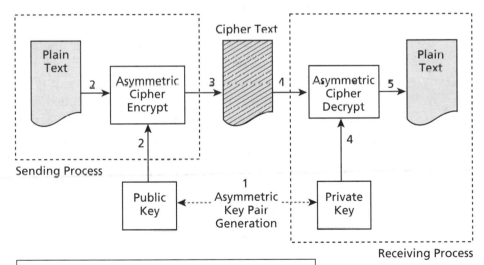

1. Secure generation of the public/private key pair, probably performed by the receiver, and distribution of the public key.
2. Encrypt the plain text under the public key.
3. Transmit or store the cipher text.
4. Receive or retrieve the cipher text and decrypt it using the private key.
5. The result should be the original plain text.

**Figure 2-4** | Public key encryption

while retaining and keeping secret the private decryption key. Senders would encrypt the data under this public encryption key. Only the intended recipient, who has the private decryption key, can then read it.

This cipher eliminates the problems associated with securely distributing symmetric keys among many entities in a large system. Only one public-private key pair is required for each entity and purpose because everyone can safely know all of the public keys. Unfortunately, two new problems arise with this technique:

1. Asymmetric encryption algorithms tend to be very slow. Thus, if the user sends a large confidential message, it may be prohibitive to encrypt all of the data with a public key algorithm. This problem is solved with "enveloped encryption" (see Section 2.8).

2. It becomes critical to determine whether you are using the right public key. If an adversary can convince you to use the adversary's public encryption key, instead of the public key for the intended recipient, then the adversary can decrypt your message. Remember this individual has the private decryption key corresponding to his or her own public key. After reading your secret message, the adversary may even be able to re-encrypt it with the intended recipient's public encryption key and forward it to the intended recipient. You and the intended recipient would never realize that the message had been compromised. Certificates address this problem of trust in public keys (see Section 2.7).

Real-world use of asymmetric ciphers also requires padding methods because asymmetric ciphers usually operate on a block of data whose size may depend on the key size. For the specific asymmetric algorithms described in Chapter 18, the padding method is described or referenced there.

## 2.5    Asymmetric Keys and Authentication

Asymmetric authentication algorithms also change the security model for signatures compared with message authentication codes. A program originating data that it wants to authenticate can send, along with that data, the same data transformed under a private key and make known the corresponding public key. (Note: Which key is public and which is private is the reverse of the confidentiality case mentioned earlier.) Then, anyone with access to the sender's public key can verify the message using the plain text and transformed text, and determine that it comes from the sender—only the sender should have the necessary private key. This technique solves the two problems mentioned in Section 2.2 for MAC symmetric key distribution, but brings the same two new problems listed in Section 2.4, efficiency and public key trust, for public key confidentiality.

Section 2.6 on digital signatures discusses ways to handle the issue of asymmetric cipher algorithm efficiency. Section 2.7 describes the use of certificates to address the critical problem of determining which public key to use.

N-bit asymmetric keys for asymmetric algorithms are usually much weaker than the corresponding-size keys for symmetric algorithms. For example, a 2400-bit asymmetric RSA key is generally considered to only be as strong as a 112-bit triple DES symmetric cipher key [Orman] while a 112-bit asymmetric key would, for many asymmetric algorithms, be quite weak. This issue does not create a problem as long as you use large enough asymmetric keys to compensate.

---

## 2.6     Digital Signatures

You can use public key authentication to produce "digital signatures." These signatures have a very desirable characteristic—namely, it is computationally infeasible for anyone without the private key to produce a signature that will verify for a given message. Modern digital signatures consist of (1) a message and (2) a message digest of that message asymmetrically transformed under a private key of the signer. See Figure 2-5.

Because message digests are short, fixed-length quantities, the slowness of public key algorithms has minimal effects on processing. The critical need to be sure you are using the right public key still exists, however, and is usually addressed by certificates.

Real digital signature systems have many more complexities than this brief description suggests. The actual quantity being secured by asymmetric transformation under a private key typically includes not just the critical message digest value, but also two other items:

- Identification of the message digest function

- Possibly other information such as date signed or key identifier

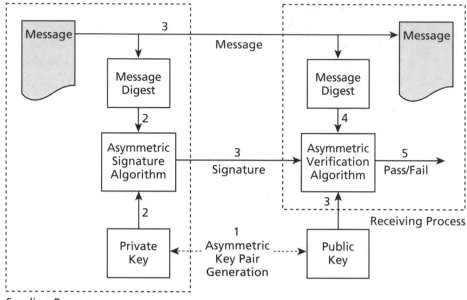

Sending Process

1. Secure generation of the public/private key pair, probably performed by the sender, and distribution of the public key.
2. Calculate the message digest of the message and encrypt it under the private key.
3. Transmit the message and the transformed digest, known as the signature, to the receiver.
4. Calculate the new message digest of the received message.
5. Verify the signature and produce a pass/fail result.

**Figure 2-5** | Digital signatures

This information is formatted so that a signature verifier can parse it. The verifier uses the asymmetric algorithm, public key, and material transformed under the private key (including the message digest value, which it computes over the plain text) to verify that the corresponding private key signed it. In addition, the overall signed message must use some known format so that the system can separate the signature and possibly key identification information from the signed message information.

## 2.7 Certificates

Certificates offer a way of providing assurance about a public key. In general, they consist of the following components:

- The public key
- Some associated information such as an identity or access authorization
- A date of issuance and expiration
- An authenticating digital signature by a "certification authority" over this information

Anyone knowing and trusting the public key of this "authority" and having the certificate can have confidence that the public key inside the certificate is associated with the identity or should have the access indicated. See Figure 2-6.

This verification can be continued through a "chain" of certificates. Cert-1 signed by entity-1 can provide trust in the public key of entity-2, whose private key can then be used to sign Cert-2, which provides trust in the public key of entity-3, whose private key can be used to sign Cert-3, and so on. If one or only a few globally known and trusted public keys exist, a hierarchical model results, as shown in Figure 2-7. Top-level certification authorities control the private keys corresponding to these top-level or "root" public keys.

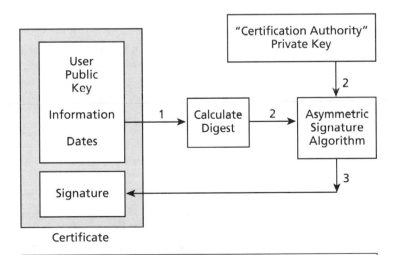

**Figure 2-6** | Certificate

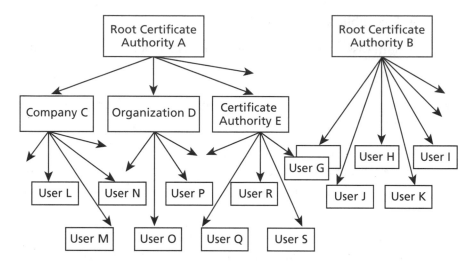

**Figure 2-7** | Certificate hierarchies

These authorities sign certificates for lower-level certification authorities, possibly through several levels, ending with bottom-level "user" certificates.

The alternative to this hierarchical model is a mesh model, as shown in Figure 2-8. With a mesh, various entities sign one another's certificates. A user can then start from a few trusted public keys and, subject to any criterion desired, chain through available certificates to gain trust in other public keys.

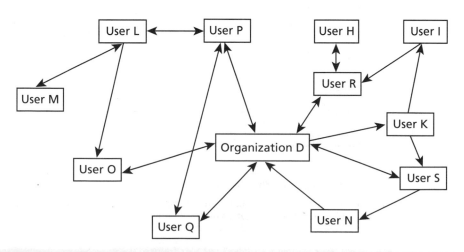

**Figure 2-8** | A certificate mesh

The most common type of certificates are X.509v3 [ISO 9594] certificates. Derived from the OSI X.500 Directory standard, they were originally intended to authenticate update authority and the like on the hypothetical global X.500 directory. The original X.509 certificates bound a public key to an X.500 identity. X.509v3 (version 3) generalizes X.509 certificates in various ways to allow for other types of more reasonable identities (such as e-mail and IP addresses) and extensions.

**Soapbox**

> X.500 identities are baroque hierarchical names, in which each level of the hierarchy consists of an arbitrary, unordered set of attribute–value pairs. They are just one of the complexities and false assumptions (such as the assumption that everyone would allow themselves to be listed in one global public directory, including companies listing all their employees) that doomed the X.500 Directory as originally conceived.

In theory, you can have an X.509v3 mesh. In fact, such certificates are normally used in a hierarchical mode. A common root is a commercial certification authority. An intermediate-level certification authority might be a company that obtained a certificate from a root and then issued certificates to its employees. All X.509 certificates and X.500 names appear in the binary ASN.1 BER or DER encoding. While it might seem odd to use such binary non-XML complexities to support XML Security, most of the existing public key infrastructures and commercial certification authorities work with X.509v3 so it is convenient to be able to use such certificates in XML Security.

Other types of certificates exist as well. Pretty Good Privacy [RFC 2440] has its own certificates that are almost always used in a mesh, although they can be employed hierarchically. A recent attempt to develop simpler standard certificates in the Internet Engineering Task Force (IETF) produced the Simplified Public Key Infrastructure (SPKI) certification system [RFC 2693]. Many people had hoped that SPKI (pronounced "spooky") would provide a greatly simplified and rationalized direct replacement for X.509v3. Instead, SPKI, while simple, made some radical changes. As a result, it has seen only limited deployment.

### Certificate Revocation Lists

Compromised private keys really do happen. For example, a private key owner may accidentally release the key or someone may steal, guess, or compute a copy of the private key and erroneously issue certificates. In this case, a certification authority issues a certificate for the wrong entity. In theory, the problem of compromised private keys or erroneously issued certificates is handled by a "revocation" mechanism. Whoever signed the original certificate signs and distributes a revocation of that certificate. In reality, such revocation systems require communication from the revoking entity to the entity trusting the certificate, and an adversary can block that communication.

To provide revocation, X.509 defines a certificate revocation list (CRL) structure. This structure is dated and carries a version number. It lists revoked certificates as of that date and time from a particular certificate issuer (except for certificates that have already expired). It also gives a date before or at which the next CRL version will be issued. Thus, for example, if you receive a signature that you trust based on a chain of certificates, you should get CRLs for all issuers in the chain. Furthermore, for any issuers for which you have only a CRL issued before the signature date, you should wait until the next CRL to see whether the certificate becomes revoked. This system is not terribly convenient, so most implementations, including the most popular browsers, ignore certificate revocation and CRLs entirely.

**History**

In January 2001, Verisign, Inc., the largest commercial certification authority, issued two of its highest-assurance-level X.509v3 certificates to some person or persons unknown who impersonated Microsoft Corporation. Thus, unless they took special precautions or obtained and followed Verisign's relevant CRL, anyone who trusted Verisign would trust these imposters to speak for Microsoft.

### Online Certificate Status Protocols

Certificates were designed in a time when offline verification was virtually the norm. With modern, always-connected technology, it should be possible to dispense with the entire certificate structure and ask a trusted online server to provide or verify trust in a key. (See Chapter 14 for a proposed XML way of achieving this goal.)

The Online Certificate Status Protocol (OCSP) represents a halfway step toward this end. It eliminates CRLs by utilizing a trusted online server to indicate whether a given certificate submitted to it remains valid [RFC 2560]. A client of such a server would have to know and trust the public key of that server. But, because such servers shield the client from complexity, the client probably needs to know only the key for one server. That server can then contact others on behalf of the client, if necessary, and forward any responses, providing its own signature to authenticate them.

For some systems (see Chapter 12), a signature may be more easily enforceable if you have checked and saved "proof" that all certificates you used to verify the signature were valid at the time. The trusted server signs and dates OCSP responses, which can be saved like CRLs.

## 2.8    Enveloped Encryption

Modern public key encryption systems that encrypt arbitrary-size messages use a combination of secret key and public key ciphers. Stated more precisely, they generate a random symmetric key to encrypt each message and then encrypt that key with a public encryption key of the intended recipient. The symmetrically encrypted message is then sent along with the asymmetrically encrypted random key. See Figure 2-9.

This type of encryption takes advantage of the more efficient symmetric cipher, avoiding the problem of the slowness of public key systems for large messages, while still gaining the more convenient key distribution model of public key cryptography. Of course, you must still ensure that you are really using the public key of the intended recipient of the encrypted messages, an issue that is commonly addressed through certificates.

If a message is sent confidentially to more than one recipient, the sender can transmit separate enveloped encryptions to each one. More commonly, senders create one enveloped encryption employing only one cipher text and symmetric key. That symmetric key then appears several times encrypted under a public encryption key of each intended recipient. These public keys need not be the same size or even use the same public key algorithm. Intended recipients use their own private keys to decrypt the appropriate public key encrypted copy of the symmetric key. They can then use the symmetric key to decrypt the confidential information.

Enveloped encryption does not authenticate the message's originator. If that service is desired, it is usually combined with a digital signature (Section 2.6). Such a digital signature can appear either inside or outside the encryption (or you can use two signatures, one in each place).

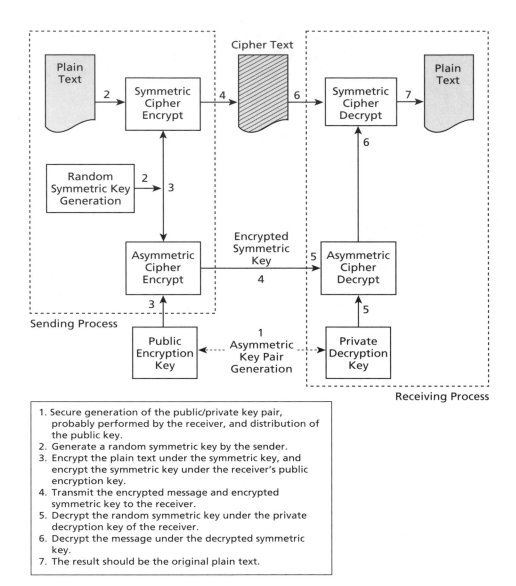

1. Secure generation of the public/private key pair, probably performed by the receiver, and distribution of the public key.
2. Generate a random symmetric key by the sender.
3. Encrypt the plain text under the symmetric key, and encrypt the symmetric key under the receiver's public encryption key.
4. Transmit the encrypted message and encrypted symmetric key to the receiver.
5. Decrypt the random symmetric key under the private decryption key of the receiver.
6. Decrypt the message under the decrypted symmetric key.
7. The result should be the original plain text.

**Figure 2-9** | Enveloped encryption

"Outside the encryption" means that the signature appears over the entire enveloped encryption structure and the signature takes the form of plain text. As a consequence, the recipient can first test the signature before decrypting the message. Depending on the exact presentation of the keying information for the signature, this process can also reveal the identity of the originator. Furthermore, the signature will not be useful without the cipher text. The recipient cannot demonstrate the validity of the signature in connection with the plain text to a third party without giving the cipher text and revealing the recipient's private decryption key, which may compromise many other messages.

Placing the signature "inside the encryption," so the plain text of the confidential information together with the signature is encrypted, is generally preferable. This strategy assures that the signature is not visible in the cipher text and so cannot reveal the originator's identity. Furthermore, the signature is valid after decryption and so can be demonstrated to a third party without compromise of any recipient private decryption key. For further discussion of these issues, see Chapter 16.

## 2.9     Canonicalization

Canonicalization is a critical aspect of digital signatures and verification. It also has limited applicability to encryption.

To be useful, signatures (and message authentication codes, if appropriate) must be secure and robust. For the signature to be secure, any "significant" change in the signed data or the signature must cause the signature to fail. For the signature to be robust, any "insignificant" change in the signed data, or the signature itself, must not cause the signature to fail. Any change allowed by normal receipt, storage, and/or transmission of the message should be considered insignificant and should not be covered by the signature. Figuring out exactly what is significant for signature purposes can prove tricky. Message digest algorithms, which are used in message authentication codes and digital signatures, reflect **any** change in their input, so you must manage their input carefully. In particular, that input should normally consist of a canonicalization of the data being secured, discarding insignificant aspects of that data.

Chapter 9 is entirely devoted to canonicalization, particularly as it pertains to XML.

## 2.10     Randomness

The keys used in digital security must be generated "randomly." For our purposes, "random" is defined as hard to guess, so this makes it more difficult to guess the key. This goal turns out to be surprisingly challenging to achieve on a computer. One strategy is to use true physical randomness such as thermal noise or radioactive decay, but it requires special hardware and usually produces random bits fairly slowly. More commonly, systems use algorithmic "pseudo-random" number generators. Unfortunately, to be unguessable, they initially require some sort of strong random seed value. Frequently such a seed can be derived from some hardware source of randomness.

Many real-world systems that did almost everything else right have been broken due to weak random numbers. Perhaps they based their random number generation on a seed that uses only the time and date. As a result, anyone with a general idea of when the seed was generated will have an embarrassingly small space to search through to find the key—possibly only a few dozen values—even if the key is 128 bits and should have $2^{128}$ equally probable values.

For a deeper and more detailed discussion of these issues, see [RFC 1750] and [Schneier].

**History**

Early versions of Netscape Navigator, although they did most everything else correctly in terms of security, depended (as have other security critical software products) on a library "random" number generator for SSL keys. On some platforms, this generator used the time of day and process ID as a seed. Its output was relatively easy to guess. This problem has, of course, been fixed. Because it drew a bit of attention, people have become more cautious about this issue. But give it a few years and likely someone will make the same mistake again. It's very easy to put in a "temporary" weak random number generator while developing a system and never get around to upgrading it.

## 2.11    Other Facets of Security

Next, we look briefly at a few other important facets of a complete security system, albeit issues that are somewhat outside the scope of digital cryptography. An overall security system is only as secure as the weakest facet.

### Key Rollover

No key should be used forever. The longer a key has been in use and the more often its uses are exposed, the greater the probability of it being compromised due to accident, subversion, or cryptanalysis. Most systems require regular key updates and a plan for nonscheduled rollover in case of known compromise. While the timing for such updates depends on the particular circumstances, most public keys should not be used for more than a year. In fact, sometimes it is reasonable to use a key—for example, an enveloped encryption symmetric key—once only.

### Physical Security

Devices and areas where keys are exposed, cryptographic computations are performed, and the plain text version of cipher text appears must be physically secure. If an adversary can obtain keys or passwords by getting them from computer memory, observing user keystrokes, or similar activities, you are sunk. Cryptographic security relies on the security of the keys. If the actual cryptographic computations can be observed, changed, or bypassed, security is lost.

### Personnel Security

In security systems of any complexity, there are always people whom you must trust. They include, but are not limited to, people with physical access to the keying material, people who implemented the software and/or hardware involved with critical operations, and people who designed the system. If operation of the system is critical or protects valuable secrets, how do you assure that these people are trustworthy?

### Procedural Security

Even with good cryptography, physical, and personnel security, what sort of administrative procedures do you have? If a security violation or compromise occurs, who reports it and what action is taken? Does anyone actually check that what is supposed to be done is being done, that encrypted data are actually secure?

**History**

One implementation of secure Telnet used a 64-bit DES key, which includes eight nominal "parity" bits. The keys consisted of 64 randomly generated bits, but the actual encryption/decryption routine ignored the supplied key and used a key of all zero bits if the parity was wrong! Consequently, more than 99.5% of the time, the same zero key was used [JIS]. This system scrambled the bits so they looked secure to a human. This code interoperated well with other copies of itself, as both ends made the same mistake, but in a way that was very insecure to anyone trying a few keys. A zero key is particularly obvious to try when attempting to decode unknown cipher text because it could result from a software or hardware failure and is one of the four "weak" keys for DES. The lesson: Constant vigilance and oversight of security systems are needed.

## 2.12    Cryptography: A Subtle Art

This chapter has presented just a brief overview of the basics of digital cryptography at a high level. Beyond the security of individual algorithms lies the question of overall system security. A secure system can be made insecure by the addition of one more operation/feature even if that operation is secure in isolation.

Technical progress in this area occurs constantly. Unless you want to make the study of this area into your life's work, we suggest you follow these guidelines:

- Do not depend on security by obscurity (i.e., the secrecy of your algorithms). Depend only on the secrecy of symmetric and private keys.

- Do not design your own basic cryptographic algorithms or formats. Use recent—but not too recent—strong algorithms and formats that have been subject to public scrutiny.

- Pay attention to such often neglected areas as randomness generation and proper canonicalization for your application.

- Keep in mind that physical security of cryptographic processing and key storage; covert channels and electromagnetic emanations that can compromise keying material or plain text; traffic analysis; operational procedures; and personnel security, all of which are beyond the scope of this book, can be crucial, depending on your threat model.

- Cross your fingers and consider actively monitoring for intrusion or compromise: No matter how careful you are, security is never perfect.

# Part II | XML Basics

Chapters 3 through 8 go into XML and some standards built on basic XML in considerable depth. Depending on how familiar you are with XML and how deeply you want to get into the subject, you may be able to skip or skim much of Part II. You can always refer back to it if you run into a question later in this book.

Chapter 3 offers some general background on XML and XML Namespaces, except for DTDs (which are covered in Chapter 4). Namespaces permit mixing XML for different sources by qualifying the names that appear.

Chapter 5 focuses on XML schemas. Both DTDs and schemas are means of specifying the allowed syntax of an application. DTDs, which were part of the original definition of XML, are covered in great depth. Schemas, a more recent addition to XML, are not covered as thoroughly but enough information is given that you will be able to understand the uses of schemas in the XML Security standards specifications. Although schemas do not completely replace DTDs, they are better adapted to use with namespaces and are used for the authoritative syntax specification in the XML Security standards.

Chapter 6 covers XPath in great depth. The XPath data model is used throughout XML Security including canonicalization, signature, and encryption (Parts III and V). Nevertheless, a full implementation of XPath is not required as part of XML Security. Unless you are very familiar with XPath, you should read most of Chapter 6. You probably don't need to study the entire function library described in Section 6.5, however.

Chapter 7 examines Uniform Resource Identifiers (URIs), the standard way to identify information and resources on the Internet, xml:base, which provides a means to the base from which relative URIs are interpreted, and XPointer, a powerful syntax for specifying pieces of information within larger XML aggregates.

Finally, Chapter 8 gives a snapshot of current state of the work involved in developing an XML Protocol framework.

# 3 | The Extensible Markup Language

This chapter provides a general overview of XML. If you are familiar with XML, feel free to skip ahead to Chapter 4.

**History**

James Clark invented the name Extensible Markup Language and its abbreviation XML. He has been quoted as saying, "XML isn't going to win any prizes for technical elegance. But it was just simple enough that it could get broad acceptance, and it has just enough Standard Generalized Markup Language (SGML) stuff in it that the SGML community felt they could embrace it." (SGML is a standard indicating how to specify a document language or tag set.)

A markup language is a mechanism for identifying structure in a document. The Extensible Markup Language Recommendation [XML] specifies a way to structure, store, and send information. It does not say anything about what information should be presented to the user, however. Rather, this meta-markup language is used for creating other languages (each called an XML "application"). As such, XML is really a grammatical system that enables the creation of customized markup languages for particular documents and domains [Harold].

**Note**

It is a quirk of XML documentation nomenclature that it uses the term "application" very liberally. In particular, computer code that reads or prints XML, generates or verifies XML signatures, or the like, is frequently called an "application," such as an "XML signature application" in the XML literature. This terminology is employed even when, in other computer contexts, the code would be referred to as a "subroutine," "library," or other term clearly indicating that it is merely one building block in a complete application or system.

An XML markup language defines tags for labeling content, and the relationship between such tags. Consider the following example:

```
<foo>. . . content of tag foo . . .</foo>
```

The XML Recommendation defines a methodology for tag creation. It specifies neither tag semantics nor a specific tag set. That is, XML specifies structure, not meaning. You can define an infinite number of markup languages based on the XML Recommendation standards.

Once defined, tags are mixed with character data to form an "XML document." An XML document can take numerous forms. For example, it can be a logical structure within a computer program or an external file in the traditional sense. Likewise, an XML document can be sent as a data stream, reported as a database result set, or dynamically generated by one application and sent to another.

## 3.1    Related Standards and Recommendations

The XML Recommendation describes the class of data objects called XML documents and loosely describes the behavior of computer programs that read or write these objects. The XML Recommendation and the standards shown in Table 3-1 identify the standards and specifications necessary to understand basic XML Version 1.0 [XML] and construct computer programs to process it.

A number of related XML recommendations from the W3C extend XML itself or provide ways to specify processing of XML. Table 3-2 lists those recommendations.

**Table 3-1** | Standards Associated with Basic XML

| Standard | Subject | Reference |
|---|---|---|
| Extensible Markup Language (XML) 1.0 (second edition) | Defines Basic XML syntax | [XML] |
| Unicode and ISO/IEC 10646 | Characters | [Unicode] |
| Internet RFC 1766 | Language identification tags | [RFC 1766] |
| ISO 639 | Language name codes | [ISO 639] |
| ISO 3166 | Country name codes | [ISO 3166] |

**Table 3-2** | XML Extension and Processing Recommendations

| Recommendation | Description | Reference |
|---|---|---|
| Namespaces in XML | Extends XML syntax to permit mixing of tags from different sources | [Names] |
| XML Base | Extends XML to provide URI bases for relative URIs | [XBase] |
| XML Path Language (XPath), Version 1.0 | A language for addressing parts of a document | [XPath] |
| XSL Transformations (XSLT), Version 1.0 | A language for transforming XML documents into other XML documents | [XSLT] |
| XML Pointer Language (XPointer) | Describes how to address a resource | [XPointer] |
| XML Linking Language (XLink), Version 1.0 | Describes how to associate two or more resources | [XLink] |
| Extensible Style Language (XSL), Version 1.0 | Defines a standard stylesheet language for XML | [XSL] |
| XML Inclusions (XInclude), Version 1.0 | Describes how to dynamically include XML or text in a document | [XInclude] |

## 3.2   XML Documents

XML documents are the class of data objects described by the XML Recommendation [XML]. All XML documents are made up of two parts:

- A prolog, which, if present, contains at least the XML declaration

- A body that contains the actual marked-up document

For example, the following is an XML document:

```
<?xml version="1.0"?> <body> content </body>
```

All XML documents have a logical and a physical structure. A document usually consists of a hierarchical structure of elements. An element consists of data (including null data) surrounded by start and end tags. In XML, you can generate an infinite number of custom tag sets for your documents.

Example 3-1 compares similar XML and HTML documents. HTML typically describes what a document looks like, whereas XML describes how a document is logically structured.

***Example 3-1***    *Comparison of similar XML and HTML documents*

| XML Example | HTML Example |
|---|---|
| `<sale-item>` | `<h1>House for Sale</h1>` |
| `<head>House</head>` | `<p align=center>Single family</p>` |
| `<type>single family</type>` | `<br><i>like new</i> 1400 sq. ft.` |
| `<cond>like new</cond>` | `<br>3 bedrooms` |
| `<size>1400 sq. ft.</size>` | `<br>1 _ baths` |
| `<bedroom>3</bedroom>` | `<br>lot size of 8000 sq. ft.` |
| `<bath>1 1/2</bath>` | `<br>asking $158,000` |
| `<lot>8000 sq. ft.</lot>` | |
| `<price>$158,000</price>` | |
| `</sale-item>` | |

The XML Recommendation defines the rules for creating the semantic tags that you use to describe data and for adding markup to documents. An XML document consists of text (data) plus XML markup. Note that an XML document is always interpreted as [Unicode]. If the document uses non-Unicode character codes, the processing agent maps them into Unicode code points when read. An XML markup language must follow standard rules that provide the following information:

- The syntax for marking up, which follows strict rules. If the syntax is not exactly right, the parser stops processing and returns an error message.

- The meaning behind the markup (standards for encoding data with information about itself).

Table 3-3 lists the components for encoding and decoding an XML document.

The processing application needs to know the syntax of the markup to determine what to do with the XML.

**Note**

The use of XML is not limited to text markup. Thanks to its extensibility, XML could just as easily apply to sound markup or video markup. For example, as text markup the tag <EMPHASIZE> might display text as bold. Used in audio markup, the same tag might produce a louder voice. Used in logical assertion markup, it might indicate an assertion with higher strength, which would prevail when conflicts with other assertions arise. The actions of tags are generally defined by the applications.

**Table 3-3** | Components Related to Encoding and Decoding Using XML

| Component | Function |
|---|---|
| XML document | A data object containing a custom markup language |
| Document Type Definition (DTD; optional) | Specifies the markup syntax—that is, what it means to be a valid tag (see Chapter 4 for more information about DTDs) |
| Schema (optional) | Specifies more detailed markup syntax and data typing (see Chapter 5 for more information about schemas) |
| Stylesheet (optional) | Usually contains the graphical user interface (GUI) instructions specifying display instructions when the XML is intended for output presentation for the processing application (see Section 3.7) |
| Display agent | Combines the DTD, stylesheet logic, and XML document, and displays it according to the rules and the data |

### 3.2.1   XML Parsing Process

To read an XML document, you need an XML parser/processor, which can be implemented as a browser, if the XML is just to be displayed, or as an application module, if it is to feed more complex processing. The XML Recommendation provides for two types of parser/processors: nonvalidating and validating. The XML Recommendation also provides for two categories of XML documents: well formed (Section 3.2.2) and valid (Section 3.2.3). An XML parser must determine whether the markup is well formed and, if a DTD is present, whether to determine if it is valid. The XML Recommendation does not require that XML documents have a DTD. All XML documents must follow the rules for being well formed or else they are, by definition, not XML documents. All XML documents do not have to be valid, but all valid documents are well formed.

- The XML processor provides access to the XML document's content and structure. An XML processor acting on behalf of the application, either independently or through a browser, reads and interprets the XML document, and, if present, the DTD, schema, and stylesheet. This processing agent uses the DTD and schema as part of the input and uses stylesheets for display output.

A nonvalidating parser checks the XML document against the well-formed constraints of XML. Note that a DTD can be present for a nonvalidating parser/processor. As described in Chapter 4, it must still expand entities that are defined in the DTD but will not provide a valid/nonvalid indication. A validating parser checks the XML document against the validity constraints of XML and any contained in the DTD.

In many applications, the parsed information ends up in an internal data structure or in a database. Later, some code may modify the data structure, synthesize new XML data structures, or retrieve information from the database and create output XML. For example, many of today's Java-based processors are designed for use with Web applications. With a Java-based XML processor, the application uses the processor classes to read in the document. Once the application reads in the document, the information in the document becomes available to Java.

Generally, parsers just go from an external representation of XML to an internal one. Some processors also have facilities to interpret stylesheets and produce various output. For example, a browser-oriented processor translates an XML document into different types of documents such as HTML, RTF, or TeX. During translation, the parser checks whether the XML document is well formed and/or confirms the validity of the XML document. When a document meets the requirements for well-formed and/or valid documents, the parser or code generator transforms it into a different document type (see Figure 3-1).

Transforming an XML document into another document type requires a translation file or stylesheet. Section 3.7 discusses stylesheets.

### 3.2.2   Well-Formed Documents

"Well formed" has an exact meaning in XML. A well-formed document adheres to the syntax rules specified by the XML 1.0 Recommendation. If the document is not well-formed and an error appears in the XML syntax, the XML processor stops and reports the presence of a fatal error. A textual object is a well-formed XML document if it meets the following criteria:

- It contains one or more elements.

- It meets all the well-formed constraints given in the XML 1.0 Recommendation [XML].

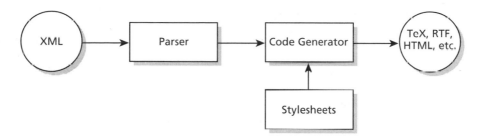

**Figure 3-1** Browser-oriented parsing process

- Each of the parsed entities directly or indirectly referenced within the document is well formed.

> **Note**
>
> A parsed entity's contents are referred to as its replacement text; this text is considered an integral part of the document.

A well-formed XML document will meet the minimum requirement of being parseable as XML. Example 3-2 shows such a document. The first line in the example is the XML declaration. The XML declaration, if present, must begin the XML document and must be in lowercase. It tells the parser that the document is XML and that it conforms to the version 1.0 specification.

> **Note**
>
> Case sensitivity is strictly observed in XML.

**Example 3-2**    *A well-formed XML document*

```
<?xml version="1.0"?>
<memo>
  <to>Jon</to>
  <from>Chris</from>
  <subject>Reminder</subject>
  <body>Three PM meeting canceled. Have a great weekend.</body>
</memo>
```

A well-formed document also adheres to the following rules:

- Elements containing data have both start and end tags For example:

```
<to>Jon</to>
```

- Elements containing no data and using a single tag end with slash greater than ("/>"). These so-called empty elements need not always end with slash greater than ("/>"). An empty element is also valid if the start tag is immediately followed by an end tag. For more information, see the discussion of elements later in this chapter. For example:

```
<memo/>
```

- A document must contain exactly one element that contains all other elements. For instance, in the preceding example:

```
<memo> . . . </memo>.
```

- Nesting of elements is allowed but elements may not overlap.

- Quotes must surround attribute values, as in the following example:

```
<termdef id="dt-dog" term='dog'/>
```

- Use of the less than ("<") and ampersand ("&") characters is limited to start tags or entity references.

- The following five predefined entity references are available to represent markup characters in content or single and double quotes:

  &amp;, &lt;, &gt;, &apos;, &quot;

### 3.2.3    Valid XML Documents

An XML document is valid if it is well formed, has an associated DTD, and complies with the constraints expressed in that DTD. The DTD defines the grammar and vocabulary of a markup language, specifying what is and what is not allowed to appear in a document—for example, which tags can appear in the document and how they must nest within one another.

An XML document can contain the DTD, the XML document can link to an external DTD, or DTD material can appear in both places. Different documents and Web sites can share external DTDs. The DTD or its reference must appear before the first element in the document.

Example 3-3 shows a well-formed and hypothetically valid XML document. This example references an external DTD. Chapter 4 discusses the details of DTDs.

**Example 3-3**   *A well-formed and valid XML document with an external DTD*

```
<?xml version="1.0"?>
<!DOCTYPE memo SYSTEM "InternalMemo.dtd">
<memo>
  <to>Jon</to>
  <from>Chris</from>
  <subject>Reminder</subject>
  <body>Three PM meeting canceled. Let's meet at Big Stick Farm
        after work</body>
</memo>
```

## 3.3    XML Document Structure

As mentioned previously, XML documents have both a logical structure and a physical structure. An XML document consists of text (data) plus the XML markup. The entire sequence of character codes in an XML document must map into allowed Unicode characters [Unicode]. An XML document consists of storage units called entities. These entities contain either parsed data or, rarely, unparsed data. Parsed data, in turn, consist of characters that form data and markup. Markup, in turn, encodes a description of the logical structure of the XML document.

Markup properties include entities, CDATA (Section 3.4.5), declarations, DTDs, elements, comments, character references, and processing instructions. Table 3-4 outlines the structure of an XML document.

**Note**

> XML works with entities, not files. As the physical representation of XML documents, entities are usually stored as files, but it is not a requirement.

## 3.4    XML Document Logical Structure

The logical structure of an XML document consists of declarations, elements, character references, comments, and processing instructions.

**Table 3-4** | Structure of an XML Document

| Structure | Consists of . . . | Part Referred to as . . . | Notes |
|---|---|---|---|
| Logical | Markup | Declarations<br>Elements<br>Attributes<br>Character references<br>CDATA sections<br>Comments<br>Namespaces<br>Processing instructions | • Explicit markup indicates each type of markup.<br>• The logical and physical structures must nest properly. |
| Physical | One or more storage units | Entities | • Entities have content and a name.<br>• They can be parsed or unparsed.<br>• They can refer to other entities.<br>• Each document has a document entity.<br>• All have content.<br>• All are identified by name, except the document entity and an external DTD subset. |

### 3.4.1   The XML Declaration

Two types of declarations exist: the XML declaration and a DTD. If you use both, the XML declaration must precede the DTD. Although the XML declaration is optional, the W3C specification suggests that you include it so that the appropriate parser, or parsing process, can interpret the document correctly. XML version information is required in an XML declaration. The version number indicates that the document conforms to that version of the XML specifications, although 1.0 is the only version defined to date.

**Note**

A working draft of [XML 1.1] has been published that proposes to make relatively modest but incompatible changes to XML at the character set level, but no structural changes. For example, it proposes adding the [Unicode] line separator character to the set of allowed white space characters and changing the default for tokens from allowing only specified characters to allowing all characters not prohibited. With this provision, as Unicode expands, so will the allowed token characters.

The XML declaration and all processing instructions begin with less than question mark ("<?") and end with question mark greater than ("?>"). XML allows you to also specify a "standalone" attribute and an "encoding" attribute that gives the character encoding in use. The XML Recommendation requires that all parsers support UTF-8 and UTF-16; parsers can support additional encodings as well. Thus the XML declaration might look something like the declarations shown in Example 3-4.

**Example 3-4**    *XML declarations*

```
<?xml version = "1.0"?>


<?xml version = "1.0" standalone="yes" encoding = "UTF-8"?>
```

The "standalone" document declaration is optional. A "standalone" value of "yes" indicates that the document does not depend on an external DTD; "no" indicates that the document may depend on an external DTD. The encoding declaration is optional and describes the character encoding currently in use. An appendix to the XML Recommendation gives heuristics whereby a parser may recognize many encodings, including UTF-8 and UTF-16, even in the absence of an encoding attribute.

**Soapbox**

> It was intended that applications for which external DTDs were inconvenient or unavailable would specify that the input must have standalone="yes". However, this approach is essentially never taken. In retrospect, it is not clear it was even worth the effort to define the standalone attribute.

### 3.4.2    Elements

An element consists of a start tag/end tag pair and any data found in between them. The start tag includes the name of an element type enclosed by a less than symbol ("<") and a greater than symbol (">"), as shown in Figure 3-2. The name of an element type is known as a generic identifier (GI).

XML documents contain data marked up with element start and end tags. Element start tags may have attributes. Elements are the most common form of markup and are extensible.

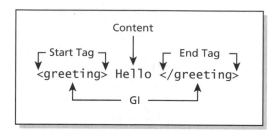

**Figure 3-2** | An element with content

- XML elements have content.

- XML elements have relationships.

- XML elements have simple naming rules.

Each XML document contains one or more elements, which can be classified into one of two categories: empty elements and elements with content. Empty elements are simply markers where something occurs. To denote an empty element, you can use start and stop tags with no content or use an "empty tag" that ends with a slash greater than ("/>"). For example, the XML equivalent to HTML's "<HR>" is "<HR/>". The trailing "/>" tells the processor that the element is empty and no matching end tag exists. See Figure 3-3.

The content of an element can consist of one or more elements, mixed content, simple text content or, as described above, no content. In Example 3-5, the <book> element contains other elements. Conversely, the <chapter> element contains mixed content—both text and other elements. The <title> and <section> elements are examples of simple content; they contain only text.

The relationships between XML elements are named according to parent and child nomenclature. In Example 3-5, <book> is the root element, whereas <title> and <chapter> are child elements of <book>. Note that <book> is also the parent element of both <title> and <chapter>.

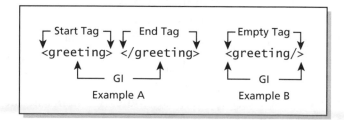

**Figure 3-3** | Two examples of empty elements

***Example 3-5***   *Element contents and relationships in an XML document*

```
<book>        ◄────────────────Root element; also parent element
  <title>XML Security</title>◄──────────Child element
  <chapter>XML and Security◄──────────Child element
    <section>Origins of XML</section>◄─────Grandchild of root
    <section>XML Goals</section>
  </chapter>
</book>
```

When creating names of elements, you should avoid using a colon (" : ") because it is reserved for use by namespaces (as described in Section 3.5). You can use any name you want because the XML Recommendation reserves no words. You should, however, try to keep element names simple and descriptive. A name can contain letters, numbers, and other characters. Do not start a name with a number, punctuation characters, or the letters "xml" in any capitalization (i.e., Xml, XML, xMl), and do not include any spaces in an element name.

**Soapbox**

It is sometimes quite annoying that XML prohibits "Names," such as element and attribute names, from starting with digits. No strong reason for this restriction exists.

### 3.4.3   Attributes

XML elements can have attributes in the start tag, just as in HTML. Attributes provide additional information for elements but do not constitute part of the element's content.

Attributes have both a name and a value. In XML, the attribute value must always be quoted. You can use either single or double quotes, but double quotes are more common. Attribute specifications may appear only within start tags and empty-element tags.

Figure 3-4 identifies the parts of an element that denote an attribute. Example 3-6 shows the attribute

```
language="latin"
```

incorporated into an XML document. Chapter 4 discusses specifying attributes in a DTD in more detail.

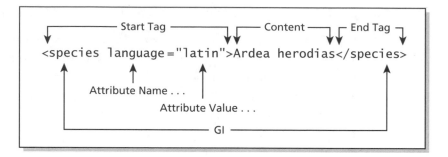

**Figure 3-4** | Example of an attribute

***Example 3-6*** *Attributes in an XML document*

```
<classification>
  <order>Ciconiformes</order>
  <family>Ardeidae</family>
  <species/>
  <name language="latin">Ardea herodias</name>
  <name language="english">Great Blue Heron</name>
  <foe>Raccoon</foe>
  <foe>Red-shouldered Hawk</foe>
</classification>
```

### 3.4.4    Special Attributes xml:space and xml:lang

The XML Recommendation defines the attributes xml:lang and xml:space. The xml:lang attribute facilitates the use of documents containing human-language–dependent text, especially if they employ multiple languages. The xml:space attribute allows elements to declare to an application whether their white space is "significant."

**Language**

You can insert the special attribute xml:lang in elements to specify the default language that the application will use in the contents and attribute values of that element in an XML document. If it is present and you are using a validating parser, you must have declared the xml:lang attribute in the DTD. The IETF [RFC 1766] specification, "Tags for the Identification of Languages," or its successor on the IETF Standards Track, defines the values of the xml:lang attribute. By convention, the language code appears in lowercase and the country code (if any) appears in uppercase.

**Soapbox**

> IETF [RFC 1766] tags are constructed from two-letter language codes as defined by [ISO 639], from two-letter country codes as defined by [ISO 3166], or from language identifiers registered with the Internet Assigned Numbers Authority [IANA-LANGCODES]. The successor to IETF [RFC 1766] will likely introduce three-letter language codes for languages not presently covered by [ISO 639].

### White Space

The use of white space in documents varies. For example, you can use spaces, tabs, and blank lines when writing code or creating markup to make them easier to read. Such white space is typically not intended to be part of the delivered version of the document. Even so, white space in the actual source code can be significant as white space in a poem is.

The XML Recommendation requires that an XML processor pass all characters that are not markup through to the application. When you attach the xml:space attribute to an element, it provides information to the application about handling white space found in that element.

**Note**

> No matter what you do, all white space that is part of element content must be passed to applications by an XML-conformant parser; an application could then make arbitrary decisions based on such white space. Without special application knowledge, all white space given to an application must be considered "significant" from a security point of view, even where the XML Recommendation says that it should be identified to the application as "insignificant."

You must declare the xml:space attribute if you use it with a validating parser. When declared, this attribute must be given as an enumerated type whose values are "default", "preserve", or both. For example:

```
<!ATTLIST poem  xml:space (default preserve) 'preserve'>
```

```
<!ATTLIST pre xml:space (preserve) #FIXED 'preserve'>
```

In this example, the value "default" indicates that applications' default white-space processing modes are acceptable for this element. The value "preserve" indicates that applications should preserve all of the white space. Chapter 4 provides more information about declarations and attributes in an XML document.

The xml:space behavior is inherited from parent elements. If an element containing an xml:space value contains other elements, they also inherit the xml:space behavior from the parent element, unless they have a xml:space attribute of their own.

### 3.4.5    CDATA Sections

CDATA—character data—is a mechanism typically used to include blocks of special characters as character data. CDATA sections provide a way to protect information from a parser. Specifically, a CDATA section specifies that all characters within it should be considered character data, whether or not they look like a tag or entity reference. A CDATA section can appear anywhere in a document where you can have character data.

CDATA sections begin with the string

```
<![CDATA[
```

and end with the string

```
]]>
```

The character string "]]>" is, of course, not allowed within a CDATA section because it would signal the end of the section. Example 3-7 shows a CDATA section that treats "<greeting>" and "</greeting>" as character data, not markup.

**Note**

CDATA is text that will *not* be analyzed by a parser, except to look for the magic CDATA termination string. The parser will not treat tags inside the text as markup, nor will it expand entities.

PCDATA, a type of element content (see Chapter 4), is text that will be parsed by a parser. In such a case, the parser will treat tags inside the text as markup and will expand entities.

***Example 3-7***    *A CDATA section*

```
<![CDATA[<greeting>Hello, world!</greeting>]]>
```

### 3.4.6    Comments

Comments are used to annotate an XML document, but are not part of the document's text content. In addition, you can use them to comment out tag sets. Although an XML processor generally ignores comments, a processor may make it possible for an application to retrieve the text of comments.

Comments begin with

```
<!--
```

and end with

```
-->
```

HTML uses the identical syntax for inserting comments into a document. For compatibility, the string "--" (double-hyphen) must not occur in a comment. Comments may appear anywhere in a document, provided the comment remains outside other markup. Example 3-8 gives several examples of comments.

***Example 3-8***    *Comments*

```
<!-- This is a comment -->
<!--
This is also a comment
-->


<!-- Begin the contributing author names -->
<name>George W. Archibald</name>
<name>James C. Lewis</name>
<!-- End the contributing author names -->
<!-- Comment out other contributing author names!
<name>Able B. Charlie</name>
<name>Delta E. Foxtrot</name>
End commenting out other contributing author names. -->
```

When using comments, observe the following guidelines:

- Never place a comment inside an entity declaration.

- Never place a comment before the XML declaration. A comment may, however, occur after the XML declaration and before the root element or after the root element.

- Never nest comments. The end of the first nested comment will terminate the outermost comment.

- Never include two hyphens in a row (--) within a comment.

- Never place a comment within a start or end tag.

### 3.4.7 Character Sets and Encoding

[ISO 10646] is the native character set of XML.

Every ISO character corresponds to a number between 0x0 to 0x10FFFF (in the hexadecimal system). Legal characters in XML are the tab, carriage return, line feed, and legal characters of [Unicode] or [ISO 10646] in the ranges 0x20 to 0xD7FF, 0xE000 to 0xFFFD, and 0x10000 to 0x10FFFF hexadecimal (i.e., all characters except for the surrogate blocks, 0xFFFE and 0xFFFF). Note, however, that some changes in this system have been proposed [XML 1.1].

All XML processors must accept the UTF-8 and UTF-16 encoding of ISO 10646.

### Special Character Strings

Text in an XML document consists of intermingled character data and markup. All text that is not markup constitutes the character data of the document. The XML Recommendation specifies that the ampersand character ("&") and the left and right angle brackets ("<" and ">") may appear in their literal form only when used as follows:

- As markup delimiters

- Within a comment

- Within a processing instruction

- Within a CDATA section

If you use these characters outside of markup, you must "escape" them using either numeric character references or special escape strings, as defined in the XML Recommendation. In addition, the XML Recommendation specifies special escape strings to allow attribute values to contain both single and double quotes (see Table 3-5). You must escape the right angle bracket (">") using "&gt;" or a numeric character reference when it appears in the string "]]>" in content and when that string does not mark the end of a CDATA section.

### Numeric Character References

Numeric character references allow you to insert into your document any legal Unicode characters including those that satisfy the following criteria:

- You cannot type the characters directly on your keyboard.

- You cannot input the characters from other available devices.

- The characters are not available in the character encoding in use.

Character references take one of two forms: decimal references that start with "&#" and hexadecimal references that start with "&#x". For example, "&#169;" is the decimal representation of the standard copyright symbol ("©"). You can represent the Greek letter pi in an XML document using the decimal representation "&#960;" or the hexadecimal representation "&#x3C0;". An XML processor must expand numeric character references immediately on parsing them and must treat them as character data.

**Note**

On a Windows machine, you can find the character code for most characters in the Keystroke field of the Character Map (see Figure 3-5).

**Table 3-5** | Predefined Special Character Strings

| Character | Escape String |
| --- | --- |
| Left angle bracket ("<") | &lt; |
| Right angle bracket (">") | &gt; |
| Ampersand ("&") | &amp; |
| Single apostrophe/single-quote ("'") | &apos; |
| Double apostrophe/double-quote (" " ") | &quot; |

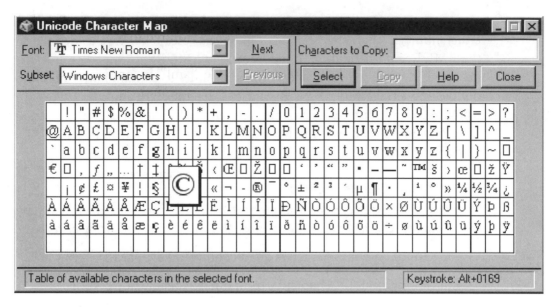

**Figure 3-5** | The Character Map showing a character code

### 3.4.8    Processing Instructions

A processing instruction (PI) is an explicit mechanism for embedding information in a document intended for an application rather than for the XML parser or browser. PIs are not part of an XML document's character data.

A processing instruction begins with a target that identifies the application to which the instruction is directed. The XML processor must pass PIs on to the appropriate application. The application then decides how to handle the instructions. Applications that do not recognize the instructions simply ignore them.

Processing instructions have the following form:

```
<?APPLICATION_NAME INSTRUCTIONS?>
```

Notice that the XML declaration that appears on the first line of an XML document looks like a processing instruction (see Example 3-4) but is not.

See Example 3-9 for another example of a processing instruction. You can declare the PI target beforehand using a NOTATION declaration as shown in this example. Chapter 4 discusses NOTATION declarations in more detail.

The PI data for the PI target application should appear in a format that the application can interpret. Note that PIs are not required to have data after the target. Only the application recognizes data following the PI target. The XML Recommendation reserves the target name "xml" in any capitalization, including mixed capitalization, for standardization in future versions of the specification.

**Example 3-9**   *Sample processing instruction*

```
<!NOTATION mybirdapp SYSTEM file://mydir/birdapp.exe>
<?mybirdapp Do_this?>
```

**History**

Processing instructions were included in XML because they appeared in [SGML] and it seemed like a good idea at the time. Today, most people wish they had been left out because they represent an unnecessary complexity, but feel they must continue to be supported for compatibility. The modern approach calls for encoding essentially all semantics using the simpler syntax of plain XML without PIs.

More radical proposals such as a "Simple XML" would omit attributes; instead, elements would be used for everything. This idea isn't likely to be adopted as a standard but you can define your XML that way if desired.

## 3.5    XML Namespaces

The intent of XML namespaces is to eliminate naming conflicts in XML documents that contain element types and attributes from multiple XML languages. Namespaces can prove useful in situations in which documents combine components from several fields that have the same name but are used in a different context. For example, the bird classification document shown previously in Example 3-6 uses the element <name> to identify a particular species of heron:

```
<name language="latin">Ardea herodias</name>
<name language="english">Great Blue Heron</name>
```

The <name> element we saw in Example 3-8 identifies the contributing authors of an article:

```
<name>George W. Archibald</name>
<name>James C. Lewis</name>
```

Each of the name elements has a different content model. In this case, the document that contains names of birds can use "name" qualified by one Uniform Resource Identifier (URI; see Chapter 7) [RFC 2396]. Figure 3-6 shows the parts of a typical HTTP URI as used in a namespace. A document that contains names of authors can use "name" qualified by another URI. The URI does not have to point to an actual file or other resource.

**Note** XML namespaces do not have any official function except providing a two-part naming system for element types and attributes. They may, however, point to a schema, text document, or other useful information.

XML namespaces are collections of names identified by a URI. You use an XML namespace in XML documents to qualify element and attribute names. A unique two-part name identifies the element and attribute names in the namespace. The XML Namespaces Recommendation [Names] defines a mapping based on the idea of a prefix. When an element type name or attribute name contains a colon, then the mapping treats the part of the name before the colon as a namespace prefix. The part following the colon gives the local name.

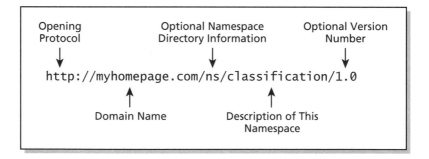

**Figure 3-6** | Parts of a namespace as shown in the form of a URI

**Soapbox** Uniform Resource Identifiers [RFC 2396] are a key Web concept, making it almost inevitable that they would be employed by the W3C as namespace identifiers. This approach has both advantages and disadvantages:

- The URI can be chosen so that it points to something useful, such as a DTD or schema. This relationship is not required, however, and some insist that namespace names should be opaque identifiers without external reference.

- The hierarchical allocation of the domain names that occur in most URIs makes it relatively easy to assure namespace uniqueness.

- The rich structure of most URIs (thanks to their path, fragment, query, and other sections) provides many dimensions of flexibility. Unfortunately, it can also lead to complexity and verbosity.

The prefix maps to a URI reference and selects a namespace. The combination of the universally managed URI namespace and the document's own namespace produces universally unique identifiers. The namespace prefix serves as a proxy for a URI reference.

**Note**

The Namespaces in XML Recommendation [Names] assigns a meaning to names containing colon characters. Authors should not use the colon in XML names except for namespace purposes, but XML processors must accept the colon as a name character.

### 3.5.1 Namespace Declarations

To declare a namespace, you use an attribute, either "xmlns" as the attribute name or "xmlns:" as a prefix to the attribute name. The attribute value is a URI and identifies the namespace (see Example 3-10). Chapter 5 also provides more information about namespace declarations.

**Example 3-10** *Associating a namespace prefix with the namespace name*

```
<?xml version="1.0"?>
<name xmlns:family='http://myhomepage.com/classification'>
  <!-- the "family" prefix is bound to
       http://myhomepage.com/classification for the "name"
       element and contents -->
```

XML and XML-related specifications reserve for their use prefixes beginning with the three-letter sequence x, m, l, in any case combination [XML].

The prefix provides the namespace prefix part of the qualified name and must have been associated with a namespace URI reference by a namespace declaration. The portion following the prefix provides the local part of the qualified name. The prefix functions as a placeholder for the namespace name.

- The prefix "xml" is by definition bound to the namespace name:

```
http://www.w3.org/XML/1998/namespace
```

- The prefix "xmlns" is used only for namespace bindings and is not itself bound to any namespace name.

### 3.5.2    Using Qualified Names

Element names are given as qualified names. Attributes may be namespace declarations, or their names may be given as qualified names.

The following two examples come from the Namespaces in XML Recommendation [Names]. Here the namespace declaration applies to the element where it is specified and to all elements within the content of that element. This relationship holds true unless it is overridden by another namespace declaration with the same prefix:

```xml
<?xml version="1.0"?>
<!-- all elements here are explicitly in the HTML namespace -->
<html:html xmlns:html='http://www.w3.org/TR/REC-html40'>
  <html:head>
    <html:title>Frobnostication</html:title>
  </html:head>
  <html:body><html:p>Moved to
    <html:a href='http://frob.com'>here.</html:a></html:p>
  </html:body>
</html:html>
```

You can declare multiple namespace prefixes as attributes of a single element:

```
<?xml version="1.0"?>
<!-- both the bk and isbn namespace prefixes
    are available throughout -->
<bk:book xmlns:bk='urn:loc.gov:books'
         xmlns:isbn='urn:ISBN:0-395-36341-6'>
    <bk:title>Cheaper by the Dozen</bk:title>
    <isbn:number>1568491379</isbn:number>
</bk:book>
```

### 3.5.3   Namespace Guidelines

Keep in mind the following guidelines when using namespaces:

- No tag may contain two attributes that have identical names or have qualified names with the same local part and with prefixes that have been bound to identical namespace names.

- Documents using namespaces must conform to the "Namespace Constraints" described in the Namespaces for XML Recommendation [Names]. For example:

  - All element types and attribute names must contain either zero or one colon.

  - No entity names, processing instruction targets, or notation names can contain any colons.

- Namespace URIs are simply identifiers. The URIs in XML namespace names can, but do not necessarily, point to schemas, information about the namespace, or anything else.

- Ronald Bourret, in *XML Namespaces Frequently Asked Questions* [Bourret], states that namespaces do not provide or define any of the following:

  - A way to merge two documents that use different DTDs

  - A way to associate XML namespaces and schema information

  - A way to validate documents that use XML namespaces

  - A way to associate element type or attribute declarations in a DTD with an XML namespace

## 3.6    XML Document Physical Structure

An instance of XML is a hierarchical set of entities. Entities constitute the physical structure of an XML document. Figure 3-7 shows the different types of entities other than the special document entity.

XML uses entities to represent special characters, to represent repetitious text, and to include the content of other files. These storage units of XML documents contain particular parts of the document [Harold]. Namely, an entity contains either text or binary data—but not both. It may be a file, a database record, or a network resource. Entities also contain either parsed or unparsed data. Parsed data consists of characters, some of which form the character data in the document, and some of which form markup.

Every entity has a unique name except the document entity. The document entity consists of the XML declaration, the DTD, and the root element, as shown in Example 3-11.

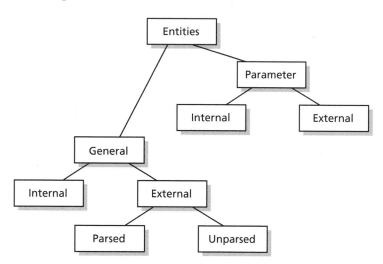

**Figure 3-7** | Entity types

***Example 3-11***    *Document entity*

```
<?xml version="1.0"?>
<!DOCTYPE memo SYSTEM "InternalMemo.dtd">
<memo>
M
</memo>
```

Entities are reusable chunks of data, much like macros, and are part of XML's inheritance from SGML. XML classifies entities into two categories: general or parameter entities. Each of those can be either an internal entity or an external entity. General external entities can be parsed or unparsed (see Figure 3-7).

You must declare an entity before you can refer to it through an entity reference. Entity references are part of the logical structure of an XML document and are described later in this chapter.

Figure 3-8 declares that the entity xml has the text contents "Extensible Markup Language". The processor reads the entity reference of "&xml;" and replaces each instance with "Extensible Markup Language".

### 3.6.1    General and Parameter Entities

General entities can appear anywhere in text or markup and are mostly used to represent larger chunks of data. External general entities can reference other documents, such as images and video clips. To insert entities into a document, you use entity references.

You declare general entities in the DTD with the markup as shown in Example 3-12. Note that the entity *name* is the abbreviation for the replacement text.

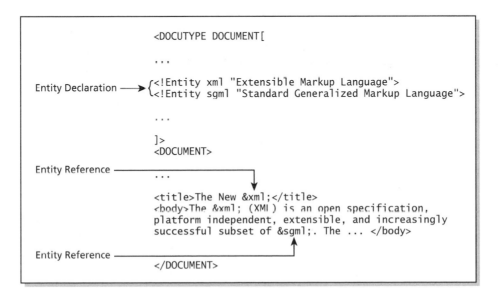

**Figure 3-8** | An entity declaration and entity reference

**Example 3-12**  *An entity declaration and entity reference*

```
<!ENTITY name "definition or replacement text">  ◄── Form
<!ENTITY BSF "Big Stick Farm">  ◄── Example


&BSF;  ◄── Entity reference
```

Parameter entities appear only in the DTD. With a parameter entity, a percent sign ("%") appears before the entity name instead of the ampersand ("&") that is used by general entities.

---

### 3.6.2  Internal and External Entities

Internal entities define the entity replacement text and are stored completely within the XML document. An internal entity is a parsed entity. That is, the processor will parse the entity's replacement text as part of the document in which a reference to it occurs.

In contrast, an external entity points to a system or public identifier. External entities acquire their content from another source located through a URI [RFC 2396]. The content of an external entity is not part of the current document. An external entity may or may not be parsed. Unparsed entities let you reference non-XML data, such as an image, from a document. An entity can be referenced at many places where it is logically inserted.

If an entity is unparsed, a "notation" must identify the type of document referenced by the entity. You must use the keyword NDATA to introduce any unparsed entity such as an image document, as follows:

```
<!ENTITY bsf1 SYSTEM http://pics.bigstickfarm.com/bsf1.gif
        NDATA GIF>
```

Figure 3-9 gives an example of each type of entity: internal, external, parsed, and unparsed.

```
Parsed Entity
with Markup ───────► <!Entity xsl "<bold>Extensible Stylesheet Language</bold>">

Internal Entity ───────► <!Entity sgml "Standard Generalized Markup Language">

External Entity ───────► <!Entity chp2 SYSTEM "http://www.myxml.com/chp2.xml">

Unparsed Entity ───────► <!Entity image SYSTEM "http://myxml.com/entity2.jpg"
                    NDATA JPG>
```

**Figure 3-9** | Internal, external, parsed, and unparsed entity declarations

### 3.6.3   Entity References

An entity reference refers to the content of a named entity. Entity references point to parsed general entities and use the ampersand ("&") as a beginning delimiter and the semicolon (";") as an ending delimiter. Parameter-entity references use the percent sign ("%") and semicolon as corresponding delimiters. You invoke parsed entities by name using entity references.

To distinguish markup elements in a document, the XML specification reserves some characters to identify the start and end of markup. For instance, the ampersand character ("&") and the left angle bracket ("<") may normally appear in their literal form only when used as markup delimiters. XML provides an alternative method to represent these characters in the content of a document. Character references allow you to insert specific characters as described in Section 3.4.7.

When using entities and entity references, note the following points:

- You should always declare entities in an XML document before referencing them.

- The text that the entity references must be well-formed XML if it is parsed.

- An entity reference cannot contain any white space although the entity replacement text may.

- References to entities may not appear in the DOCTYPE declaration.

- You should not reference an external entity from within element attributes.

- Entities may refer to other entities, but they may not be self-referential.

- Referenced text may not contain the left angle bracket ("<") character.

## 3.7   XML and Stylesheets

The XML Recommendation defines a way to structure, store, and send information, but it says nothing about how the content should be displayed. Stylesheets store information indicating how an XML document should appear to a user. For example, a stylesheet can define how the source content should be styled, laid out, and paginated onto some presentation medium. The presentation medium could be a window in a Web browser or a handheld device, or it could be printed pages in a book or other form of print media.

**Note**

Stylesheets affect security because they must be included under a signature if the signature is meant to securely indicate approval of information as presented to a user. In addition, the transform (XSLT) part of XSL, as described in Section 3.7.1, is used as a transformation algorithm to change the structure of XML being presented.

Different stylesheets can produce radically different appearances for the same document. Cascading Style Sheets and Extensible Stylesheet Language stylesheets [XSL] are both examples of stylesheet languages that you can use with XML documents. Conversely, because they can be extracted from the data, any number of XML documents can share stylesheets.

### 3.7.1   Cascading Style Sheets

Cascading Style Sheets (CSS) were introduced in 1996 as a standard way to add information about style properties to HTML documents. Two W3C documents make up the CSS family of recommendations: Cascading Style Sheets, Level 1 [CSS1], and Cascading Style Sheets, Level 2 [CSS2]. CSS is a simple declarative language that allows authors and readers to attach styles such as fonts, colors, and spacing to HTML or XML documents. The CSS language is human readable and writable, and it expresses styles in common desktop publishing terms.

CSS stylesheets "cascade," which means that authors can attach one stylesheet to the document and the reader, depending on his or her preference, can attach a different stylesheet. For example, a reader might attach a stylesheet that accommodates human or technological handicaps. Although we do not go into that level of detail here, the CSS recommendations specify the rules for resolving conflicts between different stylesheets.

CSS2 builds on CSS1 by supporting media-specific style sheets. Authors can tailor their documents for presentation on various media such as visual browsers, aural devices, printers, Braille devices, and handheld devices.

CSS allows the rendering of elements by associating them with properties such as font size, font weight, color, and values. For instance, in Example 3-13, CSS renders the "Hello" element as a block-level element in 24-point bold blue text.

**Example 3-13**   *Use of CSS*

```
Hello {
  Display: block;
  Font-size: 24pt;
  Font-weight: bold;
  Color: blue;
}
```

### 3.7.2   Extensible Stylesheet Language

The Extensible Stylesheet Language (XSL) W3C Recommendation [XSL] defines the XSL language for expressing stylesheets. XSL builds on the prior work on Cascading Style Sheets Level 1 [CSS1] and Level 2 [CSS2] and the Document Style Semantics and Specification Language [ISO 10179].

XSL was developed to give designers greater control over needed features during pagination of documents and to provide an equivalent "frame"-based structure for browsing on the Web. It also incorporates the use of the XLink language [XLink] to insert elements into XML documents that create and describe links between resources.

XSL uses the XSL Transformations [XSLT] W3C Recommendation, formatting objects, and the XML Path Language W3C Recommendation (see Chapter 6) for tree construction, format control, and pattern selection. This approach provides detailed control over the presentation of portions of the source content and the association of properties with those content portions.

An XSL stylesheet processor accepts a document or data in XML and an XSL stylesheet, then produces the presentation format of that XML source content as specified by the designer of that stylesheet. This process involves two steps:

- Constructing a result tree from the XML source tree (referred to as tree transformation). In XSL, this tree is called the element and attribute tree. It represents a formatting object as an XML element, with the properties being represented by a set of XML attribute–value pairs. The XSL Transformations W3C Recommendation [XSLT] defines tree transformation.

With tree transformation, the structure of the result tree can differ quite dramatically from the structure of the source tree. During the construction of the result tree, the source tree can be filtered and reordered. Also, an arbitrary structure and generated contents may be added. Including formatting semantics as formatting objects in the result tree specifies the desired formatting. Numerous classes of formatting objects are available for this purpose.

• Interpreting the result tree to produce formatted results suitable for presentation on a display, on paper, in speech, or onto other media.

Each formatting object represents a specification for a part of the pagination, layout, and styling information. When formatting of the entire result tree occurs, the process applies the particular specifications to the content of that formatting object. Each formatting object class represents a particular kind of formatting behavior.

Properties associated with an instance of a formatting object control the formatting of that object.

**Note**

> The XSL Recommendation [XSL] states that XSL processors must use the XML namespace mechanism [Names] to recognize elements and attributes from this namespace. Elements from the XSL namespace are recognized only in the stylesheet, not in the source document. Implementers must not extend the XSL namespace with additional elements or attributes. Instead, any extension must take place in a separate namespace.

In Example 3-14, XSL transforms the Hello element to 24-point bold blue text.

**Example 3-14**   *Use of XSL*

```
<?xml version='1.0'?>
<xsl:stylesheet xmlns:xsl="http://www.w3.org/TR/WD-xsl">
  <xsl:template match="Hello">
    <FONT COLOR="blue" SIZE=24>
      <B><xsl:apply-template/></B>
```

```
    </FONT>
   </xsl:template>
 </xsl:stylesheet>
```

### 3.7.3    XSL Versus CSS

Both XSL and CSS are formatting languages, but they differ in several respects.

CSS is a simple formatting specification. It reads each XML element as it is scanned in the document and applies styles in that order. CSS doesn't change the structure of the XML; it merely changes the visual appearance of each node. In addition, CSS does not allow the user to access or display the content of the attributes. It can apply only to the elements' content, not their attributes.

XSL is more of a real programming language. That is, it allows the user to rearrange, filter, and add elements. XSL is more flexible and powerful than CSS, and better suited to XML documents except for simple display cases. This language allows the user to access and display the content of the attributes easily. The user can take an XML document and convert it to another XML document, an HTML document, an ASCII text file, or even a proprietary text format.

# 4 | XML Document Type Definitions

Document Type Definitions (DTDs) are important in data exchange. Parties exchanging data must agree on a format, and a DTD allows the specification of that format.

DTDs are used to specify the allowed syntax of an XML application [XML], including the values of entities and special properties of attributes—for example, that an attribute is a unique element identifier (ID). Familiarity with DTDs is useful because they are a fundamental part of XML parsing. In this book, we use DTDs to specify the syntax for XML signatures and some other XML security structures.

Recently, the W3C devised a new method of syntax specification, called XML Schema [Schema], which is described in detail in Chapter 5. Schemas are used in the XML Security standards and this book as the more authoritative syntax specification. Although schemas provide a more precise description and are better suited to handling XML namespaces [Names], they do not eliminate the need for DTDs. Also, as schemas are such a recent addition to the XML arsenal, fewer tools are available for handling schemas than for working with DTDs.

**Note**

> When the DTD of some signed XML specifies default attribute values, the expanded value of entities, and so on, it is usually necessary to also sign the DTD, as discussed in Chapters 9 and 10 on canonicalization and signatures. Otherwise, an adversary could change the DTD and, in effect, change the signed XML meaning without breaking the signature.

If you are already familiar with DTDs, you can skip the rest of this chapter.

## 4.1     Introduction to DTDs

An XML document consists of a prolog and a body. The document prolog contains the XML declaration and the document type declaration for that document, both of which are optional. The document type declaration specifies the root element of the document, and it can specify the DTD. The document body contains the actual marked-up document.

The markup in an XML document describes the document's storage and logical structure and associates attributes and their values with its logical structures, as described in Chapter 3. XML DTDs provide a vocabulary and syntax for describing a document's structure. The XML Recommendation provides document type declarations to define constraints on the logical structure and to support the use of predefined storage units.

The XML Recommendation [XML] defines the XML document type declaration as containing or pointing to markup declarations that provide a grammar for a class of documents. A markup declaration serves one of four purposes:

- It is an element type declaration (see Section 4.3).

- It is an attribute-list declaration (see Section 4.4).

- It is an entity declaration (see Section 4.5).

- It is a notation declaration (see Section 4.6).

This grammar is known as a Document Type Definition. A DTD defines the allowable building blocks of an XML document; that is, it defines the document structure with a list of permissible elements, attributes, nestings, and so on.

**Note**

> To make matters confusing, you could potentially use the abbreviation "DTD" for two different terms. The document type declaration includes everything between the string "<!DOCTYPE" and the matching ">". It can contain the Document Type Definition (DTD), or it can contain part of and point to the DTD. When people talk about the document type declaration, they usually say "doctype declaration" for short [XML A].

The document type declaration can point to an external subset (a special kind of external entity) containing markup declarations, it can contain the markup declarations directly in an internal subset, or it can do both. The DTD for a document consists of both subsets taken together.

Because you can define a DTD within a document or reference and access it externally, a single DTD can apply to one document or to many documents. External DTDs, by convention, appear in an ASCII text file with the extension .dtd. For example:

```
mydtd.dtd
```

Elements and attribute declarations form a framework against which a parser can test documents to see whether they meet the format described by the DTD. Declarations communicate information to the parser about document content, such as the following:

- The allowable sequence and nesting of tags

- Attribute values, including their types and defaults

- Names of referenced external files, whether or not they contain XML, and the format of non-XML data that might be referenced

- Entities that might be present

Although XML documents are not required to have a DTD, a large percentage of the XML specification [XML] deals with various sorts of declarations that are allowed in DTDs.

All XML documents must be well formed, as described in Chapter 3. A validating XML processor can use the DTD to validate a document—that is, not only to require it to be well formed but also to determine whether the document conforms to the definitions. If the document can be parsed successfully with a validating parser and its DTD, the document is valid. To be valid, a document's DTD must specify all of its structure. XML documents read by a nonvalidating parser do not have to be valid.

## 4.2    Document Type Declarations

An XML document refers to a DTD within an XML "<!DOCTYPE>" tag. The document type declaration can do either or both of the following:

- Contain the markup declarations in an internal subset within the <!DOCTYPE> tag

- Point to an external subset containing markup declarations

The document type declaration must appear before the first element in the document. Examples 4-1 and 4-2 provide samples of internal and external DTDs.

**Example 4-1** *Internal DTD*

```
<?xml version="1.0"?>
<!DOCTYPE memo [
  <!ELEMENT memo    (to,from,subject,body)>
  <!ELEMENT to      (#PCDATA)>
  <!ELEMENT from    (#PCDATA)>
  <!ELEMENT subject (#PCDATA)>
  <!ELEMENT body    (#PCDATA)>
]>
<memo>
  <to>Jon</to>
  <from>Chris</from>
  <subject>Reminder</subject>
  <body>Three PM meeting canceled. Have a great weekend</body>
</memo>
```

**Example 4-2** *External DTD*

```
<?xml version="1.0"?>
<!DOCTYPE memo SYSTEM "memo.dtd">        ◄── DTD reference
<memo>
  <to>Jon</to>
  <from>Chris</from>
  <subject>Reminder</subject>
  <body>Three PM meeting canceled. Have a great weekend</body>
</memo>
```

In the DTDs, "memo" is the root element.

## 4.2.1 Document Type Declaration Format

The document type declaration begins with <!DOCTYPE. The name of the document's root element follows, then either of two elements: (1) the DTD contained in a pair of square brackets or (2) the SYSTEM keyword and a URI for the external DTD. You can include either an external or an internal DTD, or both. The declaration ends with a close angle bracket (">"). For example:

```
<!DOCTYPE The-name-of-root-element
  SYSTEM "URI of external DTD" [
  Internal DTD
]>
```

The SYSTEM keyword simply indicates that a URI pointing to an external DTD follows. Line breaks and white space are not significant.

### 4.2.2    Document Type Declaration Guidelines

- A DTD declares all of the valid document elements using element type declarations. A DTD always contains the rules that define the syntax for elements and, if more than one are present, the relationship between elements.

- A document type declaration contains the rules that define the syntax for attributes for any elements that have attributes.

- It may contain rules that define entities.

- It may contain rules that define notations.

### 4.2.3    Conditional Sections

The external document type declaration subset can have portions that are included or excluded as indicated by an enclosing conditional syntax (e.g., the keyword "INCLUDE" or "IGNORE"). These keywords can be the value of an entity. This syntax was commonly used in SGML document preparation systems to "comment out" portions of a DTD, but it is rarely used in modern XML. See [XML] for further details.

## 4.3    Element Type Declarations

Elements are the main structure of an XML document. An element is defined as a group of one or more subelements or subgroups, character data, EMPTY, or ANY. Element type declarations identify the names of elements, the nature of their content, and how to use them. They have the following generic syntax:

```
<!ELEMENT    elementName    elementContents >
```

Sometimes the content is text. At other times, the content consists of other elements that are arranged in a certain order or used a certain number of times. The list of contents in an element type declaration is called the content model.

### 4.3.1    Element Structures

The element rules build a hierarchy of elements that describe how one element relates to another element. XML developers use a variety of names to describe the various relationships between elements. For example, elements can be referred to as subelements, parents, children, siblings, ancestors, descendants, trees, branches, leaves, or roots. All of these are tree terms.

A parent–child relationship exists when an element type declaration gives the name of the element and the children that element may have. The content type portion of the element definition defines the parent–child relationship. The DTD can specify the precise ordering of the child elements in the document and the number of times that the document can contain the child element. Similarly, the DTD may group elements to create more detailed rules.

When an element is contained within another element, it is referred to as a descendant of that element and the containing element is referred to as the ancestor. Thus the root element is the ancestor of all elements in the document. You must list the root element first in the DTD.

### 4.3.2    Element Content Models

Content models describe the relationship of elements and child elements by using keywords and symbols. Table 4-1 lists the three types of element content models that are indicators for what the element may contain.

Elements that you define as character data or EMPTY constitute terminals, so they can have no further descendants. For example:

```
<!-- Element A is a nonterminal. -->
<!ELEMENT A (B)>
<!-- Element B is a terminal. -->
<!ELEMENT B (#PCDATA)>
<!-- Element C is a terminal. -->
<!ELEMENT C EMPTY>
```

**Table 4-1** | Element Content Model

| Element Content | Meaning |
|---|---|
| (other elements) | A list of elements that can be nested within parentheses. |
| ANY | This element may contain zero or any combination of elements from this DTD or data. It takes the following content model form:<br>`<!ELEMENT elementName ANY>` |
| EMPTY | This element contains no data or elements. It takes the following content model form:<br>`<!ELEMENT elementName EMPTY>` |
| #PCDATA | This element contains parsed character data. It takes the following form:<br>`<!ELEMENT elementName (#PCDATA)>` |

**The ANY Content Model**

The keyword ANY is shorthand for mixed content that can contain all declared elements from the DTD. Although the ANY model is very useful, excessive use of this content model can make it difficult to limit document structures. XML document designers can use ANY as a placeholder or where extensibility is important. Listing ANY is useful for root elements of unstructured documents. For example, your DTD might include the following element type declaration:

```
<!DOCTYPE Chapter [
   <!ELEMENT Chapters ANY>
   <!ELEMENT Chapter (NUMBER | TITLE | #PCDATA)>
   <!ELEMENT NUMBER (#PCDATA)>
   <!ELEMENT TITLE (#PCDATA)>
]>
```

Your XML code would then include an element such as the following:

```
<Chapter>
        <NUMBER>10 </NUMBER>
        <TITLE> Cliché </TITLE>
        All good things come to those who wait
</Chapter>
```

### The EMPTY Content Model

You use the keyword EMPTY to declare an empty element. EMPTY means that the element has no child elements or character data. Such an element contains only attributes but no text. You can use an EMPTY element as a flag. Declaring an element to be EMPTY means that all instances of it must be empty. Note that an element with PCDATA or optional child elements may sometimes be empty. With the EMPTY content model, your DTD might include the following element declaration:

```
<!ELEMENT Part EMPTY>
```

Your XML code would then include an element such as the following:

```
<Part/>
```

### The #PCDATA Content Model

The presence of #PCDATA in an element type declaration means that the element can contain any valid character data. PCDATA is text occurring in a context in which markup and entity references such as "&amp;" may occur. No restriction constrains what the text can contain. For example, you might declare elements containing character data as containing only character data:

```
<!ELEMENT A (#PCDATA)>
```

Alternatively, you might declare them as containing a mixture of character data and elements:

```
<!ELEMENT A (#PCDATA | B | C)*>
```

The term "PCDATA," which stands for "Parsed Character DATA," is inherited from SGML. It means the XML processor parses the text in the XML document following the element tag looking for more markup tags.

**Soapbox**

A computer finds "mixed content" (content in which both PCDATA and elements are allowed) inherently more complex to parse than either element-only or PCDATA-only content. Furthermore, if mixed content did not exist, then XML could have rules saying the following:

- Arbitrary white space (spaces, new lines, and so on) is always allowed between two start tags, between an end tag and a start tag, and between two end tags.

- A parser never gives this white space to an application.

In other words, it would be easy to format XML with pretty indentation without having to worry about changing significant white space or breaking signatures. The possibility of mixed content and the requirement that all white space in content be given to the application makes white space problematical, however. See Chapter 9 for further discussion of this problem.

### 4.3.3    Frequency Indicators

The XML Recommendation [XML] specifies optional characters that follow an element name or list and that govern the frequency of that element or list item in the document. Table 4-2 lists the frequency indicators that can apply to an element content model. The absence of such an operator means that the element or content particle must appear exactly once.

The XML Recommendation requires that you use only one frequency indicator with each element name or group in parentheses. Of course, you can also use frequency indicators within groups and again for the entire group, which makes it possible to nest groups of elements.

### 4.3.4    Multiple Elements Within an Element

Generally, content models are built on a grouping of multiple elements. You can group elements by sequence, by alternative, or by both means. Table 4-3 lists the symbols that you can use to order multiple elements within an element's contents. You use the symbols to separate the list of child elements. Elements that contain only other elements have element-only content; elements that contain both other elements and #PCDATA have mixed content.

**Table 4-2** | Element Frequency Indicators

| Element Content | Meaning |
| --- | --- |
| (none) | This element must appear once and only once. |
| + (plus sign) | This element can occur once or several times. |
| * (asterisk) | This element can occur zero, once, or several times. |
| ? (question mark) | This element can occur zero or once. |

**Table 4-3** | Ordering Multiple Elements

| Element Content | Meaning |
|---|---|
| \| (vertical bar) | Select one from several elements: OR, as in "this or that." For example, (THIS \| THAT \| THOSE) means that only one of the choices of THIS, THAT, or THOSE can occur. |
| , (comma) | Each subsequent element follows the preceding element. Strictly ordered; analogous to an AND. For example, (YEAR, MONTH, DAY) means that a YEAR element must be followed by a MONTH element, followed by a DAY element. (YEAR, MONTH, DAY, DAY) means the same except that the content must contain exactly two DAY elements. |
| Space as a separator | No particular order of the listed elements is required. For example, (ElementA ElementB ElementC) means that all must appear but can do so in any order. |

### 4.3.5    General Guidelines for Element Type Declarations

Element content models (all the stuff in the parentheses) describe the element definitions. The ANY content model can prove useful during document conversion, but you should avoid using it in a production environment because it disables content checking in the affected element.

- If the content model is mixed, place #PCDATA first. Separate the following elements with vertical bars. The entire group must be optional.

- Begin elements with either a letter, an underscore ("_"), or a colon (":"). Follow that character with a combination of letters, numbers, periods ("."), colons, underscores, or hyphens ("-"). Do not include any white space. No tag should begin with "xml" in any capitalization. While technically the first character in a tag name may be a colon, in practice you should use colons only with namespaces, as explained in Chapter 3.

- To make processing easier and the DTD easier to read, use parentheses to group elements into recognizable sets.

- Separate child elements with spaces if the child elements are not required to appear in a specific order in the XML document—for example, (FIRST SECOND THIRD).

- Separate child elements with commas to force them to appear in a specific order in the XML document—for example, (FIRST, SECOND, THIRD).

- To indicate a choice, separate child elements with vertical bars ( "|" )—for example, (FIRST | SECOND | THIRD).

## 4.4    Defining Attributes in DTDs

Attributes provide additional information about elements and can be used for a wide variety of tasks. They make it possible to define the relationships between elements, no matter where they appear in the document. You can declare all attributes for an element in one declaration, or you can declare the attributes via several element declarations.

Start tags and empty element tags can contain attributes, which take the form of name–value pairs separated by an equals sign ("="). "<!ATTLIST>" declares an attribute in the DTD. To declare attributes in the DTD, use the following general format:

```
<!ATTLIST   ELEMENT_NAME   ATTRIBUTE_NAME   TYPE   DEFAULT_VALUE>
```

- ELEMENT_NAME is the name of the element in which the attribute appears.

- ATTRIBUTE_NAME is the name of the attribute.

- TYPE identifies the kind of attribute in use for this element.

- DEFAULT_VALUE is the value that the parser uses if the document creator specifies none.

### 4.4.1    Attribute Types

Ten kinds of attribute types are available in XML 1.0. As shown in Table 4-4, an attribute type identifies the kind of content for an attribute. During validation, the processor examines the attribute values in the document to determine whether they conform to the requirements of the attribute type that is assigned to the element.

**Table 4-4** | Attribute Types

| Type | Attribute Value and Meaning |
|------|------------------------------|
| CDATA | The value is character data consisting of any string of legal XML characters. CDATA is text that is not markup and does not include ampersands ("&"), less than signs ("<"), or quotation marks ("""). Use escaped characters such as &amp;, &lt;, or &quot; to include those forbidden characters. |
| ENUMERATED | A value from a list of possible values delimited by the vertical bar symbol. The value must appear in an enumerated list. The document author chooses only one such value. The keyword ENUMERATED is not actually used. |
| ID | The value is a unique ID for the element such that no other ID type attribute in the document shares this value. ID attributes can never have fixed default values. If an element has multiple attributes, only one can be of type ID. The attribute value for type ID must be a valid XML name. |
| IDREF | The value is the ID of another element. It specifies that the value of one attribute refers to an element found elsewhere in the document, where the value of the IDREF is the ID value of the referenced element. |
| IDREFS | A list of tokens separated by white space, each of which is an IDREF. |
| ENTITY | The name of an entity declared in the DTD. The value is an entity. The attribute value must match the name of an external unparsed entity. An image is an example of an ENTITY attribute where the binary data is available from another URL. |
| ENTITIES | Same as ENTITY except that multiple entities can be declared in the DTD, as long as they are separated by white space. The value is a list of entities. The attribute values must match the names of external unparsed entities. |
| NMTOKEN | Restricts the value of the attribute to a valid XML name token. The attribute value must contain letters, digits, periods, dashes, underscores, combining characters, or extenders. No white space or other characters can appear. NMTOKEN can be useful when you need to map an |

**Table 4-4** | *continued*

| | |
|---|---|
| | attribute value to a name that isn't part of XML but does meet the requirements for XML name tokens. |
| NMTOKENS | The value is a list of valid XML name tokens. This attribute is less common than, but similar to, NMTOKEN, except that multiple name values can appear; these name values must be separated from each other by white space. |
| NOTATION | The value is a name of a notation. You can declare one or more names of notations in the DTD when certain consequences should follow from the attribute. The keyword NOTATION must be followed by a list of notation identifiers. |

**Soapbox**

The ID attribute is very convenient for labeling elements but inconvenient in that it requires a DTD and a validating processor. This idea violates one of the goals of XML: It is desirable that documents be usable without a DTD. The flexibility of being able to name the ID attribute for an element anything you want is more or less useless. Given that at most one ID attribute can exist for any element, it would have been better to just pick a fixed name or use some unique syntax for it, such as a double equals sign followed by the ID label; then you would not need a DTD: "<element =="tag123" OtherAttribute="foo"/>".

### Enumerated Attribute Type

Example 4-3 shows a DTD that includes an enumerated attribute type. "FICTION" is the default attribute value in this example.

***Example 4-3*** *Enumerated attribute*

```
<?xml version = "1.0" encoding="UTF-8" standalone = "yes"?>
    <!DOCTYPE LIBRARY_DEPARTMENTS [
        <!ELEMENT LIBRARY_DEPARTMENTS ANY>
        <!ELEMENT CATAGORY EMPTY>
        <!ATTLIST CATAGORY TYPE (FICTION |
                                 BIOGRAPHY |
                                 HISTORY |
                                 PHILOSOPHY) "FICTION">
    ]>
```

```
<LIBRARY_DEPARTMENTS >
<CATAGORY TYPE = "BIOGRAPHY"/>
<CATAGORY TYPE = "HISTORY"/>
<CATAGORY/>
</LIBRARY_DEPARTMENTS >
```

The case of an attribute name is important. Document authors often declare multiple attributes for a single element. Attributes can hold only simple strings and must appear in the start tag for an element. Note the following:

- You may not include attributes in end tags.

- You must surround attribute values with quotes (single or double).

- You must begin an attribute name with a letter.

Document authors can attach a special attribute named xml:space to an element to signal their intention that the application should preserve the white space in that element or handle it using the application default. For a document containing this attribute to be valid, its author must include this attribute in the DTD. Declare this attribute as an enumerated type where one or both of "default" and "preserve" are the values.

### 4.4.2   Attribute Defaults

Specifying a default value for an attribute ensures that the attribute will receive a value even if the XML document didn't include it. Four types of attribute defaults exist, as shown in Table 4-5. The syntax for attribute defaults has the following format:

```
<!ATTLIST element-name attribute-name attribute-type
        "default-value">
```

## 4.5   Entity Reference Declarations

Entities are variables that define shortcut names. The parsing process replaces them with common text. You can declare entities either internally or externally.

"General entities" are entities for use within the document content (see Section 4.5.1). The XML Recommendation refers to these entities using the

**Table 4-5** | Attribute Default Values

| Value | Explanation |
| --- | --- |
| #DEFAULT value | The attribute's default value. |
| #REQUIRED | Document authors must include the attribute value in the element. Use a required attribute when you do not have an option for a default value but still want to force the attribute to be present. |
| #IMPLIED | Use of the #IMPLIED attribute is optional. Use an implied attribute when you do not have an option for a default value and you do not want to force the author to include an attribute. |
| #FIXED value | The attribute value is fixed. A fixed value does not allow document authors to change the attribute value. If a document author includes another value, the XML parser returns an error. |

unqualified term "entity." By comparison, "parameter entities" are parsed entities for use only within the DTD (see Section 4.5.2). General and parameter entities occupy different namespaces; a parameter entity and a general entity with the same name are two distinct entities.

## 4.5.1   Internal General Entity Reference Declarations

You define internal general entity references in the DTD by using an "<!ENTITY>" declaration. General entity values cannot contain a percent sign ("%"), ampersand ("&"), or double quote (" ""), unless these characters are inserted through character references. The syntax for an entity declaration has the following format, where "name" is the abbreviation for the replacement text:

```
<!ENTITY name "replacement text">
```

Make sure to enclose the replacement text in quotes, as it might contain white spaces.

You can use general entity references in the DTD only where their use will be part of document content. In other places in the DTD, you must use parameter entities as described in Section 4.5.2.

### 4.5.2 Parameter Entity Reference Declarations

Parameter entity references are similar to general entity references except that they begin with a percent sign ("%") and can appear only in the DTD. Developers frequently use parameter entities to encapsulate part of a declaration that is used frequently and has multiple variants. Parameter entity references also prove useful when multiple elements use the same content model—for example, when you want to share common lists of children and elements between elements. You must declare parameter entity references before using them.

A parameter entity reference declaration has the following syntax:

```
<!ENTITY % name "replacement text">
```

By using parameter entities, you can shorten the declarations of other elements and attributes. For example, you can place parameter entity references in an internal DTD subset when they provide whole declarations. You can place parameter entities inside a declaration in an external DTD subset to define content models, element names, and other parts of declarations in the DTD subset.

## 4.6 Notation Declarations

Notation declarations provide labels for content in a document. The XML Recommendation [XML] requires that the DTD contain all notation declarations for a document. You use notations to identify file types or for a variety of other tasks. Notations can identify the following items by name:

- The format of unparsed entities
- The format of elements that bear a notation attribute
- The application to which a processing instruction is addressed

Notation declarations provide a name for the notation, which you can then use in entity and attribute-list declarations and specifications. Notation declarations can also provide a name for an external identifier for the notation that allows an XML processor or its client application to locate a helper application capable of processing data in the specified notation.

Only one notation declaration can declare a particular name. The XML Recommendation stipulates that XML processors must provide applications with the name and external identifier or identifiers of any notation declared and referred to in an attribute value, attribute definition, or entity declaration. XML documents, however, can declare and refer to notations for which notation-specific applications are not available on the system where the XML processor or application is running.

**Note**

Use of notations is not common in modern XML and can cause problems with canonicalization. See the limitations listed in Chapter 9 on canonicalization.

# 5 | XML Schema

XML Schema [Schema] is a way of describing the allowable syntax of XML. This chapter briefly describes schemas that conform to this standard because of their use as the authoritative descriptions of XML Digital Signature, Encryption, and other constructs. Additionally, schemas are new enough that even people familiar with other aspects of XML or SGML, such as DTDs, may not be familiar with them.

**Soapbox**

> XML Schema offers a number of advantages, particularly in comparison with DTDs (see Chapter 4):
>
> - It is generally not difficult to guess what simple Schema descriptions mean.
>
> - Schemas are well integrated with namespaces [Names].
>
> - They provide finer-grained control over both data types and structures. That is, a schema provides stronger typing.
>
> - Schemas are part of XML. Of course, by definition, DTDs are also part of XML, but they have their own special syntax. In contrast, XML schemas are expressed in terms of ordinary, garden-variety XML syntax of elements and attributes. This fact makes it easier to manipulate and make assertions about schemas, and schemas can be used to describe themselves.
>
> There are a number of bad, or at least surprising, things about XML Schema:
>
> - The XML documentation on schemas is huge! The current Schema Recommendation has three parts that total about 400 printed pages.
>
> - Schemas don't fully replace DTDs. In particular, they do not provide the equivalent to DTD entities, although the "group" construct makes some attempt in this direction. In fact, the XML Schema Recommendation goes so far as to require use of a DTD to define "%p;" and "%s;" (prefix and suffix) entities so they expand into the namespace prefix in use for the elements defined by the schema. That this point surprised so many people may indicate a failure to properly set expectations for schemas.

- Schemas don't provide some fairly obvious facilities. Suppose you want to have the allowed content of an element depend on the presence or perhaps the value of an attribute—a common preference, and something that would have been desirable at least one place in XML Security. Perhaps such a feature will appear in the next, presumably even larger, version of the Schema Recommendation.

Whether you like the Schema Recommendation or not, use of it is clearly on the rise. In the future, schemas will be the way that W3C recommendations and an increasing number of applications describe their XML [Schema].

**History**

Schemas "came out" during the development of the XMLDSIG recommendation. The XMLDSIG working group decided to provide both DTD and schema syntax, with Schema serving as the authoritative description. Other W3C working groups made their own decisions, sometimes based on whether they had the resources to convert. In any event, it seems clear that future W3C work will use schemas, as the XML Encryption and XKMS W3C working groups already are.

## 5.1    Overview

A **schema** is a model for describing the structure of information. An XML schema is an XML language that defines a class of XML documents and describes the possible arrangement of tags and text in a valid document. Schemas can be the basis for machine validation of document structure. An "instance" of a schema is an XML document that meets the constraints of that schema. As an XML schema may describe another XML schema, it can be, somewhat confusingly, referred to as an instance of a schema.

The W3C Schema Recommendation language uses namespaces and reconstructs and refines the capabilities found in XML 1.0 DTDs (see Chapter 4). Schemas, unfortunately, do not fully replace DTDs. DTDs are a lower-level mechanism. According to the fundamental definition of XML 1.0 [XML], the parsing of XML input for an application automatically invokes any DTD present. Even nonvalidating parsers must pay attention to the internal subset DTD and implement entities and default values.

Trying to condense 400 pages of the formal specification into this chapter would be a losing battle. Instead, the goal here is to selectively cover only enough material to enable the reader to understand the schema constructs used in this book and a little more for background. Many features are not covered here, but are described more fully in the recommendation [Schema].

This chapter uses the following namespace for XML Schema elements and attributes:

```
xmlns:xs="http://www.w3.org/2001/XMLSchema"
```

All schemas have, as their root, the element "schema" in that namespace.

Section 5.2 covers the basics of the schema simpleType and complexType constructs. Section 5.3 actually specifies elements and attributes with these type constructs. In Section 5.4, we consider how schemas work with namespaces [Names]. A few miscellaneous aspects are left for Section 5.5.

## 5.2   Types

A fundamental concept of schema is that of a type. In this section, we discuss named types. You can also use anonymous types, as detailed in Section 5.3.

### 5.2.1   simpleType

A simpleType is a named type that cannot contain element content and cannot carry attributes. All attributes have a simpleType. Elements that are empty or have only text content are also simpleTypes. The Schema Recommendation provides a large number of predefined simpleTypes, the most general of which is "string." Most of these types have fairly descriptive names, such as "integer," "dateTime," and "anyURI." XML Security uses the "base64Binary" simpleType extensively; it indicates an octet stream encoded in base-64 [RFC 2045]. All of the special attribute types declarable in DTDs, such as ID, NMTOKENS, and IDREF, are also available as simpleTypes.

You can define additional simpleTypes by placing restrictions on existing simpleTypes. Such restrictions can affect various "facets" of the simpleType, such as its range of values, pattern of characters, or limitations on certain enumerated values, as explained in [Schema]. For instance, Example 5-1 defines a type for U.S. Social Security numbers of the form *ddd-dd-dddd*, where *d* is a digit.

**Example 5-1**   *Use of a simpleType*

```
<xs:simpleType name="SSN" >
  <xs:restriction base="xs:string>
    <xs:pattern value="\d{3}-\d{2}-\d{4}" />
  </xs:restriction>
</xs:simpleType>
```

### 5.2.2   complexType

A complexType can contain element content and carry attributes. The content permitted by the complexType itself is approximately modeled by the content of the complexType element. In Example 5-2, any element of type test1 must have a "bar" attribute and contain two children elements, foo1 and foo2, in that order. Also, foo1 can have any text content, foo2 has text content that looks like an integer, and the "bar" attribute must have a value that looks like the SSN type shown in Example 5-1.

**Example 5-2**   *Use of a complexType*

```
<xs:complexType name='test1'>
  <xs:sequence>
    <xs:element name='foo1' type='xs:string'/>
    <xs:element name='foo2' type='xs:integer'/>
  </xs:sequence>
  <xs:attribute name='bar' type='SSN'/>
</xs:compexType>
```

You can use <xs:choice/> instead of <xs:sequence/> to indicate that only one out of a series of possibilities should appear. In addition, you can nest these two mechanisms. All but the outer one may include minOccurs and maxOccurs attributes, which default to 1, to permit optionality or multiple occurrences.

To allow mixed text and element content in a complexType, add the

```
mixed="true"
```

attribute to the xs:complexType start tag.

To indicate that a complexType has only attribute content and not element content, simply omit any list of elements.

## 5.3    Elements and Attributes

An occurrence of xs:element specifies an element. It must have a "name" attribute or a "ref" attribute, but not both. If a "name" attribute appears, then a "type" attribute can appear. The value of a "type" attribute is the name of a type, either simple or complex; it specifies that the element will be of that type. The value of a "ref" attribute is the name of a global element; it indicates that the element being specified, presumably as part of a structure, has the same name and type as does the global element. In the absence of either a "type" or "ref" attribute, the element specification must contain an anonymous type (described later), or it will default to type "anyType" (also described later).

Schema elements come in two flavors, global and local. An xs:element element specifies both:

- For a global element, the xs:element appears as a child of xs:schema.

- For a local element, the xs:element appears as a grandchild of xs:schema or deeper descendant.

Typically, local element specifications are descendants of a global xs:element or xs:complexType. A global element can appear as the top-level element of an instance of the schema and must be defined with a "type" attribute.

A local element may have a minOccurs and/or maxOccurs attribute added to its xs:element specification to indicate the range of allowed occurrences. If minOccurs='0', the element is optional. You cannot restrict global elements in this manner. In effect, global elements, when used at the top level, always act as if they are specified with

```
minOccurs='0' maxOccurs='unbounded'
```

which indicates that no upper bound restricts the number of occurrences. For local elements, the default for both minOccurs and maxOccurs is 1. Although you cannot apply these limits to global elements, you can apply them to an appearance, through the "ref" attribute mechanism, of a global element within a complexType.

Local elements are, in some sense, qualified by their ancestors up to the global element in which they occur. That is, different instances of the same local element name with different types can exist as long as they occur with different ancestors or within different global elements. This idea is similar to the way in which attributes can be local to their element.

Example 5-3 illustrates some of these features. It includes the following items:

- A global element "foo," which is of type "bar"

- A complexType "bar," which has at least one and a maximum of 42 "intB" local element children, and zero or one "DT" local element children, and which permits text content to be mixed with that element content

- A global element "owT," which is of type "charlie"

- A complexType "charlie," which consists of either a "foo" element child or an "NM" local element child whose contents are of type NMTOKENS

Either "foo" or "owT" could appear at the top level of an instance of this schema.

**Example 5-3**   *Elements schema*

```
<xs:schema>

<xs:element name="foo" type="bar">
<xs:complexType name="bar" mixed="true">
  <xs:sequence>
    <xs:element name="intB" type="xs:integer" maxOccurs="42">
    <xs:element name="DT" type="xs:dateTime" minOccurs="0">
  </xs:sequence>
</xs:complexType>

<xs:element name="owT" type="charlie">
<xs:complexType name="charlie">
  <xs:choice>
    <xs:element ref="foo">
    <xs:element name="NM" type="NMTOKENS">
  </xs:choice>
</xs:complexType>

</xs:schema>
```

Attributes are usually local, as they are specified inside an element schema. Nevertheless, you can have global attributes with a schema, which you specify with an "xs:attribute" element at the top level inside the root "xs:schema" element. You can use such global attributes in any element defined by the schema.

Local attributes do not have minOccurs or maxOccurs attributes on their specifications, but they can have a "use" attribute that can have "required" or "optional" or "prohibited" for its value. A "use" attribute cannot appear in a global attribute. All global attributes are, in effect, optional for all elements specified by the schema.

Values for an attribute or element can appear in a schema via the optional "default" and "fixed" attributes. Only one of these attributes may occur, however. A "fixed" attribute specifies the value or content that the attribute or element must have if it appears. Schemas treat "default" somewhat differently for attributes and elements. If an attribute is missing but the schema specifies a default value, then the attribute is inserted with that value. If the attribute is present but has a null value, a default does not disturb that value.

On the other hand, for elements, a missing element is not created with a default value. Only if the element is present but has null content does the default have any effect—namely, it fills in the content of that element instance with the default value.

Example 5-4 illustrates some of these features of attributes in schemas. It defines three items:

- A global attribute called "atlas" of type IDREF

- A global element called "Top" of type "TT"

- A complex type "TT" that has empty content but an optional "Middle" attribute that, if present, has a URI as its value, and a "Bottom" attribute that, if absent, is inserted with a default value of "abc"

The global attribute "atlas" can also appear on the Top element.

**Example 5-4** *Attributes schema*

```
<xs:schema>

<xs:attribute name="atlas" type="IDREF"/>

<xs:element name="Top" type="TT"/>
<xs:complexType name="TT">
  <xs:attribute name="Middle" type="anyURI" use="optional"/>
  <xs:attribute name="Bottom" type="string" default="abc"/>
</xs:complexType>
</xs:schema>
```

### Groups

The Schema Recommendation provides a mechanism for expressing groups of elements or groups of attributes so that they can be incorporated into types more easily. The xs:group element is somewhat like xs:complexType. It can appear at the top level and contain the same sort of content. It can then be instantiated inside a complexType by using an xs:group element with a "ref" attribute, thereby giving the name of the top-level xs:group. The effect is as if the top-level xs:group content had appeared in full when the "ref" was invoked.

The same sort of thing is possible with attributes using the xs:attributeGroup element. Such an element inside a complexType can invoke a top-level xs:attributeGroup by giving its name in a "ref" attribute.

### Anonymous Types

Both xs:element and xs:attribute may have, as their content, a type structure without a "name" attribute. This "anonymous type" can be either a simpleType or, for elements, a complexType.

### anyType

With schemas, the special type "anyType" is the root of all simpleTypes and complexTypes and is the least restricted type. Thus, if we declare an element

```
<xs:element name="foo" type="anyType"/>
```

it can be anything from empty to arbitrary mixed content.

### Any, anyAttribute

The xs:any element may appear in a content model where we want additional flexibility. It enables you to restrict any valid XML content depending on the xs:any elements attributes. The processContents attribute can have "skip" or "lax" or "strict" as its value:

- With skip, no validity checking is done, and the contents are skipped over.

- With lax, checking is done on an opportunistic basis, but anything not understood is skipped.

- With strict, everything must be validated or an error occurs.

A "namespace" attribute consists of a list of allowable namespaces or classes of namespaces for "any" content, separated by white space. The list can include specific namespaces, "##any" to indicate that all namespaces are acceptable, "##local" to permit unqualified content, or "##other" to indicate that all namespaces except the targetNamespace (see below) are acceptable. "##targetNamespace" is also acceptable as a synonym for the targetNamespace.

- The attributes minOccurs and maxOccurs can be added to an "any" element.

- "anyAttribute" is a similar construct for attributes with the same "namespace" and "processContents" attributes possible.

## 5.4    Namespaces

Schemas are reasonably well integrated with namespaces. The xs:schema element, for example, should normally have a targetNamespace attribute. It indicates the namespace in which the elements and attributes defined by the schema should appear. If no such attribute exists, the schema is intended for unqualified names—perhaps to validate some XML designed before namespaces were recommended.

When a targetNamespace exists, that namespace must qualify all global elements and attributes. Local elements and attributes are a different matter, however. By default, they are unqualified and, in effect, get their namespace from their nearest global ancestor. But either or both of the elementFormDefault and attributeFormDefault attributes on the xs:schema element may be set to "qualified." Doing so requires that local elements or attributes, respectively, appear qualified with a namespace prefix bound to the targetNamespace. Any particular local element or attribute specification can override these defaults by using the "form" attribute on that specification with the value "qualified" or "unqualified" as appropriate.

The xs:include element provides a way to include parts of a schema that reside in different files. Within the content of xs:schema, you can say

```
<xs:include schemaLocation="http://example.com/schemaPart.xsd"/>
```

or something similar to include the schema content from that file as if it were present in the place of the xs:include element. You can include more than one file, and included files can themselves include other files.

The xs:redefine element is similar to include. However, as part of the body of an xs:redefine element, you can include specifications of types, elements, and so on that will override the particular components in the material being included.

Finally, you can use the xs:import element to input components from other namespaces. Each xs:import element must have a "namespace" attribute, which identifies the remote namespace of the components to be imported. It may also contain a schemaLocation attribute with a URI value to help in locating the remote schema. A normal xmlns attribute on the xs:schema element binds this remote namespace to a local prefix. Then, when components appear with that prefix, the schema will attempt to import that particular component from the remote schema. Although multiple xs:import elements may exist, they must be the first children of xs:schema, appearing before any other children.

## 5.5   Miscellaneous Aspects of Schemas

Several additional aspects of schemas don't fit too well into the preceding discussions.

### Abstractness

Any element or type can be made "abstract" by adding an

```
abstract="true"
```

to the "element" or "simpleType" or "complexType" element where the element or type is specified. Thus you cannot directly use the type or element in an instance of XML; rather, you can use it only in the specification of other types or elements. The "abstract" type/element has "false" as its default value.

### Annotations

You can insert "annotations" into a schema for human or automated consumption. These annotations use the xs:annotation element and are fairly obvious when they occur.

## 5.6   Parts Not Covered

This chapter did not cover many parts of the Schema Recommendation. When the discussion focused on only a few items from a long list, such as the list of basic simpleTypes, we have mentioned the existence of these additional items. Note, however, that some capabilities are generally not mentioned elsewhere:

### Schema in Instances

You can insert schema constructs into actual instances of XML—for example, to indicate the type of an element by adding an attribute. Such schema constructs in instances use a different schema namespace defined for that purpose. As we use schemas only to provide descriptive models for specification and expository purposes, this capability is not relevant.

### List Types

You can create types that consist of lists of instances of simpleTypes separated by white space.

### Union Types

You can create types that are unions of basic simpleTypes and combine them with list types.

### Restrictions on Type Derivation

You can specify a type so that you cannot derive other types from it or so that, in derivation, you cannot change certain facets of the type.

### All

You can create a complicated extension of groups with complicated restrictions.

### Nillable Elements

"Nillable" elements provide a method for declaring that it is valid for an instance of an element to be empty despite the element's type appearing to prohibit it.

### Unique/Key Values

A schema can indicate that certain attribute values or element contents within a specified scope must be unique values. In addition, it can indicate that certain, possibly composite values act as "keys" or references to keys in a manner somewhat similar to ID and IDREF.

### Deriving Types from Complex Types

You can specify a complex type by restricting or extending a complex type.

### Element Substitution

You can declare an element to be substitutable for another element.

# 6 | XPath: A Basic Building Block

The XML Security standards need a data model for and means of expressing operations on XML, particularly extraction of subdocuments. This need could entail modeling parsed XML and sending input to an application from an external encoding or XML that an application constructs internally and has not yet output.

For example, an XML document might represent a user form. Assume that a user fills in several fields that XML elements represent and then wants to digitally sign those fields. As Chapter 10 describes in detail, the signature object needs some method of specifying or pointing to these fields. XPath provides the necessary data model and method.

**Soapbox**

It might seem that meeting this goal would be easy because one data model would be in use throughout the XML standards, or at least throughout the XML standards issued by the W3C. After all, the W3C promotes tight integration of its standards activities, and its working group charters include mandatory review by related W3C working groups. In reality, the XML Recommendation, XML [Infoset], different levels of the Document Object Model [DOM], XPath, and so on all have somewhat different data models. Matters get even worse when you consider XML schema augmented infosets [Schema].

The XPath data model was chosen for two reasons:

- Subdocument extraction is necessary for both XML digital signatures and XML encryption: in the first instance when a subdocument is extracted for signing, and in the second instance when a subdocument is extracted for decryption. Both need a language such as XPath or XPointer (which is based on XPath) to express these operations.

- The data model must preserve literal prefix names, because these names can appear in patterns within attribute values or element content for XSLT and other XML standards, and they must be output as read or generated.

Given these requirements and this view of the best XML data model, it is not surprising that XML canonicalization is also based on XPath.

**History**

> XPath is closely related to XSLT and XPointer. XPath was developed when it was found that both XSLT and XPointer need similar capabilities. XPath's initial goal was to support both of them.

Because XML canonicalization, signatures, and encryption all make use of XPath, at least for expository purposes, a general understanding of XPath is important to understanding these XML security standards. See Figure 6-1.

If you are already familiar with XPath, you can skip this chapter. If you want more details on XPath, see the XPath Recommendation [XPath]. It assumes that XPath is operating on a node-set produced from an entire document. In XML Security, however, an XPath node-set often exists for a document subset.

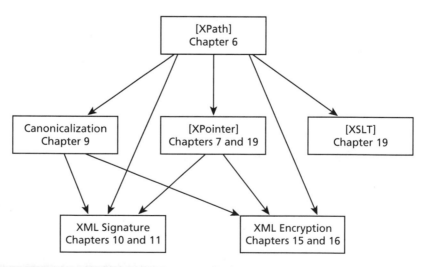

**Figure 6-1** | Some dependencies on XPath

The use of XPath to describe some operations in XML Security does not imply that the application must implement the full capabilities of XPath. Rather, an application typically needs only a subset of these features. Any method that produces the same results is considered acceptable.

## 6.1    Introduction to XPath

An XPath expression specifies a part of any XML object to which it is applied.

XPath models XML as a hierarchical tree of nodes. The best way of thinking of this structure is to say the following: An XPath operation takes an XPath node-set (or XML converted into an XPath node-set) and then tags certain nodes in that set as being selected. As long as you stay in the world of XPath node-sets, the entire original node-set remains accessible through XPath operations that can find related nodes from any starting node in the set. For example, XPath operations can find ancestor or descendant nodes. As soon as you leave the XPath world with a selected node-set, all nodes not output are lost. In XML Security, the nodes output exactly match those selected. For other uses of XPath, the nodes output might consist of the selected nodes and all nodes for which a selected node is an ancestor. For example, losing the nodes not output could occur when printing a selected node-set or using the selected nodes and original node-set to construct a new XML object.

## 6.2    Data Model

The XPath data model is relatively simple. Any XML document or object is a set of nodes of one of seven types (listed below). These nodes are organized into a hierarchical tree. In addition to this tree structure, a linear ordering of the nodes is maintained; this ordering is called "document order."

The document order of nodes matches the order in which the first character of that node appears in the document character string form. Thus an element node precedes all of its children, because the element start tag's opening left angle bracket occurs before all element content, attributes, or namespace declarations. By convention, the root node, which has no character representation, comes first in document order:

- Root node
- Element nodes

- Attribute nodes

- Namespace nodes

- Text nodes

- Processing instruction nodes

- Comment nodes

Note that no provision is made for DTDs or the XML declaration. In effect, XPath takes the point of view that DTDs and the XML declaration are part of the external form of XML. After reading XML into an application, the DTD and declaration have already been taken into account and are no longer useful. Similarly, the parsing of characters into an XPath node-set removes external artifacts such as CDATA sections and character references. Example 6-1 and Figure 6-2 provide an example of some XML and the resulting XPath data model.

***Example 6-1***    *External XML*

```
<?xml version="1.0" ?>
<example>qwert yuiop<ens:foo xmlns:ens="http://bar.example">
<bar a='b' c='d'/><bar/>
<!--fun--></ens:foo><![CDATA[more text]]></example>
<!--more fun-->
```

The following sections describe the seven node types in XPath, including the string value and extended name for each node type. In XPath, every node has a "string value" and some have "extended names"; both of these values are accessible through XPath functions, as described in Section 6.5.

### 6.2.1    Root Nodes

Every XPath node-set has one and only one root node for its tree. The top-level element of an XML document, often called the "root element," is a child of the XPath root node in the XPath node-set for that document. It is necessary to provide the root node because comments and processing instructions can appear both before and after the root element. The root node is the parent of such outside-of-document nodes. Many uses of XPath are intended to also apply to general external parsed entities and so allow multiple element children of the root node.

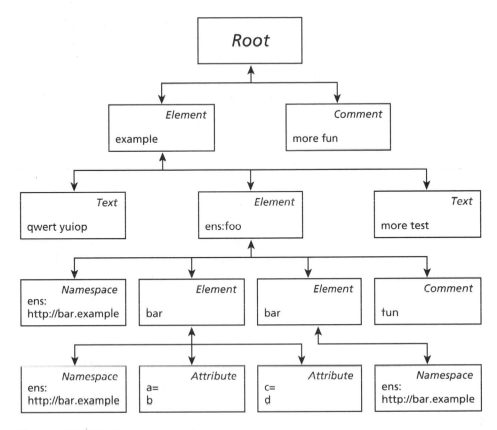

**Figure 6-2** | XPath data model

The root node has no parent. Every other node in an XPath node-set has exactly one parent.

The string value of the root node is the concatenation of the string value of all text node descendants of the root nodes organized in document order. Root nodes do not have extended names.

---

### 6.2.2 Element Nodes

An element node exists for each element in the original XML object. The XPath string value of an element is the concatenation of the string values of all of its text node descendants. For example, the text value of

```
<e>(one<!--two--> three<f g="hijklmnop">four <?five
    six?>seven</f>nine) xyz</e>
```

is

```
(one threefour sevennine) xyz
```

The extended name of an element node is its local name and the URI of its namespace, if any. It may consist of the namespace bound to its namespace prefix if one is present or the default namespace if no prefix is present. The URI of the extended name is null only if no namespace prefix exists and the default namespace is null or not declared in scope.

### 6.2.3    Attribute Nodes

Every element node has an associated and possibly empty set of attribute nodes. (Namespace declarations are not attributes, although they may look like them.) Although XPath considers the element to be the parent of its attribute nodes, it does not consider the attribute nodes to be children or descendants of their element. As a consequence, to access the attribute nodes, an application must use different XPath operations than the application uses to access children. This treatment of attributes in XPath differs from that found in the Document Object Model [DOM]: DOM does not treat elements as the parents of their attributes.

Because the XPath model is invoked after XML has been parsed by an application on input, the XPath node-set includes the default attributes. Attributes in the xml namespace, which affect all descendants of an element until they are overridden, such as xml:lang, nevertheless appear only as single attribute nodes for the elements in whose start tags they occur.

The string value of an attribute node is the normalized attribute value. See [XML].

The extended name of an attribute is its local name and the URI of its namespace if it has a namespace prefix. The URI part of the extended name is null if no namespace prefix is present.

### 6.2.4    Namespace Nodes

As shown in Example 6-1 and Figure 6-2, namespace declarations do not simply create namespace nodes attached to the element in whose start tag the namespace declaration occurs. Rather, XPath creates namespace nodes below all descendant elements of that element, except at and below element nodes where a new namespace declaration with the same prefix overrides the ancestral declaration.

**Note**

> Perhaps XPath decided to replicate the namespace declaration nodes over descendant elements to make it easier to access the set of namespace declarations in scope. In reality, this choice destroys information. Consider Example 6-2. After parsing and conversion to an XPath node-set, it is no longer possible to tell that the namespace declaration of prefix "x" appeared on element "B." Because of the namespace declaration at element "A," XPath would have created a namespace node at all descendants of "A" and "B," even if that same namespace declaration had not occurred at "B." Similarly, after conversion to an XPath node-set, you can't tell whether this declaration occurred on elements "C" or "D" in the input. This problem makes canonicalization more difficult, as explained in Chapter 9.

The string value of a namespace node is the namespace URI that is bound to the prefix. Thus the string value of the namespace nodes created in Example 6-2 is

```
http://foo.example/bar
```

As you might guess, the extended name for a namespace node has the prefix and the local name and the URI as the namespace. If the declaration involves the default prefix, the local name is null.

**Example 6-2**   *XPath and namespaces*

```
<x:A xmlns:x="http://foo.example/bar">
  <x:B xmlns:x="http://foo.example/bar">
    <x:C><D/></x:C>
  </x:B>
</x:A>
```

### 6.2.5   Text Nodes

Character content appears as text nodes. Text nodes always have at least one character in them, and a text node in the full XPath node-set never has an adjacent text node. Contiguous text in the original input, however long, appears as a single text node. An XPath selection, however, can select two or more text nodes without select intervening nodes of other types. Processing these nodes can, therefore, result in processing of two or more text nodes in a row.

The character data in a text node is the internal application version. Thus CDATA sections have already been processed, the character referred to replaces character references, and so on. For example, the external representation

```
&quot;<![CDATA[>"<]]>&amp;&quot;
```

appears as a text node with content

```
">"<&"
```

The string value of a text node is its character data. A text node has no extended name.

---

### 6.2.6 Processing Instruction Nodes

The extended name of a processing instruction is the target name of the processing instruction with a null URI. The string value of a processing instruction is the part of the instruction that occurs after the target and after any white space separating it from the target. The string value does not include the terminating "?>". Thus

```
<?foo  ?>
```

has a null string value, whereas

```
<?bar Bokm 42 yZgv?>
```

has the string value "Bokm 42 yZgv".

Note that any processing instructions in the DTD and the XML declaration do not appear as nodes of any sort in the corresponding XPath node-set. Other than that, a processing instruction node corresponds to each processing instruction in the external XML. (Although the XML declaration looks like a processing instruction, it is defined not to be one.)

### 6.2.7    Comment Nodes

A comment node does not have an extended name. The string value of a comment comprises everything between the opening "<!--" and closing "-->". For example, the string value of

```
<!---->
```

is null, whereas that of

```
<!--Four score and Seven.-->
```

is "Four score and Seven."

## 6.3    Location Paths

Location paths are a particular kind of expression that yields a node-set. Because they are so important, we will discuss them first, before general XPath expressions. Two kinds of location paths exist: relative and absolute.

**Relative Location Paths**

The evaluation of a relative location path occurs relative to some current context node. It consists of one or more location steps. If multiple steps are present, they are separated by slashes ("/").

The evaluation of these location steps goes from left to right, with the information being passed along consisting of a selected node-set. The node-set fed into the first or leftmost (and possibly only) location step consists of just the context node. The evaluation of a particular node step occurs for each node in the input node-set that the location steps to its left produce.

The node step can eliminate a node, produce a set of nodes, or produce a single node, which can be the same as or different from its input. The results obtained from evaluating a location step for each input node are merged into a node-set. This set then serves as the input for the next location step or as the value of the location path if no more location steps appear to the right. (See the upper part of Figure 6-3.)

**Absolute Location Paths**

An absolute location path begins with a forward slash character ("/"), which represents the root node of the document containing the context node. If the absolute location path consists of just a slash, it selects only this root node.

If a relative location path follows the slash, the path name evaluates to that relative path location with the initial input of this root node.

**Abbreviated Location Paths**

For convenience, abbreviations are available for commonly used parts of absolute and relative locations paths, as described in Section 6.3.5.

### 6.3.1   Location Steps

Every location step consists of three parts, as shown in the lower part of Figure 6-3:

- An *axis,* which specifies the data model relationship between the input node and the nodes that are subject to the node test. The simplest axis, "self," passes the input node to the node test.

- The *node test* can filter the nodes selected by the axis to nodes of a certain type or name.

- *Predicates* are enclosed in square brackets ("[ ]") and apply further tests that can eliminate nodes.

You separate the axis from the node test with a double colon ("::"). Both are always present in a location step, although some abbreviations can substitute for the axis and node test or just for the axis (see Table 6-3). Predicates are optional.

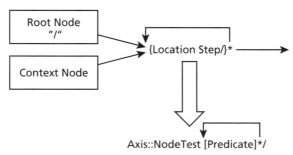

*Zero or more occurences.

**Figure 6-3** | Location paths and steps

### 6.3.2   Axes

The axis portion of a location step takes each input node to that step and coverts it to zero or more nodes with a particular data model relationship to the input node. Table 6-1 lists the 13 axes defined by XPath.

**Table 6-1** | XPath Axes

| Axis | Description |
|------|-------------|
| `ancestor::` | The node-set consisting of the parent of the context node, the parent of that node, and so on. Always includes the root node unless the context node is the root node, in which case the result is the empty node-set. |
| `ancestor-or-self::` | Same as the "ancestor::" axis except that it also includes the context node. |
| `attribute::` | The node-set of the attributes of the context node. It produces the empty set if the context node is not an element, or it is an element with no attributes. |
| `child::` | The children of the context node. Attributes and namespace nodes are not considered children. |
| `descendant::` | The node-set consisting of the children of the context node, the children of the children, and so on. Attributes and namespace nodes are not considered children. |
| `descendant-or-self::` | Same as the "descendant::" axis except that it also includes the context node. |
| `following::` | The set of all nodes that appear after the context node in document order, excluding attribute nodes, namespace nodes, and descendant nodes. |
| `following-sibling::` | The node-set of the children of the context node's parent that appear after the context node in document order. However, If the context node is an attribute or namespace node, the "following-sibling::" axis is empty. |
| `namespace::` | The node-set of the namespace declarations for which the context node is the parent. It consists of the empty set if the context node is not an element or if it is an element with no namespace declarations. |

*(continued)*

**Table 6-1** | *continued*

| | |
|---|---|
| `parent::` | The node-set consisting of the one node that is the parent of the context node, unless the context node is the root; in that case, it produces the empty node-set. |
| `preceding::` | The set of all nodes that appear before the context node in document order, excluding attribute nodes, namespace nodes, and descendant nodes. |
| `preceding-sibling::` | The node-set of the children of the context node's parent, which appear before the context node in document order. If the context node is an attribute or namespace node, the "preceding-sibling::" axis is empty. |
| `self::` | The identity axis. It produces the node-set consisting of the context node. |

### 6.3.3   Node Tests

The node test portion of a location step applies a test to the name or type of each node in the node-set produced by the axis. Table 6-2 lists the node tests found in XPath. Several are defined in terms of the "principal node type" of the axis. That type is "element" except for the "attribute::" and "namespace::" axes, where the principal node types are "attribute" and "namespace," respectively.

For example,

```
following::text()
```

is the set of all the text nodes in the document after the context node ignoring descendants. By comparison,

```
/descendant::n1:foo
```

is the set of all elements with name "foo" in the namespace bound to the prefix "n1" in the document containing the context node.

### 6.3.4   Predicates

One or more predicates, each inside square brackets, can optionally appear in a location step after the node test. Each predicate is evaluated, and nodes are

**Table 6-2** | XPath Node Tests

| Node Test | Description |
|---|---|
| `::node()` | Does nothing. It selects all nodes of any type from the axis output. |
| `::*` | Selects all nodes with the same type as the principal node type of the axis. |
| `::text()` | Selects only text nodes. |
| `::comment()` | Selects only comment nodes. |
| `::processing-instruction()` | Selects only processing instruction nodes. |
| `::processing-instruction(Literal)` | Selects only processing instruction nodes with a target equal to *Literal*. |
| `::QName` | Selects nodes only if their expanded names have the same local part and namespace URI as the expansion of *QName*.<br><br>A *QName* is a possibly namespace-qualified name. It is interpreted as an expanded-name, with the prefix being expanded based on the expression context in the same way as attribute names are expanded. That is, if no namespace prefix exists, the namespace URI is null. An error occurs if *QName* uses an unbound namespace prefix. |
| `::NCName:*` | Selects nodes only if their expanded names have a namespace URI matching that to which the *NCName* prefix is bound. An error occurs if it is not bound to a namespace. The local part of the name can be anything legal for an XML local name. |

selected only if all predicates present evaluate to "true." However, the truth values of numeric predicate expressions are specially determined. In particular, if the "position" of the node (defined below) matches the numeric value of the predicate, the predicate is considered "true." If they are not equal, the predicate is considered "false" and the node is not selected.

"Position" is the location at which a node appears in an axis, starting at 1, in document order for a forward axis, and in reverse document order for a reverse axis.

- A forward axis can contain nodes only at or after the context node in document order.

- A reverse axis can contain nodes only at or before the context node in document order.

Except for the "self::" axis, where it doesn't matter, only the ancestor, ancestor-or-self, preceding, and preceding-sibling axes use a reverse document order.

Thus

```
[position()=7]
```

and

```
[3+4]
```

have the same effect as predicates—namely, selecting only the seventh position node in the location step axis.

```
/descendant::*[starts-with(local-name(),"de")]
```

selects all elements whose local names start with "de" in the document containing the context node.

### 6.3.5   Abbreviated Notation

Table 6-3 lists the abbreviations available in XPath.

The shortest way in XPath to select all nodes in a node-set is as follows:

```
( //. | //@* | //namespace::* )
```

XPath does not consider attributes and namespace nodes to be descendants of an element. Thus the attributes and namespaces must be gathered separately. This expression occurs frequently in connection with XML Security, particularly during canonicalization.

## 6.4   Expressions

Expressions in XPath include the sorts of structures, operators, and data types found in most computer languages, albeit with a few differences. This section gives an overview of these distinguishing features. Consult the XPath Recommendation [XPath] for the full details. Note that location paths can

**Table 6-3** | XPath Abbreviations

| Abbreviation | Description |
|---|---|
| | **Examples** |
| `//` | Equivalent to the location step `/descendant-or-self::node()/` Because this path is defined as ending with a slash, it cannot occur at the end of a location path. Because it is defined as starting with a slash, when it occurs at the beginning of a location path, that path is absolute. |
| | `//self::node()` |
| | An abbreviated absolute location path for all of the elements, comments, and processing instructions in a document. |
| | `child::foo//self::bar` |
| | All "bar" elements that are descendants of a "foo" element child of the context node. |
| `@` | Equivalent to the axis `attribute::` |
| | `//@*` |
| | All attribute nodes in a document. |
| | `@foo` |
| | The "foo" attribute of the context node. |
| `..` | Equivalent to `parent::node()` |
| | `../child::comment()` |
| | All comment children of the context node's parent. |
| | `//self::foo/..` |
| | All parents of "foo" elements in the current document. |
| `.` | Equivalent to `self::node()` Sometimes useful in conjunction with `//`. |
| | `.//` |
| | All elements, comments, and processing instructions under the context element. |
| | `//.` |
| | All elements, comments, and processing instructions in the document. |

(continued)

**Table 6-3** | *continued*

| default axis is child | `child::`<br>Can be omitted. |
|---|---|
| | `foo//bar`<br>All "bar" elements that are descendants of a "foo" element child of the context node. |
| | `//foo/bar`<br>All "bar" elements that are children of "foo" elements in the document. |

appear in expressions, and expressions can appear in location paths as predicates (see Section 6.3.4).

The evaluation of XPath expressions occurs in a context. This context consists of a node, position, and set of variable bindings. Section 6.3 discussed nodes and positions as they apply to location paths. XPath does not support looping or assignment constructs, although you can achieve a limited repetition effect by using an axis in a location step. While the context node and position can be different at different places in evaluating an XPath expression, particularly inside a location path, the context variable bindings do not change during the evaluation of an expression.

Location paths always produce a node-set, which can be empty.

### 6.4.1 Function Calls

The syntax for a function call has the typical format: the function name followed by zero or more comma-separated arguments (parameters) in parentheses. For example:

```
example(parameter1, parameter2)
```

When the type of a particular parameter is fixed as "string," "number," or "boolean," and a different type of parameter is supplied, the type is converted as if by calling the "string( )," "number( )," or "boolean( )" function, respectively. An error occurs if a parameter of any other type is supplied when the program expects a "node-set"–type parameter.

Section 6.5 provides a full list of the core library functions. Particular applications of XPath may supplement this library. Node tests (listed in Section 6.3.3) that look like function calls are considered to be special instances of the XPath syntax, not separate functions.

### 6.4.2    Operators

This section lists all of the operators available in XPath expressions except for the operators that are part of the syntax of location paths, such as the slash and double colons. If the values presented to an operator are of the wrong type, they are converted, or else generate an error. Note that some operators, such as the left angle bracket ("<"), must be encoded as a character reference or the like ("&lt;") if they occur in an XML attribute value or element content.

**( )**    Operators have precedence and association direction as described in [XPath] but can be overridden or clarified by explicit grouping via parentheses.

#### Node-Set Operators

**|**    The vertical bar character produces the union of the node-sets appearing before and after it.

#### Boolean Operators

Boolean operators appear syntactically between two operands.

**or**    The logical "or" of the Boolean values appearing before and after it. When the left operand is true, the right operand is not evaluated.

**and**    The logical "and" of the Boolean values appearing before and after it. When the left operand is false, the right operand is not evaluated.

For the comparison operators shown below, if both operands are node-sets, then the comparison is true if either of the following conditions applies:

- If one operand contains any node whose string value compares as true with the string value of any node in the other operand.

- If one operand is a node-set and the other is a string, number, or boolean, then the comparison is true if any node in the node-set compares as true with the other operand after being converted by the "string( )," "number( )," or "boolean( )" function, respectively.

= Tests for equality between its operands. If neither operand is a node-set, both are converted to the same type as follows:

- If either is a Boolean value, the other operand is converted to a Boolean value.

- If neither is a Boolean value, but one operand is a number, the other is converted to a number.

- If neither is a Boolean value or a number, then both operands are converted to strings.

!= Tests for inequality between its operands. Use the same rules as for "=" if neither operand is a node-set.

For the following comparison operators, if neither is a node-set, then both are converted to numbers and compared according to [IEEE 754].

< True if the left operand is less than the right operand.

> True if the left operand is greater than the right operand.

<= True if the left operand is less than or equal to the right operand.

<= True if the left operand is greater than or equal to the right operand.

### Arithmetic Operators

Double-precision 64-bit floating-point numbers use the [IEEE 754] system of binary floating-point arithmetic. It includes positive and negative infinity, positive and negative zero, and "Not-a-Number" (NaN). The numeric operators, if necessary, convert operands as if by calling the "number( )" function.

**div** The left operand divided by the right operand. (A slash ("/") cannot be used for division because it separates location path steps.)

**mod** The remainder of the left operand divided by the right operand with truncation, not rounding.

+ The sum of the left and right operands. The unary plus is not supported.

- The left operand minus the right operand. It may be used as a unary operator with only a right operand that produces the same result as if the left operand had been zero. Because XML permits you to use this character inside names, it may be necessary to insert white space before a minus sign: "x-y" is a single token and "x- y" is two tokens separated by a space, whereas "x -y" and "x - y" are x minus y.

## 6.5    Function Library

All XPath implementations must include certain core functions. For particular applications, this function library may be augmented. For example:

- XML canonicalization adds the function "here( )". (See Chapter 9.)

- XPointer adds several functions and data types. (See Chapter 7.)

Of course, the various operators that can appear in XPath expressions may also be considered as functions invoked by the operator's syntax rather than the usual functional syntax. XPath does not consider the node tests listed in Section 6.3.3, which look like function calls (such as "text( )"), to actually be functions.

The rest of this section describes the functions in function prototype format. An italicized data type before the function name gives the type of output. The function name appears in boldface type. Each parameter is represented by its italicized data type. Where a question mark ("?") appears after a parameter data type, it indicates that the parameter is optional.

### 6.5.1    Node-Set Functions

Node-set-related functions are listed here in alphabetic order by function name, followed by a description of their output.

**Note**  The "id" function, in its simplest mode with a string parameter, and the "count" function are particularly important to XML Security.

*number* **count** (*node-set*)

The number of nodes in the parameter.

*node-set* **id** (*object*)

The element with a unique ID equal to the parameter if the parameter is a string. If the parameter is a node-set, it consists of the set of elements, each with a unique ID equal to the string value of any member of the node-set. For other parameter types:

- The parameter is converted to its string value, which is treated as a list of tokens separated by white space

- The result is the set of elements with unique IDs equal to any of those tokens

*number* **last**( )

A number equal to the context size of the expression evaluation context.

*string* **local-name**(*node-set?*)

The local part of the expanded name of the first node, in document order, in the parameter node-set. If the parameter node-set is null or if the first node has no expanded name, the function returns a null string. If the parameter is omitted, the function acts as if the parameter were a node-set containing only the context node. For example:

```
local-name ( <foo:bar xmlns:foo="http://xyz.example"/> ) = "bar"
```

*string* **name** (*node-set?*)

The prefix-qualified name representing the first node, in document order, in the parameter node-set. If the parameter node-set is null or if the first node has no expanded name, the function returns a null string. If the parameter is omitted, the function acts as if the parameter were a node-set containing only the context node. For example:

```
name ( <foo:bar xmlns:foo="http://xyz.example"/> ) = "foo:bar"
```

**Note**

In the case where multiple prefixes are bound by namespace declarations to the same URI, XPath permits the return of any of these prefixes as part of the qualified name. However, XML Security **requires** that the prefix returned always be the original prefix appearing in the XML before conversion to an XPath node-set. Otherwise, conversion of XML to an XPath node-set would destroy the information regarding what prefix was originally used. As a consequence, the XPath node-set could not be printed consistently.

*string* **namespace-uri** (*node-set?*)

The URI of the expanded name of the first node, in document order, in the parameter node-set. (It will be null except for element and attribute nodes that have namespaces.) If the parameter node-set is null or if the first node has no expanded name, the function returns a null string. If the parameter is omitted, the function acts as if the parameter were a node-set containing only the context node. For example:

```
namespace-uri ( <foo:bar xmlns:foo="http://xyz.example"/> )
                 = "http://xyz.example"
```

*number* **position**( )

A number equal to the context position of the expression evaluation context.

---

### 6.5.2    String Functions

The string functions either return a string result or require string parameters. They are listed in alphabetic order here by function name, followed by a description of their output.

*string* **concat** (*string, string, string*ˈ )

The concatenation of its parameters. The "*" indicates that additional string parameters may be present.

*boolean* **contains** (*string, string*)

True if its second parameter appears as a substring of its first parameter; otherwise, false.

*string* **normalize-space** (*string?*)

Its parameter, or the string value of the context node if its parameter is omitted, with leading and trailing white space deleted and each internal contiguous run of white space converted to one space.

*boolean* **starts-with** (*string, string*)

True if its first parameter starts with its second parameter; otherwise, false.

*string* **string** (*object*?)

Converts the object to a string. If the object is a node-set, the function returns the string value of the first node in the set in document order or the empty string if the node-set is empty.

*number* **string-length** (*string*?)

The length of the parameter or, if the parameter is omitted, the length of the string value of the context node.

*string* **substring** (*string, number, number*?)

That part of its first parameter starting at the position specified by the second parameter and continuing for the third parameter number of characters or until the end of the first parameter if the function call omits the third parameter. Following are some examples:

```
substring ("12345", 2, 2) = "23"
substring ("12345", 4, 99) = "45"
substring ("12345", -1, 3) = "1"
```

*string* **substring-after** (*string, string*)

The remainder of the first parameter after the second parameter's first occurrence within the first parameter, or the empty string if there are no such occurrences.

*string* **substring-before** (*string, string*)

The part of the first parameter that comes before the second parameter's first occurrence within the first parameter, or the empty string if there are no such occurrences.

*string* **translate** (*string, string, string*)

Returns the first parameter with occurrences of characters that also appear in the second parameter replaced by the corresponding character in the third parameter. If no corresponding character occurs in the third parameter, because the third parameter is shorter than the second parameter, the character is simply deleted from the first parameter. For example:

```
translate ( "123456", "156", "IV") = "I234V"
```

### 6.5.3    Boolean Functions

Boolean functions yield a Boolean result. They are listed alphabetically by function name here, followed by a description of their return value.

*boolean* **boolean** (*object*)

Converts its parameter to a Boolean value according to the following rules:

- A node-set is true only if it is nonempty.

- The Boolean function passes through its parameter if that parameter is a Boolean value.

- A string is true only if it is of nonzero length.

- A number is true only if it is nonzero and not NaN (Not a Number) [IEEE 754].

- For other types of parameters, the results depend on the type.

*boolean* **false**( )

Returns the "false" Boolean value.

*boolean* **lang** (*string*)

The parameter must be a language tag [RFC 1766]. This function returns true if the context node's language is the same as or is a more specific language than the parameter. The language of the context node is determined by looking for an xml:lang attribute there or at the nearest ancestor node with an xml:lang attribute. If no xml:lang attribute can be found, the function returns the "false" Boolean value.

Language tags consist of a primary tag followed by zero or more subtags separated by hyphens. All tags are case insensitive—for example, "fr," "NO-nynorsk," and "en-US-brooklyn." A language tag is a more specific language tag than the parameter if it consists of the parameter extended by one or more subtags.

*boolean* **not** (*boolean*)

Returns true if its parameter is false; otherwise, returns false.

*boolean* **true**( )

Returns the "true" Boolean value.

### 6.5.4 Number Functions

Number functions yield a numeric result. They are listed alphabetically by function name here, followed by a description of their return value.

*number* **ceiling** (*number*)

Returns the smallest (closest to minus infinity) integer that is not less than its parameter.

*number* **floor** (*number*)

Returns the largest (closest to plus infinity) integer that is not greater than its parameter.

*number* **number** (*object?*)

Converts its parameter to a number and then returns that number. If the optional parameter is omitted, the function acts as if that parameter were the node-set consisting of the context node. Conversion of various types of parameters occurs as follows:

- Boolean "true" and "false" values are converted to 1 and 0, respectively.

- A string representing a number is converted to the nearest [IEEE 754] number. Leading and trailing white space characters are ignored. Other strings are converted to NaN (Not a Number).

- A node-set is first converted to a string, as if by a call to the "string" function, then that string is converted as above.

- All other types of parameters are converted in a type-dependent fashion.

*number* **round** (*number*)

Returns the integer that is closest to its parameter. If the parameter is exactly midway between two integers, it is rounded toward plus infinity.

*number* **sum** (*node-set*)

Converts each node in the parameter into its string value, converts that value to a number, and finally returns their sum.

# 7 | URIs, xml:base, and XPointer

An important aspect of XML Security, as well as of the World Wide Web in general, is the ability to point to a wide variety of data objects. As Section 7.1 describes, Uniform Resource Identifiers (URIs) offer a way to achieve this goal. Because URIs can be relative to some assumed base location/name, you need a method for specifying such a base when it might default incorrectly, as noted in Section 7.2. Finally, when you need to point to part of an XML document, you can invoke the expressive power of XPath (discussed in Chapter 6) through the fragment part of a URI reference using the XPointer mechanism, the topic of Section 7.3.

If you are thoroughly familiar with URIs, xml:base, and XPointer, you can skip this chapter. If you are generally familiar with these topics and don't want to get too deep into their details right now, you might consider skipping ahead and referring back to this chapter when necessary.

Note that XLink is a related XML Recommendation [XLink] that provides a flexible mechanism, including the association of semantics with a pointer. In XML Security, the surrounding XML security structures specify the meaning of a pointer such as a URI. For this reason, XML Security does not need or use XLink.

## 7.1    URIs

A Uniform Resource Identifier [RFC 2396] is the fundamental way to name or locate something in the World Wide Web. Formally, URIs represent the union of Uniform Resource Locators and Uniform Resource Names [RFC 2141].

### 7.1.1 URI Syntax

The most general syntax for a URI is

```
Scheme ":" scheme-specific-part
```

If the scheme-specific-part starts with a double slash ("//"), the URI is called a "generic URI." In this case, a specific substructure to the scheme-specific-part is implied as follows:

```
Scheme "://" authority path [ "?" query ]
```

Here square brackets surround the optional parts, italics indicate variables, and quoted text indicates fixed characters.

The scheme name is case independent and must start with a letter. The remainder of the scheme name can consist of any combination of letters, digits, periods ("."), hyphens ("-"), and plus signs ("+"). The most common scheme seen by users is "http:"; it indicates a pointer to a resource the user can obtain through the Hypertext Transfer Protocol (HTTP; [RFC 2616]).

### Authorities

According to the specification of URIs, the "authority" portion is scheme dependent and can be null. Thus a scheme can have its own registry, and URIs using that scheme could potentially use names in that registry as their authority section. As a practical matter, however, almost all authority sections seen in real life are "server"-based. That is, they rely on the specification of a server computer on the Internet. When desired, they can refer to particular accounts and/or ports at such computers as described below.

The general syntax for a server-based URI authority portion is

```
[ [ userInfo "@" ] host [ ":" portNumber ] ]
```

Unless the authority is null, it must always specify a host (computer). It can be optionally preceded by user information and an at sign ("@"), where the user information identifies a user or account at that host. A colon and a port number can also follow it.

The user information could consist of a user name or an account number. On many systems, it is structured as follows:

```
UserName [ ":" Password ]
```

This syntax indicates that a user name is optionally followed by a colon and a password. Use of this format to send plain text passwords is dangerous and not recommended except in the extraordinary circumstance that the "password" is intended to be public knowledge.

The host specification can consist of either a numeric address or a domain name [RFC 1034, 1035] to be looked up to find the address. Domain names are a dotted sequence of labels such as "server.example.mp.us" or "www.example.com". Numeric addresses can appear in several formats. The Internet is currently based on version 4 of the Internet Protocol (IPv4), which uses 32-bit addresses [RFC 791]. Version 6 (IPv6), which uses 128-bit addresses, is being slowly deployed, however [RFC 2460]. Numeric host addresses must follow one of the standardized formats:

- A "dotted quad" takes the form x.y.z.w, where each letter is an integer in the range 0 to 255. This form represents the IPv4 host address with four bytes of those integer values in that order (i.e., $w + z*2^8 + y*2^{16} + x*2^{24}$). Example: "10.0.0.1".

- An integer in the range 0 to $2^{32} - 1$ represents an IPv4 host with that address. Example: "167772161", which has the same meaning as 10.0.0.1.

- Numeric IPv6 addresses within square brackets can be represented in a flexible format that preferably consists of hexadecimal chunks of four digits [RFC 2373]. Example: "[1080:0:0:0:8:800:200C:417A]". (A number of abbreviations are available, such as squeezing out one run of zeros by using "::", as in "[1080::8:800:200C:417A]".)

**History**

Internet protocols historically differentiated between numeric addresses and domain names in user input by placing numeric addresses inside square brackets—for example, "[10.0.0.1]". Although no all-numeric domain names existed, that might be confused with numeric addresses because no numeric top-level domain names (the last label in a domain name) were allowed, they might be created in the future. The initial URL design violated this principle by using a naked dotted quad, thereby leaving no way to distinguish this type of name from certain all-numeric domain names. For compatibility reasons, this format had to be carried forward into URIs. As a result, it will be very difficult to ever create general-use numeric top-level domain names.

The optional port number part of the authority information indicates how to obtain the resource from the specified host by using the "scheme". Typically communication with the server occurs through the Transmission Control Protocol (TCP; [RFC 793]) or some other method in which a numeric port or other designator selects the type of server process initially contacted. For example, TCP port 80 is assigned to HTTP, so a server expects to speak HTTP on a connection established for a request arriving addressed to that port. The port number optional field, when present, specifies the port to connect to at the server. For example:

```
http://www.example.com:8000/foo/bar/
```

specifies that an HTTP connection will use port 8000 at the computer specified by "www.example.com", instead of port number 80, which is typically assigned to HTTP.

**Note**

The complex design of the authority portion of URIs—particularly the choice to put the optional user information first—enables semantic security attacks that work because few users will understand what a complex authority portion really means. For example, <http://www.navy.mil@167772161/page.html> looks like a URI pointing to a Web page of the U.S. Navy because users are accustomed to believing the domain name that appears immediately after "//". In fact, it is a pointer to the host at numeric address 167772161, which is presumably run by imposters. The identifier "www.navy.mil" will merely be provided to that host as a user name and probably ignored. Browsers should check for such semantic attacks and warn the user. The Opera browser [Opera] does so, but Netscape Navigator and Internet Explorer do not.

**Soapbox**

It's too late to change URIs, but it would have been better if the host portion always came first.

### Paths

A URI path consists of a slash ("/") followed by one or more path segments separated by slashes. Each path segment consists of a string that can take parameters after a semicolon (";"), although the use of such parameters is extremely rare. For example:

```
http://foo.example/pub/seg1/bar
http://bar.example/seg2/seg3;rare/seq4
```

Path segments are considered hierarchical. They look like file names on some systems and may even be implemented that way, but this need not be. The service at the designated host can generally choose how it interprets paths, with the exception of the few rules in [RFC 2396]. These rules provide for special handling of the special path segments consisting of period (".") and double period (".."). For example, "./" does nothing if the period appears as a full segment and "segment/../" does nothing. In effect, the double period backs up one level.

### Queries

The query component of a generic URI occurs at the end of the URI. A question mark ("?") precedes the query component. It is handled opaquely and passed on to the service addressed by the rest of the URI. The most common coding in the query portion consists of a name–value pair format in which the values are quoted strings and the pairs are separated with the ampersand ("&") character. The "mailto:" scheme [RFC 2377] uses this coding, for example. It is also commonly used for "http:" and related schemes that pass on their information to Common Gateway Interface (CGI) programs to calculate a response. For example:

```
http://foo.example/path?a="value"&bar="foo"
```

Services using this format of query also sometimes encode a space as a plus sign ("+"), because spaces are prohibited and standard URI character escaping encodes a space as three characters.

### 7.1.2   Relative URIs

In XML, pointers often point elsewhere in the same document or to other documents on the same host or even within the same directory. Similar pointers within an HTML Web page might point to other places in the HTML code or other files that reside on the same host. You can easily create such pointers by omitting the "scheme://<authority>" portion of the URI and as much of the beginning of the "<path>" portion as appropriate. A base URI then supplies this omitted prefix.

For URIs found inside retrieved XML or HTML, the base URI defaults to the URI that retrieves the document or page. For example, if a page is retrieved from "http://foo.example/path/page/" and contains the relative URI "gifs/ picture.gif", then that relative URI converts by default to the following absolute URI:

```
http://foo.example/path/page/gifs/picture.gif
```

Use of relative URIs provides another advantage: You can move a Web resource or set of resources around in a file system or even between computers. The Web resource will still work if its internal references are relative.

If an entity expansion actually moves some XML into a document, however, it may change the base URI from its former location to that of the document. This switch changes the meaning of relative URIs. In XML, you can fix the base URI for converting relative to absolute URIs by using the xml:base attribute (see Section 7.2).

### 7.1.3   URI References and Fragment Specifiers

A URI can point to a part or fragment of a resource. You indicate this fact by adding a fragment specifier to the end of the URI. The result is formally called a "URI Reference," although the term "URI," whose formal definition excludes URI References, is frequently stretched in practice to include them. For example, the schema (Chapter 5) restriction of a character string to "anyURI" includes URI References.

URI References have the following syntax:

```
<scheme>:<scheme-specific-part>#<fragment>
```

The generic URI reference syntax is

```
<scheme>://<authority><path>?<query>#<fragment>
```

The interpretation of the "fragment" portion depends on the type of data pointed to. When that type is XML, the format of the fragment specifier is XPointer (see Section 7.3).

### 7.1.4   URI Encoding

Trying to write a URI in XML sounds simple—until you look at the process closely. First, the original URI specification did not define how to encode anything other than ASCII characters in URIs [ASCII]. Second, if the encoding of a URI is a sequence of octets, no specification dictates what octets with a value higher than x7F (127 decimal) mean.

HTML did, however, provide a rule for encoding characters that URIs or parts thereof do not allow. For example, if a particular label in a path needs to contain a space or a question mark (possibly because those characters occur in a file name), you encode the character as a percent sign ("%") followed by the two hex digits for the value of that character—for example, "%20" for space and "%3F" for question mark ("?"). These disallowed characters were ASCII characters so the question of how to handle a value that wouldn't fit into one octet didn't arise.

The rules for encoding arbitrary Unicode characters [Unicode] in URIs follow:

1. Determine all characters in the URI that are not allowed. They include all non-ASCII characters, such as all characters with a character value exceeding 127, and the extended characters listed in Section 2.4 of [RFC 2396]. Exceptions are square brackets ("[ ]"), which are restored by [RFC 2732], the octothorpe ("#"), and the percent sign ("%").

2. Convert each disallowed character in the original URI to UTF-8 [RFC 2279] as one or more octets.

3. For the octet sequences produced in Step 2, search for disallowed characters and replace them with the percent sign ("%") followed by the two-hexadecimal-digit encoding given earlier in this section.

4. Replace each disallowed character in the original URI with the results of the two-stage expansion described in Steps 2 and 3.

For example,

```
http://example.com/foo bar©.htm
```

would be encoded as

```
http://example.com/foo%20bar%57%33.htm
```

**Note**

These steps describe the general URI encoding. The URI usage context may require further encoding. For example, if the URI is used in XML, you must further encode the ampersand ("&") and less than sign ("<").

**History**

> The exact specification of the encoding rules for URIs was forced by the development of digital signatures, with their stringent canonicalization requirements. These rules first appeared in an XML digital signature document. At this point, the same description of URI encoding appears in at least the XMLD-SIG, XML Base, and XML Pointer Language documents.

## 7.2    xml:base

Before they can actually be used, relative URIs must be resolved into absolute URIs. A "base" URI is added as the initial portion of the absolute URI. Thus a URI such as

```
website/images/picture.jpg
```

if it appears in an HTML Web page fetched from

```
https://foo.example.com/projects/
```

would be interpreted as

```
https://foo.example.com/projects/website/images/picture.jpg
```

This base information can be obtained from four sources [RFC 2396]:

1. Base URI information embedded in the document containing the relative URI

2. The URI of the object immediately containing the relative URI

3. The URI used to retrieve the overall object in which the relative URI appears

4. A base URI defined by the application context

Lower-numbered sources in this list dominate higher-numbered ones. XML security does not use Source 4 . Sources 2 and 3 are sometimes the same, but one URI might retrieve an enclosing object while the relative URI occurs within a nested object that has a different, possibly more specific URI.

To set embedded base URI information, you can use "xml:base". As Source 1 in the list, it dominates all other base URI sources. In particular, xml:base occurs as an attribute and sets the URI base at that node and all descendant nodes until it reaches one that overrides it. The XML in Example 7-1 produces the effective absolute URIs shown in Table 7-1. While this example uses "href", other attributes can have a URI in their value; likewise, URIs can be present in text content and processing instructions.

***Example 7-1***   *Base, relative, and absolute URIs*

```
<foo xml:base="https://example.com/1/">
  <bar href="data.jpg" id="A"/>
  <bar href="image.gif" id="B" xml:base="ftp://10.0.0.1/">
    <charlie href="delta/description.txt" id="C"/>
    <charlie href="http://xyz.example/cgi/" id="D"/>
  </bar>
  <bar href="../2/3/" id="E"/>
</foo>
```

You determine base URIs as follows:

- The base URI for relative URIs appearing in an xml:base attribute value is the base URI for the parent of the element where the xml:base attribute appears, if one exists in the document or external entity. Otherwise, it is the URI of the document or external entity.

- The base URI for relative URIs appearing in attributes other than xml:base is the base URI of the element in which the attribute appears.

- The base URI for relative URIs appearing in text is the base URI of the element containing that text.

**Table 7-1** | Effecive URIs from Example 7-1

| Element ID Where "href" Is Found | Effective URI | Notes |
|---|---|---|
| A | https://example.com/1/data.jpg | |
| B | ftp://10.0.0.1/image.gif | |
| C | ftp://10.0.0.1/delta/description.txt | |
| D | http://xyz.example/cgi/ | The absolute URI is not affected by the base. |
| E | https://example.com/2/3/ | ".." in the relative path backs up over "1/" in the base URI path. |

- The base URI for relative URIs appearing in processing instructions is the base URI for the parent of the processing instruction, if one exists in the document or external entity. Otherwise, it is the URI of the document or external entity.

## 7.3    XPointer

XPointer is the syntax you use for the most general addressing of parts of an XML object [XPointer]. When an HTTP URI references XML, any fragment specifier to select a portion of the XML is written in XPointer syntax. XPointer can also be called explicitly to extract a subset of data (see Chapter 19). Note that XPointer does not include any way to point into the DTD or XML declaration for a document.

XPointer extends XPath so that you can use it in the following ways:

- As a fragment identifier in a URI reference

- To locate information by string matching

- To address points and ranges within XML

**Note**

In XML Security URIs, you should rarely encounter anything other than very simple XPointers. The implementation might delegate URI retrieval and fragment specifier processing to separate code with somewhat unpredictable results. For this reason, the XML Security standards discourage use of XPointer fragment specifiers in favor of using the explicit "Transforms" mechanism provided. (While you can invoke the full power of XPointer in such transforms, full support for it is optional. Even full support of XPath, on which XPointer builds, is merely recommended, not mandatory.)

### XPointer Encoding

When an XPointer contains special characters that have significance to XPointer but that should be treated as data, a circumflex ("^") prefixes the special characters. One example would be an unbalanced parenthesis—either "(" or ")"—appearing in a literal string. Due to this use, circumflex itself must be considered a special character and occurrences of a literal circumflex doubled ("^^"). For example,

```
xpointer( string-range ( /., "f)^" ) )
```

would be encoded as follows:

```
xpointer( string-range ( /., "f^)^^") )
```

The preceding rule applies only to general XPointer encoding. An XPointer must also be URI encoded (see Section 7.1.4) if it is used in a URI and XML encoded if it appears in XML. So, for example,

```
xpointer(string-range(//example,"André :-)"))
```

would always be XPointer encoded for the unbalanced parenthesis in the "smiley" as follows:

```
xpointer(string-range(//example,"André :-^)"))
```

If it appeared as such in an XML attribute value delimited by double quotes and encoded in US ASCII, you would escape the double quotes and the accented "é":

```
xpointer(string-range(//example,&quot;Andr&#xE9; :-^)&quot;))
```

If it appeared generally as a URI reference fragment specifier, you would encode the space, double quotes, circumflex, and accented "é":

```
xpointer(string-range(//example,%22Andr%C3%A9%20:-%5E)%22)
```

## 7.3.1   Forms of XPointer

XPointer has three possible forms:

- Full XPointers

- Bare names

- Child sequences

### Full XPointers

A full XPointer can be complicated, but you will rarely encounter the full form. It consists of a sequence of one or more parts that can optionally be separated by white space. Each part has the following format:

```
scheme(string-with-balanced-parentheses)
```

The "xpointer" and "xmlns" schemes are defined below. The "string-with-balanced-parentheses" means any string where all parentheses—both "(" and ")"—are properly nested, except for those escaped with the circumflex ("^"), as described earlier. Full XPointer parts end with a close parenthesis that matches the open parenthesis after the scheme name.

If multiple parts are present, they are evaluated from left to right until one succeeds. If all parts fail, then the full XPointer fails. As yet undefined schemes are permitted for future expansion. Encountering a scheme you do not understand is equivalent to a failure of that part. (This scheme-based system allows other data types than general XML to define their own schemes.)

You use the "xmlns" scheme to set up the namespace context for XPointer expression evaluations occurring farther to the right. The parenthesized string immediately after this scheme must consist of a namespace prefix followed by a namespace URI. Do not use quotation marks around the URI. For example:

```
xmlns(foo=http://bar.example/x)
```

The "xmlns" scheme adds its namespace declaration to the namespace context and then "fails" so that evaluation proceeds to the next part of the full XPointer to its right. If two "xmlns" parts try to bind the same prefix, the one evaluated later (the one farther to the right) overrides the first. Those "xmlns" parts that attempt to bind the "xml" prefix are ignored. Instead, the prefix is always bound to "http://www.w3.org/XML/1998/namespace"; this binding is always part of the namespace context for evaluating XPointer expressions.

The "xpointer" scheme does the obvious thing—namely, it interprets the parenthesized string immediately after it as an XPointer expression. If it is evaluated without error and yields a nonempty location-set, then that result is the value of the entire full XPointer.

You can use the ability to provide a sequence of XPointer parts for various purposes. The following example shows general fail-over from one XPointer expression to another. It finds all "foo" elements that don't have a foo descendant or, if no such foo elements are present, all "bar" elements that do not have any children.

```
xpointer(//*foo[not(.//foo)])xpointer(//*bar[not(./*)]
```

**Bare Names**

In comparison with a full XPointer, it is difficult to get much simpler than a bare name. A bare name is pretty much like it sounds—just a token. It refers to the element with that token as an ID. In other words, the bare name fragment specifier

```
#foo
```

is the same as the full XPointer fragment specifier

```
#xpointer(id("foo"))
```

**Child Sequences**

A child sequence consists of a series of one or more decimal numbers preceded by a slash ("/") and separated by slashes. No white space is permitted. The sequence may be optionally prefixed with a bare name. Two example fragment specifiers are shown here:

```
#/2/7/18/2/8
#pi/3/14/
```

Such sequences can only locate elements. They do so by using each number to index into the children of the element found by the previous step. The starting point is the root element, if the child sequence starts with a slash, or the element that the name as an ID specifies (if it starts with a name). The preceding examples are therefore equivalent to the following:

```
#xpointer(/*[2]/*[7]/*[18]/*[2]/*[8])
#xpointer(id("pi")/*[3]/*[14])
```

### 7.3.2   The XPath Extensions

XPath deals only with nodes. XPointer extends XPath, however, so that it can handle more general locations. The locations permitted include a pointer into the middle of text as well as more general ranges, such as might result from a user clicking and dragging on a screen display of XML to include parts of two elements with different parents. In summary, the extensions to XPath have the following effects:

• The concepts of a node and a node-set are extended to include a location and a location-set. In effect, the two location types of "point" and "range" have the same status as node types and appropriate extensions are made to node tests and the definitions of axes. While evaluating an expression, the context location is extended so that it can consist of a point or range. Also, you can use the XPath "[*number*]" predicate to select values from a set of points and ranges.

- The extensions provide extended rules for establishing the XPath evaluation context.

- Numerous additional functions are added, as listed in Section 7.3.3. A special-case extension applies to the expression syntax for the "range-to," as explained with that function's definition.

- The root node may have multiple child elements. This principle allows XPointers into general external parsed entities, which might consist of multiple top-level elements.

### Location Extension: Point

XPointer adds the "point" type to XPath, defined as follows:

- A point is defined as an index and a container node. It always points before the first item in the container, between two items in the container, or after the last item in the container.

- If the container is an element or root node, the items are its children.

- If there are N children, an index of zero points just before the first child; an index of N points just after the last child; and an index of X, where $0 < X < N$, points between child X and X + 1. Such a point into children is called a "node-point."

- If a container does not have children but does have a string value, then the index points between characters in that string value. If the string value length is N, an index of zero points just before the first character; an index of N points just after the last character; and an index of X, where $0 < X < N$, points between character X and X + 1. Such a point into text is called a "character-point."

You need to be careful about thinking of a "point" as just a location in the external representation of XML. For example, consider "<a>xyz</a>". It is an element node with a child text node. The point using this element as container and index 1 is the point just after the text node. The point using the text node as a container and index 3 is the point just after the last character in the text. Although the two are different points, a poorly designed user interface might display them indistinguishably on a computer screen.

A point location does not have an expanded name. It does have a null string value.

The XPath set of node tests is extended to include "point( )" so that points can be selected from a location-set. The axes of a point are location-sets defined as follows:

- The "self::" axis contains the point itself.
- The "parent::" axis contains the point's container node.
- The "ancestor::" axis contains the point container node and its ancestors.
- The "child::", "descendant::", "preceding-sibling::", "following-sibling::", "attribute::", and "namespace::" axes are empty.
- Although they are not defined in the XPointer document, one would presume that the "descendant-or-self::" axis contains just the point itself, that the "ancestor-or-self::" axis is the union of the "self::" and "ancestor::" axes, and that the "following::" and "preceding::" axes are empty.

### Location Extension: Range

XPointer adds to XPath the "range" type. A range is simply defined as two points: the start point and the end point of the range. The start point must not follow the end point, and both must appear in the same XML document. The range represents the XML content and structure between its points.

If the container node of one point of a range is an element, text, or root, then the container node of the other point must also be one of these three types. If the container node of one such point is any other type, then both the start and end point must reside within the same node.

For example, you can have a range that appears within the string value of a processing instruction, where both points have the processing instruction as their container node. Alternatively, for a range from a processing instruction to (and including) an immediately following element, the points of the range might have as their container nodes the parents of the processing instruction and element. You could not, however, have a range from inside the text content of a processing instruction to inside the text content of a following element.

A range with the same start and end point is called a collapsed range. A range location does not have an expanded name.

The string value of a range depends on the nature of its points. If both are character-points in the same container node, the string value is—just as you would expect—the characters between the start and end points. Otherwise, the string value consists of the characters in text nodes for which the character is found after the start point and before the end point. For example, in

```
<a>1#23<b attribute='value'>foo</b>xy#z</a>
```

the string value of a range from just after the first octothorpe ("#") to just before the second would simply be

```
23fooxy
```

In the same example, the string value of the range from just before element "a" to just after element "a" is

```
1#23fooxy#z
```

The XPath set of node tests is extended to include "range( )" so that ranges can be selected from a location-set.

The axes of a range are the same as the axes of the start point of that range.

### Covering Ranges

XPointer defines the concept of a covering range. A covering range that encompasses any type of location can be found as follows:

- The covering range of a range is that range.

- The covering range for a point is the collapsed range starting and ending with that point.

- For the root node, the start and end points of the covering range have the root node as their container. The index of the start point is zero, and the index of the end point is the number of children of the root.

- For an attribute or namespace node, the start and end points of the covering range have the attribute or namespace node as their container. The index of the start point is zero, and the index of the end point is the length of the string value of the attribute or namespace node.

- For all other kinds of nodes, the start and end points of the covering range have the parent of that node as their container. The index of the start point is the number of preceding sibling nodes, and the index of the end point is one greater than the start point. Thus the covering range of an element is the pair of node-points to just before and just after that element.

### Document Order

XPointer extends the XPath concept of "document order" to include points and ranges.

First, a "preceding node" is defined for all points as follows:

- For a node-point with a nonzero index X, the preceding node is the Xth child of the container node.

- For a node-point with a zero index, the preceding node is the container node, unless it has attributes or namespaces. In that case, it is the last attribute or namespace declaration.

- For a character-point, the preceding node is its container node.

Using these definitions, you can find document orderings that XPath does not specify:

- A node is located before a point if it is before or the same as the preceding node of that point. Otherwise, it is found after the point.

- The document order of a node and a range matches the document order of that node and the start point of the range.

- The document order of two points matches the document order of their preceding nodes. If they are identical, the point with the smaller index comes first. (If both the preceding node and the indices of the points are equal, they are the same.)

- The document order of a point and a range matches the document order of that point and the start point of the range.

- The document order of two ranges matches the document order of their start points, unless they have the same start point. In that case, it is the document order of their end points.

### Initialization of Evaluation Context

The evaluation of XPointer expressions occurs in the same way as the evaluation of XPath expressions, albeit with a few changes:

- The context location is initialized to a root node. For a URI reference fragment specifier XPointer expression, it is the root node of the document that the rest of the URI specifies. For other XPointer use—for example, the XPointer transform described in Chapter 19—the initial root node is specified by the application.

- The context position and size are initialized to 1.

- An empty set of variable bindings is used.

- The library of functions matches that defined in Chapter 6 for XPath and Section 7.3.3.

- A set of namespace declarations is provided, as described earlier in this chapter.

### 7.3.3   XPointer Functions

The following functions have been added to the core XPath function library for the evaluation of XPointer expressions. In this section, the function name appears in boldface, preceded by the data type of the result in italics. Parameters are represented by their data type in italics. Parameters are followed by a question mark when they are optional.

**Note**

A location-set is a superset of a node-set. Nodes are also locations. Thus, wherever a parameter is shown as being of type *location-set,* you may supply a node-set without a data type mismatch occurring.

*location-set* **end-point** (*location-set*)

The result is a point for each location in the input as specified by the following rules:

- For an input point, the output element is the same point.

- For an input range, the output element is the end point of the range.

- For a root or element node input, the output is the point just after the last child of the input. That is, the output point has a container node of the input node and an index of the number of children of the input.

- For a text, comment, or processing instruction node, the output is the point just after the end of the text content. That is, the output point has a container of the input node and an index of the length of the string value of the input.

- For an attribute or namespace node, the XPointer in which this function appears fails.

### *location-set* **here**( )

This function fails if the XPointer where it appears is not in XML. If it is in XML, then the function returns a location-set with a single member. If the XPointer expression being evaluated occurred in a text node, then the function returns the parent element. Otherwise, it returns the node containing the XPointer, presumably an attribute or processing instruction node. (When an XPointer occurs as element content, it isn't actually in that element but rather appears in a text child of that element.)

### *location-set* **origin**( )

This function provides addressing relative to the origin of the link traversed to reach the document containing the XPointer. It returns a location-set with a single member—the element from which the traversal was initiated. An error occurs if you invoke this function where no such traversal has occurred or the document from which traversal occurred is not XML. You cannot use this function in a URI reference fragment identifier where a URI is also provided, unless that URI identifies the same resource from which the traversal was initiated. See [XLink] for more information on traversal.

### *location-set* **range** (*location-set*)

This function returns the ranges covering all items in the input. A covering range is added to the output for each member of the input.

### *location-set* **range-inside** (*location-set*)

This function returns the ranges covering the contents of all items in the input. For every input item that is a range or point, that range (or the collapsed range of the point) is added. For all other types of input item, a range is added with that item as the container node and a start point index of zero. The end point index is the number of children of that item or, if the input item is of a type that cannot have children, the length of the string value of the item.

*location-set* **range-to** (*location-set*)

Range-to is a special function in terms of the way in which it makes use of the context. For each location in the context, it returns a range from the start point of the context location to the end point found by evaluating its parameter with that context location. A special-purpose extension to the XPath syntax permits the use of a range-to in place of an axis specifier and node test in a location path step. For example, to obtain a range from the element with the ID "label1" to the element with the ID "label2" you can write the following code:

```
xpointer(id("label1")/range-to(id("label2")))
```

As another example, if portions of a document have been marked by EdStart and EdEnd elements, ranges covering all such pairs could be found with the following code:

```
xpointer(//EdStart/range-to(following::EdEnd[1])))
```

*location-set* **start-point** (*location-set*)

This function returns a point for each location in the input as specified by the following rules:

- For an input point, the output element is the same point.

- For an input range, the output element is the start point of the range.

- For a root or element node input, the output is the point just before the first child of the input. That is, the output point has a container node of the input node and an index of zero.

- For a text, comment, or processing instruction node, the output is the point just before the first character of the text content. That is, the output point has a container of the input node and an index of zero.

- For an attribute or namespace node, the XPointer in which the function appears fails.

*location-set* **string-range** (*location-set, string, number?, number?*)

For each item in the input location-set, the function searches the string value of that item for the second parameter. For each nonoverlapping occurrence found, it adds a range to the output location-set. This range consists of two character-points encompassing the occurrence of the string if the optional numeric third and fourth parameters are absent.

If one numeric parameter is present, the function returns the position of the first character of the resulting range adjusted by that parameter relative to the beginning of the matched string. A single numeric parameter value of 1 indicates no adjustment.

If a second numeric parameter is present, it specifies the length of the resulting range in characters. The default, in the absence of a second numeric parameter, is that the resulting range extends to include the last matched character. If the numeric parameters are such that the resulting range would extend beyond either end of the string value, the XPointer part in which the function appears fails.

# 8 | SOAP

SOAP is a simple, extensible XML protocol framework for communication between distributed peer processes [SOAP]. It does not define specific application semantics. This book includes a discussion of SOAP for the following reasons:

- Chapter 11 uses SOAP as an example of the application profiling of XMLDSIG authentication.

- The XML key management protocol (XKMS), as described in Chapter 14, commonly uses SOAP.

- Some problems related to exclusive versus inclusive canonicalization were first actually encountered in connection with SOAP use. SOAP illustrates these problems, as described in Chapter 9.

- SOAP is an example of a protocol use of XML (see Appendix E)

An understanding of SOAP is not necessary to achieve a general understanding of XML digital signatures (Chapter 10) or XML encryption (Chapter 15). If you are already familiar with SOAP, you can skip this chapter.

Section 8.1 introduces SOAP. Next, Section 8.2 specifies the basic structure of SOAP messages, explains how they are exchanged and processed, and considers error handling under SOAP. Section 8.3 describes the syntax for encoding information being sent with this protocol as well as a method for indicating other encoding syntaxes. In Section 8.4, the binding of SOAP to particular transport protocols, including HTTP, is considered [RFC 2616]. Finally, Section 8.5 describes a method of performing remote procedure calls through SOAP.

## 8.1    Introduction to SOAP

SOAP originally stood for Simple Object Access Protocol, but it is no longer restricted in any way to object access or object-oriented use. Starting with version 1.2, the acronym is no longer officially spelled out; that is, "SOAP" is just a name. Although it originated from an industrial consortium, the XML Protocol Working Group of the W3C now has change control for new versions of SOAP. Here we give an overview of the features that SOAP includes and excludes, examine its relationship to XML, and list the basic SOAP namespaces.

### 8.1.1    Features Included and Excluded

Draft Version 1.2 [SOAP] includes the following:

- A definition of a general structure for messages
- A general processing specification for handling SOAP messages from an originator through zero or more intermediate nodes to an ultimate destination
- A method for returning error and status indications
- A specification for encoding a variety of data types into those messages
- A specification for sending messages over lower-level transport protocols, particularly HTTP
- A description of one way to use SOAP for remote procedure calls

To achieve its goals of simplicity and extensibility, SOAP excludes the following features (and some others not listed here):

- Grouping or batching of multiple messages
- Transmission of objects-by-reference
- Distributed garbage collection (which, as a practical matter, is required if objects are transmitted by reference)

An application based on SOAP can add features through SOAP Headers.

### 8.1.2    Relation of SOAP to XML

SOAP imposes substantial restrictions on the XML it uses. In particular, SOAP messages (i.e., documents) must obey the following restrictions:

- Processing instructions are prohibited.
- All elements and attributes must be appropriately namespace qualified.

- DTDs are prohibited. SOAP applications must simply know the SOAP DTDs and schemas.

- No schema processing can be required. This restriction, along with the "no DTDs" rule, means that all attributes or elements intended must be explicitly present and cannot be supplied by default.

Also, note that SOAP defines some global attributes that you can use in any SOAP namespace element. In particular, you can use "id" of type ID, and "href" of schema type anyURI. The "id" attribute uniquely identifies an encoded element and the "href" attribute references a value.

**Soapbox**

The SOAP restrictions on and assumptions about the XML used are relatively strong. In this respect, SOAP is somewhat similar to BEEP [RFC 3080], which prohibits any character or entity references other than the five predefined character references in [XML]. It's a bit suspicious that "protocol" uses of XML tend to immediately throw overboard a substantial amount of the "richness" of XML this way. Thus you can't just transparently include XML from other realms of interest inside such "XML" protocols without considering the possibility that it might violate the protocol framework's severe restrictions. If XML had been simpler, perhaps protocols would be more inclined to use it without major surgery.

### 8.1.3   Basic SOAP Namespaces

The following namespaces are part of the basic mechanisms of the SOAP version 1.2 draft. Additional namespaces are used in connection with encoding and remote procedure calls.

The SOAP envelope syntax, discussed in Section 8.2, has the namespace identifier

```
http://www.w3.org/2001/12/soap-envelope
```

The SOAP MustUnderstand Fault has the namespace identifier

```
http://www.w3.org/2001/12/soap-faults
```

The SOAP Upgrade element that you use in connection with version negotiation has the namespace identifier

```
http://www.w3.org/2001/12/soap-upgrade
```

> Do not confuse the "MustUnderstand" fault and the "mustUnderstand" attribute that differ in terms of the capitalization of their names.

## 8.2    SOAP Envelope, Message Exchange, and Processing Model

The fundamental communicating entities from SOAP's point of view are "nodes," as shown in Figure 8-1. A SOAP message start at the original sender node, proceeds through zero or more intermediate nodes, and terminates at the ultimate receiver node. A message always has a top-level element, "Envelope," in the soap-envelope namespace.

Although SOAP does not provide message routing, it fundamentally recognizes that messages can pass through intermediate nodes on the way to their destinations.

This protocol does not have a traditional versioning label. If a SOAP node receives a message with an unrecognized top-level element (anything other than Envelope) or namespace, however, it must generate a SOAP VersionMismatch Fault (see Section 8.2.4).

### 8.2.1    SOAP Messages

SOAP messages contain an optional Header element and a mandatory Body element. Each of these items can contain Blocks, as shown in Figure 8-2. The

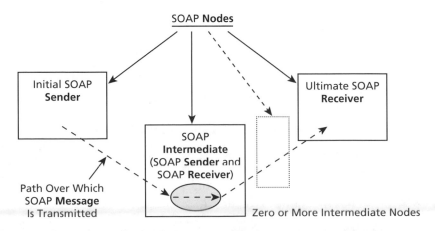

**Figure 8-1** | Message transmission model

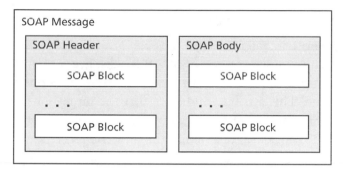

**Figure 8-2** | SOAP message structure

SOAP Header extends SOAP messages. For example, a Header Block could be used for authentication as described in Chapter 11.

Example 8-1 shows a simple SOAP message consisting of a Header and a Body, with each containing one Block.

***Example 8-1***   *Simple SOAP message*

```
<env:Envelope xmlns:env="http://www.w3.org/2001/12/soap-envelope">
  <env:Header>
    <foo:control xmlns:foo='http://www.example.net/protocol'>
      <foo:example attribute="value"/>
    </foo:control>
  </env:Header>
  <env:Body>
    <foo:data xmlns:foo='http://www.example.net/protocol'>
      ...y8gaGp5WVtMODq7b29bGxjI4OIBH...
    </foo:data>
  </env:Body>
</env:Envelope>
```

SOAP has quite liberal rules regarding what you can include as an attribute at the Envelope or Header/Body level. The meaning of such attributes, beyond those actually defined by SOAP, is unclear. It is best to extend SOAP through Block elements or attributes at the Block level or below rather than through such high-level element attributes.

### 8.2.2    SOAP Actors

As noted earlier, a SOAP message has two parts, the Header and the Body, each of which consists of SOAP Blocks. Every SOAP Header Block can have an optional "actor" attribute in the soap-envelope namespace with a URI value. This attribute indicates that the target for that Block is a node that fulfills the role of that actor. Header Blocks with no "actor" attribute and all Body Blocks are targeted to the ultimate receiver node. (SOAP Body Blocks cannot have an "actor" attribute.)

Nodes take on the role of "actors," where a URI identifies each actor. A SOAP node can fulfill the role of many actors. Every SOAP node must act in the role of the special SOAP actor:

```
http://www.w3.org/2001/12/soap-envelope/actor/next
```

No SOAP node may act in the role of the special SOAP actor:

```
http://www.w3.org/2001/12/soap-envelope/actor/none
```

Header Blocks for the "none" actor consequently have the following characteristics:

- They pass through to the ultimate destination.

- They are never formally operated on.

- They can contain information that other processing uses.

A SOAP node that fulfills the role of the "anonymous" actor is an ultimate receiver. It may seem natural for actor names to be related to the host name of the node where the actors run and to be useful in routing messages. In reality, SOAP imposes no such restrictions and does not provide any routing. (Note: A transport to which SOAP is bound would normally provide routing, as discussed in Section 8.4.)

A particular SOAP Block is understood at a particular SOAP node if the node implements and conforms to the semantics of that Block. The namespace-qualified apex element name in that Block indicates which semantics are in use. A requirement that a Block be understood can be imposed through the "mustUnderstand" attribute in the soap-envelope namespace. If that attribute is present at a block with the value "true," then a SOAP node fulfilling the role of the actor specified by the Block (or the ultimate destination if the Block specifies no actor):

- Must properly process the SOAP Block on which it appears, or

- Cannot process any part of the SOAP message and must return a Fault.

Example 8-2 shows a SOAP message with two Header Blocks and one Body Block. Each Header Block has an "actor" attribute, and one such Block has a mustUnderstand attribute value of "true."

**Example 8-2**   *A SOAP message with actors*

```
<env:Envelope
  xmlns:env="http://www.w3.org/2001/12/soap-envelope">
  <env:Header>
    <foo:control xmlns:foo-'http://www.example.net/protocol'
                 env:actor='http://example.net/protocol/control'>
      <foo:example attribute="value"/>
    </foo:control>
    <bar:priority xmlns:bar-'http://www.example.net/protocol'
                  env:actor='http://priority.test'
                  env:mustUnderstand='true'>
      <bar:level>high</foo:level>
    </bar:priority>
  </env:Header>
  <env:Body>
    <foo:data xmlns:foo='http://www.example.net/protocol'>
      y8gaGp5WVtMODq7b29bGxjI4OIBH...
    </foo:data>
  </env:Body>
</env:Envelope>
```

Although the standard defines the SOAP Header and Body as separate elements, they are, in fact, related. There is no difference between a Block appearing in the Body, where it cannot have an "actor" or "mustUnderstand" attribute, and the same Block appearing in the Header with no "actor" attribute and a "mustUnderstand" attribute value of "true." A Block with no actor attribute is targeted at the actor identified with a null URI—that is, the anonymous actor. The presence of such an actor indicates an ultimate receiver SOAP node.

### 8.2.3  SOAP Processing

The processing at a SOAP node must be equivalent to the following steps:

1. Identify the roles in which the node will act.

2. Identify all mandatory Header Blocks targeted to the node (with an actor attribute specifying a role filled by the node).

3. If the node does not understand any of the mandatory Header Blocks targeted to it, generate a SOAP MustUnderstand fault (see Section 8.2.4). Generating such a fault must stop further processing of the SOAP message. If this step generates a fault, the application must not generate a fault that relates to the contents or existence of the body.

   a. Process all Header Blocks targeted at the node and, if it is the ultimate destination, the body as well. SOAP does not specify the order of processing Blocks, although a Header Block might do so. A node may ignore nonmandatory Header Blocks targeted at it.

   b. Generate any new SOAP messages required.

4. If the node is an intermediate node, remove all Blocks targeted at the node from the message, regardless of whether they were processed or ignored; add any new Blocks needed; and forward the message. The processing of a Block and its removal may result in the addition of a similar Block, a different Block, or no Block.

Failure while processing a SOAP message at a node produces exactly one Fault.

### 8.2.4  SOAP Faults

SOAP nodes return error or status information to a node from which they have received a message. They send back a SOAP message with a Body Block consisting of the Fault element in the soap-envelope namespace. Fault has two mandatory child elements, "faultcode" and "faultstring," and two optional child elements, "faultactor" and "detail."

- The "faultstring" element has text content that is intended to be a human-readable explanation.

- The "faultactor" element (fault actor) has a URI as its content to identify the actor at which the Fault occurred. It is optional only for ultimate receivers. All intermediate nodes generating a Fault element must provide a "faultactor" in any such Fault.

- The "detail" element provides application-dependent additional information on a Fault generated by processing a message Body. You should not include this element for Header Block errors. Rather, the application must include it if the Body contents could not be processed successfully. Its presence indicates that the ultimate receiver at least processed some of the Body. The content and attributes of the "detail" element are application dependent. It can have an "encodingStyle" attribute. All element children of a "detail" element are called detail entries.

- The "faultcode" element contains a namespace-qualified name.

Table 8-1 lists the values of "faultcode" defined by the SOAP specification. All of these values appear in the soap-envelope namespace. For the "Sender" and "Receiver" values, more information may be present in the Fault "detail" child element. An example "faultcode" might be

```
<faultcode xmlns:foo="http://example.com">foo:problem</faultcode>
```

**Table 8-1** | Values of Faultcode

| Value | Reason |
|---|---|
| VersionMismatch | The top-level element or its namespace is not recognized. |
| MustUnderstand | A node is unable to process the Header Block targeted at it with a mustUnderstand attribute value of "true." |
| DTDNotSupported | The SOAP message contains a DTD. |
| DataEncodingUnknown | A Block has an encodingStyle attribute with an unknown value. |
| Sender | A SOAP node has detected an error in the form or content of an incoming message. The message should not be re-sent as is. |
| Receiver | A SOAP node has detected an error that appears to be unrelated to the form or content of the message it is processing—for example, lack of resources or inability to communicate with some other node whose services are required. |

### VersionMismatch Faults

The SOAP version really refers to the SOAP Envelope version. More common than an envelope version change is requiring a particular extension by a Header Block with a mustUnderstand attribute of "true" for that extension. If the server does not support the extension, the SOAP node must return a "MustUnderstand" Fault.

In the much less common case of change in the envelope structure, a SOAP node may support multiple envelope structure versions. If it receives a message with a root element it does not understand, its "VersionMismatch" Fault response should include a Header Block consisting of an "Upgrade" element in the following namespace:

```
http://www.w3.org/2001/12/soap-upgrade
```

The content of the "Upgrade" element is an ordered list of the envelope versions supported by the server, starting with the most preferred and ending with the least preferred.

The lack of an "Upgrade" element may indicate that the server supports only SOAP version 1.1.

### MustUnderstand Faults

When a SOAP node returns a "MustUnderstand" Fault, the message should include Header Blocks that indicate which Blocks were not understood. These Header Blocks consist of the "Misunderstood" element in the

```
http://www.w3.org/2001/12/soap-faults
```

namespace. This Misunderstood element has a "qname" attribute, whose value is the namespace-qualified name of the element that was not understood. A namespace declaration in the Misunderstood element or an ancestor thereof must also bind the namespace prefix used by the qualified name. See Example 8-3.

**Example 8-3**  *Misunderstood fault*

```
Original Message:

<env:Envelope
  xmlns:env="http://www.w3.org/2001/12/soap-envelope">
  <env:Header>
    <foo:extension
```

```
       xmlns:foo='http://www.example.illegal/protocol'
       env:mustUnderstand='1'/>
</env:Header>
  <env:Body>...</env:Body>
</env:Envelope>


Resulting "Misunderstood" Fault:

<env:Envelope
  xmlns:env="http://www.w3.org/2001/12/soap-envelope">
  <env:Header>
    <f:Misunderstood
      xmlns:f="http://www.w3.org/2001/12/soap-faults"
      f:qname='foo:extension
      xmlns:foo='http://www.example.illegal/protocol'/>
</env:Header>
  <env:Body>
    <env:Fault>
      <faultcode>env:mustUnderstand</faultcode>
      <faultstring>Never heard of "foo"</faultstring>
    </env:Fault>
  </env:Body>
</env:Envelope>
```

## 8.2.5   SOAP Envelope and Fault Schemas

Below is the schema for the SOAP Envelope element and for its Header and Body children from <http://www.w3.org/2001/12/soap-envelope> adapted for shorter lines. The version of a SOAP Envelope is indicated by its namespace. If a node receives a SOAP message with an Envelope element namespace it does not understand, it responds with a VersionMismatch Fault. The following also includes a schema for Fault.

```
<!-- Schema defined in the SOAP Version 1.2 Part 1 specification
     17 December 2001 Working Draft:
     http://www.w3.org/TR/2001/WD-soap12-part1-20011217/
   $Id: soap-envelope.xsd,v 1.1 2001/12/14 13:35:22 ylafon Exp $

   Copyright 2001 W3C (Massachusetts Institute of Technology,
   Institut National de Recherche en Informatique et en
```

```
<xs:schema
  xmlns:xs="http://www.w3.org/2001/XMLSchema"
  xmlns:tns="http://www.w3.org/2001/12/soap-envelope"
  targetNamespace="http://www.w3.org/2001/12/soap-envelope" >

<!-- Envelope, header and body -->
<xs:element name="Envelope" type="tns:Envelope" />
<xs:complexType name="Envelope" >
  <xs:sequence>
    <xs:element ref="tns:Header" minOccurs="0" />
    <xs:element ref="tns:Body" minOccurs="1" />
  </xs:sequence>
  <xs:anyAttribute namespace="##other" processContents="lax" />
</xs:complexType>

<xs:element name="Header" type="tns:Header" />
<xs:complexType name="Header" >
  <xs:sequence>
    <xs:any namespace="##other" minOccurs="0"
                               maxOccurs="unbounded"
                               processContents="lax" />
  </xs:sequence>
  <xs:anyAttribute namespace="##other" processContents="lax" />
</xs:complexType>

<xs:element name="Body" type="tns:Body" />
<xs:complexType name="Body" >
```

```
  <xs:sequence>
  <xs:any namespace="##any" minOccurs="0" maxOccurs="unbounded"
         processContents="lax" />
  </xs:sequence>
  <xs:anyAttribute namespace="##any" processContents="lax" >
  <xs:annotation>
    <xs:documentation>
Prose in the spec does not specify that attributes are allowed
on the Body element
          </xs:documentation>
  </xs:annotation>
  </xs:anyAttribute>
</xs:complexType>


<!-- Global Attributes.  The following attributes are intended
to be usable via qualified attribute names on any complex type
referencing them.   -->
<xs:attribute name="mustUnderstand" type="xs:boolean"
              default="0" />
<xs:attribute name="actor" type="xs:anyURI" />


<xs:simpleType name="encodingStyle" >
  <xs:annotation>
    <xs:documentation>
'encodingStyle' indicates any canonicalization conventions
followed in the contents of the containing element.
For example, the value
'http://schemas.xmlsoap.org/soap/encoding/'
indicates the pattern described in SOAP specification
    </xs:documentation>
  </xs:annotation>
  <xs:list itemType="xs:anyURI" />
</xs:simpleType>


<xs:attributeGroup name="encodingStyle" >
  <xs:attribute name="encodingStyle"
                type="tns:encodingStyle" />
</xs:attributeGroup>
```

```
<xs:element name="Fault" type="tns:Fault" />
<xs:complexType name="Fault" final="extension" >
  <xs:annotation>
    <xs:documentation>
Fault reporting structure
      </xs:documentation>
  </xs:annotation>
  <xs:sequence>
    <xs:element name="faultcode" type="xs:QName" />
    <xs:element name="faultstring" type="xs:string" />
    <xs:element name="faultactor" type="xs:anyURI"
                                    minOccurs="0" />
    <xs:element name="detail" type="tns:detail"
                                minOccurs="0" />
  </xs:sequence>
</xs:complexType>

<xs:complexType name="detail">
  <xs:sequence>
    <xs:any namespace="##any" minOccurs="0"
                                maxOccurs="unbounded"
          processContents="lax" />
  </xs:sequence>
  <xs:anyAttribute namespace="##any" processContents="lax" />
</xs:complexType>

</xs:schema>
```

## 8.3    SOAP Encoding

SOAP assumes that many applications based on it will want to send encoded data labeled with its type—whether a simple type, such as character string, integer, and floating-point number, or a compound type, such as array and structure. In the case of a remote procedure call (Section 8.5), such data would consist of parameters or results. SOAP is very general, however, and has many other possible uses requiring the transmission, within XML, of typed, encoded data.

### 8.3.1    The encodingStyle Attribute

The specific encoding detailed in the SOAP specification is not fundamental to SOAP. To indicate how data are encoded, SOAP defines a very general mechanism based on its global encodingStyle attribute, which appears in the

```
http://www.w3.org/2001/12/soap-envelope
```

namespace. This attribute, which can appear on any data element, specifies the encoding that the content of that element and all descendants use until it is overridden with another encodingStyle attribute. This inheritance resembles the scoping rules for "xml:lang" and the like.

The value of this attribute is not just, as you might guess, one URI, but a list of URIs separated by white space. These URIs are given in order from the most restrictive to the most general. The encoded data are converted to whatever local internal representation is convenient by trying the first encoding and, if the conversion encounters errors because the data do not conform to that encoding, then trying the second encoding, if a second encoding is given, and so on.

The encoding defined in the SOAP specification is assigned the following URI:

```
http://www.w3.org/2001/12/soap-encoding
```

The specification defines meanings for this URI, the null URI, and extensions of this soap-encoding URI. A null URI represents a disclaimer of any information about the encoding of data; its primary use on an element is to cancel an encodingScope inherited from an ancestor. A URI with the soap-encoding URI as a prefix can only be associated with a narrower encoding defined by restricting the soap encoding.

### 8.3.2    The http://www.w3.org/2001/12/soap-encoding Encoding

The encoding specified in detail in [SOAP] is very general and powerful, providing complete mechanisms for simple types, structs, arrays, sparse arrays, enumerations, polymorphic accessors, compound types, and so on. The type labels defined in this way can be used in schemas or to directly label elements as to the type of their content. It is beyond the scope of this chapter to give all the intricate details of this process; see [SOAP] for further information. The schema for the encoding defined in the SOAP specification appears in Appendix F.

## 8.4       SOAP Transport Binding and HTTP

To actually get SOAP messages from one node to another, you must use some underlying transport protocol, such as HTTP [RFC 2616] or SMTP [RFC 2821, 2822]. The extent to which you must augment or restrict the transport protocol varies depending on how closely the native mechanism of the protocol matches the needs of SOAP.

By convention, most TCP/IP-based protocols have a default "port" number—for example, port 80 for HTTP and port 25 for SMTP. Servers that support a protocol normally have, listening on the default port, a process that handles incoming service requests. The SOAP specification recommends the use of a different port number when you use an existing transport protocol with SOAP. This recommendation reflects the fact that the service being requested is SOAP service, rather than the service for which the transport protocol was originally intended. For example, HTTP was originally developed to support Web browsing. Although you can accommodate both that use and SOAP on the default HTTP port 80, it is simpler and more efficient to have separate processes servicing and optimized for these different kinds of requests on different ports.

### 8.4.1    Transport Message Exchange Patterns

The XML Protocol Working Group is developing a general model for transport mechanism patterns and their binding to SOAP. Such patterns describe the following aspects of transport:

- The life cycle of transport exchange messages

- The temporal order and causal relationships of multiple messages being exchanged

- Normal and abnormal termination of message exchange

The Transport Message Exchange Pattern (TMEP) model is complex; readers are referred to [SOAP] for its detail. The only TMEP specified thus far is the Single-Request-Response TMEP, named in the current draft by the URI "http://www.example.org/2001/12/soap/transport-mep-single-request-response."

## 8.4.2    The SOAP HTTP Binding

The Hypertext Transfer Protocol [RFC 2616] is a convenient protocol to use for SOAP. HTTP is based on a request–response model that works well when the single request–response TMEP is being used in SOAP. However, the semantic match is not complete, so some interpretation is required [SOAP]. For example, HTTP intermediaries (such as proxies) are not necessarily SOAP intermediaries.

**Soapbox**

Although it is not mentioned in the SOAP specification, one reason SOAP uses HTTP is that firewalls are ubiquitously configured to let HTTP pass through. This approach is very convenient when you are trying to get from a client or peer inside one firewall out through the general Internet to a server or peer inside another firewall. It is much less desirable from a security point of view, however. SOAP can access very general interfaces, including remote procedure calls to system facilities, for example.

The increasing tendency to layer protocols on top of HTTP makes firewall filtering at the protocol level useless because it requires that you choose one of three options:

1  Having the firewall block a fundamental protocol such as HTTP or SMTP

2. Letting the protocol through and then worrying about securing all machines inside the firewall

3. Making the firewall more complex and knowledgeable by having it look inside the protocol and try to figure out if the contained message, perhaps SOAP, is safe

In general, option 1 is too painful and option 2 is probably the appropriate choice, as the "hard exterior shield and soft, insecure inside" security model is a proven loser. Of course, this brings up an obvious question: Why are you paying for a fancy firewall? People therefore tend to choose option 3, which leads to a spiral of evasion measures and countermeasures and decreased firewall reliability resulting from the increased complexity.

When carrying SOAP in HTTP, you must take three considerations into account:

- You can use only the HTTP "POST" method.

- You must label the body (i.e., the SOAP message) with the "application/soap" MIME type.

- You may include a "SOAPAction:" HTTP Header in requests and "required-SOAPAction:" in responses, for optimization purposes.

You use the SOAPAction Header as a optional hint to optimize processing. It takes a URI, which can be relative or absolute. If the URI is relative, interpret it using the HTTP Request-URI as a base. If a SOAP receiver does not require it, it must ignore the absence of this Header or the presence of an incorrect SOAPAction Header. Conversely, if a SOAP receiver requires this Header, and none is present or the receiver does not recognize the one provided, it must respond with the following HTTP error status code:

```
427 "SOAPAction Required"
```

An HTTP response with this 427 status code may have a Required-SOAPAction Header that gives a URI that a SOAPAction Header can use in a resubmission of the HTTP request. The following example shows a SOAPAction request Header:

```
SOAPAction: "http://www.foo.example/path#fragment"
```

The following example shows a Required-SOAPAction response Header:

```
Required-SOAPAction: "example://www.bar.example?query"
```

[SOAP] contains detailed tables describing how to create and respond to other HTTP error codes. These responses generally preserve the existing HTTP semantics of the codes.

## 8.5   SOAP Remote Procedure Call

One application that can be built on top of SOAP is remote procedure calling (RPC). In fact, it was one of the main motivations for the definition of SOAP. This section describes the RPC specification given in [SOAP] but others are possible.

An initial SOAP message indicates a procedure call request. The SOAP message then returned is the remote procedure response—presumably a return value or error indication.

### 8.5.1   SOAP HTTP Remote Procedure Call

Using SOAP for an RPC works independently of the transport used to carry and the encoding in use within the SOAP messages involved. However, it was anticipated that the SOAP encoding (see Section 8.3) and the HTTP protocol binding (Section 8.4) would be commonly used. In the case of HTTP, an RPC naturally uses an HTTP request and the response uses an HTTP response.

To call a remote procedure, you must have the following information:

- The URI of the target SOAP node
- The remote procedure name
- The parameters to the procedure or method

The HTTP Header includes the URI. The parameters appear as an element in a SOAP Body Block with the same name and type as the remote procedure. They are modeled as structs, with elements having the same names as the "in" and "in/out" parameters. Those names should appear in the same order as they do in the procedure. The remote procedure's response also appears as a SOAP Body Block, with an element name matching the procedure name. Such a Block contains a similar struct, whose first element should have the "result" name in the

```
http://www.w3.org/2001/12/soap-rpc
```

namespace specified in the schema described later in this section. The Block can have additional elements named for "out" or "in/out" parameters. The procedure must return a result element unless its return value is "void." A procedure cannot return both a result and a Fault. You can define the procedure so that, for missing parameters, it returns a result or a Fault as desired.

You can also include the following optional information:

- A procedure signature
- Optional Header data

In the latter case, you would include optional Header data as an additional SOAP Header Block. It could, for example, be a transaction identification or an indication that debugging information is requested.

Use whatever protocol binding you have set up to carry the invocation to, and the result back from, the remote procedure.

### 8.5.2 Remote Procedure Call Faults

Returning a Fault, as described in Section 8.2.4, indicates failure of the remote procedure. The following rules apply in such a case. When a conflict occurs, the first applicable rule appearing below dominates. The "env" and "rpc" namespace prefixes represent the appropriate prefixes for the SOAP envelope and SOAP remote procedure call namespaces, respectively.

1. Generate an "env:Server" Fault if the problem is temporary, such as a transient lack of resources.

2. Generate an "env:DataEncodingUnknown" Fault if the procedure encounters an encoding it does not recognize.

3. Generate an "rpc:ProcedureNotPresent" Fault if no such procedure exists at the server.

4. Generate an "rpc:BadArguments" Fault if a mismatch between the type and the number of supplied parameters makes it impossible to run the remote procedure.

5. Generate other application-specific Faults as needed.

### 8.5.3 Remote Procedure Call Schema

The schema for an RPC is trivial, because the only thing that must be defined is the element used for returning a procedure result. All other data, including procedure parameters, can be transmitted with existing SOAP mechanisms.

```
Schema definition:


<schema xmlns="http://www.w3.org/2001/XMLSchema"
        targetNamespace="http://www.w3.org/2001/12/soap-rpc" >


  <element name='result' />


</schema>
```

### 8.5.4  Mapping Application Parameter Names into XML

The RPC technique given earlier implies that you can turn application parameter names into valid XML names. If the characters in the application name are valid XML name characters, this transformation usually isn't a problem. You can mostly solve name conflicts by qualifying them with a namespace [Names]. Even with qualification, however, all names starting with "xml" in any capitalization are reserved. The [SOAP] draft suggests the following procedure to solve this:

1. Map each character in the application name into Unicode characters [Unicode]. If no obvious mapping exists, use an application-determined mapping.

2. Scan through the results from Step 1.

   a. If the first three letters of the application name are "xml" in any capitalization, including mixed capitalization, output

   ```
   _xFFFF_
   ```

   and then proceed as normal. The "xml" characters will be valid XML name characters and will be copied over.

   b. If you encounter an underscore character ("_") followed by a lowercase x in the application name, output the underscore as

   ```
   _x005F_
   ```

   and then proceed as normal. The x character will be a valid XML name character and will be copied over.

   c. If you encounter an illegal character for an XML name or, in the first position, an illegal character for the first character of an XML name, replace it with

   ```
   _xUUUUUUUU_
   ```

   where UUUUUUUU is the hexadecimal encoding, using capital A–F, for the 32-bit Unicode value for the character. An exception occurs when the top 16 bits are zero, in which case you replace the character with

   ```
   _xUUUU_
   ```

   where UUUU is the similar hex encoding of the bottom 16 bits of the character's Unicode value.

d. Otherwise, just copy the application name character to the XML name being constructed.

For example, the following five comma-separated parameter names in a hypothetical application

```
foo, Axml, xmlA, y_x, &>
```

would map into

```
foo, Axml, _xFFFF_xmlA, y_005F_x, _x0024__x003E_
```

# Part III | Canonicalization and Authentication

Congratulations! You have made it through the introductory parts of this book. Now our look at the real XML Security parts begins.

Part III deals with authentication—that is, digital signatures, message authentication codes, and the like. For a language as malleable as XML, a critical part of any nontrivial authentication is canonicalization. Chapter 9 goes into that topic in great depth.

Armed with an understanding of canonicalization, we then dive into the XML Digital Signature standard (XMLDSIG) in Chapter 10.

Chapter 11 gives several examples of profiling XMLDSIG for particular applications. You should view XMLDSIG as a toolbox. Almost any particular use will require restrictions on the wide range of things you can do with XMLDSIG; some will also require extensions to XMLDSIG.

Finally, Chapter 12 gives a snapshot of the effort under way to specify XML-based digital signatures that will conform to European government directives and qualify thereunder as trusted.

# 9 | XML Canonicalization: The Key to Robustness

What is canonicalization? It is the extraction of the "standard form" of some data and the discarding of "insignificant" aspects of the data's surface representations, usually by restricting all surface representation choices to a single option. For example, ordinary ASCII text files appear on modern computers with a variety of conventions to indicate end-of-line. If you want to calculate a signature over such a file and then verify it when the file moves to a different platform with a different end-of-line convention, the signer and verifier need to use the canonicalized file with a standard end-of-line.

In principle, the standard form of data and the aspects considered insignificant depend on the particular application. However, for most types of data, such as ASCII text or XML, a standard canonicalization, perhaps with a few variations, tends to become widespread. Over time, many applications for which canonicalization is important adopt that standard. This chapter and the official documents [Canon, Exclusive] describe the canonicalizations that have been adopted so far for XML.

Getting just the right canonicalization is one of the most important, yet trickiest aspects of digital authentication. Proper canonicalization of the data being signed is essential in all nontrivial cases to ensure robust and secure signatures. Less commonly known is the fact that it can also make encryption more useful. Thus, canonicalization of XML data is a significant consideration for any type of signature over or encryption of such XML data (see Sections 9.1 and 9.2), including the XML Digital Signature and XML Encryption standards.

Two primary versions of XML canonicalization exist, both of which produce as output a "printing" or "serialization" of the XML in the UTF-8 character encoding. The first, inclusive version, known as Canonical XML [Canon], incorporates into the output the XML context of the subdocument being canonicalized. The second version, known as Exclusive XML Canonicalization

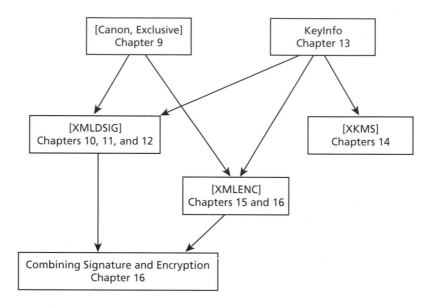

**Figure 9-1** | Chapter dependencies after the basics

[Exclusive], excludes the XML context of the subdocument from the output, as far as it practically can.

Section 9.3 describes the standardized canonicalizations of XML viewed as the transformation of arbitrary, well-formed XML into XML output. Sections 9.4 and 9.5 give the full formal specifications of the XML canonicalizations, and Section 9.6 describes their limitations.

Figure 9-1 shows how later chapters depend on this chapter.

**History**

The Canonical XML specification originated in the W3C Core XML Group. Later, it was discovered that XMLDSIG was the most vitally concerned user of Canonical XML. As a result, the canonicalization effort was transferred to the XMLDSIG Working Group where that specification [Canon], which is now a full W3C Recommendation, was completed under the authorship of John Boyer. (John works in Victoria, British Columbia, and one of the XMLDSIG meetings occurred there. This meeting included high tea at the Empress Hotel, which is highly recommended.)

Actual experience showed that, all too often, when signed XML moved from one document to another, signatures broke due to changes in XML context. This problem arose frequently in protocol applications including use of SOAP.

To solve this problem, Exclusive XML Canonicalization was designed to minimize the dependence of a canonical form on context [Exclusive]. The XMLDSIG Working Group carried out the work on exclusive canonicalization.

## 9.1   Canonicalization—Essential for Signatures Over XML

Assume we have some data we want to sign. We calculate a digital signature, as described in Chapter 10, over the data using some key and algorithm. Next, we store the data and the digital signature or send them to another place. After subsequently retrieving or receiving the data, we expect the verification of the digital signature to indicate whether the data remains the "same." It might seem that what it means to say that two instances of XML are the "same" is clear. In the real world, however, this determination turns out to be a difficult question.

The calculation of modern digital signatures involves signing a sequence of eight-bit binary bytes or octets. If the data being signed already consist of a fixed sequence of bytes (e.g., a JPEG image), then we're probably fine. But if the data actually consists of XML or even plain text, it is not so easy to ensure that the verifier will perform the verification calculations with the same sequence of octets used by the signer. See Figure 9-2.

Let's look at some text as a simple example. If we send it from one application to another as text, quite often we find changes such as the following:

- The line-ending characters may have changed.

- Spaces at the ends of lines may have been removed or added.

- Horizontal tab characters may have been converted into spaces, or vice versa.

- The encoding may have changed so that different bits represent what we think of as the same "character."

- Long lines may wrap or words may flow from one line to another.

A signature calculated over text will not verify over the text modified in these ways because the modified text consists of a different byte sequence. Signing a canonical (or "normalized" or "standardized") form of the text solves this problem. For example, you might pick a standard line ending and convert all

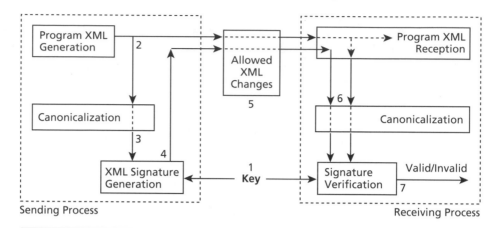

1. Keying material is generated and distributed (could be symmetric or asymmetric).
2. Application generates XML to be transmitted.
3. Canonicalization algorithm produces a standard serialization of the XML.
4. Canonicalized XML data and key are combined into XML digital signature.
5. XML data and signature are transmitted. Changes allowed by XML specification primarily happen during serialization for transmission and parsing at reception.
6. Canonicalization algorithms specified in the XML signature are used to canonicalize the XML data and signature.
7. XML signature is verified over the canonicalized data using the key.

**Figure 9-2** | Canonicalization: XML signature over XML data

line endings to it, use a standard character encoding, or employ another tactic. Chapter 17 describes a Minimal Canonicalization, which does just that; it is appropriate for data treated as text but is inadequate for data treated as XML.

With insufficient canonicalization, signatures become brittle. In such a case, any trivial change in the surface form of data will cause them to fail, even if the change is insignificant for that application. Conversely, with excessive canonicalization, signatures become insecure. A signature is then verifiable even after significant changes in the meaning of the data if excessive canonicalization discards those changes. For example, discarding accents on characters before they are fed into a signature algorithm would enable an attack, undetectable by signature checking, in which a name in a message is changed to refer to someone else whose name differs only in character accents. As you can see, achieving robust and secure signatures requires just the right canonicalization.

### 9.1.1    Some Simple Aspects of XML Canonicalization

XML is, of course, even more flexible than text. When it is being read, the XML Recommendation [XML] specifies which data passes to the application and which data is discarded. For example, it includes the following provisions:

- White space between attributes in an element start tag is not passed to the application.

- Attributes are inherently unordered, so their original order is discarded.

XML canonicalization must precisely specify all choices for such discarded formatting. That way, if two instances of XML provide the same data to an application and their external representations are canonical, then their external representations will be byte-for-byte identical. As a result, a signature over one can be verified over the other representation.

## 9.1.2    The Problems with XML White Space

Readable formatting is supposed to be an advantage of XML. If you use white space for formatting, three cases arise. Consider the example

```
<a><b c="d">foo8 foo9</b><e f="ghijklmno">bar</e></a>
```

where element "a" is specified in the DTD you are using as having only element content, not mixed element and text content.

The first type of white space, which you can freely add, occurs in many places inside the start and end tag. For example,

```
<a><b       c="d"
>foo8 foo9</b
><e          f="ghijklmno"
>bar</c
></a >
```

is the same as the one-line example given earlier, according to the basic XML specification. The additional white space inside the start and end tags isn't passed to an application reading this XML, so it can't be significant. XML canonicalization simply specifies a fixed way of handling such spacing so that the XML is always serialized in the same way.

To see the second type of white space, consider the following example:

```
<a><b c="d">
    foo8
    foo9
```

```
</b><e f="ghijklmno">
    bar
</e></a>
```

Here white space has been added to the actual text content. It is considered significant white space under the XML Recommendation [XML], must be passed along to the application exactly, and is not altered by XML canonicalization. Changing it will break a signature (unless, for example, you use a nonstandard canonicalization that strips all leading and trailing white space from text content and changes all internal runs of white space to, say, a single space).

The trickiest case is the third and last type of white space. Consider the following example:

```
<a>
    <b c="d">foo8 foo9</b>
    <e f="ghijklmno">bar</e>
</a>
```

Here white space has been added inside element "a" but outside the elements that are the content of "a". Because our DTD specified "a" to have only element content, this extra white space is considered insignificant. The XML recommendation, however, requires that it be passed to the application, albeit flagged as "insignificant." Thus an application can act as it chooses when it encounters such white space. Furthermore, if the DTD had provided that "a" had mixed content (text and elements), this white space would be significant. If the DTD is not accessible and we use a nonvalidating parser, we would have no way of telling the status of this white space!

XML canonicalization has chosen to handle this problem by assuming that the second and third types of white space must be exactly retained and serialized unchanged from their appearance in the text nodes of an input XPath node-set.

### 9.1.3   The Problems with XML Namespaces

XML namespaces [Names] enrich XML but also provide another range of options that appear, by definition, identical in meaning. For example, a namespace prefix declaration affects all child nodes unless a child node redeclares the prefix. Thus, if a namespace is set up at the apex node of some XML and child nodes do not redeclare the prefix, then it is immaterial whether redundant identical declarations of that prefix also appear in the children.

Are the prefixes themselves significant? You might think not, assuming that they are just dummy symbols bound to a URI. In reality, XPath and other expressions can explicitly match prefix names, and such expressions can appear inside attribute values or text content or even be calculated dynamically. For this reason, in general, you must consider namespace prefix names to be significant and not altered by canonicalization.

**History**

> Some early canonicalization efforts used generated symbols, such as "n1," "n2," "n3," and so on, to normalize namespace prefixes before these problems were noticed [C14N-20000119].

As references to namespace prefixes can lurk in text, attribute values, and other locations, it is generally impossible to determine algorithmically whether a namespace prefix is actually referenced by some XML. On the other hand, problems can arise if you assume that all namespace declarations in scope might be used and so need to be copied into a descendant element, if that element and its content are being canonicalized. In particular, if the element moves to a different ancestor context, as frequently happens with protocols, its canonicalization may change because different namespace declarations are inherited from ancestors. A signature over it will then break.

### A Simple Example

For an example of the type of problem that changes in XML context can cause for signatures, consider the following:

```
<n1:elemX xmlns:n1="http://b.example">
  content
</n1:elemX>
```

It is then wrapped in another element:

```
<n0:pdu xmlns:n0="http://a.example">
  <n1:elem1 xmlns:n1="http://b.example">
  content
</n1:elem1>
</n0:pdu>
```

The first XML code appears in canonical form. Assume, however, that the XML is wrapped as in the second case for protocol transmission. The sub-document with elem1 as its apex node can then be extracted with an XPath expression:

```
(//. | //@* | //namespace::*)[ancestor-or-self::n1:elem1]
```

In this expression, the parenthesized part selects every node; the predicate in square brackets filters these nodes to those with the name or with an ancestor with the name "elem1" (Chapter 6).

Applying Canonical XML, which is inclusive, to the XPath node-set created in this way gives the following (except for line wrapping to fit this document):

```
<n1:elem1 xmlns:n0="http://a.example"
          xmlns:n1="http://b.example">
  content
</n1:elem1>
```

Note that Canonical XML has included the n0 namespace because it includes namespace context. This change would mean that a signature over "elem1" based on the first, unwrapped instance would not be verifiable.

### General Problems with Reenveloping

As a more complete example of the changes in the Canonical XML form that can occur when you change the enveloping context of an element, consider the following:

```
<!-- Case one -->

<n0:local xmlns:n0="foo:bar"
          xmlns:n3="ftp://example.org">
  <n1:elem2 xmlns:n1="http://example.net"
            xml:lang="en">
    <n3:stuff xmlns:n3="ftp://example.org"/>
  </n1:elem2>
</n0:local>
```

The following case arises when you change the enveloping of elem2:

```
<!-- Case two -->

<n2:pdu xmlns:n1="http://example.com"
        xmlns:n2="http://foo.example"
        xml:lang="fr"
        xml:space="retain">
  <n1:elem2 xmlns:n1="http://example.net"
            xml:lang="en">
    <n3:stuff xmlns:n3="ftp://example.org"/>
  </n1:elem2>
</n2:pdu>
```

Assume that you produce an XPath node-set from each of these two cases by applying the following XPath expression:

```
(//. | //@* | //namespace::*)[ancestor-or-self::n1:elem2]
```

Applying Canonical XML to the node-set produced from the first XML code yields the following serialization (except for line wrapping to fit in this document):

```
<n1:elem2 xmlns:n0="foo:bar"
          xmlns:n1="http://example.net"
          xmlns:n3="ftp://example.org"
          xml:lang="en">
    <ns3:stuff></ns3:stuff>
  </n1:elem2>
```

Although the identical octet sequence in both pieces of external XML above represents elem2, the Canonical XML version of elem2 from the second case would be (except for line wrapping so it will fit into this document) as follows:

```
<n1:elem2 xmlns:n1="http://example.net"
          xmlns:n2="http://foo.example"
          xml:lang="en"
          xml:space="retain">
    <n3:stuff xmlns:n3="ftp://example.org"></n3:stuff>
  </n1:elem2>
```

The change in context produces many changes in the subdocument as serialized by the inclusive Canonical XML. In the first example, "n0" has been included from the context, and the presence of an identical "n3" namespace declaration in the context has elevated that declaration to the apex of the canonicalized form.

In the second example, "n0" has gone away but "n2" has appeared, "n3" is no longer elevated, and an xml:space declaration has appeared, due to changes in context. Not all context changes have an effect, however. In the second example, the presence at ancestor nodes of an xml:lang and "n1" prefix namespace declaration has no effect because of existing declarations at the elem2 element.

This sort of change of context is typical of protocols and can easily lead to signatures that can not be validated. To help with this situation, Exclusive XML Canonicalization [Exclusive] is used. The physical form of elem2 as extracted by the XPath expression above and then subjected to Exclusive XML Canonicalization is, in both cases (except for line wrapping so it will fit into this document), as follows:

```
<n1:elem2 xmlns:n1="http://example.net"
          xml:lang="en">
   <n3:stuff xmlns:n3="ftp://example.org"></n3:stuff>
  </n1:elem2>
```

As you see, a signature using Exclusive XML Canonicalization would not be broken by the change in context and would be verifiable.

### 9.1.4    Canonicalization Is Required for XML Data

XML canonicalization is more complex than the previous discussion has suggested, as will be explained later. When we are concerned with XML digital signatures, at least part of the signature itself must be canonicalized, because it is XML, as must the signed data if it is being handled as XML. See Figures 9-2 and 9-3. Even if a binary format signature, such as PKCS#7 [RFC 2315], is calculated over XML data that is being handled as XML, canonicalization remains vital because such XML handling can change the surface form of the XML, as shown in Figure 9-4.

## 9.2    Canonical XML and XML Encryption

Modern encryption algorithms work with sequences of eight-bit bytes (octets). As a consequence, any XML document or portion of a document

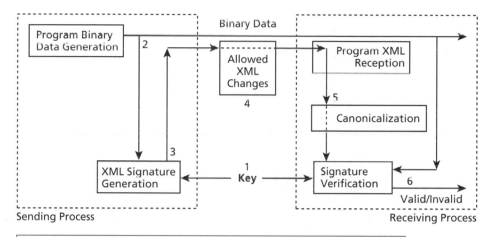

1. Keying material is generated and distributed (could be symmetric or asymmetric).
2. Application generates binary data to be transmitted.
3. Binary data and key are combined into XML digital signature.
4. Binary data and signature are transmitted. Changes allowed by XML specification primarily happen during serialization for transmission and parsing at reception of the XML signature.
5. Canonicalization algorithm specified in the XML signature is used to canonicalize the XML signature.
6. XML signature is verified over the binary data using the key.

**Figure 9-3** | Canonicalization: XML signature over binary data

being encrypted must be converted to such a format by, for example, "printing" or serializing it.

The normal reason for encrypting XML (or any other data) is so that some authorized application can later decrypt it and use the information. If the XML will always be decrypted back into the same environment, then it will normally provide the same information and be faithfully decrypted. Maintaining the same environment means maintaining the same character encoding, namespace prefix bindings, scoped value for xml:lang, xml:base if relevant, and perhaps additional application environment factors. However, if the application decrypts the XML into a different environment, it may be incorrectly parsed because its character encoding differs from that used by the parser. Decrypting into a different environment could also provide meaningless or corrupted information due to changes in environmental factors such as namespace bindings. See Figure 9-5.

Use of Canonical XML ensures that XML is in a standard character encoding (UTF-8). The inclusive canonical output incorporates all standard XML

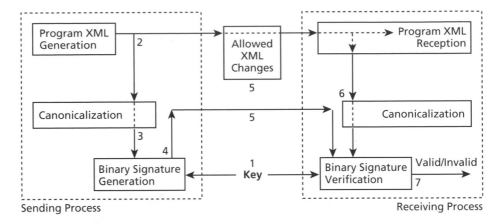

1. Keying material is generated and distributed (could be symmetric or asymmetric).
2. Application generates XML to be transmitted.
3. Canonicalization algorithm produces a standard serialization of the XML.
4. Canonicalized XML data and key are combined into binary signature.
5. XML data and binary signature are transmitted. Changes allowed by XML specification primarily happen during serialization for transmission and parsing at reception.
6. The same canonicalization algorithm is used to canonicalize the XML data.
7. Binary signature is verified over the canonicalized  XML data using the key.

**Figure 9-4** | Canonicalization: binary signature over XML data

environmental factors, such as namespace declarations and values of all attributes in the xml namespace. (Section 9.6 describes some limitations.) Decryption into a different environment is then much safer. Because the character encoding of the decrypted XML is known, it can be parsed into data structures or changed to the appropriate encoding for insertion into enveloping XML.

These considerations apply for any type of encryption of XML data, including the XML Encryption standard described in Chapter 15.

## 9.3    Transformative Summary

This section describes the changes that XML canonicalization makes to non-canonical XML. They are described as transformation rules to convert the external representation of non-canonical XML into an external canonicalized XML representation. The rules are divided into input/read, output/print, and inherited attribute and namespace rules, although in some cases the rule involves several of these aspects. See Figure 9-6.

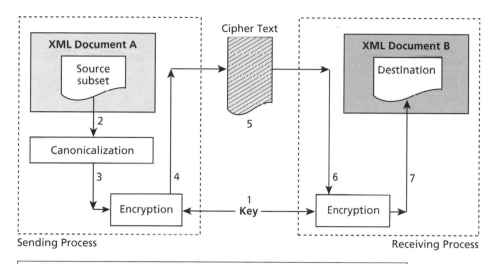

1. Keying material is generated and distributed (could be symmetric or asymmetric).
2. XML data are selected from Document A context.
3. XML data are serialized by canonicalization algorithm to include or exclude context depending on the system designer's intent.
4. Canonicalized XML data are encrypted under the key.
5. Encrypted data are transmitted.
6. Encrypted data are decrypted under the key.
7. XML is inserted in new Document B context.

**Figure 9-5** | Canonicalization and encryption

This perspective on XML canonicalization helps to intuitively understand the canonical form of XML, but it is not a likely implementation. Rather, canonicalization is typically applied to XML that has already been read into or created as an internal representation by the application. XML canonicalization implementations commonly use the specification given in Section 9.5

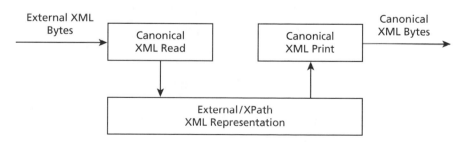

**Figure 9-6** | Canonical XML: transformative view

to generate a Canonical XML serialization from the XPath data model described in Section 9.4. When any conflicts or incompleteness is noted in Section 9.3, you should look to Sections 9.4 and 9.5 for instructions.

For a discussion of the reasoning behind canonicalization rules whose justification this chapter does not explain, see [Canon] and [Exclusive].

### 9.3.1    Input/Read Rules

All of the rules in this section apply to both Canonical XML and Exclusive XML Canonicalization.

#### Remove Declarations

The XML declaration and DTD are removed, including any comments or processing instructions that may have resided inside the DTD.

#### Reference Replacement

Parsed entity references and character references are replaced by their definitions.

For example, using both this and the previous rule,

```
<?xml version=1.0">
<!DOCTYPE  Doc <!-- comment -->
          <!ENTITY foo "supercalifragilisticexpialidocious" >
          ] >
<example>abc &foo;itis &x31;&quot;&x32;</example>
```

is input as follows:

```
<example>abc supercalifragilisticexpialidociousitis 1"2</example>
```

#### Line Breaks

Line breaks are converted to a new line (<u>x0A</u>), even though they may have originally been a carriage return (<u>x0D</u>) or the sequence carriage, return new line (<u>x0Dx0A</u>). The exact rule is that all <u>x0D</u> characters are converted to <u>x0A</u> unless they are immediately followed by <u>x0A</u>, in which case they are dropped.

#### CDATA Sections

CDATA sections are intended to offer a convenient way to include odd characters in XML content. Because alternatives are available for representing such characters in XML content, however, XML canonicalization chose to eliminate CDATA sections. Any special characters exposed through this approach are input as if they were character references. For example,

```
<Example>x<![CDATA[ & this<< is; just& data> ]]>y</Example>
```

is input as if it was

```
<Example>x &amp; this&lt;&lt; is; just&amp; data&gt; y</Example>
```

### Attribute Value Normalization

Attribute values are normalized as if by a validating processor. This procedure involves several ordered steps:

1. All line breaks are normalized as for any other part of XML (see the earlier rule).

2. Start with a normalized value consisting of the empty string.

3. For each character, entity reference, or character reference in the unnormalized attribute value, beginning with the first and continuing to the last, do the following:

   - For a character reference, append the referenced character to the normalized value.

   - For an entity reference, recursively apply this Step 3 to the replacement text of the entity.

   - For any of the white space characters horizontal tab (x09), new line (x0A), carriage return (x0D), or space (x20), append a space character (x20) to the normalized value.

   - For any other character, append the character to the normalized value.

4. If the attribute type is not CDATA, then, in the normalized value, discard any leading and trailing space (x20) characters and replace any internal sequences of the space (x20) character by a single space (x20) character.

If the unnormalized attribute value contains a character reference to a white space character other than space (x20), the normalized value contains the referenced character itself (x09, x0A, or x0D). In contrast, it is normalized to the space character if the attribute value had the white space character itself rather than a reference to it.

**Soapbox**

> This distinction in white space processing between CDATA and non-CDATA attributes is a harmful complication because it makes processing more DTD dependent, thereby violating one of XML's goals (see Chapter 1). It wouldn't have mattered which way the attribute white space normalization was handled, but it should have always been specified as one way or the other.

XML canonicalization mandates normalizing as if by a validating processor, which requires that you know the attribute type. If it is unknown, the only safe assumption is that the attribute is of type CDATA. This assumption preserves information and satisfies the XML Recommendation's requirement for nonvalidating XML processors that do not know the attribute type.

For example,

```
[!DOCTYPE Doc [ <!ENTITY    a    "bc">
                <!ENTITY    d    "&a;&xD;">
                <!ATTLIST   Elem
                            X    NMTOKENS
                            Y    CDATA> ] >
<Elem X="   z &d;z   " Y="   z &d;z   "/>
```

is input as follows:

```
<Elem X="z a z" Y="   z a#xDz   "/>
```

### Inclusion of Default Attributes

Default attributes are added to elements. For example,

```
<!DOCTYPE Doc [ <!ATTLIST   Elem
                            z    #IMPLIED   "FooZ"> ] >
<Elem a="FooA">content</Elem>
```

is input as follows:

```
<Elem a="FooA" z="FooZ">content</Elem>
```

### 9.3.2    Output/Print Rules

All of the rules in this section apply to both Canonical XML and Exclusive XML Canonicalization.

## Document Encoding

The XML Recommendation [XML] permits a variety of encodings. Different encodings use different bit patterns for the same logical character and would, therefore, produce different digital signature values. Canonical XML always employs the UTF-8 character encoding [RFC 2279]. The XML standard requires that all XML parsers support this encoding, along with UTF-16 [RFC 2781]. With either of these encodings, you can omit the "encoding" declaration in the prolog XML declaration.

For example,

```
<?xml version="1.0" encoding="ISO-8859-1"?>
<Document>&#174;</Document>
```

is output as follows:

```
<Document>xC2xAE</Document>
```

This two-octet sequence is the UTF-8 encoding for the Unicode character for registered trademark ("®") which was represented by the character entity "&#174;".

## White Space Outside the Document

XML permits comments and processing instructions to appear before and after the top-level document element. Canonicalization eliminates white space between such items, and between them and the document element; the exception is that it assures a new line (x0A) after each such item appearing before the document element and before each such item appearing after the document element. For example,

```
<!-- comment1--><document>stuff</document><?Foo bar ?>
<!-- comment2-->
```

is output as follows:

```
<!-- comment1-->
<document>stuff</document>
<?Foo bar ?>
<!-- comment2-->
```

### Empty Elements

XML permits an element with no content to be represented two ways. First, it can appear with one angle bracket pair and a slash before the close angle bracket. Alternatively, it can be given as a start tag and an end tag with nothing between. In canonicalized XML, empty-element tags are replaced by start tag, end tag pairs.

For example,

```
<Example/>
```

is output as follows:

```
<Example></Example>
```

### Attribute and Namespace Ordering

Namespace declarations are given in alphabetic order by prefix, followed by attributes in alphabetic order by namespace URI and then by attribute name.

For example,

```
<E  Z3="a" B:A1="x" D:C2="9"
 xmlns:B="http://example.com" xmlns:D="ftp://ftp.example"/>
```

is output as follows:

```
<E xmlns:B="http://example.com" xmlns:D="ftp://ftp.example"
   Z3="a" D:C2="9" B:A1="x"></E>
```

The attribute D:C2 appears before B:A1 because ordering is primarily by namespace URI, not by namespace prefix. This approach groups together attributes under the same URI even if they have different prefixes. (Note: White space within the E element start tag in this example is not correctly portrayed due to the limited line length in this book.)

### Attribute Value Delimiters

Attribute values can be delimited with either single or double quotes in XML. For Canonical XML, these delimiters are always double quotes.

For example,

```
<Example Attribute='xyzzy'>content</Example>
```

is output as follows:

```
<Example Attribute="xyzzy">content</Example>
```

### White Space Inside Start and End Tags

White space inside element start tags is normalized to a single space (x20) before each namespace declaration and attribute. White space inside end tags is eliminated.

For example,

```
<Example    az="lmnop"
              foo="bar"                    >baz</Example       >
```

is output as follows:

```
<Example az="lmnop" foo="bar">baz</Example>
```

### White Space in Processing Instructions

Inside processing instructions (PIs), white space is normalized to a single space (x20) between the target name and the string value, if the string value is not null. If the string value is null, all white space after the target name is discarded.

For example,

```
<?Target1                ?><?
     target2
     String        ?>
```

is output as follows:

```
<?Target1?><?target2 String?>
```

### White Space in Content

All white space in content is retained, including all white space between any combination of element start and end tags.

### Special Characters in Text Output Encoded

Special characters, such as the ampersand ("&"), less than ("<"), and double quote ("""), are encoded as character entities in output. The exact details depend on whether the output is text content, an attribute value, a comment string, or a processing instruction string, as detailed in Section 9.5.

### 9.3.3 Inherited Attribute and Namespace Declaration Rules

By far, the most complex aspects of XML canonicalization relate to the handling of namespace declarations and xml namespace attributes such as xml:lang. These aspects are the only area where Canonical XML and Exclusive XML Canonicalization differ. This subsection gives an overview of these differences.

#### xml Namespace Attribute Inheritance

Consider the following XML, where we want to canonicalize "example" and all nodes below it:

```
<foo xml:lang="en" xml:base="http://example.com/">
  <example a="b">
    <bar xml:lang="fr" href="abc/def#123>
      content
  </bar></example></foo>
```

Exclusive XML Canonicalization will serialize the attributes only where they are shown, so no xml:lang or xml:base attribute would exist in its canonicalization of "example". The inclusive Canonical XML, however, would produce the following output:

```
<example a="b" xml:lang="en" xml:base="http://example.com/">
    <bar xml:lang="fr" href="abc/def#123>
      content
  </bar></example>
```

Some other outcome might also be desired—perhaps only one of the two xml namespace attributes shown on "foo" being carried down to the canonicalization of "example". To accomplish this goal, the application designer needs to either create a customized canonicalization or arrange that the desired attribute be added to "example" and then use Exclusive XML Canonicalization.

#### Namespace Declaration Inheritance and Superfluous Declaration Deletion

XPath maps namespace declaration over all descendant element nodes, except at and below element where a different declaration of the same namespace prefix appears, as described in Chapter 6. Thus, if you did not take any "thinning" action, all of these namespace declarations would be output by canonicalization. Typically, the deeper an XML structure, the more bottom-level elements would be cluttered with namespace declarations accumulated from their ancestors, most of which would be superfluous.

Namespace declarations can be superfluous for several reasons. A declaration that the prefix "xml" represents "http://www.w3.org/XML/1998/namespace", for instance, is considered superfluous because it is always bound to that URI. Likewise, a declaration that the default namespace is null is superfluous at a top-level node. Furthermore, if canonicalization will output a namespace declaration at an element, it would be superfluous to output a declaration of the same prefix with the same URI at a descendant node, unless an intervening declaration changes the binding of that prefix.

For example,

```
<Z:ElemA xmlns:Z="http://foo.example" xmlns=""
         xmlns:xml="http://www.w3.org/XML/1998/namespace">
   <ElemB xmlns:Z="http://foo.example"
          Z:attrib="105">content</ElemB>
</Z:ElemA>
```

is output as follows:

```
<Z:ElemA xmlns:Z="http://foo.example">
    <ElemB Z:attrib="105">content</ElemB>
</Z:ElemA>
```

While it is always reasonable to suppress superfluous namespace declarations below an element in canonicalization output that has the same declaration on it, how do you decide which nonsuperfluous declarations to output?

Canonical XML [Canon] says to output all of the namespace declarations that appear in the XPath node-set for each node in the output unless superfluous. This group always includes all namespace declarations appearing in the XPath node-set for an apex node.

Exclusive XML Canonicalization [Exclusive] says to select for output namespace declarations only at those nodes where the declared prefix is visible before a local element or attribute name. Not all such selected declarations may be output, because an identical output ancestor declaration may make them superfluous. In addition, because some namespace declarations may be needed even though they are not visible, you may supply an optional list of namespace prefixes to the Exclusive XML Canonicalization. Namespace declarations using prefixes on this list are treated as specified for Canonical XML. In particular, if a declaration of any such prefixes is in scope for the apex node, that namespace declaration will be output at the apex node.

---

## 9.4    The XML Canonicalization Data Model

XML canonicalization uses an extension of the XPath data model. For example, all adjacent text content in input is combined into a single text node and CDATA section boundaries are discarded.

The formal definitions of standard XML canonicalizations state that they use an extension of the XPath data model and take two or three inputs. The first must be either an XPath node-set or a sequence of octets. The second is a Boolean flag that indicates whether to preserve comments. The third, which only applies to Exclusive XML Canonicalization, is a list of namespace prefixes to be treated inclusively. If the first parameter is an octet sequence, it is parsed as XML into an XPath node-set and so must be well formed XML. See Figure 9-7.

XPath provides a "name( )" function for element and attribute nodes that returns the name of the node with the namespace prefix, if one is present. When multiple namespace prefixes are associated with the same namespace URI at a node, XPath makes it an implementation option whether the original parsed prefix, if any, is guaranteed to be returned by name( ). Note that XML canonicalization **requires** returning the original prefix. One reason for this mandate is that XPath, XPointer, and XSLT, which can be used in XMLDSIG transforms and elsewhere in XML applications, can search on and match exact prefix names. For this reason, XML canonicalization output, as described in Section 9.5, must always produce the same prefix for the same XML. Otherwise, digital signatures using canonicalization would break.

The specification does not require actual implementation of the full XPath standard to support the XML canonicalization, but it is recommended.

**History**

XPath was chosen as the data model for canonicalization for two reasons:

1. It retains namespace prefixes, an ability that appears to be essential to retaining data of significance to XPointer, XSLT, and similar processing.

2. XPath processing is a powerful tool in application filtering of data to be signed, provides a language for formally expressing the mandatory Enveloped Signature Transform, and serves as the foundation of XPointer and XSLT.

DOMHASH [RFC 2803] provides a different approach to canonicalization and hashing, although it is primarily of historical interest. DOMHASH is based on the DOM data model and was designed before XPath existed because IOTP v1.0 [RFC 2801, 2802] needed XML digital signatures. At that time, no standard for XML digital signatures existed. Future versions of IOTP are committed to using XMLDSIG.

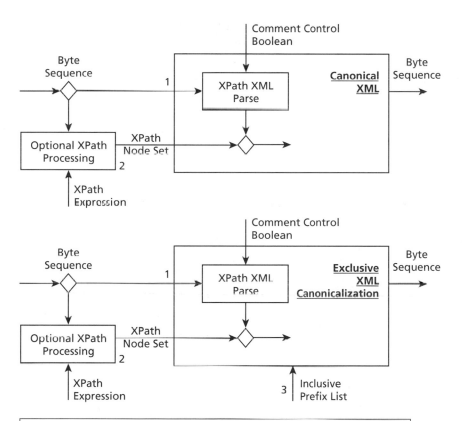

1. Input to XML canonicalization may be a byte sequence. In that case, it is parsed and comments may or may not be discarded, depending on which version of the standard canonicalization algorithms is called.
2. Alternatively, an XPath node set in provided, in which case the algorithm version has no effect on comments.
3. For Exclusive Canonicalization only, a list of namespace prefixes to be handled inclusively can be provided as well.

**Figure 9-7** | Canonical XML flows

### 9.4.1 Node-Set

Most XPath applications consider an XPath node to represent the entire document tree below that node (sometimes ignoring certain descendant node types, such as comments and processing instructions). In XML canonicalization, however, an XPath node indicates only that item and none of its children and, if it is an element, none of its attribute or namespace declarations. For example, the XPath node-set produced by the XPath expression

```
id("foo")
```

would represent just the element with that ID type attribute. For canonical XML purposes, it would not include that element's contents, child elements, attributes, or namespace declarations, if any.

In the XPath Recommendation, the execution of XPath expressions produces XPath node-sets. It therefore makes sense to consider XML canonicalization to work that way when its input consists of a byte stream being parsed as XML. In that case, whether comments will be included in the output can be rolled into the XPath expression that calculates the node-set to be output:

Without comments:

```
(//.[not(self::comment()] | //@. | //namespace::*)
```

With comments:

```
(//. | //@. | //namespace::*)
```

The XMLDSIG security recommendation requires support for the inclusive Canonical XML without comments and recommends support for Canonical XML with comments (although later work found that Exclusive XML Canonicalization is more appropriate for most signatures). With XML Encryption, all the standard canonicalizations are considered optional. In these cases, if you implement XML canonicalization so that it takes an XPath node-set as input and uses even a simplified XPath processor, then you can easily control comments by using various XPath expressions. Such an implementation also makes it easy to achieve many other effects or document subsets. For example, you could produce a canonical version of an XML document with comments left in but processing instructions and a particular element (e.g., Elem1) removed with the following code:

```
(//. | //@. | //namespace::*)[not(self::pi() or self::Elem1)]
```

Note that applying an XPath expression to an XML node-set results in a selected XPath node-set that, in some sense, remains linked to all of the XPath nodes in the original set. Although the expression will have selected a subset of nodes, the resulting node-set can, until it leaves the XPath or equivalent environment, remain subject to XPath parent, child, sibling, or other operations that can recover all the original nodes. Application of an XPath expression to an XML object first converts the object to an XPath node-set, and the above observations then apply to this node-set.

You can use various techniques to select complete document subsets. For example, consider the following:

```
id("foo")
```

To actually select the document subset whose apex is the element with ID "foo," you could use the following:

```
(//. | //@* | //namespace::* )
[ count(id("foo")|ancestor-or-self::node()) =
  count(ancestor-or-self::node()) ]
```

This code selects all nodes and then applies the predicate inside the square brackets. The predicate allows only nodes for which the node with ID "foo" appears in the ancestor-or-self path (i.e., for which the node with ID "foo" is the node in question or an ancestor thereof). Thus it selects the entire subdocument of which the "foo" node is the apex.

## 9.4.2    Document Order

The XPath Recommendation describes XPath node-sets as unordered. Nevertheless, except for attribute and namespace nodes, XPath associates a document order with each of them. XML canonicalization uses the XPath definition of document order, which states that one syntactic item precedes another in document order if its first character appears before the first character of the other item. Note that XML canonicalization extends this document order by giving namespace and attribute nodes document order positions greater than those of their parent element, but less than the positions of any of child elements. It also gives attribute nodes of an element document order positions greater than those of namespace nodes of the same element.

### 9.4.3    Alphabetic Order for Namespaces and Attributes

Alphabetic comparisons are based on the character's Unicode value. Names are considered left-justified. Shorter names sort before longer names that start with the same characters as the shorter name. For example, "foo" sorts before "foobar." This approach results in exactly the same ordering as left-justified sorting of the names in the UTF-8 encoding if you consider each octet to be an unsigned integer—that is, sorting shorter UTF-8 byte sequences before longer ones that start with the same bytes as the shorter sequence. For example, the following three Unicode character strings ("W3", "©", and "©!") are in alphabetic order as Canonical XML defines it:

```
U+0057 U+0033
U+00A9
U+00A9 U+0021
```

The ordering is the same for their UTF-8 encoding:

```
0x57 0x33
0xC2 0xA9
0xC2 0xA9 0x21
```

An element's namespace nodes are ordered alphabetically by the associated prefix name. Its attributes are ordered by namespace URI first, and then by attribute name. Unqualified attributes are ordered before those qualified with a namespace. Although it might seem to be more natural to sort by prefix and local name, sorting attributes by URI first was chosen to group together attributes with the same URI, even if they use different prefixes. This system more closely adheres to the spirit of XML namespaces.

## 9.5    Formal Generative Specification

The formal description of XML canonicalization is to create an XPath node-set data model of the XML document or subset, as described in Section 9.4, and then generate the external XML representation according to the rules given in this section. This generative process starts at the root node and uses the UTF-8 character encoding. You can use any other processing that produces the same external sequence of octets in place of the specification provided here.

Note that the result is not guaranteed to be well-formed XML. For example, the XPath node-set could, in addition to the always-present root node, contain only text or only attribute nodes. Nevertheless, XML canonicalization is most commonly used with node-sets that do yield well-formed XML. Such node-sets are always produced, for example, when either of the standard XML canonicalization XPath expressions given in Section 9.4.1 is applied to well-formed XML.

When the output of XML canonicalization is well formed, then applying the same XML canonicalization again to that output does not change it. That is, this operation is idempotent. Such a feature is considered valuable in a method of canonicalization because, in complex processing, it is difficult to avoid the possibility of canonicalizing data more than once.

### 9.5.1    The Root Node

The root node is the parent of the entire document or document subset. The output is the result of processing each of the child nodes under the root node in document order and, within element start tags, processing the namespace and attribute nodes having that element as a parent, in the order described below. Processing generates no XML declaration, DTD information, or byte order mark (BOM, an artifact of [Unicode]).

### 9.5.2    Element Nodes

If the element appears in the node-set, then output the following items in the order given here. If the element is not present in the node-set, then omit items 1, 2, 5, 7, 8, and 9 and output items 3, 4, and 6.

1. An open angle bracket ("<")

2. The element name (with the namespace prefix, if one is present)

3. The result of processing the Element Node Namespace Axis section

4. The result of processing the Element Node Attribute Axis section

5. A close angle bracket (">")

6. The result of processing the child nodes of the element that appear in the node-set (in document order)

7. An open angle bracket and forward slash ("</")

8. The element name (with the namespace prefix, if one is present)

9. A close angle bracket (">")

### Element Node Namespace Axis

Process each node that appears in the element's namespace axis in alphabetical order by prefix, as described in Section 9.4.3. The processing of each namespace node is described in Section 9.5.4.

### Element Node Attribute Axis

Process each node that appears in the element's attribute axis alphabetically by URI and local part, as described in Section 9.4.3. Section 9.5.3 describes the processing of each attribute node.

---

### 9.5.3    Attribute Nodes

If the attribute node is not present in the node-set, output nothing. If the attribute node appears in the node-set, output the following items in the order given below. Namespace declarations are not considered to be attributes; Section 9.5.4 describes their handling. Special considerations apply to attributes in the xml Namespace.

1. A space (x20) character

2. The attribute name (with the namespace prefix, if one is present)

3. The two-character sequence equals sign, double quote ("=")

4. The XPath string value of the node modified as described below

5. A double quote (""")

Modify the string value in item 4 with the following substitutions:

- Replace ampersand ("&") with the five-byte character reference for ampersand ("&amp;").

- Replace open angle bracket with the four-byte character reference for open angle bracket (&lt;).

- Replace double quote (""") with the six-byte character reference for double quote ("&quot;").

- Replace horizontal tab (x09) with the five-byte character reference for horizontal tab ("&#x9;").

- Replace new line (x0A) with the five-byte character reference for new line ("&#xA;").

- Replace carriage return (x0D) with the five byte character reference for carriage return ("&#xD;").

### Special Handling of Attributes in the xml Namespace

The preceding description is accurate for Exclusive XML Canonicalization. In Canonical XML, however, we want to include ancestor environment characteristics that might affect the XML being canonicalized. For this reason, Canonical XML imports to each apex element (i.e., each element that is a child of the root node) all ancestor xml namespace attributes (e.g., xml:lang, xml:space, or xml:base) that are in scope and do not already appear at that apex element. Such imported attributes are output as described earlier in this section for other attributes.

---

### 9.5.4   Namespace Nodes

If a namespace node is not part of the node set, output nothing. If it is part of the node-set, however, special criteria are applied to determine whether outputting the namespace node will have an effect. Nothing is output if the namespace node would have no effect.

Keep in mind that on input, XPath propagates a namespace declaration down to all of its descendants, creating namespace nodes for each one, until it reaches a node where the same prefix is given a different namespace value. (The same thing happens with the default namespace—it is just like a namespace assigned to the null prefix except that when you use the null prefix, and the colon is omitted.)

XML canonicalization considers a namespace node to have no effect at the current node if it meets any of the following criteria:

- It is a duplicate namespace declaration (same prefix and URI) of a namespace declaration at the first ancestor element in the node-set above the current node.

- It is a declaration that the default namespace is a null URI and the current node is the apex output node.

- It is a declaration of the "xml" prefix, as that should always be "http://www.w3.org/XML/1998/namespace".

If a namespace node does have effect and appears in the node-set, it is output in the same way as an attribute node described in Section 9.5.3, with the following exceptions:

- The namespace prefix fills the role of an attribute name.

- "xmlns:" fills the role of a namespace prefix.

- For the default namespace, "xmlns" fills the role of an attribute name with no prefix.

Which namespace nodes are considered to affect the output differs between Canonical XML and Exclusive XML Canonicalization as follows:

- In Canonical XML, all namespace nodes at an apex element are considered to have an effect and appear in the node-set unless they are a declaration of the xml prefix or of a null default namespace URI.

- In Exclusive XML Canonicalization, namespace nodes are considered to have an effect and appear in the node-set at any element where their namespace prefix is visible in the element name or the name of an attribute, unless they are a declaration of the xml prefix or of a null default namespace URI at an apex. Occurrences of the same namespace declaration on ancestor nodes have no effect unless they are accompanied by visible use of the prefix.

- Namespace nodes are treated as specified in Canonical XML, rather than Exclusive XML Canonicalization, if their prefixes appear on the inclusive namespace prefix list parameter to Exclusive XML Canonicalization.

## 9.5.5   Text Nodes

If the text node is not part of the node-set, output nothing. If it appears in the node-set, output the XPath string value of the text node with the following substitutions:

- Replace ampersand ("&") with the five-byte character reference for ampersand ("&amp;").

- Replace open angle bracket ("<") with the four-byte character reference for open angle bracket ("&lt;").

- Replace close angle bracket (">") with the four-byte character reference for close angle bracket ("&gt;").

- Replace carriage return (x0D) with the five-byte character reference for carriage return ("&#xD;").

---

### 9.5.6   Processing Instruction Nodes

If the processing instruction (PI) does not appear in the node-set, output nothing. If the PI is part of the node-set, output the following in the order given:

1. A new line character (x0A) if the PI is a child of the root node, there is at least one element node child of the root node, and the PI node appears after the last element node child of the root in document order

2. The two-character opening PI sequence less than, question mark ("<?")

3. The PI target name of the PI node

4. If the string value of the PI node is not null, a space character (x20) and then that string value encoded as described in Section 9.5.5 for a text node

5. The two-character closing PI sequence question mark, greater than ("?>")

6. A new line character (x0A) if the PI is a child of the root node, there is at least one element node child of the root node, and the PI node appears before the first element node child of the root in document order

---

### 9.5.7   Comment Nodes

If the comment does not appear in the node-set, output nothing. If the comment is part of the node-set, output the following in the order given:

1. A new line character (x0A) if the comment is a child of the root node, there is at least one element node child of the root node, and the comment node appears after the last element node child of the root in document order

2. The four-character opening comment sequence of less than, exclamation point, hyphen, hyphen ("<!--")

3. The XPath string value of the comment node encoded as described in Section 9.5.5 for a text node

4. The three-character closing comment sequence of hyphen, hyphen, greater than ("-->")

5. A new line character (x0A) if the comment is a child of the root node, there is at least one element node child of the root node, and the comment node appears before the first element node child of the root in document order

## 9.6      Limitations of XML Canonicalization

XML canonicalization provides, where possible, a canonical form based on the XML and XML Namespace standards. That is, it strives to change all cases of the "same" XML, according to these standards, into identical sequences of octets. Of course, what is considered the "same" inherently depends on the particular application.

Ignoring such issues as changes in ancestor bindings that appear not to be used in a subdocument to be signed, consider the foo2:bar element:

```
<wrapper xmlns:foo2="http://example.com"
         xmlns:foo3="ftp://x.example">
  <foo2:bar attribute="value">content</foo2:bar>
</wrapper>
```

If the foo2:bar element and its content are signed, should we assume that foo2 is intended to always represent the namespace to which it is bound in the start tag of the wrapper element? Even Exclusive XML Canonicalization would include the namespace binding of foo2 from the wrapper element, because it is visibly used. But suppose that the application merely thought of foo2 as a selector between the two namespaces bound to prefixes in a wrapper element start tag, with the other selector being foo3. The application designer might expect to be able to move this foo2:bar element to a different context, where foo2 and foo3 are bound to different namespace URIs, and have it select from the new pair of namespaces that also have bar elements. For example:

```
<NewWrapper xmlns:foo2="https://10.1.2.3"
            xmlns:foo3="http://x42.net">
  <foo2:bar attribute="value">content</foo2:bar>
</NewWrapper>
```

This way to use namespaces in an application might seem a little odd, but is certainly consistent with the way many people and XML standards view the "real" XML—that is, as the surface character sequence. Conversely, other people and standards view the "real" XML as a logical tree structure without surface representation artifacts such as CDATA sections and namespace prefixes. The application designer might want to sign the foo2:bar element, send it in a message, verify the signature at the destination, and then insert it in a different wrapper for interpretation. To accomplish this goal without the XML subdocument being "changed" from this application designer's point of view, a custom canonicalization is needed. The two existing standard canonicalizations rely on the premise that they need to include the visibly used namespace binding in the foo2:bar start tag to avoid changing context effects. Of course, it is exactly those effects on which this application designer is counting in this hypothetical case! Canonicalization algorithms cannot read the application designer's mind, so the application designer must specify the appropriate canonicalization.

Beyond this situation, in some cases canonicalization does not take into account some application-level equivalence as described in Section 9.6.1. Also, some important considerations arise with Unicode character normalization, which is deliberately left outside XML canonicalization (as discussed in Section 9.6.2). In addition, canonicalized XML may not always be operationally equivalent to its non-canonical input. Section 9.6.3 describes these situations and explains how to minimize the potential operational and security problems. Finally, the inclusion or exclusion of ancestor namespace declaration and/or xml namespace attributes can result in problems requiring adjustment, as described in Section 9.6.4.

### 9.6.1    Application Equivalences

Often, two instances of XML are equivalent from the point of view of an application but XML canonicalization does not turn them into the same external representation. For example, the following may have the same meaning for some applications but different meaning and effects for other applications:

```
<ex>   1</ex>          <!-- example A -->
<ex>00001</ex>         <!-- example B -->
<ex>1.0e0   </ex>      <!-- example C -->
```

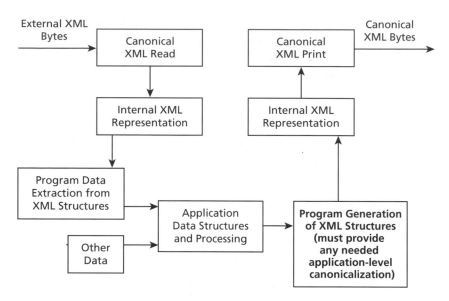

**Figure 9-8** | XML application processing and canonicalization

If examples A through C are passwords, they are very different. If A and B are just meant to be integers, they are the same. For a numeric calculator application that recognizes scientific notation, examples A through C may be the same.

Usually no problems occur where XML simply flows through storage or communications channels and a signature is then verified. (See Figure 9-6.) For more complex protocol cases, where, for example, fields are stored in a database and later retrieved to reconstitute XML over which a signature is verified, applications usually must determine and rigorously adhere to their own canonical forms. (See Figure 9-8.)

In the future, a "deeper" XML canonicalization may be specified based on knowledge of data types for XML content, perhaps derived from XML Schema [Schema].

### 9.6.2    Character Normalization

Canonical XML does not perform Unicode character normalization. In many cases, multiple representations represent the "same" character—for example a precomposed character versus a sequence. It is recommended that applications creating new XML always generate text in Unicode Normalization Form C [NFC].

It would be inappropriate for canonicalization to normalize characters within the Unicode domain for the following reasons:

- An application might act differently for different representations, yet the signature would still be considered valid if character sequences were normalized. For example, a person's name might have an accented character, and a simple-minded table lookup might fail if representation of that character were changed. Signature validation with canonicalization would not detect this change in representation of canonicalization-normalized characters.

- As more characters are added to Unicode, the cases that would need to be handled for normalization continue to grow.

- The resources in processing and program memory needed to handle all normalization cases could be nontrivial.

Conversely, it is appropriate for an application to normalize characters upon their generation. An application is likely to know the appropriate NFC or other normalization it would like to use for its repertoire of characters. Also, it is easier to generate character-normalized text initially than it is to check for all possible non-normalized sequences and convert them to their normal form.

### 9.6.3   Operational Nonequivalence

It would be desirable for the replacement of XML by a canonicalization to have no application effect. This is particularly true because the XML digital signature, using a canonicalization, will not change if that canonicalization replaces a document or subset. Neither type of XML canonicalization makes a change when applied to output of that canonicalization, assuming that the comment inclusion flag remains the same in both cases. Thus the canonicalizations of the original XML and of the original XML with replacement canonicalization will be identical, as will their digital signatures. This signature equivalence could pose a security problem if the operational differences between the original and canonicalized XML violate a security policy, as signature checks would not detect them.

The next three sections discuss particular cases where original and canonicalized XML may be operationally nonequivalent and suggest corrective actions that can be taken.

### Notations and Unparsed External Entities

Because XML canonicalization discards the DTD, NOTATION declarations are discarded along with the binding of such entities to a URI as well as the attribute type that binds the attribute value to an entity name. These features are rarely used, however, and it is recommended that applications use a URI attribute value to reference unparsed data.

### Attribute Types

Because XML canonicalization eliminates XML DTDs, output will not include information about attribute types. For example, ID nodes no longer have that type, so XPath expressions over the output using the "id( )" function cease to operate, except for applications with built-in type knowledge. This problem does not arise with attributes of type ENTITY or ENTITIES. Entity replacement and the rules concerning notations and unparsed external entities cover such attributes.

Applications for which DTD elimination might create a problem due to subsequent XML processing of canonical output can simply prefix that output with appropriate external and/or internal DTD information. Keep in mind that after adding such information, the output will no longer be canonical. Applications that are affected by DTD information should sign and verify the signature on such information as well as the signature on the XML to which the DTD applies.

### Relative URIs

Documents containing relative URIs have an operational meaning that depends on their base URI. The base URI is the URI used to access the document, except inside the scope of an xml:base attribute when xml:base is supported as described in Chapter 7. For example, if an XHTML Web page contains relative URI references to images, then the URI used to fetch the images depends on the URI used to access the initial Web page. In addition, if external general parsed entity references contain relative URIs, canonicalization will import such entities without changing the URIs. In the canonical form, the initial base URI for such external entities will be changed from the external entity location to the location of the XML into which canonicalization imports them.

An application can overcome these problems in either of two ways:

- It can always use absolute URIs.

- It can support and use the xml:base attribute at the top level of documents and external general parsed entities to fix the URI base.

**Note**

> The W3C formally disapproves of relative URIs as namespaces. The Canonical XML Recommendation supports this disapproval by requiring that an error be returned when canonicalizing XML containing a relative URI namespace and by prohibiting the use of a parser that automatically converts relative URI namespaces to absolute URIs.

### 9.6.4    Exclusion/Inclusion of Ancestor Namespace Declarations and xml Namespace Attributes

As mentioned previously, XML's correct operation may depend on making the appropriate choice between including and excluding namespace declarations and xml namespace attributes that appear on ancestor nodes above the portion of XML being canonicalized. The application designer must select a particular strategy: use Canonical XML, use Exclusive XML Canonicalization, or use a "home brew" canonicalize. With the last choice, keep in mind that for any other process to verify the signature, it must implement the chosen canonicalization algorithm. If the designer chooses Canonical XML or Exclusive XML Canonicalization, other adjustments can be made as well.

The XML being canonicalized may depend on the effect of xml namespace attributes, such as xml:lang and xml:space, appearing in ancestor nodes. To avoid problems due to the non-importation of such attributes into an enveloped document subset with Exclusive XML Canonicalization, the attributes must

- Be explicitly given in the apex nodes of the XML document subset being canonicalized,

- Always be declared with an equivalent value in every context in which the XML document subset will be interpreted, or

- Be imported by Canonical XML, which is inclusive.

Also, the XML being canonicalized may depend on the effect of XML namespace declarations where the namespace prefix being bound is not visibly utilized. For example, the evaluation of an attribute whose value is an XPath expression might depend on namespace prefixes referenced in that expression.

To avoid problems with the omission of such namespace declarations due to Exclusive XML Canonicalization,

- The XML must be modified so that the namespace prefix used is visible,

- The namespace declarations must appear and be bound to the same values in every context in which the XML will be interpreted,

- The prefixes for such namespaces must appear in the InclusiveNamespacePrefix List, or

- Canonical XML, which is inclusive, must be used.

# 10 | XML Signatures and Authentication

XML digital authentication is accomplished by means of XML data structures called digital signatures, as described in this chapter.

**Note**

> For simplicity, readability, and historical reasons, the term "signature" in this book usually refers to the general class of digital authentication values. Strictly speaking, "digital signature" refers to authentication values based on public key systems. Symmetric secret key authentication values are more properly called "authentication codes"; this book uses that term, or "authenticator," when referring to that type of authentication.

After an introduction to the XML Digital Signatures standard [XMLDSIG] in Section 10.1, Section 10.2 discusses the detailed syntax of digital signatures. Section 10.3 gives four examples of their use. You can read Sections 10.2 and 10.3 in either order, depending on whether you prefer to learn first from examples or from detailed specifications.

The signed data processing model and the Transforms element are sufficiently important that they are described separately in Section 10.4.

Section 10.5 provides the processing rules for signature generation and verification.

Section 10.6 examines a number of warning and security considerations in the use of XML digital signatures.

## 10.1    Introduction to XML Digital Signatures

What does a digital signature "mean"?

In reality, it merely associates some data with a "key." The application that generates the signature must have access to the data to be signed and the signature generation key. Later, an application can verify the signature if it has access to the signed data and to the signature verification key. (The verification key may or may not be the same as the generation key, depending on the kind of authentication in use.) If the signature is verified, the verifier knows that either some application with the generation key has produced the signature or an adversary has broken the cryptographic algorithms. Let's assume good cryptographic algorithms and good control over who has a copy of the key. If data are signed at some place and time and later verified at a different place or time, you can be confident of two things:

1. It was signed with the key.

2. It has not been modified from its original value.

Note that these points do not mention "meaning" at all. Any "meaning" given to a digital signature, beyond strongly connecting some data with a key, is an interpretation imposed by a particular application. True, it is common for the signed "data" to include structures intended to be interpreted as assertions. For example, such an assertion could be a claimed date of signing or an indication of whether some "person" who should have control over the key and its use is stating, agreeing to, or merely witnessing the data. It is very tempting, if the data appears to be human-readable text and the key is associated in some way with a particular person, to conclude that that person is "saying" what appears to be in the data. But perhaps some secure channel computer process is working on behalf of the person who has signed the data just for integrity assurance during transport without any idea of what the data "says." Or perhaps a computer program has been duped into signing the data. In any case, from the point of view of the mechanics of generating and validating signatures, the data consist of just a pile of 1s and 0s; all "human meaning" interpretations take place at a higher application level.

### Why a New Form of Signature?

One preliminary question you might ask is, "Why create a new format for signatures?" After all, things work with existing signature formats. For example, the binary format in PKCS#7 [RFC 2315] uses [ASN.1, DER] syntax, and the binary format in PGP [RFC 2240] uses its own binary syntax. If you want a printable form of these binary signature blobs, you could encode them into ordinary printable characters by using base-64 [RFC 2045] or the like.

For XML systems, the signature object itself must conform to XML syntax. Only then can you use XML tools to manipulate pieces of it, have it easily point into other XML structures so you can sign parts of XML documents, easily point into it and make assertions about it or parts of it, and use XML tools to display it.

**History**

During the development of the XMLDSIG standard, several people joined the working group mailing list and posted messages that said something like the following: "What in the world are you guys doing? You should just define a simple XML envelope to go around Z, and everyone's problem will be solved. I'm shocked that you are defining a new signature format that will be a lot of work for me to implement. . . ."

Z was always the correspondent's favorite existing binary signature standard. Of course, it was different for each person who posted such a note! These people just wanted something like a <PKCS/signature/> element, for which the content was a PKCS7 binary blob encoded into printing characters. That would have meant—using PKCS7 as an example—that everyone implementing XMLDSIG would need not just an XML parser and generator but also one for ASN.1/DER. Useful signature properties or the like would be opaquely buried inside this binary blob rather than being accessible and manipulatable XML. In other words, what these people wanted wasn't XML signatures but their own favorite non-XML signature with a very thin XML veneer.

The key characteristic of XML Digital Signatures (XMLDSIG) is that the signature object itself appears in XML syntax. The data being signed can consist of XML, but that is not required. The data could also be a binary file such as a GIF image or the result of querying a database through a URI or, because one XMLDSIG Signature element can authenticate multiple pieces of data, all of these at the same time. XML digital signatures can sign anything you can reference through a URI (see Chapter 7). Even more flexibly, they can sign anything you can derive with an algorithmic transformation from data that a URI references!

### Enveloping, Enveloped, and Detached Signatures

As well as varying by data type, you can classify things that XMLDSIG signs as to whether the data being signed appears in one of the following places:

- Inside the XMLDSIG element, which is called an enveloping signature (see Figure 10-1).

- Outside of, but surrounding, the XMLDSIG element, which is called an enveloped signature (see Figure 10-2).

- Outside and disjoint from the XMLDSIG element, which is called a detached signature (see Figure 10-3). Note that detached signed data can appear either in the same document as the XMLDISG element or elsewhere.

Because XMLDSIG elements can sign multiple pieces of data, they can be any two or all three of these kinds of signatures—enveloping, enveloped, or detached—at the same time.

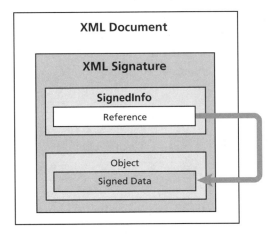

**Figure 10-1** | An enveloping signature

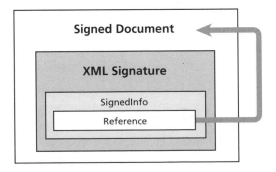

**Figure 10-2** | An enveloped signature

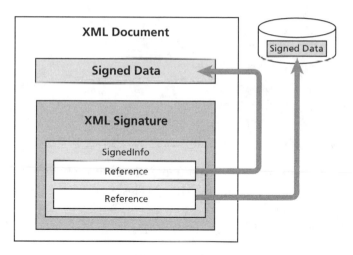

**Figure 10-3** | A detached signature over two data items

## 10.2   XML Signature Syntax

This section describes the XML digital signature syntax and discusses formal DTD and schema syntaxes as alternative descriptions of it. A certain context is assumed for the DTDs and schemas that appear in later subsections. In particular, the DTD context is assumed to be as follows:

```
<!-- XMLDSIG DTD context -->


<!--
The following entity declarations enable external/flexible
content in the Signature content model.

#PCDATA emulates schema:string; when combined with element types
it emulates schema mixed="true".

% foo.ANY permits the user to include their own element types
from other namespaces, for example:
<!ENTITY % KeyValue.ANY '| ecds:ECDSAKeyValue'>
    ...
<!ELEMENT ecds:ECDSAKeyValue (#PCDATA)  >
-->


<!ENTITY % Object.ANY ''>
<!ENTITY % Method.ANY ''>
```

```
<!ENTITY % Transform.ANY ''>
<!ENTITY % SignatureProperty.ANY ''>
<!ENTITY % KeyInfo.ANY ''>
<!ENTITY % KeyValue.ANY ''>
<!ENTITY % X509Data.ANY ''>
<!ENTITY % PGPData.ANY ''>
<!ENTITY % SPKIData.ANY ''>
```

As explained in the comment, the entity declarations offer a way to gain extensibility. Essentially, later DTDs' (external or internal subset) ENTITY declarations can append new permitted elements if the XMLDSIG DTD is interpreted before such later DTDs.

The XML schema context is assumed to be as follows:

```
<?xml version="1.0" encoding="utf-8"?>
<!-- XMLDSIG Schema context -->
<!DOCTYPE schema PUBLIC "-//W3C//DTD XMLSchema 200102//EN"
                        "http://www.w3.org/2001/XMLSchema.dtd"
[
<!ATTLIST schema
          xmlns:ds CDATA #FIXED
          "http://www.w3.org/2000/09/xmldsig#">
<!ENTITY dsig 'http://www.w3.org/2000/09/xmldsig#'>
<!ENTITY % p ''>
<!ENTITY % s ''>
] >

<schema xmlns="http://www.w3.org/2001/XMLSchema"
        xmlns:ds="http://www.w3.org/2000/09/xmldsig#"
        targetNamespace="http://www.w3.org/2000/09/xmldsig#"
        version="0.1" elementFormDefault="qualified">
```

**Note**

The somewhat mysterious "p" and "s" entities are part of the way [Schema] is defined and affect DTD processing of XML schemas. They stand for "prefix" and "suffix," respectively, and are needed because the DTD for XML schema is full of things like "xmlns&s;=…" and "<&p;foo>…</&p;foo>". If you don't set them, they default from the DTD for XML schema to "xs:" and ":xs".

### Versioning

Most signature standards include a version field in their signature structure, but XMLDSIG does not. Instead, it uses the namespaces [Names] feature of XML for this purpose. The standard defines the current XMLDSIG in the "http://www.w3.org/2000/09/xmldsig#" namespace. A new XMDSIG standard would use a new namespace.

### The ds:CryptoBinary Simple Type

Arbitrary-length integers (e.g., "bignums") appear in XML as encoded octet strings. Schema syntax represents these using the ds:CryptoBinary simple type.

Starting with such a "bignum," you first convert the integer to a "big endian" bit sequence. You then pad the bit sequence with leading zero bits so that the total length is a multiple of 8. Next, you remove any leading octets that are zero, so that the high-order octet is always nonzero. This sequence is then base-64 [RFC 2045] encoded. (The conversion from integer to octet string is equivalent to the PKCS#1's I2OSP [RFC 2437] with minimal length.)

"Bignum" values such as RSAKeyValue and DSAKeyValue use this type. If a value can be of type base64Binary or ds:CryptoBinary, it is specified as base64Binary. For example, if the signature algorithm is RSA or DSA, then SignatureValue represents a bignum and could be ds:CryptoBinary. If HMAC-SHA1 is the signature algorithm, however, SignatureValue is a fixed-size binary quantity where leading zero bytes should be preserved. For this reason, SignatureValue is specified to be of type base64Binary.

Following is the schema for ds:CryptoBinary:

```
<!-- CryptoBinary Schema -->

<simpleType name="CryptoBinary">
    <restriction base="base64Binary"/>
</simpleType>
```

DTDs have a much cruder concept of data type than XML schemas, and CryptoBinary is not used in them.

### Algorithms

Six elements that specify algorithms can appear as descendants of the Signature element: CanonicalizationMethod, SignatureMethod, DigestMethod,

Transform, and, within a KeyInfo type element, AgreementMethod and EncryptionMethod. For more details on algorithms, see Chapter 17.

**URI Representation**

XML Security uses URI [RFC 2396] attribute values in several places. For example, it uses attribute values to identify algorithms in algorithm role elements, to point to data in Reference elements, and to identify data types in Reference and RetrievalMethod elements. You need to take care when encoding URIs as attribute values, as explained in Chapter 7.

### 10.2.1   The Signature Element

Let's look at the structure of the XMLDSIG element. Example 10-1 provides a skeletal XML version of just about the simplest possible Signature element. (See the preface for a description of skeletal XML.)

***Example 10-1***   *Skeletal Signature element*

```
<Signature>     <!-- simplified skeletal Signature element-->
    <SignedInfo>
        (CanonicalizationMethod)
        (SignatureMethod)
        <Reference>
            (DigestMethod)
            (DigestValue)
        </Reference>
    </SignedInfo>
    (SignatureValue)
</Signature>
```

Although this example is very simple, we can see a few things. Inside the Signature element, we have the actual SignatureValue and SignedInfo. Inside SignedInfo we have a SignatureMethod and a Reference.

The Reference specifies the data we are signing. The DigestMethod algorithm digests the data, and the resulting DigestValue appears inside the Reference element. A digest of data is analogous to a unique fingerprint calculated from and representing the data (see Chapter 2). It is also usually much shorter than the data. For all practical purposes, then, signing the digest is as good as signing the original data. The verifier can verify the signature on the digest, check whether the digest corresponds to the data, and consider the signature verified on the data.

### Signature Element Syntax

The actual DTD syntax of the Signature element is as follows:

```
<!-- Signature DTD -->


<!ELEMENT Signature (SignedInfo, SignatureValue,
                     KeyInfo?, Object*) >
<!ATTLIST Signature
        xmlns   CDATA   #FIXED
                        'http://www.w3.org/2000/09/xmldsig#'
        Id      ID      #IMPLIED >
```

In schema notation, it has the following form:

```
<!-- Signature Schema -->


<element name="Signature" type="ds:SignatureType"/>
<complexType name="SignatureType">
    <sequence>
        <element ref="ds:SignedInfo"/>
        <element ref="ds:SignatureValue"/>
        <element ref="ds:KeyInfo" minOccurs="0"/>
        <element ref="ds:Object" minOccurs="0"
                 maxOccurs="unbounded"/>
    </sequence>
    <attribute name="Id" type="ID" use="optional"/>
</complexType>
```

### 10.2.2   The SignedInfo Element

The most complex parts of an XML digital signature are usually the Signed-Info element and the KeyInfo element. They provide information on the data and the key for the signature, respectively. SignedInfo is described follows; Chapter 13 describes KeyInfo.

The SignedInfo element DTD syntax is as follows:

```
<!-- SignedInfo DTD -->


<!ELEMENT SignedInfo (CanonicalizationMethod,
                SignatureMethod, Reference+)  >
<!ATTLIST SignedInfo
          Id    ID      #IMPLIED >
```

In schema notation, it has the following form:

```
<!-- SignedInfo Schema -->

<element name="SignedInfo" type="ds:SignedInfoType"/>
<complexType name="SignedInfoType">
    <sequence>
        <element ref="ds:CanonicalizationMethod"/>
        <element ref="ds:SignatureMethod"/>
        <element ref="ds:Reference" maxOccurs="unbounded"/>
    </sequence>
    <attribute name="Id" type="ID" use="optional"/>
</complexType>
```

During signature verification, the SignedInfo element bundles together the following items:

- The signature algorithm in SignatureMethod

- The Reference elements that point to the item or items being signed

- The CanonicalizationMethod that is used on SignedInfo itself

The following subsections discuss each of these elements.


### The CanonicalizationMethod Element

Modern signature algorithms operate on a sequence of eight-bit bytes or octets. SignedInfo is, of course, XML that has been read into or constructed by an application. It must be converted to a sequence of octets so that it can be signed using the SignatureMethod algorithm. The XML standard requires that much of the external surface representation of SignedInfo be thrown away, as it is read in, and not given to that application. Even so, the signature verification application must use the same sequence of octets for SignedInfo that the signing application uses.

The CanonicalizationMethod converts SignedInfo into a sequence of octets. Standard XML canonicalizations have been developed that handle the most common canonicalization requirements of XML, as discussed in Chapter 9.

The way in which you present the SignedInfo to the canonicalization method depends on that method.

- XML-based canonicalization algorithms must receive an XPath node-set formed from the document containing the SignedInfo and indicating the SignedInfo, its descendants, and the attribute and namespace nodes of SignedInfo and its descendant elements.

- Text-based canonicalization algorithms (such as line-ending and charset normalization) should be provided with the UTF-8 octets that represent the well-formed SignedInfo element, from the open angle bracket ("<") of the start tag to the close angle bracket (">") of the end tag, with all descendant markup and character data appearing between those tags. Use of text-based canonicalization of SignedInfo is not recommended because it can easily lead to interoperability problems.

For resource-constrained applications that do not implement XML canonicalization but rather use a text canonicalization, the standard recommends that they be implemented to generate canonicalized XML as their output serialization. This approach will mitigate interoperability and security concerns.

**Note**

Signature applications should exercise caution in accepting and executing arbitrary CanonicalizationMethod algorithms. The canonicalization method could potentially rewrite the URIs of the Reference elements being validated or massively transform SignedInfo so that validation would always succeed (e.g., converting it to a trivial signature with a known key over trivial data). Because CanonicalizationMethod appears inside SignedInfo, in the resulting canonical form, it could erase itself from SignedInfo or modify the SignedInfo element so that it appears to later analysis that a different canonicalization function was used! Thus a Signature that appears, after canonicalization, to authenticate the desired data with the desired key, DigestMethod, and SignatureMethod, could actually be meaningless if you use a capricious CanonicalizationMethod.

Consider the following example CanonicalizationMethod:

```
<CanonicalizationMethod
    Algorithm="http://www.w3.org/TR/xml-exc-c14n"/>
```

The value of the Algorithm attribute specifies the algorithm; its implicit input is SignedInfo. You can specify any needed explicit parameters as element content (see Chapter 17).

**History**

Early in the development of XMLDSIG, a substantial camp of paper-oriented people (see Appendix E) insisted on the creation of a "do nothing" canonicalization or some minimal canonicalization based on the external character representation of SignedInfo. Others argued that the XMLDSIG standard should just require use of the Canonical XML algorithm. As a consequence, CanonicalizationMethod was included and made mandatory to avoid defaulting to one of these choices, and to enable the use of other options.

It turned out that no standard XML tools at the time supported any good way to preserve and get pointers into the external byte stream, making null and/or minimal canonicalization very difficult to implement. When it became necessary to advance XMLDSIG to a standardization level that required multiple interoperable implementations, no one had implemented any canonicalization except Canonical XML. Then some real-world application problems caused by the context-inclusive nature of Canonical XML arose. An option to avoid these problems, in so far as possible, was then provided by the Exclusive XML Canonicalization algorithm, which is the most appropriate approach to use over signed XML data, including SignedInfo.

**Soapbox**

In theory, perhaps the flexibility provided by the CanonicalizationMethod element should not be necessary for XMLDSIG. After all, SignedInfo and its contents are all standardized parts of XMLDSIG, and its canonicalization requirements should be known. Although you can do some bizarre and complicated things with a custom CanonicalizationMethod, that is generally not a good idea and may bring on interoperability problems. Nevertheless, it turned out that providing this flexibility was the right choice, as problems arose with Canonical XML. Almost all CanonicalizationMethod elements should specify Exclusive XML Canonicalization, as in the preceding example.

The syntax for the CanonicalizationMethod element is as follows:

```
<!-- CanonicalizationMethod DTD -->


<!ELEMENT CanonicalizationMethod (#PCDATA %Method.ANY;)* >
<!ATTLIST CanonicalizationMethod
          Algorithm    CDATA      #REQUIRED >
```

In schema notation, it has the following form:

```
<!-- CanonicalizationMethod schema -->

<element name="CanonicalizationMethod"
         type="ds:CanonicalizationMethodType"/>
<complexType name="CanonicalizationMethodType" mixed="true">
   <sequence>
       <any namespace="##any" minOccurs="0"
                          maxOccurs="unbounded"/>
       <!-- (0,unbounded) elements from (1,1) namespace -->
   </sequence>
       <attribute name="Algorithm" type="anyURI" use="required"/>
</complexType>
```

## The SignatureMethod Element

The SignatureMethod element specifies the algorithm that is applied to the canonicalized SignedInfo and the signing key, as implicit inputs, to produce the SignatureValue as its output.

An example of a SignatureMethod element is as follows:

```
<SignatureMethod
    Algorithm="http://www.w3.org/2000/09/xmldsig#rsa-sha1"/>
```

The syntax for SignatureMethod is as follows:

```
<!-- SignatureMethod DTD -->

<!ELEMENT SignatureMethod (#PCDATA | HMACOutputLength
                       %Method.ANY;)* >
<!ATTLIST SignatureMethod
          Algorithm CDATA #REQUIRED >
```

In schema notation, it has the following form:

```
<!-- SignatureMethod schema -->

<element name="SignatureMethod" type="ds:SignatureMethodType"/>
<complexType name="SignatureMethodType" mixed="true">
    <sequence>
        <element name="HMACOutputLength" minOccurs="0"
                type="ds:HMACOutputLengthType"/>
        <any namespace="##other"
            minOccurs="0" maxOccurs="unbounded"/>
        <!-- (0,unbounded) elements from
            (1,1) external namespace -->
    </sequence>
    <attribute name="Algorithm" type="anyURI" use="required"/>
</complexType>
```

## 10.2.3  The Reference Element

Reference elements in SignedInfo specify which data is being signed. At least one Reference element must appear in SignedInfo, but there can be more. The syntax for each Reference is as follows:

```
<!-- Reference DTD -->

<!ELEMENT Reference (Transforms?, DigestMethod, DigestValue) >
<!ATTLIST Reference
        Id      ID      #IMPLIED
        URI     CDATA   #IMPLIED
        Type    CDATA   #IMPLIED >
```

In schema notation, it has the following form:

```
<!-- Reference schema -->

<element name="Reference" type="ds:ReferenceType"/>
<complexType name="ReferenceType">
    <sequence>
        <element ref="ds:Transforms" minOccurs="0"/>
        <element ref="ds:DigestMethod"/>
```

```
            <element ref="ds:DigestValue"/>
    </sequence>
    <attribute name="Id" type="ID" use="optional"/>
    <attribute name="URI" type="anyURI" use="optional"/>
    <attribute name="Type" type="anyURI" use="optional"/>
</complexType>
```

The optional Id attribute makes it easier to point to the Reference from else-where.

The attribute named URI, if present, must have a URI [RFC 2396] as its value. It is considered optional because sometimes you can determine the location of a data item to be signed from the application context without any explicit pointer. To avoid confusion, you can omit the URI attribute on only one Reference within a SignedInfo. XMLDSIG applications must be able to parse Uniform Resource Identifier (URI) syntax, as specified in Chapter 7.

The standard recommends that XMLDSIG applications support the "http:" access scheme. Retrieval based on an "http:" URI must comply with redirect status codes that may be returned. If multiple URIs of different levels of specificity exist for the same resource, you should use the most specific one to minimize the chance of the signature or application breaking because it receives a different version of the data. For example, the first of the following two URIs is preferred:

```
http://www.w3.org/2000/06/interop-pressrelease.html.en
http://www.w3.org/2000/06/interop-pressrelease
```

The optional Type attribute, if present, also has a URI [RFC 2396] value that represents the type of the data to which the Reference applies. The Type has no effect on Signature verification as defined in XMLDSIG but might be used by other processing. For example, in some application context, Manifest elements (Section 10.2.7) might need special processing. If, in that application, the Type attribute is always present for Manifest element data, the program could use it to decide whether to specially retrieve and process that data.

The Type attribute applies to the item being pointed at, not its contents. For example, a reference that points to an Object element containing a SignatureProperties element is still of type "http://www.w3.org/2000/09/xmldsig#Object." On the other hand, a pointer that points directly to that same SignatureProperties element should identify it as of type "http://www. w3.org/2000/09/xmldsig#SignatureProperties." The XMLDSIG standard considers the Type information advisory and requires no validation of it.

### The Transforms Element

Transforms provide a powerful mechanism to indicate processing of the data before they are digested. You might want to extract a subset of the data, for example, if that is all you want to sign. Transforms are part of a data pipeline starting from retrieval, going through possible transform operations, and ending with the DigestMethod, are discussed in Section 10.4.

### The DigestMethod Element

DigestMethod is a required element in a Reference that identifies the digest algorithm to be applied to the signed data. This element uses the standard algorithm syntax described in Chapter 17.

If the result of the data fetch and application of Transforms is an XPath node-set (or sufficiently functional replacement implemented by the application), then the application must convert it to a sequence of octets on which the DigestMethod can operate (see Section 10.4). If the data fetch and application of Transforms results in an octet stream, then no conversion is needed. The application applies the digest algorithm to the resulting octet stream.

The syntax for DigestMethod is as follows:

```
<!-- DigestMethod DTD -->


<!ELEMENT DigestMethod (#PCDATA %Method.ANY;)* >
<!ATTLIST DigestMethod
          Algorithm      CDATA    #REQUIRED >
```

In schema notation, it has the following form:

```
<!-- DigestMethod schema -->

<element name="DigestMethod" type="ds:DigestMethodType"/>
<complexType name="DigestMethodType" mixed="true">
    <sequence>
        <any namespace="##other" processContents="lax"
            minOccurs="0" maxOccurs="unbounded"/>
    </sequence>
```

```
        <attribute name="Algorithm" type="anyURI" use="required"/>
</complexType>
```

### The DigestValue Element

The DigestValue is a mandatory element in Reference that contains the encoded value of the digest output from DigestMethod. The digest is always encoded in base-64 [RFC 2045]. The syntax for DigestMethod is as follows:

```
<!-- DigestValue DTD -->

<!ELEMENT DigestValue (#PCDATA) >
<!-- base64 encoded digest value -->
```

In schema notation, it has the following form:

```
<!-- DigestValue schema -->

<element name="DigestValue" type="ds:DigestValueType"/>
<simpleType name="DigestValueType">
    <restriction base="base64Binary"/>
</simpleType>
```

### Reference Examples

Example 10-2 shows a simplified enveloping signature data Reference, where "foo" [RFC 3092] is the ID of a signed XML element included in an Object element later in the signature.

**Example 10-2**  *Enveloping Reference element*

```
<Reference URI="#foo">
    <DigestMethod
     Algorithm="http://www.w3.org/2000/09/xmldsig#sha1"/>
    <DigestValue>qZk+NkcGgWq6PiVxeFDCbJzQ2J0=</DigestValue>
</Reference>
```

Example 10-3 shows a simplified enveloped signature Reference where the null URI refers to the entire document containing this Reference. Here, the enveloped-signature transform exempts the signature from trying to cover itself.

**Example 10-3** *Enveloped Reference element*

```
<Reference URI="">
    <Transforms><Transform Algorithm=
"http://www.w3.org/2000/09/xmldsig#enveloped-signature"/>
    </Transforms>
    <DigestMethod
     Algorithm="http://www.w3.org/2001/04/xmldsig-more#md5"/>
    <DigestValue>qZk+NkcGgWq6PiVxeFDCbJ==</DigestValue>
</Reference>
```

Example 10-4 shows a detached signature where it is assumed that the file referenced by the URI contains base-64 encoded data. The signature covers the decode of that data, and the Reference element itself can be referred to conveniently by its ID.

**Example 10-4** *Detached Reference element*

```
<Reference Id="a123" URI="ftp://foo.example/bar.b64">
    <Transforms>
        <Transform
         Algorithm="http://www.w3.org/2000/09/xmldsig#base64"/>
    </Transforms>
    <DigestMethod
     Algorithm="http://www.w3.org/2001/04/xmldsig-more#md5"/>
    <DigestValue>qZk+NkcGgWq6PiVxeFDCbJ==</DigestValue>
</Reference>
```

### 10.2.4  The SignatureValue Element

The SignatureValue element stores the actual binary signature value. This value is calculated over the canonicalized SignedInfo using SignatureMethod and the signing key. The value is encoded as base-64. The syntax of the SignatureValue element is as follows:

```
<!-- SignatureValue DTD -->

<!ELEMENT SignatureValue (#PCDATA) >
<!ATTLIST SignatureValue
        Id      ID      #IMPLIED>
```

In schema notation, it has the following form:

```
<!-- SignatureValue schema -->


<element name="SignatureValue" type="ds:SignatureValueType"/>
<complexType name="SignatureValueType">
    <simpleContent>
        <extension base="ds:base64Binary">
            <attribute name="Id" type="ID" use="optional"/>
        </extension>
    </simpleContent>
</complexType>
```

### 10.2.5   The KeyInfo Element

The KeyInfo element provides information to help the verifier find the appropriate verification key. Chapter 13 describes this element, which is used for both signatures and encryption.

### 10.2.6   The Object Element

The Object element provides a convenient envelope for putting data inside a Signature element but outside SignedInfo. It provides a convenient way to give the MIME type of the data [RFC 2045], such as "text/html" or "image/gif," and its encoding. Binary objects will normally be encoded in base-64. Object is an optional element that may occur multiple times. While Signature provides for Object elements to appear only in a specific place within it, applications can use Object outside of Signature if desired.

Example 10-5 demonstrates use of the Object element.

**Example 10-5**   *Object element*

```
<Signature>
    <SignedInfo>
        ...
    </SignedInfo>
    <Object Encoding="http://www.w3.org/2000/09/xmldsig#base64"
            Id="8abc"
```

```
            MimeType="image/jpeg">
        W1OWlgjBwUSmppX3...
     </Object>
</Signature>
```

The Object element syntax is as follows:

```
<!-- Object DTD -->

<!ELEMENT Object (#PCDATA|Signature|SignatureProperties|Manifest
            %Object.ANY;)* >
<!ATTLIST Object
        Id          ID      #IMPLIED
        MimeType    CDATA   #IMPLIED
        Encoding    CDATA   #IMPLIED >
```

In schema notation, it has the following form:

```
<!-- Object schema -->

<element name="Object" type="ds:ObjectType"/>
<complexType name="ObjectType" mixed="true">
    <sequence minOccurs="0" maxOccurs="unbounded">
        <any namespace="##any" processContents="lax"/>
    </sequence>
    <attribute name="Id" type="ID" use="optional"/>
    <attribute name="MimeType" type="string" use="optional"/>
    <attribute name="Encoding" type="anyURI" use="optional"/>
</complexType>
```

The Id attribute provides a convenient way of referencing the Object from elsewhere—for example, from a Reference in SignedInfo or from a Manifest.

The MimeType attribute is purely advisory, and the signature standard requires no checking of this attribute. Applications that require strong control of type and encoding for signature verification should probably specify Transforms that produce the type and encoding they want.

If an application wants to exclude the start and end tags of Object from digest calculation, a Reference must identify the actual data inside the Object element. This task may be easy to perform for XML data inside Object if it has an ID. For non-XML text data, the program must use a Transform to remove the Object tags. Exclusion of the object tags would be necessary in a case where the signature must remain valid if the data object moves from inside a signature to outside the signature (or vice versa), or if the content of the Object is an encoding of an original binary document and you want to extract and decode it so as to sign the original representation.

**Soapbox**

> The Object element is very useful for putting arbitrary data objects inside an enveloping Signature in a controlled way. It does not do much good, however, when its content is just a Manifest, SignatureProperties, or Signature element. The consensus of the working group was that it provided some useful isolation of stuff that "isn't part of the signature." At the time, tremendous opposition arose in the working group to anything resembling "signature properties." The Object element was kind of a purgatory in which to further exile them. It merely creates a wasted level of element wrapping. Manifest, SignatureProperties, and Signature should have been allowed at the same level in Signature as Object.

### 10.2.7  The Manifest Element

A Manifest element closely resembles a SignedInfo except that it contains only References and the application has control over what happens if verification of the DigestValue in some References fails. You could use Manifest elements to advantage in the following cases, if you have access to this optional feature:

- You are signing multiple pieces of data and want to know for each one whether verification has failed. If the data are all pointed to from References inside SignedInfo, then XMLDSIG requires them to all be verified with failure returned if any Reference fails. When the References appear in a Manifest, however, the application decides which to check and how to treat failure in verifying the DigestValue. The application also decides how to handle other failures, such as data or key not obtainable.

- You want to sign the same list of pieces of data with multiple keys or SignatureMethod algorithms. To do so, you can use multiple Signatures. Of course, if the list of References inside each Signature is large, the resulting code gets very unwieldy. For multiple data items that are the same in multiple Signatures, you can abstract them into a Manifest element, then include a Reference to that Manifest in each Signature, as long as your application will verify them all.

The syntax for the Manifest element is as follows:

```
<!-- Manifest DTD -->


<!ELEMENT Manifest (Reference+) >
<!ATTLIST Manifest
         Id   ID   #IMPLIED >
```

In schema notation, it has the following form:

```
<!-- Manifest schema -->

<element name="Manifest" type="ds:ManifestType"/>
<complexType name="ManifestType">
    <sequence>
        <element ref="ds:Reference" maxOccurs="unbounded"/>
    </sequence>
    <attribute name="Id" type="ID" use="optional"/>
</complexType>
```

The optional Id attribute is one way to reference a Manifest element from a Reference element or another Manifest element.

## 10.2.8 The SignatureProperties Element

The SignatureProperties element holds additional information relevant to the Signature itself or cryptographic parts of it such as a DigestValue. Examples of such information would be the time of calculation or the serial number of a hardware device used in the calculation. The syntax of SignatureProperties is as follows:

```
<!-- SignatureProperties DTD -->


<!ELEMENT SignatureProperties (SignatureProperty+) >
<!ATTLIST SignatureProperties
        Id      ID          #IMPLIED >


<!ELEMENT SignatureProperty (#PCDATA %SignatureProperty.ANY;)* >
<!ATTLIST SignatureProperty
        Target  CDATA       #REQUIRED
        Id      ID          #IMPLIED >
```

In schema notation, it has the following form:

```
<!-- SignatureProperties Schema -->

<element name="SignatureProperties"
        type="ds:SignaturePropertiesType"/>
<complexType name="SignaturePropertiesType">
    <sequence>
        <element ref="ds:SignatureProperty"
                 maxOccurs="unbounded"/>
    </sequence>
    <attribute name="Id" type="ID" use="optional"/>
</complexType>


<element name="SignatureProperty"
        type="ds:SignaturePropertyType"/>
<complexType name="SignaturePropertyType" mixed="true">
    <choice maxOccurs="unbounded">
        <any namespace="##other" processContents="lax"/>
        <!-- (1,1) elements from (1,unbounded) namespaces -->
    </choice>
    <attribute name="Target" type="anyURI" use="required"/>
    <attribute name="Id" type="ID" use="optional"/>
</complexType>
```

Note that the required Target attribute in SignatureProperty points to the element to which the property applies. It will usually be the Id of a Signature or Reference element.

**History**

The contents of a SignatureProperty element are traditionally called "signature attributes" in other types of digital signatures. (The name has nothing to do with XML attributes.) Often, such properties are associated with a "criticality flag." In such a case, if a verifier does not understand a property, it can proceed anyway if the flag says it is not critical, but verification must fail if the flag says that property is critical. This approach sounds reasonable, but the XMLDSIG working group explicitly decided not to provide for such a flag, for three reasons:

• Having a criticality flag leads to endless arguments, when a property is defined, as to whether it should be critical.

- There is no way to enforce the flag on receivers. In other words, protocols are misleading if they claim that such a flag, outside of a closed system, is anything other than a request.

- There always seem to be special circumstances under which something flagged as critical needs to be ignored and/or something not flagged as critical needs to cause failure.

### 10.2.9   Comments and Processing Instructions

XML comments and processing instructions are not used by and have no special significance in Signature elements or any of the elements defined in this chapter. If you use Exclusive XML Canonicalization or Canonical XML for your CanonicalizationMethod, you can freely add and delete comments from the SignedInfo element without affecting the signature. Standard canonicalizations do not automatically eliminate processing instructions, so messing with them will likely break signatures. Similarly, if you do not canonicalize away comments within SignedInfo or signed XML, signatures will be sensitive to changes in comments.

## 10.3    XML Signature Examples

This section provides four examples of XML digital signatures, starting with simple cases and working toward more complex cases. Two of the examples are protocol oriented, and two are form/paper oriented.

### 10.3.1   Simple Protocol Example

Assume you want to efficiently secure protocol messages between two parties. One technique would be to use efficient shared secret key message authentication, like that shown in Example 10-6. In this example, the Data element in a protocol message needs to be authenticated. Because we assume that it is an established connection for a simple protocol, the sender and receiver have already agreed on a key, and thus no KeyInfo is present.

**Example 10-6**   *Simple protocol signature*

```
[L01] <PDU>
[L02]    <Data>...</Data>
```

```
[L03]    <Signature>
[L04]      <SignedInfo>
[L05]        <CanonicalizationMethod
[L06] Algorithm="http://www.w3.org/2001/10/xml-exc-c14n#"/>
[L07]        <SignatureMethod Algorithm=
[L08] "http://www.w3.org/2001/04/xmldsig-more#hmac-md5"/>
[L09]        <Reference>
[L10]          <DigestMethod
[L11] Algorithm="http://www.w3.org/2001/04/xmldsig-more#md5"/>
[L12]          <DigestValue>Zu0kJL/V1YVZWWdnZ71fXw==
                </DigestValue>
[L13]        </Reference>
[L14]      </SignedInfo>
[L15]      <SignatureValue>w5smJq3//01VVUvd3d0BAQ==
              </SignatureValue>
[L16]    </Signature>
[L17] </PDU>
```

[L02] The element that needs to be authenticated.

[L03] Beginning of the authenticating Signature element, which extends to L16.

[L04] Beginning of the element across which the SignatureMethod is actually applied and which is linked to the data by a digest.

[L05/06] How the SignedInfo is canonicalized when verifying the signature. Exclusive XML Canonicalization, as specified, is usually the appropriate algorithm for signatures.

[L07/08] The authentication algorithm. It is applied, using the shared secret key, to SignedInfo to produce the SignatureValue. It includes performing the MD5 hash algorithm on the results of applying the CanonicalizationMethod to SignedInfo.

[L09] This Signature element has only one Reference to authenticated information. Because of the simple nature of this protocol and previous agreement between the parties, no "URI=" attribute is needed. The receiver knows that the Data element is being authenticated.

[L10/11] The algorithm applied to the data to be authenticated. Because the data consist of parsed XML (the Data element), the data will automatically be subject to Canonical XML, producing a standardized serialization to feed to the MD5 hash algorithm.

[L12] The hash value output of MD5 in base-64.

[L15] The authentication value output of the HMAC-MD5 in base-64.

### 10.3.2 Simple Document Example

Example 10-7 shows a simple case of a more document-oriented signature.

***Example 10-7*** *Simple document signature*

```
[L20] <Document...>
[L21]   <Field1 ...>
[L22]     ...myriad content...
[L23]   </Field1>
[L24]   <Field2>...<subF2>...<subsubF2 a="b"/>...</subF2>...
        </Field2>
[L25]   <Signature>
[L26]     <SignedInfo>
[L27]       <CanonicalizationMethod Algorithm=
        "http://www.w3.org/TR/2001/REC-xml-c14n-20010315"/>
[L28]       <SignatureMethod Algorithm=
        "http://www.w3.org/2001/04/xmldsig-more#rsa-sha1"/>
[L29]       <Reference URI="">
[L30]         <Transforms><Transform Algorithm=
        "http://www.w3.org/2000/09/xmldsig#enveloped-signature"/>
            </Transforms>
[L31]         <DigestMethod
        Algorithm="http://www.w3.org/2000/09/xmldsig#sha1"/>
[L32]         <DigestValue>Szbv70MrKxJjY6bx8daFhQjV1fk=
            </DigestValue>
[L33]       </Reference>
[L34]     </SignedInfo>
[L35]     <SignatureValue>
            yFw+PrsMDBmvr0kaGme1tVwQEOLa2qiIiCZycoFDQ+jQ0F
            58fHf4+BGAgA8mJvRLS067u/Sbm8NDQ18GBsoPDw=
          </SignatureValue>
[L36]     <KeyInfo><X509Data><X509Certificate>
            zPrj46nf38G5ufIEBG7w8G5dXVaEhNBZWaqMjJiwsL/Dwz
```

```
            UhTdO1pVYTF1bPz/rj4y/s7GNtbdaHh9t3dzxRUfqHh6Qj

            ...

            </X509Certificate></X509Data></KeyInfo>
[L37]    </Signature>
[L38] </Document>
```

[L20] This document has an embedded signature that covers all of the document except for the signature itself.

[L21/24] Assorted complex document content.

[L25] The signature, which extends to L37.

[L26] The actual element SignedInfo to which the SignatureMethod is applied. It extends to L34.

[L27] The canonicalization algorithm used to serialize SignedInfo—that is, Canonical XML.

[L28] The signature algorithm—in this case, the RSA algorithm coupled with the SHA-1 hash (see Chapter 17 for information on algorithms).

[L29] The Reference to the data signed. The null URI indicates the entire document in which this Reference element appears. The Reference extends to L33.

[L30] Because a signature cannot sign itself, you must specify a transform to drop the signature out of the data being signed.

[L31] The SHA-1 hash that links the data to the SignedInfo.

[L32] The base-64 representation of the SHA-1 hash of our document after the Transforms drop out the Signature element.

[L35] The base-64 encoding of the output from the SignatureMethod (including SHA-1) applied with our private key to the serialization of SignedInfo by the specified CanonicalizationMethod.

[L36] To make this signature verifiable by users with whom we do not have a prior relationship, we include an X509 Certificate with our public key. If someone believes that certificate, presumably because he or she can trace it back through a chain of certificates to a trusted Certification Authority, the user will trust our signature as well.

### 10.3.3 More Complex Protocol Example

Example 10-8 and Figure 10-4 show a more complete example of a simple protocol message. This example features two Reference elements and uses a Manifest element. In addition, it includes a hypothetical Routing element, which might influence the path followed by the object from source process to destination process. Likewise, it has a hypothetical Hopcount element, whose integer content is decremented for each application node through which it is transmitted, so that excess forwarding (probably a routing loop) can be detected and the object discarded or logged. Because Hopcount and Routing have no significance for the destination and the Hopcount element must change anyway, they are not signed. In actual use, the code might include more signed parts with different signatures and signers and intended for different ultimate recipients after forwarding.

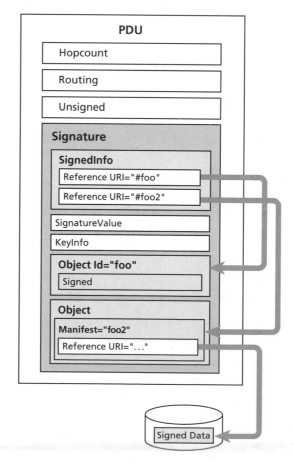

**Figure 10-4** | Complex protocol signature example

**Example 10-8**   *More complex protocol signature*

```
[L10]  <PDU>
[L41]    <Hopcount>3</Hopcount>
[L42]    <Routing>...</Routing>
[L43]    <unsigned>...</unsigned>
[L45]    <Signature>
[L46]      <SignedInfo>
[L47]        <CanonicalizationMethod Algorithm=
[L48] "http://www.w3.org/2001/10/xml-exc-c14n#"/>
[L49]        <SignatureMethod Algorithm=
      "http://www.w3.org/2000/09/xmldsig#hmac-sha1"/>
[L50]        <Reference URI="#foo">
[L51]          <DigestMethod Algorithm=
      "http://www.w3.org/2000/09/xmldsig#sha1"/>
[L52]          <DigestValue>...</DigestValue>
[L53]        </Reference>
[L54]        <Reference URI="#foo2" Type=
      "http://www.w3.org/2000/09/xmldsig#Manifest">
              <DigestMethod Algorithm=
      "http://www.w3.org/2000/09/xmldsig#sha1"/>
              <DigestValue>...</DigestValue>
            </Reference>
[L55]      </SignedInfo>
[L56]      <SignatureValue>...</SignatureValue>
[L57]      <KeyInfo><KeyName>xyz</KeyName></KeyInfo>
[L58]      <Object Id="foo" >
             <signed>...</signed>
           </Object>
[L59]      <Object><Manifest Id="foo2">
[L60]        <Reference URI="ftp://bar.example/data.bin">
               <DigestMethod Algorithm=
      "http://www.w3.org/2000/09/xmldsig#sha1"/>
               <DigestValue>...</DigestValue>
             </Reference>
           </Manifest></Object>
[L61]    </Signature>
[L62} </PDU>
```

[L40] A more complex protocol data unit extending to L62.

[L41/43] A variety of unsigned material, including the "unsigned" element, which might consist of protocol data such as performance or debugging information whose inclusion in the signature would perturb what was being studied.

[L45] The authentication structure, which extends to L61.

[L46] The SignedInfo element actually authenticated, which is linked to the authenticated data by digests. It extends to L55.

[L47] The canonicalization algorithm applied to serialize SignedInfo.

[L49] The authentication algorithm applied to SignedInfo and a secret shared key.

[L50] The first of two References. The URI attribute provided points to the Object element later in the Signature. It extends to L53.

[L51/52] The hash algorithm and hash value that cryptographically link the SignedInfo to the first piece of data being authenticated.

[L54] The second Reference, which points to a Manifest found later in the Signature. The hash of the Manifest element itself, under the hash function given, is included, linking the Manifest to this SignedInfo.

[L56] The base-64 encoded value of the SignatureMethod applied to the shared secret key and the serialization of SignedInfo by Canonicalization-Method.

[L57] Identification of the shared secret key by name.

[L58] The Object element that holds the signed protocol information present in the PDU.

[L59] An Object element wrapping a Manifest. This Manifest element refers to a data file elsewhere and gives the hash value and hash algorithm that produces that value when applied to that file. It links the file contents to this Manifest, which can be used to cryptographically authenticate a later retrieved copy of the file. If the file has been directly referenced from SignedInfo, then XMLDSIG would require that it be retrieved and its hash verified as part of core Signature verification.

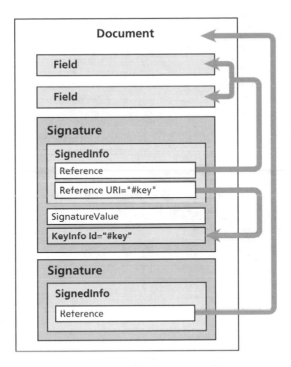

**Figure 10-5** | Complex document/form example

## 10.3.4  More Complex Form Example

As our last example, we consider a more complex form with two signatures: an "applicant" and an "office" signature (see Example 10-9 and Figure 10-5). Most real-world forms would be substantially more complex than this one, having more structures, probably more different namespaces, and so on. For simplicity, we have used unqualified names for the elements in our examples.

*Example 10-9*   *More complex document/form signature*

```
[L80] <Document...>
[L81]   <Field ...>... </Field>
[L82]   <Field>...<subF2>...<subsubF2 a="b"/>...</subF2>...
        </Field>
[L83]   <Signature> <!-- Applicant -->
          <SignedInfo>
[L84]       <CanonicalizationMethod .../>
[L85]       <SignatureMethod .../>
```

```
[L86]          <Reference URI="">
[L87]             <Transforms><Transform Algorithm=
         "http://www.w3.org/TR/1999/REC-xpath-19991116">
                     <XPath>
             (//.|//@*//namespace::*)[ancestor-or-self::Field]
                  </XPath></Transform></Transforms>
                  <DigestMethod>...</DigestMethod>
                  <DigestValue>...</DigestValue>
               </Reference>
[L88]          <Reference URI="key">...</Reference>
            </SignedInfo>
            <SignatureValue>...</SignatureValue>
[L89]       <KeyInfo Id="key"><X509Data><X509Certificate>
            cxeFhewnJ0+Xlwv09OZcXKVJSfQYGHnX1wSnp9Plyzj...
            </X509Certificate></X509Data></KeyInfo>
[L90]    </Signature>
[L91]    <Office ...>...</Office>
[L92]    <Signature> <!-- Office -->
[L93]       <SignedInfo><CanonicalizationMethod .../>
            <SignatureMethod .../>
[L94]          <Reference URI="">
[L95]             <Transforms><Transform Algorithm=
         "http://www.w3.org/2000/09/xmldsig#enveloped-signature"/>
                  </Transforms>
                  <DigestMethod>...</DigestMethod>
                  <DigestValue>...</DigestValue>
               </Reference>
            </SignedInfo>
            <SignatureValue>...</SignatureValue>
[L96]       <KeyInfo><X509Data><X509Certificate>
            qUDa2mPi4ikODuC2tv4NDeoUFNZxceRzcxsVFRUfH6Y...
            </X509Certificate></X509Data></KeyInfo>
[L97]    </Signature>
[L98] </Document>
```

[L80] Our more complex form, which extends to L98.

[L81/82] Fields filled in by an applicant. All use the element name Field, so presumably you can tell by attributes or content which is which.

[L83] The applicant's signature, extending to L90.

[L84/85] The CanonicalizationMethod applied to SignedInfo and the SignatureMethod used in the applicant signature.

[L86] The first Reference for the applicant signature. It starts with the entire document containing this Reference due to the null URI specified.

[L87] A transform that cuts down what the applicant signs to just nodes that have a "Field" element as an ancestor. In this example, those nodes include exactly those fields that the applicant filled in and wants to sign.

[L88] A second Reference in the applicant's signature, whereby the applicant also signs the keying information provided.

[L89] The applicant provides an X.509 certificate to back up the applicant's signature.

[L91] Information added to the form by the office.

[L92] The signature, by the office over the entire form, including the applicant data and signature, but excluding the office signature itself. It extends to L97.

[L93] The SignedInfo, the CanonicalizationMethod used to serialize it, and the SignatureMethod used by the office.

[L94] The Reference to the entire document for the office signature.

[L95] A transform, identified by its well-known URI, to drop out the office signature itself so that the office does not try to sign its own signature, which does not work.

[L96] The office's key information.

---

## 10.4    Transforms and the Use of XPath

The raw data retrieved, based on the URI attribute in the Reference element or application context, is passed along through a pipeline of the Transforms, if any. The DigestMethod, which is effectively the last step in this pipeline, produces the DigestValue. See Figure 10-6. At each stage in the pipeline, the data can take one of two forms: a sequence of octets or an XPath node-set. Each Transform algorithm requires one of these forms as implicit input; the final DigestMethod requires an octet sequence for input.

This process sounds straightforward, but some complexities arise. We consider them next.

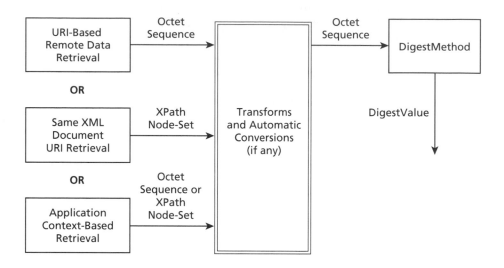

**Figure 10-6** | The data pipeline

---

### 10.4.1 The "XPath" Data Model

Implementation of XPath in an XMLDSIG application is recommended. Signature applications do not need to conform to the XPath specification [XPath] to conform to XMLDSIG.

The XPath data model definitions, such as node-sets, and XPath syntax are used within this chapter to describe functionality for applications that want to sign XML processed as XML, instead of as an octet stream for signature generation. This approach is almost always necessary when processing the SignedInfo element. An XPath implementation provides one way to implement these features, but it is not required. Applications can use a functional replacement for a node-set and implement only those XPath expression behaviors required for XMLDSIG. This book uses XPath terminology without including this qualification on every point.

---

### 10.4.2 Dereferencing the URI

The start of the data pipeline occurs when data are fetched, using the value of the URI attribute to the Reference element or based on application context. Two different cases arise in terms of the dereferencing of a Reference element URI:

1. Same-document references

2. Other references

### Same-Document References

In this type of reference, the URI is null or consists of a fragment. It is the only type of reference that produces a node-set. For example:

```
URI=""
URI="#name"
```

Dereferencing a same-document URI results in an XPath node-set suitable for use by Exclusive XML Canonicalization or Canonical XML. More precisely, dereferencing a null URI results in an XPath node-set that includes every noncomment node of the XML document containing a Reference element with this URI attribute. In a fragment URI, the characters after the number sign character ("#") conform to the XPointer syntax (see Chapter 7). The occurrence of a simple name as the fragment of a same-document reference, such as "#name" in the preceding example, is a "bare name XPointer" and refers to every noncomment node of the XML subdocument whose apex is the element with that "name" as its ID.

When processing an XPointer same-document reference, the application behaves as if the root node of the XML document containing the URI attribute were used to initialize the XPointer evaluation context. The location-set result of the XPointer processing is converted to a node-set through the following steps:

1. Discard the point nodes.

2. Replace each range node with all XPath nodes having full or partial content within the range.

3. Replace the root node with its children (if it appears in the node-set).

4. Replace any element node E with E plus all descendants of E (text, comment, processing instruction, or element) and all namespace and attribute nodes of E and its descendant elements.

5. If the URI is not a full XPointer, then delete all comment nodes.

Step 4 is necessary because XPointer typically indicates a subtree of an XML document's parse tree using just the element node at the root of the subtree. XML canonicalization treats a node-set as a set in which the absence of descendant nodes leads to the omission of their representative text from the canonical form.

Step 5 is performed for null URIs, bare name XPointers, and child sequence XPointers. When Exclusive XML Canonicalization and Canonical XML are called with a node-set, they process the node-set as is. Only when they are called with an octet stream do they invoke their own XPath expressions, depending on whether the default or the "WithComments" version was called. To retain comments while selecting an element by an ID, use the following full XPointer:

```
URI='#xpointer(id('name'))'
```

To retain comments while selecting the entire document, use the following full XPointer:

```
URI='#xpointer(/)'
```

This XPointer contains a simple XPath expression that includes the root node, which Step 4 replaces with all nodes of the parse tree (all descendants, plus all attributes, plus all namespace nodes). Support for these two forms of simple XPointers is recommended for XML signature applications. All other XPointer support is optional.

### Other References

All other references produce an octet sequence. These references include all non-null URIs without a fragment specifier and fragment specifiers with non-null URI prefixes, even if to an XML document. If a following transform requires node-set input, however, the octet sequence will be parsed as XML.

When a URI reference ends with a fragment specifier, the data's MIME type defines the meaning of the fragment. Even for XML documents, a proxy might perform the URI dereferencing—including the fragment processing. If fragment processing is not performed in a standard way, the retrieved data could differ, thereby breaking signatures. Consequently, you should avoid URI attributes that include fragment identifiers and carry out the processing with an additional XPath Transform.

You should support the same-document XPointers shown next as mentioned earlier, if you also intend to support any canonicalization that preserves comments. (Otherwise, you must use the "#foo" fragment form that will remove comments before the canonicalization can be invoked.)

```
#xpointer(/)
#xpointer(id('ID'))
```

All other support for XPointers is optional, especially all support for bare name and other XPointers in external resources. After all, the application may not have control over how the fragment is generated (leading to interoperability problems and verification failures).

The following examples demonstrate what the URI attribute identifies and how it is dereferenced:

```
URI="http://example.com/foo.xml"
```

This code identifies the octet sequence that represents the external resource "http://example.com/foo.xml." It is probably an XML document, given its file extension.

```
URI="http://example.com/foo.xml#bar"
```

This code identifies the element with ID attribute value "bar" of the external XML resource "http://example.com/foo.xml," provided as an octet stream. For the sake of interoperability, it would be better to obtain the "bar" element using an XPath transform rather than a URI fragment. The XML signature standard does not require support for bare name XPointer resolution.

### 10.4.3   The Data Pipeline

Table 10-1 shows what automatic transform, if any, occurs for all combinations of the output format from one stage of processing and required input to the next stage.

In any case where the automatic transform is the wrong choice, you can add an explicit transform to bridge the data formats. This situation is most likely

**Table 10-1** | Data Pipeline Format Transition Rules

| Output Format of Previous Stage | Input Format Required | Automatic Transform |
| --- | --- | --- |
| Octet sequence | Octet sequence | None |
| Octet sequence | XPath node-set | XML parse |
| XPath node-set | Octet sequence | Canonical XML |
| XPath node-set | XPath node-set | None |

to occur when the automatic transform is Canonical XML, and its effect of stripping out comments or incorporating XML context is not desired. Thus, for some applications, you must specify Exclusive XML Canonicalization to make the signature more robust against changes in the XML context of signed XML. For others, you might need to specify the "with comments" version of either Canonical XML or Exclusive XML Canonicalization if the signature must cover comments.

### 10.4.4   Transforms Element Syntax

The syntax for the Transforms element is as follows:

```
<!-- Transforms DTD -->


<!ELEMENT Transforms (Transform+)>


<!ELEMENT Transform (#PCDATA|XPath %Transform.ANY;)* >
<!ATTLIST Transform
          Algorithm    CDATA     #REQUIRED >


<!ELEMENT XPath (#PCDATA) >
```

In schema notation, it has the following form:

```
<!-- Transforms Schema -->


<element name="Transforms" type="ds:TransformsType"/>
<complexType name="TransformsType">
    <sequence>
        <element ref="ds:Transform" maxOccurs="unbounded"/>
    </sequence>
</complexType>


<element name="Transform" type="ds:TransformType"/>
<complexType name="TransformType" mixed="true">
    <choice minOccurs="0" maxOccurs="unbounded">
        <any namespace="##other" processContents="lax"/>
        <!-- (1,1) elements from (0,unbounded) namespaces -->
        <element name="XPath" type="string"/>
```

```
    </choice>
    <attribute name="Algorithm" type="anyURI" use="required"/>
</complexType>
```

## 10.5    Processing Rules

The XMLDSIG standard defines the steps required to produce a Signature element and verify a Signature element. These steps are not very surprising, as the following subsections explain.

### 10.5.1  Signature Generation

Signature generation consists of two parts. First, you need to generate the Reference elements to go into SignedInfo. Second, you need to construct SignedInfo, sign it, and create the Signature element. These steps must occur in that order.

Although the XML Digital Signature standard does not require it, real-world XMLDSIG subroutine libraries will probably include an entry for generating a Manifest element as well as a Signature element. This entry would involve exactly the same Reference element generation as described here; instead of then building a Signature, however, it would wrap the References in a Manifest element with an optional application-provided Id attribute. You could then use the Manifest element as data for a higher-level Reference or Manifest element and/or include in an Object element within a Signature.

### Reference Generation

Each Reference describes one piece of data being signed. For each Reference, four steps are taken:

1. Obtain the raw data associated with the Reference and URI to be given. (Omit the URI if the verifier will know the URI from the application context; this omission is allowed for only one Reference in any Signature element.)

2. Apply any Transforms, as determined by the application, to produce the actual data signed. The result of the last Transform, or of Step 1 if no Transforms are present, should consist of a sequence of octets. If it

would otherwise be an XML node-set, serialize the result with Canonical XML. If you want a different canonicalization, such as Exclusive XML Canonicalization, add it as an explicit last (or only) Transform.

3. Calculate the DigestValue over the data obtained in Step 2 using the application-provided DigestMethod.

4. Create the Reference element from the URI (if it must be specified), Transforms (if any), DigestMethod, and DigestValue.

### Signature Generation

Using the Reference elements generated earlier, generate the Signature element as follows:

1. Create the SignedInfo using the application-determined CanonicalizationMethod and SignatureMethod elements and the Reference elements generated earlier.

2. Apply the CanonicalizationMethod to the SignedInfo.

3. Using the application-determined signing key, apply the SignatureMethod to the canonicalized SignedInfo, thereby producing the SignatureValue.

4. Construct the Signature element using the SignedInfo element already generated, the SignatureValue, a KeyInfo element if needed, and any Object elements needed.

### 10.5.2   Signature Verification

Just as signature generation occurs in two phases, so signature verification takes place in two separate sets of steps. First, the Signature element is verified. Second, the Reference elements within SignedInfo inside the Signature are verified. These steps can occur in either order.

Although the XML Digital Signature standard does not require it, real-world XMLDSIG libraries will probably include an entry for validating the Reference elements in a Manifest. This validation occurs in the same way as Reference verification in SignedInfo (described later in this section), except that no explicit canonicalization takes place. Also, failure and success of individual Reference elements inside a Manifest must be reported to the application so it can decide what to do, whereas failure of any Reference within SignedInfo causes Signature verification to fail by definition.

Attempts to verify a Signature element could fail for many reasons, even if the signature is, in some sense, actually valid. For example, a particular verifier might not have implemented some optional parts of the XMLDSIG standard, it might be unable or unwilling to execute the specified algorithms or get data pointed at by a specified URI, or the actual Signature or Reference verification might fail. Subroutine libraries implementing XMLDSIG should provide different error messages for different failure conditions.

**Signature Verification**

Signature verification authenticates the SignedInfo material. It requires the following steps:

1. Obtain the verification key using the KeyInfo element or the application context. (If KeyInfo is used to determine the key, it should be signed through a Reference in SignedInfo for greater security.)

2. Apply the CanonicalizationMethod to the SignedInfo and SignatureMethod elements.

3. Using the verification key and canonicalized SignatureMethod obtained in Step 2, verify the SignatureValue over the canonicalized SignedInfo. SignatureValue comparisons must be done numerically or using the binary octet sequence. Do not use text comparison of base-64 encodings, because they may fail due to discrepancies in their white space conventions.

**Note**

The SignatureValue elements in two different XML signatures over the same data with the same keying material and algorithms may differ due to different white space in DigestValue elements or the deliberate use of randomness for padding in algorithms.

**Reference Verification**

Reference verification authenticates the data signed against the digests in SignedInfo. It requires the following steps:

1. Using CanonicalizationMethod, canonicalize SignedInfo. (This step isn't necessary unless a custom CanonicalizationMethod changes the Reference elements. Using such a custom CanonicalizationMethod is probably a bad idea.)

2. For each Reference in the canonicalized SignedInfo, do the following:

- Obtain the data to be digested. Depending on the application context, you could dereference the URI attribute value and apply any Transforms, retrieve the data from a local cache, or use some other means.

- Digest the data using the DigestMethod specified by the canonicalized Reference element.

- Compare the result with the DigestValue in the canonicalized Reference element. If they disagree, verification for that Reference has failed. The DigestValue comparison must be done numerically or using the binary octet sequence. Do not use text comparison of base-64 encodings, because they may fail due to discrepancies in their white space conventions.

## 10.6    Security of Signatures

Because the XMLDSIG standard provides a very flexible digital signature mechanism, there are lots of ways to misuse it and produce insecure or misleading results. When designing a system using XMLDSIG, you should consider the factors discussed in this section.

### 10.6.1  Transforms

The Transforms mechanism makes it easy to sign data derived from processing the content of an identified resource. For instance, an application might wish to sign a form, but permit users to enter limited field data without invalidating a previous signature on the form. The application could use an XPath-based Transform to exclude those portions that the user will change. Transforms can also include encoding changes, canonicalization instructions, or even XSLT and user-defined transforms. Note the following three cautions with respect to this feature:

- Only what is signed is secure.

- Only what is "seen" should be signed.

- "See" what is signed.

The XMLDSIG standard does not require that the signed data be obtained by applying each step of the indicated transforms during signature verification. Some applications may be satisfied with verifying an XML signature over a cached copy of already transformed data. Other applications might require that content be freshly dereferenced and transformed. The approach required depends on the purpose of the signature and is part of secure design.

### Only What Is Signed Is Secure

Obviously, signatures over a transformed document do not secure any information discarded by transforms: Only what is signed is secure.

When signing XML, use of canonicalization (as described in Chapter 9) is critical. It can ensure that all internal entities and visibly used XML namespaces are expanded within the data being signed. All entities are replaced with their definitions, and the canonical form generally includes or excludes the namespace that an element would otherwise inherit, as appropriately selected by the application designer.

Failure to canonicalize XML content is generally a bad idea. The resulting applications are arguably not XML applications, as they do not strictly follow the XML Recommendation [XML]. Nevertheless, to have a chance of working, such applications should satisfy two criteria:

- They should not use internal entities.

- They should represent namespaces explicitly within the content being signed.

Some applications depend upon the integrity of the element type definitions associated with the XML instance being signed. Such an application should sign those definitions as well—for example, the schema, DTD, or natural language description associated with the namespace/identifier.

Information that is not signed but is merely part of an envelope containing signed information is obviously not secured. For instance, unsigned recipient headers accompanying signed information within an encrypted envelope do not have their authenticity or integrity protected.

### Only What Is "Seen" Should Be Signed

If the intent of signing is to convey the judgment or consent of a user (an automated mechanism or person), then it is normally necessary to secure, as closely as possible, the information as presented to that user. Applications could accomplish this by literally signing what was shown a user, such as a screen image. However, the result would be difficult for subsequent software to manipulate. Instead, applications can sign the data along with whatever filters, style sheets, client profile or other information that affects its presentation. But there are practical limits. For example, if the data were viewed through a browser, it would be reasonable to secure any style sheets used and perhaps the browser version. However, it would almost certainly not be practical or worthwhile to sign and preserve a complete copy of the browser and operating system that the browser was running on.

### "See" What Is Signed

In a context where a user is seeing and approving something, the user should sign only what he or she "sees." Persons and automated mechanisms that trust a transformed document on the basis of a valid signature should operate over the data that were transformed and signed, not the original, pre-transformation data.

This recommendation applies to transforms specified within the signature as well as those that are part of the document itself. For instance, if an XML document includes an embedded style sheet [XSLT], then the transformed document should be presented to the user and signed. When a document references an external style sheet or external data having a visible effect, then a signature Reference should also sign the content of that external resource. Failure to do so could permit later change of that external data, thereby altering the resulting document without invalidating the signature.

Some applications might operate over the original or intermediary data. In such a case, they should be careful about potential weaknesses that can occur between the original and transformed data. This kind of a trust decision about the character and meaning of the transforms creates a situation in which a system designer needs to exercise caution. Consider a canonicalization algorithm that normalizes character case (lowercase to uppercase) or character composition ("e and accent" to "accented-e"). An adversary could introduce changes that are normalized and therefore inconsequential to signature validity but material to a Document Object Model (DOM) processor.

For instance, by changing the case of a character, you might influence the result of an XPath selection or database query. A serious risk is introduced if that change is normalized for signature verification but the processor operates over the original data and returns a different result than intended. Consequently, while it is recommended that all documents operated on and generated by signature applications appear in "normal form C" [NFC], encoding normalization should not occur as part of a signature transform operation.

## 10.6.2  Check the Signature Security Model

XMLDSIG provides signature algorithms based on public key signatures and keyed hash authentication codes. These algorithms rely on substantially different security models. Furthermore, XMLDSIG permits user-specified algorithms that may utilize still other models. (See also Chapter 2 on this topic.)

With public key signatures, any number of parties can hold the public key and verify signatures, even though only the parties with the private key can create signatures. It is preferable to minimize the number of holders of the private key, keeping it as close to one holder as practical. An important issue is confidence by verifiers in the public key used and its binding to the entity or capabilities represented by the corresponding private key. Certificate or online authority systems usually address this issue.

Keyed hash authentication codes, based on secret keys, usually work much more efficiently than do public keys in terms of the computational effort required. Unfortunately, all verifiers need to have the same key as the signer with such systems, which means that any verifier can forge signatures.

XMLDSIG permits user-provided signature algorithms and keying information designators. Such user-provided algorithms might have other security models. For example, methods involving biometrics depend on physical characteristics of the authorized user that cannot be changed in the same way that public or secret keys can be; they might have other security model differences as well.

## 10.6.3  Signature Strength

The strength of a particular signature (i.e., how difficult it is to forge a signature on new or altered data) depends on all links in the security chain. They include, but are not limited to, the following:

- The signature and digest algorithms in use

- The strength of the key generation [RANDOM] and key size

- The security of key and certificate authentication, distribution, and storage mechanisms

- The certificate chain validation policy for certificate-based systems

- Protection of cryptographic processing from hostile observation and tampering

A system's overall security also depends on the security and integrity of its operating procedures, its personnel, and the administrative enforcement of those procedures. All factors mentioned in this section are important to the overall security of a system; most, however, are beyond the scope of the XML Signature, Encryption, and other XML Security recommendations.

### 10.6.4  Algorithms and Executable Content Caution

Applications must exercise care when executing the various algorithms specified in an XML digital signature. They must also exercise care when processing any "executable content" that might be provided to such algorithms as parameters, such as [XSLT] transforms. A trusted library will usually implement the algorithms specified by the standards. Even there, however, perverse parameters might cause unacceptable processing or place overwhelming demands on memory. Application-defined algorithms might warrant even more care.

# 11 | Profiling XMLDSIG for Applications

Any particular application of XMLDSIG requires a specific profiling of XMLDSIG. That is, it requires a specification of the following issues:

- How the signature or signatures fit syntactically into the application documents and/or protocol messages

- What the signature or signatures mean semantically

- What specifications or limits apply to the composition and use of the signature or signatures such as limitations on algorithms, types of keying information, ways to extend them (if allowed), and so on

The XMLDSIG standard merely provides cryptographic linking between signed data and the key used to sign that data. A higher application level must specify the Signature meaning.

When developers design security into an application from the beginning, they should integrate this profiling of XMLDSIG (and perhaps XML Encryption) into the general specification of the application. XML Key Management (see Chapter 14) is an application that uses XMLDSIG as a building block and so integrates a profile of how XMLDSIG will be used into its general specification. P3P (Platform for Privacy Preferences) and SOAP (see Chapter 8) are two examples of initially insecure applications for which separate profiles have been written. These profiles, which exist as separate W3C Notes, are described in this chapter. Because neither is a standard yet, changes or replacements may occur before a security profile emerges as a standard for P3P or SOAP.

This chapter assumes familiarity with the XML Digital Signature standard (see Chapter 10). Some familiarity with P3P and SOAP will also be helpful.

## 11.1    P3P XMLDSIG

P3P, the Platform for Privacy Preferences [P3P], provides a syntax for Web sites to specify their privacy policies in a standard format. A privacy policy indicates what information the Web site retains and how it uses that information. P3P seeks to inform Web services users of the available policies of the sites they visit. Users can select among the available policies or refuse to use the offered service if no acceptable policy is acceptable. The intention in standardizing the expression of privacy policies is to enable the automation of such decisions.

Clearly, user assurance of the authenticity of such privacy policy information is desirable for any user who wants to have confidence in the policy descriptions and, potentially, the ability to call on third parties to take action if such policies are violated.

### 11.1.1    Linkage of XMLDSIG to P3P Semantics

Although P3P policies appear in XML, P3P's syntax does not permit the inclusion of signatures in its constructs. However, the [P3P-Sec] W3C Note profiles a way to "assure" a P3P policy with an enveloping or detached XML digital signature. This assurance means that the specified dispute service enforces the signed P3P policy using the specified remedies, as long as the signature key matches the dispute service key.

You accomplish this goal by specifying an "Assures" element that appears within a SignatureProperty element in a SignatureProperties element. The signing of such a SignatureProperties by a Reference from a Signature element binds the assurance to the key employed for this signing.

In addition, the "verification" attribute of a "disputes" clause in the P3P policy can point to a signature containing an Assures element. The signature can then be found starting with the policy, as shown in Example 11-1.

Applications must use additional mechanisms to determine whether the application can trust that the key belongs to the dispute service. In addition, anyone depending on a signature should confirm that the key size and type and algorithms in use provide adequate security for the user's purposes.

***Example 11-1*** *P3P policy with signature verification*

```
http://www.example.org/p3p.xml

<POLICY xmlns="http://www.w3.org/2000/09/15/P3Pv1"
discuri="http://www.example.com/PrivacyPracticeBrowsing.html">
...
<DISPUTES-GROUP>
  <DISPUTES resolution-type="independent"
    service="http://www.PrivacySeal.example.org"
    short-description="PrivacySeal.example.org"
    verification="http://www.example.org/Signature.xml">
    <IMG src="http://www.PrivacySeal.example.org/Logo.gif"
        alt="PrivacySeal's logo"/>
    <REMEDIES><correct/></REMEDIES>
  </DISPUTES>
</DISPUTES-GROUP>
<STATEMENT>
  <PURPOSE><admin/><develop/></PURPOSE>
  <RECIPIENT><ours/></RECIPIENT>
  <RETENTION><stated-purpose/></RETENTION>
  <DATA-GROUP>
   <DATA ref="#dynamic.clickstream.clientip"/>
   <DATA ref="#dynamic.http.useragent"/>
  </DATA-GROUP>
</STATEMENT>
</POLICY>
```

## 11.1.2  Specific Assurance Syntax

The syntax of the Assures element follows:

```
Schema Definition:

<?xml version='1.0'?>

<!DOCTYPE schema SYSTEM
                'http://www.w3.org/1999/XMLSchema.dtd'>
<schema
targetNamespace='http://www.w3.org/2001/02/xmldsig-p3p-profile'
```

```
version='0.1'
xmlns='http://www.w3.org/2000/10/XMLSchema'
xmlns:profile='http://www.w3.org/2001/02/xmldsig-p3p-profile'
elementFormDefault='qualified'>

<element name='Assures'>
  <complexType>
    <all>
      <element ref='profile:P3P-Policy' minOccurs='0' />
      <element ref='profile:Signature' minOccurs='0' />
    </all>
    <attribute name='via' type='URI'/>
    <attribute name='Id' type='ID' use='optional'/>
  </complexType>
</element>

<element name='P3P-Policy'>
  <complexType>
    <sequence>
      <any namespace='http://www.w3.org/2000/10/18/P3Pv1'/>
    </sequence>
    <attribute name='Id' type='ID' use='required'/>
  </complexType>
</element>

<element name='Signature'>
  <complexType>
    <sequence>
      <any namespace='http://www.w3.org/2000/09/xmldsig#'/>
    </sequence>
    <attribute name='Id' type='ID' use='required'/>
  </complexType>
</element>

</schema>
```

### 11.1.3   P3P XMLDSIG Use

Applications and users can use the P3P profiled XML signature in several ways; some examples follow. Other arrangements are also possible.

**Detached Signature Element**

A Signature element can appear separately that points to and provides assurance for a P3P policy. Example 11-2 shows a made-up Signature element that signs a P3P policy through its first Reference and then signs the semantic assertion that this policy is assured through its second Reference.

***Example 11-2***   *Detached P3P signature*

```
<Signature Id="Signature1"
           xmlns="http://www.w3.org/2000/09/xmldsig#">
  <SignedInfo>
    <CanonicalizationMethod
Algorithm="http://www.w3.org/TR/2000/WD-xml-c14n-20000907"/>
    <SignatureMethod
     Algorithm="http://www.w3.org/2000/09/xmldsig#dsa-sha1"/>
    <Reference URI="http://www.foo.example/p3p.xml">
      <Transforms>
        <Transform
Algorithm="http://www.w3.org/TR/2000/WD-xml-c14n-20000907"/>
      </Transforms>
      <DigestMethod
        Algorithm="http://www.w3.org/2000/09/xmldsig#sha1"/>
      <DigestValue>V3CLi8jBwTEODuttbdtXV5e3t6k=</DigestValue>
    </Reference>
    <Reference URI="#Assurance1"
Type="http://www.w3.org/2000/09/xmldsig#SignatureProperties">
      <DigestMethod
Algorithm="http://www.w3.org/2000/09/xmldsig#sha1"/>
      <DigestValue>/GgdHYV6emaoqH8UFIdgYKFMTBE=</DigestValue>
    </Reference>
  </SignedInfo>
  <SignatureValue>
    Kslvb0xDQ05DQzMeHnXc3GTk5C08PJEJCdeHh6b8/Ijp6Sp1ddRqag==
  </SignatureValue>
```

```
<KeyInfo>
  <DSAKeyValue>
    ...KeyInfo of the Disputes Service...
  </DASKeyValue>
</KeyInfo>
<Object>
  </SignatureProperties>
    <SignatureProperty Id="Assurance1"
                       Target="#Signature1"
      xmlns="http://www.w3.org/2000/09/xmldsig#">
      <Assures Policy="http://www.foo.example/p3p.xml"
xmlns="http://www.w3.org/2001/02/xmldsig-p3p-profile"/>
    </SignatureProperty>
  </SignatureProperties>
</Object>
</Signature>
```

### Enveloping Signature/Assures

Rather than referencing an external policy, the Signature element can also enclose the policy by adding another Object within the Signature to contain it. The Assures element can also directly enclose the policy. These arrangements are relatively straightforward, so this book does not provide a specific example of them.

### 11.1.4   Limitations

For P3P to succeed, widespread compatibility and interoperability are clearly desirable. Consequently, the P3P XMLDSIG profile places stringent limitations on the signatures that you use in this context. The following list identifies these limitations and the identifying URIs for allowed choices.

1. The only CanonicalizationMethod allowed is Canonical XML, http://www.w3.org/TR/2000/WD-xml-c14n-20001011.

2. Only two SignatureMethod algorithms are allowed:

   • DSA, http://www.w3.org/2000/09/xmldsig#dsa-sha1

   • RSA, http://www.w3.org/2000/09/xmldsig#rsa-sha1

3. The only DigestMethod allowed is SHA-1, http://www.w3.org/2000/09/xmldsig#sha1.

4. Only two Transforms are allowed:

- Canonical XML,
  http://www.w3.org/TR/2000/WD-xml-c14n-20000907.

- P3P Statement to HTML/English XSLT. This specification provides an [XSLT] instance that changes a P3P statement into an HTML page using English to describe that statement. It is available from http://www.w3.org/2001/02/xmldsig-p3p-profileenglish.xsl.

5. Only two KeyInfo formats are allowed:

- DSAKeyValue, http://www.w3.org/2000/09/xmldsig#dsa-sha1

- RSAKeyValue, http://www.w3.org/2000/09/xmldsig#rsa-sha1

## 11.2   SOAP XMLDSIG

Chapter 8 describes the SOAP protocol framework. The W3C Note [SOAP-Sec] specifies a method for including XML digital signatures in SOAP messages. As you might expect from the generality of the SOAP syntax, the method is also fairly general. Limitations would likely be found in further profiling for specific applications based on SOAP.

The [SOAP-Sec] document accomplishes this goal by providing a SOAP Signature element so that an application can freely include it as a SOAP Header Block. This element has as its content a single XML digital signature and may have the additional attributes of SOAP blocks as well. Also, SOAP defines a global "id" attribute that applications can use in elements to be signed; as a consequence, they can be conveniently cited in XMLDSIG Reference elements. See the following schema definition:

```
Schema definition:

<schema
  xmlns="http://www.w3.org/1999/XMLSchema"
  xmlns:SOAP-SEC=
    "http://schemas.xmlsoap.org/soap/security/2000-12"
  targetNamespace=
    "http://schemas.xmlsoap.org/soap/security/2000-12"
  xmlns:ds="http://www.w3.org/2000/09/xmldsig#"
  xmlns:env="http://schemas.xmlsoap.org/soap/envelope/">
```

```
<import namespace="http://www.w3.org/2000/09/xmldsig#"/>
<import
 namespace="http://schemas.xmlsoap.org/soap/envelope/"/>

<element name="Signature" final="restriction">
  <complexType>
    <sequence>
      <element ref="ds:Signature" minOccurs="1"
                                  maxOccurs="1"/>
    </sequence>
    <attribute name="id" type="ID" use="optional"/>
    <attribute ref="env:actor" use="optional"/>
    <attribute ref="env:mustUnderstand" use="optional"/>
  </complexType>
</element>

<attribute name="id" type="ID"/>

</schema>
```

### 11.2.1 Processing Rules

The SOAP application signature profile provides the following rules and recommendations:

1. Multiple SOAP signature blocks are permissible in a SOAP header and may sign separate or overlapping elements.

2. All XMLDSIG Reference elements must point to material within the enclosing SOAP Envelope element or within the enclosing SOAP message package.

3. A SOAP application receiving a SOAP message with SOAP signature blocks addressed to it—either explicitly or because it is the final destination—must examine the SOAP signature. If the "mustUnderstand" attribute is set or the application chooses to do so, it attempts to validate the signature. Depending on the particular application, SOAP may report a signature failure to the sender.

4. Canonicalization is performed in context. That is, if inclusive canonicalization is carried out, SignedInfo will have at least the SOAP envelope and security namespace declarations.

5. Because SOAP intermediaries can add to, delete from, or reorder blocks in a SOAP message, you must take care in using XPath or the like to avoid brittle signatures that will break due to insignificant changes of this sort.

## 11.2.2   SOAP Signature Example

Example 11-3 shows a SOAP Envelope with a signature in it.

***Example 11-3***   *SOAP signature*

```
<env:Envelope
  xmlns:env="http://schemas.xmlsoap.org/soap/envelope/">
  <env:Header>
    <SOAP-SEC:Signature
      xmlns:SOAP-SEC=
        "http://schemas.xmlsoap.org/soap/security/2000-12"
      env:actor="http://foo.example/bar"
      env:mustUnderstand="1">
      <ds:Signature
        xmlns:ds="http://www.w3.org/2000/09/xmldsig#">
        <ds:SignedInfo>
          <ds:CanonicalizationMethod
Algorithm="http://www.w3.org/TR/2000/CR-xml-c14n-20001026"/>
          <ds:SignatureMethod
Algorithm="http://www.w3.org/2000/09/xmldsig#dsa-sha1"/>
          <ds:Reference URI="#Body">
            <ds:Transforms>
              <ds:Transform
Algorithm="http://www.w3.org/TR/2000/CR-xml-c14n-20001026"/>
            </ds:Transforms>
            <ds:DigestMethod
Algorithm="http://www.w3.org/2000/09/xmldsig#sha1"/>
            <ds:DigestValue>j6lwx3rvEPO0vKtMup4NbeVu8nk=
            </ds:DigestValue>
          </ds:Reference>
        </ds:SignedInfo>
        <ds:SignatureValue>
          rMzv774yMoCLi8kHB23q6rva2hs5Ore
          amqFwcFDg4AaXl0qhoYQGBg==
```

```
            </ds:SignatureValue>
          </ds:Signature>
        </SOAP-SEC:Signature>
      </env:Header>
      <env:Body
        SOAP-SEC:id="Body"
        xmlns:SOAP-SEC=
        "http://schemas.xmlsoap.org/soap/security/2000-12">
          <m:GetLastTradePrice
            xmlns:m="http://example.com/trade">
            <m:symbol>EXAMPLE</m:symbol>
          </m:GetLastTradePrice>
      </env:Body>
    </env:Envelope>
```

# 12 | ETSI "Advanced" XML Signatures

The European Telecommunications Standards Institute (ETSI) is developing extensions to the XML Digital Signature Recommendation (see Chapter 10) so that the resulting extended signatures will meet the European Directive requirements for valid electronic signatures for electronic commerce purposes [Directive]. This chapter describes the extensions as an example of one way to build a higher-level "trust" structure on the basic XMLDSIG structure.

The discussion in this chapter is based on ETSI's July 2001 draft, XML Advanced Electronic Signatures [XAdES], which uses the following namespace:

```
http://www.etsi.org/names/TS/101903/v1.1.1#
```

**Soapbox**

I don't know about you, but I'm always suspicious of things called "new" or "advanced." What will they call the next, more advanced version?

ETSI assumes the existence of trusted service providers, including time stamping services and certificate authorities. Another assumption relates to the existence of signature policy issuers. The ETSI draft is aimed, to a great extent, at convincing an independent arbiter of the validity of a signature. It assumes that all signatures with which it deals will be public key signatures with keying material in X.509 [ISO 9594] certificates.

**Soapbox**

The sheer size and complexity of the ETSI draft should give pause to those who think it should be easy to establish "trust" and "meaning" from a document (see Appendix E) point of view.

The schema information given is this chapter assumes the following preface:

```
<?xml version="1.0" encoding="UTF-8"?>
<schema targetNamespace=
        "http://uri.etsi.org/names/TS/101903/v1.1.1#"
 xmlns:xsd="http://www.w3.org/2001/XMLSchema"
 xmlns="http://uri.etsi.org/names/TS/101903/v.1.1.1#"
 xmlns:ds="http://www.w3.org/2000/09/xmldsig#"
 elementFormDefault="qualified"
 >
```

## 12.1    Levels of XAdES Signature

The ETSI draft defines a series of augmented XML signatures, each of which builds on and requires all information required by the previous type of augmented XML signature. The levels are as follows:

- XAdES (XML Advanced Electronic Signature)

- XAdES-T (XAdES with additional time stamp)

- XAdES-C (XAdES-T with complete validation data references)

- XAdES-X (XAdES-C with extended validation data)

- XAdES-XL (XAdES-X with complete validation data information)

- XAdES-A (XAdES-XL with one or more embedded archival time stamps)

The validation of an electronic signature according to the ETSI draft criterion requires not only the signature, but also a signed signature policy, various signature properties, and validation data such as certificates, revocation status information, and time stamps. The signer or the verifier may collect this validation data. Higher-level ETSI advanced signatures include the data in the extended signature object.

The signature policy specifies the requirements for a signature to meet a particular business need, including both technical and procedural requirements. It also covers signature creation and validation.

### 12.1.1  XAdES

The first level of advanced signature is built on an XMLDSIG structure by adding one enveloped Object element that has either a QualifyingProperties or a QualifyingPropertiesReference child. QualifyingProperties is used to directly include properties in the signature and can occur zero or one time. QualifyingPropertiesReference indirectly includes properties stated elsewhere and can occur zero or more times. All QualifiedProperties and Qualified-PropertiesReferences in a signature must occur within the same Object element. QualifyingProperties in turn has two children, SignedProperties and UnsignedProperties.

SignedProperties, whether directly present in a QualifyingProperties element or indirectly present though a QualifyingPropertiesReference element, must be the target of a Reference element in the Signature being enhanced. Furthermore, the Reference must use the Type attribute with a value of

```
http://uri.etsi.org/01903/v1.1.1#SignedProperties
```

Mandatory contents of the SignedProperties element of an XAdES are as follows:

- A reference to the certificate with the signer's public key that the signer selected for this XAdES. While XMLDSIG is concerned primarily with cryptographic security, XAdES focuses on trust. As a consequence, it must know the exact certificate used because policy constraints apply to that certificate and because revocations are done at a certificate level. (See Section 12.3.2.)

- A reference to the signature policy to be used, so a verifier can use the same policy as the signer. (See Section 12.3.3.)

- The time at which the signer claims to have created the signature. (See Section 12.3.1.)

In addition, SignedProperties can contain the following optional contents.

- An indication of the content format so that the verifier will interpret the signed data properly. (See Section 12.3.5.)

- A commitment type. It is required only if the signature policy indicates that more than one commitment type is possible, which alters the intention of the signature (e.g., proof of origin, proof of receipt). (See Section 12.3.6.)

- Any additional information that the application requires the signature policy to sign.

- The claimed or certified role assumed by the signer in creating the signature. (See Section 12.3.8.)

- Contact information for the signer as claimed by the signer. (See Section 12.3.7.)

- A content time stamp to prove the signature was created after that time. (See Section 12.3.9.)

See Figure 12-1.

## 12.1.2  XAdES-T

To build an XAdES-T (time stamped) from an XAdES, you need to obtain a time stamp across the signature (see Section 12.4.1) and add it as a child of the UnsignedProperties element of the XAdES. See Figure 12-1.

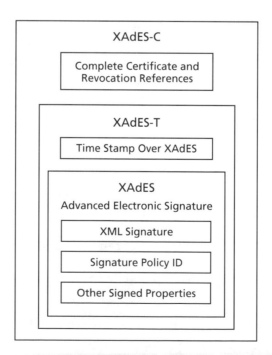

**Figure 12-1** | XAdES, XAdES-T, and XAdES-C

### 12.1.3  XAdES-C

To build an XAdES-C (complete) from an XAdES-T, you must add references to the full set of data supporting the validity of the signature. (Refer to Sections 12.4.2 and 12.4.3.) That is, you must add references to all certificates in the certification path to be used by the verifier with certificate revocation lists or OCSP tokens for each issuer, showing that the certificates have not been revoked. You add this information as a child of the UnsignedProperties element of the XAdES-T. See Figure 12-1.

### 12.1.4  XAdES-X

When an XAdES-C is "complete," you can add extended validation information to it to produce an XAdES-X (extended) or XAdES-XL signature. See Figure 12-2.

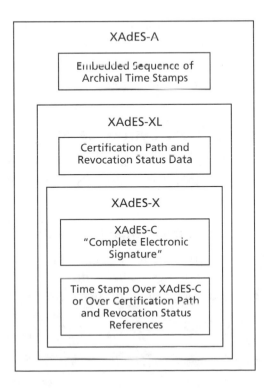

**Figure 12-2** | XAdES-A, XAdES-XL, and XAdES-X

To build an XAdES-X, you add a time stamp over the entire XAdES-C structure or over the references to the complete set of validating data that the XAdES-C requires, as Sections 12.4.4 and 12.4.5 describe.

### 12.1.5  XAdES-XL

An XAdES-XL (extended long-term) is a long-term version of XAdES-X. In the long run, you may not be able to dereference the references to validation data that XAdES-C requires. The XAdES-XL, therefore, requires that you include the actual validation data, not just references to it (as Sections 12.4.6 and 12.4.7 specify) as a child element of the UnsignedSignatureProperties element. See Figure 12-2.

### 12.1.6  XAdES-A

An XAdES-A (archival) is built from an XAdES-XL or an earlier XAdES-A by time stamping the XAdES-XL or earlier XAdES-A as Section 12.4.8 specifies. This time stamping should be done with stronger keys and stronger/newer algorithms than are used in the signature being stamped. This approach proves that the signature was created before that time and ensures that it will remain valid against later key compromise or later algorithm weakness as long as the last time stamp itself is still strong. See Figure 12-2.

## 12.2    XAdES Signature Syntax Basics

This section covers the basic elements for expressing and containing the additional information to create ETSI advanced signatures.

### 12.2.1  Qualifying and Qualifying Reference Properties

QualifyingProperties elements serves as a container for the SignedProperties and UnsignedProperties elements described below while QualifyingPropertiesReference elements point to such elements. Their schema is as follows:

```
<!-- Start QualifyingProperties -->


<xsd:element name="QualifyingProperties"
              type="QualifyingPropertiesType"/>
<xsd:complexType name="QualifyingPropertiesType">
```

```
<xsd:sequence>
 <xsd:element name="SignedProperties"
              type="SignedPropertiesType"
              minOccurs="0"/>
 <xsd:element name="UnsignedProperties"
              type="UnsignedPropertiesType"
              minOccurs="0"/>
</xsd:sequence>
<xsd:attribute name="Target" type="xsd:anyURI"
              use="required"/>
<xsd:attribute name="Id" type="xsd:ID" use="optional"/>
</xsd:complexType>

<!-- End QualifyingProperties -->

<!-- Start QualifyingPropertiesReference-->

<xsd:element name="QualifyingPropertiesReference"
             type="QualifyingPropertiesReferenceType"/>
<xsd:complexType name="QualifyingPropertiesReferenceType">
 <xsd:sequence>
  <xsd:element name="Transforms" type="ds:TransformsType"
              minOccurs="0"/>
 </xsd:sequence>
 <xsd:attribute name="URI" type="xsd:anyURI"
                use="required"/>
 <xsd:attribute name="Id" type="xsd:ID" use="optional"/>
</xsd:complexType>

<!-- End QualifyingPropertiesReference-->
```

## 12.2.2  Signed and Unsigned Properties

The SignedProperties and UnsignedPropreties elements include the additional information required that make a signature qualify as an XAdES. The SignedProperties element, in turn, has SignedSignatureProperties and SignedDataObjectProperties children. The UnsignedProperties element has UnsignedSignatureProperties and UnsignedDataObjectProperties children.

The schemas for these elements appear below.

### The SignedProperties Element

```
<xsd:element name="SignedProperties"
             type="SignedPropertiesType" />


<xsd:complexType name="SignedPropertiesType">
  <xsd:sequence>
    <xsd:element name="SignedSignatureProperties"
             type="SignedSignaturePropertiesType"/>
    <xsd:element name="SignedDataObjectProperties"
             type="SignedDataObjectPropertiesType"/>
  </xsd:sequence>
  <xsd:attribute name="Id" type="xsd:ID" use="optional"/>
</xsd:complexType>
```

### The UnsignedProperties Element

```
<xsd:element name="UnsignedProperties"
             type="UnsignedPropertiesType" />


<xsd:complexType name="UnsignedPropertiesType">
  <xsd:sequence>
    <xsd:element name="UnsignedSignatureProperties"
             type="UnsignedSignaturePropertiesType"
             minOccurs="0"/>
    <xsd:element name="UnsignedDataObjectProperties"
             type="UnsignedDataObjectPropertiesType"
             minOccurs="0"/>
  </xsd:sequence>
  <xsd:attribute name="Id" type="xsd:ID" use="optional"/>
</xsd:complexType>
```

### The SignedSignatureProperties Element

```
<xsd:element name="SignedSignatureProperties"
             type="SignedSignaturePropertiesType" />


<xsd:complexType name="SignedSignaturePropertiesType">
  <xsd:sequence>
```

```
    <xsd:element name="SigningTime"
type="xsd:dateTime"/>
    <xsd:element name="SigningCertificate"
                type="CertificateIDListType"/>
    <xsd:element name="SignaturePolicyIdentifier"
                type="SignaturePolicyIdentifierType"/>
    <xsd:element name="SignatureProductionPlace"
                type="SignatureProductionPlaceType"
             minOccurs="0"/>
    <xsd:element name="SignerRole" type="SignerRoleType"
             minOccurs="0"/>
  </xsd:sequence>
</xsd:complexType>
```

## The SignedDataObjectProperties Element

```
<xsd:element name="SignedDataObjectProperties"
                type="SignedDataObjectPropertiesType" />


<xsd:complexType name="SignedDataObjectPropertiesType">
  <xsd:sequence>
    <xsd:element name="DataObjectFormat"
                type="DataObjectFormatType"
                minOccurs="0" maxOccurs="unbounded"/>
    <xsd:element name="CommitmentTypeIndication"
                type="CommitmentTypeIndicationType"
                minOccurs="0"
                maxOccurs="unbounded"/>
    <xsd:element name="AllDataObjectsTimeStamp"
                type="TimeStampType"/>
    <xsd:element name="IndividualObjectsTimeStamp"
                type="TimeStampType"/>
  </xsd:sequence>
</xsd:complexType>
```

## The UnsignedSignatureProperties Element

```
<xsd:element name="UnsignedSignatureProperties"
                type="UnsignedSignaturePropertiesType" />
```

```xsd
<xsd:complexType name="UnsignedSignaturePropertiesType">
  <xsd:sequence>
    <xsd:element name="CounterSignature"
                 type="ds:SignatureType"
                 minOccurs="0"/>
    <xsd:element name="SignatureTimeStamp"
                 type="TimestampType"
                 minOccurs="0" maxOccurs="unbounded"/>
    <xsd:element name="CompleteCertificateRefs"
                 type="CompleteCertificateRefsType"
                 minOccurs="0"/>
    <xsd:element name="CompleteRevocationRefs"
                 type="CompleteRevocationRefsType"
                 minOccurs="0"/>
    <xsd:choice>
      <xsd:element name="SigAndRefsTimeStamp"
                   type="TimestampType"
                   minOccurs="0" maxOccurs="unbounded"/>
      <xsd:element name="RefsOnlyTimeStamp"
                   type="TimestampType"
                   minOccurs="0" maxOccurs="unbounded"/>
    </xsd:choice>
    <xsd:element name="CertificatesValues"
                 type="CertificatesValuesType"
                 minOccurs="0"/>
    <xsd:element name="RevocationValues"
                 type="RevocationValuesType"
                 minOccurs="0"/>
    <xsd:element name="ArchiveTimeStamp"
                 type="TimestampType"
                 minOccurs="0" maxOccurs="unbounded"/>
  <xsd:sequence>
</xsd:complexType>
```

## The UnsignedDataObjectProperties Element

```xsd
<xsd:element name="UnsignedDataObjectsProperties"
             type="UnsignedDataObjectsPropertiesTypes" />


<xsd:complexType name="UnsignedDataObjectPropertiesType">
  <xsd:sequence>
```

```
    <xsd:element name="unsignedDataObjectProperty"
            type="AnyType"
            minOccurs="0" maxOccurs="unbounded"/>
  </xsd:sequence>
</xsd:complexType>
```

## 12.2.3  Basic Elements

The ETSI signature schema specifies a number of basic types, which are described in the following sections.

### The AnyType Data Type

AnyType is a complete wildcard. You can put whatever you want into an element with this type, including mixed content and arbitrary attributes.

```
<!-- Start AnyType  >

<xsd:element name="Any" type="AnyType" />

<xsd:complexType name="AnyType" mixed="true">
  <xsd:sequence>
    <xsd:any namespace="##any"/>
  </xsd:sequence>
  <xsd:anyAttribute namespace="##any"/>
</xsd:complexType>
```

### The ObjectIdentifierType Data Type

Object identifiers (OIDs) are hierarchically allocated unique identifiers that are used heavily in ASN.1 and ASN.1-based ISO standards (e.g., X.509v3). Elements with this type not only let you specify an OID but also give a text description, corresponding URI, and so on.

```
<!-- Start ObjectIdentifierType -->

<xsd:element name="ObjectIdentifier"
            type="ObjectIdentifierType" />

<xsd:complexType name="ObjectIdentiferType">
  <xsd:sequence>
    <xsd:element name="Identifier" type="IdentifierType"/>
```

```
      <xsd:element name="Description" type="xsd:string"
                   minOccurs="0"/>
      <xsd:element name="DocumentationReferences"
                   type="DocumentationReferencesType"
                   minOccurs="0"/>
   </xsd:sequence>
</xsd:complexType>

<xsd:complexType name="IdentifierType">
  <xsd:complexContent>
    <xsd:extension base="xsd:anyURI">
      <xsd:attribute name="Qualifier"
                     type="QualifierType"
                     use="optional"/>
    </xsd:extension>
  </xsd:complexContent>
</xsd:complexType>

<xsd:simpleType name="QualifierType">
  <xsd:restriction base="xsd:string">
    <xsd:enumeration value="OIDAsURI"/>
    <xsd:enumeration value="OIDAsURN"/>
  </xsd:restriction>
</xsd:simpleType>
<xsd:complexType name="DocumentationReferencesType">
  <xsd:sequence maxOccurs="unbounded">
    <xsd:element name="DocumentationReference"
                 type="xsd:anyURI"/>
  </xsd:sequence>
</xsd:complexType>
```

### The EncapsulatedPKIValueType Data Type

This type is supplied for elements that contain binary ISO public key infrastructure items. It permits arbitrary binary content, encoded in base-64 [RFC 2045].

```
<!-- Start EncapsulatedPKIDataType -->

<xsd:element name="EncapsulatedPKIData"
             type="EncapsulatedPKIDataType" />
```

```
<xsd:complexType name="EncapsulatedPKIDataType">
  <xsd:complexContent>
    <xsd:extension base="base64Binary">
      <xsd:attribute name="Id" type="xsd:ID"
                     use="optional"/>
    </xsd:extension>
  </xsd:complexContent>
</xsd:complexType>
```

## The TimeStampType Data Type

Time stamps are a very important part of ETSI advanced signatures. You send a digest of the data you want time stamped to a Timestamp Authority. This authority signs and returns the data, with the result including the digest value, identity of the authority, and time of the stamping. It proves that the data existed before the time of stamping.

```
<!-- Start TimeStampType -->

<xsd:element name="TimeStamp"
             type="TimeStampType" />

<xsd:complexType name="TimeStampType">
  <xsd:sequence>
    <xsd:element name="HashDataInfos"
                 type="HashDataInfoType">
                 maxOccurs="unbounded"/>
    <xsd:choice>
      <xsd:element name="EncapsulatedTimeStamp"
                   type="EncapsulatedPKIDataType"/>
      <xsd:element name="XMLTimeStamp" type="AnyType"/>
    </xsd:choice>
  </xsd:sequence>
</xsd:complexType>

<xsd:complexType name="HashDataInfosType">
  <xsd:sequence>
    <xsd:element name="Transforms"
                 type="ds:TransformsType"/>
```

```
                    minOccurs="0"/>
  </xsd:sequence>
</xsd:complexType>
```

Each HashDataInfo element uses the usual XML Security reference URI and optional Transforms element to provide input for computing the hash sent to the Timestamp Authority.

## 12.3    XAdES Signature Elements Syntax

This section describes the elements used to build an XAdES signature.

### 12.3.1   The SigningTime Element

SigningTime is a time stamp over the entire signature. It uses the schema dateTime type. Only one SigningTime element can appear in the signature. Its schema is as follows:

```
<!-- Start SigningTime element -->

<xsd:element name="SigningTime" type="xsd:dateTime"/>
```

### 12.3.2   The SigningCertificate Element

The SigningCertificate element is the source of the signer identity. Legal entities can have multiple certificates that the same or different certificate authorities issue containing the same key. As a signed property of the signature, the one SigningCertificate incorporated in an ETSI advanced signature remains protected against substitution so that the identity, policy, and restrictions within the certificate will be accessible to the verifier. Its schema follows:

```
<!-- Start SigningCertificate -->

<xsd:element name="SigningCertificate"
             type="SigningCertificateType">

<xsd:complexType name="SigningCertificateType">
  <xsd:sequence>
    <xsd:element name="Certs" type="CertIDType"/>
```

```
                        maxOccurs="unbounded"/>
    </xsd:sequence>
 </xsd:complexType>


<xsd:complexType name="CertIDType">
  <xsd:sequence>
    <xsd:element name="CertDigest"
                 type="DigestAlgAndValueType"/>
    <xsd:element name="IssuerSerial"
                 type="ds:X509IssuerSerialType"/>
  </sequence>
 </xsd:complexType>


<xsd:complexType name="DigestAlgAndValueType">
  <xsd:sequence>
    <xsd:element name="DigestMethod"
                 type="ds:DigestMethodType"/>
    <xsd:element name="DigestValue"
                 type="ds:DigestValueType"/>
  </xsd:sequence>
 </xsd:complexType>
```

The first certificate identified by the Certs element is the certificate used to verify the signature. You can omit the issuer and serial number if the signature has a KeyInfo element with an X509Data child that contains an X509IssuerSerial element.

Any additional certificates that the Certs element identifies limit the set of authorization certificates that are used during signature validation.

## 12.3.3  The SignaturePolicyIdentifier Element

An ETSI advanced signature must contain exactly one SignaturePolicyIdentifier element that sets the rules for signature creation and validation and, as a signed property, is cryptographically bound to the signature. Its schema follows:

```
<!-- Start SignaturePolicyIdentifier -->


<xsd:element name="SignaturePolicyIdentifier"
             type="SignaturePolicyIdentifierType">
```

```
<xsd:complexType name="SignaturePolicyIdentifierType">
  <xsd:choice>
    <xsd:element name="SignaturePolicyId"
                 type="SignaturePolicyIdType"/>
    <xsd:element name="SignaturePolicyImplied">
  </xsd:choice>
</xsd:complexType>

<xsd:complexType name="SignaturePolicyIdType">
  <xsd:sequence>
    <xsd:element name="SigPolicyId"
                 type="ObjectIdentifierType"/>
    <xsd:element name="SigPolicyHash"
                 type="DigestAlgAndValueType"/>
    <xsd:element name="SigPolicyQualifiers"
                 type="SigPolicyQualifiersListType"
                 minOccurs="0"/>
  </xsd:sequence>
</xsd:complexType>

<xsd:complexType name="SigPolicyQualifiersListType">
  <xsd:sequence>
    <xsd:element name="SigPolicyQualifier"
                 type="AnyType"
                 maxOccurs="unbounded"/>
  </xsd:sequence>
</xsd:complexType>
```

The policy may be implied by what is being signed or by external data, for which case the SignaturePolicyImplied empty element is provided.

The SigPolicyID element uniquely identifies a version of the policy.

The optional SigPolicyQualifier element contains information qualifying the signature policy. Two types of such information have been defined to date [RFC 2459]:

• A URL from which a copy of the policy can be obtained

• A user notice to be displayed when the signature is verified

The schema for indicating these values follows:

```
Schema Definition:

<xsd:element name="SPUri" type="xsd:anyUri"/>
<xsd:element name="SPUserNotice"
            type="SPUserNoticeType"/>


<xsd:complexType name="SPUserNoticeType">
  <xsd:sequence>
    <xsd:element name="NoticeRef"
                type="NoticeReferenceType"
                minOccurs="0"/>
    <xsd:element name="ExplicitText" type="xsd:string"
                minOccurs="0"/>
  </xsd:sequence>
</xsd:complexType>


<xsd:complexType name="NoticeReferenceType">
  <xsd:sequence>
    <xsd:element name="Organization" type="xsd:string"/>
    <xsd:element name="NoticeNumbers"
                type="IntegerListType"/>
  </xsd:sequence>
</xsd:complexType>


<xsd:complexType name="IntegerListType">
  <xsd:sequence>
    <xsd:element name="int" type="xsd:integer"
                minOccurs="0"
                maxOccurs="unbounded"/>
  </xsd:sequence>
</xsd:complexType>
```

ExplicitText is text to be displayed. NoticeRef is information with which the notice could be extracted from a notices file, if necessary.

## 12.3.4   The CounterSignature Element

Some signatures may be valid under their signature policy only if they or their signed data are countersigned by appropriate entities. In some cases, the ordering or the determination of whether one party signs the other's signature may not be important, as when two parties sign a contract. In other cases, as a notary attesting to a signature, it may be vital.

Independent parallel signatures can exist as separate signature elements; however, where one signature must cover another, ETSI Advanced XML Signatures provides the CounterSignature element. This element contains one or more signatures and is added as one of the UnsignedProperties of the signature that it covers. The CounterSignature covers the SignatureValue of this signature. A CounterSignature can itself have a CounterSignature, and this layering can continue for any depth needed.

Its schema follows:

```
<!-- Start CounterSignature -->

<xsd:element name="CounterSignature"
             type="CounterSignatureType"/>

<xsd:complexType name="CounterSignatureType">
  <xsd:sequence>
    <xsd:element name="CounterSigInstance"
                 ref="ds:SignatureType"
  </xsd:sequence>
</xsd:complexType>
```

### 12.3.5  The DataObjectFormat Element

In many contexts, it is important to ensure that the user receives data in the format intended by the signer. Otherwise, a bad guy might be able to use some clever "pun." For example, perhaps some data was signed after the signer approved the data in a vector graphics format, but the same data played to the verifier in an audio format means something completely different.

Each DataObjectFormat gives the format of a single signed data item, so multiple DataObjectFormat elements can be included. The element supports lots of format types: a text description for human consumption, an Object Identifier, a MIME type [RFC 2045], and an encoding URI. About the only thing a DataObjectFormat element doesn't provide is a URI encoded type, which can be put in the ds:Type attribute of the ds:Reference element. Thus you can have five different "type" values for the same object.

**Soapbox**

> Having many different type designators for the same object is probably a bad idea. What if they are inconsistent?

The schema for the DataObjectFormat element follows:

```
<\!-- Start DataObjectFormat -->

<xsd:element name="DataObjectFormat"
             type="DataObjectFormatType"/>

<xsd:complexType name="DataObjectFormatType">
  <xsd:sequence>
    <xsd:element name="Description" type="xsd:string"
                 minOccurs="0"/>
    <xsd:element name="ObjectIdentifier"
                 type="ObjectIdentifierType"
                 minOccurs="0"/>
    <xsd:element name="MimeType" type="xsd:string"
                 minOccurs="0"/>
    <xsd:element name="Encoding" type="xsd:anyURI"
                 minOccurs="0"/>
  </xsd:sequence>
  <xsd:attribute name="ObjectReference" type="xsd:anyUri"
                 use="required"/>
</xsd:complexType>
```

### 12.3.6  The CommitmentTypeIndication Element

The CommitmentTypeIndicator says what the signers have bound themselves to. It can be explicit or implied from the semantics of the signed object. If explicit, it can be specified as part of the signature policy or registered for global use.

This SignedSignatureProperty applies to a particular data item, as indicated by the required ObjectReference attribute. Thus multiple CommitmentTypeIndication elements can refer to different data items.

This element's schema follows:

```
<!-- Start CommitmentTypeIndication -->

<xsd:element name="CommitmentTypeIndication"
            type="CommitmentTypeIndicationType"/>

<xsd:complexType name="CommitmentTypeIndicationType">
  <xsd:sequence>
    <xsd:element name="CommitmentTypeId"
            type="ObjectIdentifierType"/>
    <xsd:choice>
      <xsd:element name="ObjectReference"
                  type="xsd:anyURI"
                  minOccurs="0"
                  maxOccurs="unbounded"/>
      <xsd:element name="AllSignedDataObjects"/>
    </xsd:choice>
    <xsd:element name="CommitmentTypeQualifiers"
                type="CommitmentTypeQualifiersListType"
                minOccurs="0"/>
  </xsd:sequence>
</xsd:complexType>

<xsd:complexType name="CommitmentTypeQualifiersListType">
  <xsd:sequence>
    <xsd:element name="CommitmentTypeQualifier
                type="AnyType"
                minOccurs="0"/>
          maxOccurs="unbounded"/>
  </xsd:sequence>
</xsd:complexType>
```

The CommitmentTypeId element precisely identifies the type of commitment made by the signer. ETSI document TS 101 733 defines the following commitment possibilities:

- Proof of origin: a combination of proof of creation, proof of approval, and proof of sender

- Proof of receipt: the signer has received the contents of the signed data object

- Proof of delivery: the signing service provider has placed the signed data object in a local store accessible to the recipient

- Proof of sender: the signer has sent the signed data object (but not necessarily created or approved it)

- Proof of approval: the signer has approved the contents of the signed data object

- Proof of creation: the signer has created the signed data object (but not necessarily approved or sent it)

The CommitmentTypeQualifiers element provides a means to include additional qualifying information on the commitment made by the signer.

### 12.3.7   The SignatureProductionPlace Element

The SignatureProductionPlace element is a SignedSignatureProperty that can include a bunch of information about the signer at the time of the signature. It is optional, and an ETSI signature can include no more than one such element.

```
<!-- Start SignatureProductionPlace -->

<xsd:element name="SignatureProductionPlace"
          type="SignatureProductionPlaceType" />


<xsd:complexType name="SignatureProductionPlaceType">
  <xsd:sequence>
    <xsd:element name="City"
              type="xsd:string"
              minOccurs="0"/>
    <xsd:element name="StateOrProvince"
              type="xsd:string"
              minOccurs="0"/>
    <xsd:element name="PostalCode"
              type="xsd:string"
              minOccurs="0"/>
```

```
        <xsd:element name="CountryName"
                    type="xsd:string"
                    minOccurs="0"/>
  </xsd:sequence>
</xsd:complexType>


<!-- End SignatureProductionPlace -->
```

### 12.3.8  The SignerRole Element

Sometimes it is critical to know the "role" that someone is playing when he or she signs an object. For example, is the person signing as a vice president authorized to bind a company? The optional SignerRole provides two ways to indicate the signer's role: through a list of claimed roles or through an attribute certificate that binds the signer's identity to a role attribute.

This signed property qualifies the signer. The schema for the SignerRole element follows:

```
<!-- Start SignerRole -->

<xsd:element name="SignerRole" type="SignerRoleType">

<xsd:complexType name="SignerRoleType">
  <xsd:sequence>
    <xsd:element name="ClaimedRoles"
                type="ClaimedRolesListType"
                minOccurs="0"/>
    <xsd:element name="CertifiedRoles"
                type="CerifiedRolesListType"
                minOccurs="0"/>
  </xsd:sequence>
</xsd:complexType>

<xsd:complexType name="ClaimedRolesListType">
  <xsd:sequence>
    <xsd:element name="ClaimedRole" type="AnyType"
            maxOccurs="unbounded"/>
  </xsd:sequence>
</xsd:complexType>
```

```
<xsd:complexType name="CertifiedRolesListType">
  <xsd:sequence>
    <xsd:element name="CertifiedRole"
                 type="EncapsulatedPKIDataType"
                 maxOccurs="unbounded"/>
  </xsd:sequence>
</xsd:complexType>

<!-- End SignerRole -->
```

### 12.3.9  The AllDataObjectsTimeStamp and IndividualDataObjects-TimeStamp Elements

These signed properties qualify the signed data object(s) and may occur multiple times in an ETSI signature. Their schema follows:

```
Schema Definition:

<xsd:element name="AllDataObjectsTimeStamp"
             type="TimeStampType"/>
<xsd:element name="IndividualObjectsTimeStamp"
             type="TimeStampType"/>
```

## 12.4    Validation Data Syntax

This section describes additional elements that you can add to an XAdES to produce higher levels of trusted signatures.

### 12.4.1  The SignatureTimeStamp Element

A SignatureTimeStamp is a time stamp over the signature to prove that it existed before the stamped time. The intention is to show that the signature existed and was valid when dependence was made on it—even if any keys involved in the signature are later revoked. This element may be applied to an XAdES to produce an XAdES-T or to an existing XAdES-T to produce a new XAdES-T that contains multiple time stamps. Its schema follows:

```
Schema Definition:

<xsd:element name="SignatureTimeStamp"
             type="TimeStampType"/>
```

### 12.4.2   The CompleteCertificateRefs Element

A long-term signature needs to have its validation data conveniently accessible, including the following items:

- References to the complete certificate chain involved, or the certificates themselves.

- References to the complete set of revocation information, or the revocation information itself, needed to prove the signature valid at the time dependence was made on the signature. These data can include certificate revocation lists (CRL) and Online Certificate Status Protocol (OCSP) tokens.

If the validation data includes all references, it converts an XAdES-T into an XAdES-C. The CompleteCertificateRefs element described here contains the Certificate references, and the CompleteRevocationRefs element (see Section 12.4.3) includes the revocation information.

If you include the certificates and revocation data directly rather than through reference, it converts an XAdES-T or XAdES-C into an XAdES-A suitable for archival storage. You can include full certificates through the CertificateValues element (see Section 12.4.6); you can include full revocation data through the RevocationValues element (see Section 12.4.7).

The schema for CompleteCertificateRefs follows:

```
<!-- Start CompleteCertificateRefs -->

<xsd:element name="CompleteCertificateRefs"
             type="CompleteCertificateRefsType">

<xsd:complexType name="CompleteCertificateRefsType">
  <xsd:sequence>
    <xsd:element name="CertRefs" type="CertIDListType" />
  </xsd:sequence>
  <xsd:attribute name="ID" type="xsd:ID" use="optional"/>
</xsd:complexType>
```

### 12.4.3   The CompleteRevocationRefs Element

You include the CompleteRevocationRefs element in an XAdES-C as described in Section 12.4.2. Its schema follows:

```xml
<!-- Start CompleteRevocationRefs -->

<xsd:element name="CompleteRevocationRefs"
             type="CompleteRevocationRefsType"/>
<xsd:complexType name="CompleteRevocationRefsType">
  <xsd:sequence>
    <xsd:element name="CRLRefs"
                 type="CRLRefsType"
                 minOccurs="0"/>
    <xsd:element name="OCSPRefs"
                 type="OCSPRefsType"
                 minOccurs="0"/>
    <xsd:element name="OtherRefs"
                 type="OtherCertStatusRefsType"
                 minOccurs="0"/>
  </xsd:sequence>
  <xsd:attribute name="Id" type="xsd:ID" use="optional"/>
</xsd:complexType>

<xsd:complexType name="CRLRefsType">
  <xsd:sequence>
    <xsd:element name="CRLRef"
                 type="CRLRefType"
              maxOccurs="unbounded"/>
  </xsd:sequence>
</xsd:complexType>

<xsd:complexType name="CRLRefType">
  <xsd:sequence>
    <xsd:element name="DigestAlgAndValue"
                 type="DigestAlgAndValueType"/>
    <xsd:element name="CRLIdentifier"
                 type="CRLIdentifierType"
                 minOccurs="0"/>
  </xsd:sequence>
</xsd:complexType>

<xsd:complexType name="CRLIdentifierType">
  <xsd:sequence>
```

```
      <xsd:element name="Issuer" type="xsd:string"/>
      <xsd:element name="IssueTime" type="xsd:dateTime" />
      <xsd:element name="Number" type="xsd:"integer"
                   minOccurs="0"/>
    </xsd:sequence>
    <xsd:attribute name="URI" type="xsd:anyUri"/>
                   use="optional"/>
  </xsd:complexType>

  <xsd:complexType name="OCSPRefsType">
    <xsd:sequence>
      <xsd:element name="OCSPRef"
                   type="OCSPRefType"
                   maxOccurs="unbounded"/>
    </xsd:sequence>
  </xsd:complexType>

  <xsd:complexType name="OCSPRefType">
    <xsd:sequence>
      <xsd:element name="OCSPIdentifier"
                   type="OCSPIdentifierType"/>
      <xsd:element name="DigestAlgAndValue"
                   type="DigestAlgAndValueType"
                   minOccurs="0"/>
    </xsd:sequence>
  </xsd:complexType>

  <xsd:complexType name="OCSPIdentifierType">
    <xsd:sequence>
      <xsd:element name="ResponderID" type="xsd:string"/>
      <xsd:element name="ProducedAt" type="xsd:dateTime"/>
    </xsd:sequence>
    <xsd:attribute name="URI" type="xsd:anyUri"
                   use="optional" />
  </xsd:complexType>

  <xsd:complexType name="OtherCertStatusRefsType">
    <xsd:sequence>
      <xsd:element name="OtherRef" type="AnyType"
```

```
              maxOccurs="unbounded"/>
    </xsd:sequence>
</xsd:complexType>
```

As you can see by the three allowed contents of the CrlOcspRef element, it can accommodate references to CRLs, OCSP responses, and other forms of revocation data.

### 12.4.4 The SigAndRefsTimeStamp Element

You use the SigAndRefsTimeStamp element to time stamp the certificates and revocation information used to validate a signature at a particular time. It protects against later compromise of the certificate chain or Certification Authority key. Including this element advances an XAdES-C to an XAdES-X. Its schema follows:

```
Schema Definition:

<xsd:element name="SigAndRefsTimeStamp"
             type="TimeStampType"/>
```

### 12.4.5 The RefsOnlyTimeStamp Element

If an ETSI advanced signature does not contain the complete certificates and revocation information, but rather references to them, then you can include the RefsOnlyTimeStamp element to advance an XAdES-C to an XAdES-X. Its schema follows:

```
Schema Definition:

<xsd:element name="RefsOnlyTimeStamp"
             type="TimeStampType"/>
```

### 12.4.6 The CertificateValues Property Element

You use the CertificateValues element to collect all certificates starting from some trusted point down to, but not including, the signer's certificate. This element is included in the XAdES-XL long-term signature format; that format requires all information used in signature verification. There is no reason to sign this element because the certificates contain their own signature covering all relevant data. The schema for the CertificateValues element follows:

```
<!-- Start CertificateValues -->

<xsd:element name="CertificateValues"
            type="CertificateValuesType"/>
<xsd:complexType name="CertificateValuesType">
  <xsd:choice minOccurs="0" maxOccurs="unbounded">
    <xsd:element name="EncapsulatedX509Certificate"
                type="EncapsulatedPKIDataType"
    <xsd:element name="OtherCertificate" type="AnyType"
  </xsd:choice>
  <xsd:attribute name="Id" type="xsd:ID" " use="optional"/>
</xsd:complexType>
```

### 12.4.7 The RevocationValues Property Element

Revocation information can include certificate revocation lists (CRLValues) and responses from an online certificate status server (OCSPValues). Additionally, the standard provides a placeholder for other revocation information (OtherValues) for future use.

Certificate revocation lists (CRLValues) consist of a sequence containing at least one certificate revocation list. Each EncapsulatedCRLValue contains a DER-encoded X.509v2 CRL encoded in base-64.

OCSP Responses (OCSPValues) consist of a sequence containing at least one OCSP Response. The EncapsulatedOCSPValue element contains the base-64 encoding of a DER-encoded OCSP Response.

You must include the full revocation information in the XAdES-XL ETSI advanced signature format using the RevocationValues element. The schema for the RevocationValues element follows.

```
<!-- Start RevocationValues -->

<xsd:element name="RevocationValues"
            type="RevocationValuesType"/>
```

```
<complexType name="RevocationValuesType">
  <xsd:sequence>
    <xsd:element name="CRLValues" type="CRLValuesType"
                 minOccurs="0"/>
    <xsd:element name="OCSPValues" type="OCSPValuesType"
                 minOccurs="0"/>
    <xsd:element name="OtherValues"
                 type="OtherRevocationValuesType"
                 minOccurs="0"/>
  </xsd:sequence>
  <xsd:attribute name="Id" type="xsd:ID"
                 use="optional"/>
</xsd:complexType>

<xsd:complexType name="CRLValuesType">
  <xsd:sequence>
  <xsd:element name="EncapsulatedCRLValue"
               type="EncapsulatedPKIDataType"
               maxOccurs="unbounded"/>
  </xsd:sequence>
</xsd:complexType>
<xsd:complexType name="OCSPValuesType">
  <xsd:sequence>
    <xsd:element name="EncapsulatedOCSPValue"
                 type="EncapsulatedPKIDataType"
                 maxOccurs="unbounded"/>
  </xsd:sequence>
</xsd:complexType>

<xsd:complexType name="OtherRevocationValuesType">
  <xsd:sequence>
    <xsd:element name="ObjectIdentifer"
                 type="ObjectIdentiferType"/>
    <xsd:element name="OtherValue" type="AnyType"/>
                 maxOccurs="unbounded"/>
  </xsd:sequence>
</xsd:complexType>

<!-- End RevocationValues -->
```

### 12.4.8   The XAdESArchiveTimestamp Element

You use the XAdESArchiveTimestamp element to secure archival signatures. As time passes, old signatures become less reliable due to improvements in cryptanalysis, advances in brute-force computing, and potential compromise. To improve this situation, before the signature weakens too much, you can use a Trusted Service Provider (TSP) to obtain a strong time stamp that will prove that the signature existed before the weakening. TSPs will normally use more secure algorithms/keys and, as time passes, will provide ever stronger signatures. Multiple TSP archival signatures can be obtained over time as necessary.

Each XAdESArchiveTimestamp must cover all of the following:

- Required qualifying properties for an XAdES

- SignatureTimestamp elements

- The CompleteCertificateRefs element

- The CompleteRevocationRefs element

- The CertificateValues element (if it is located elsewhere, this information must be fetched and included)

- The RevocationValues element (if it is located elsewhere, this information must be fetched and included)

- The XAdESCCompleteTimestamp element, if present

- The XAdESCRefOnlyTimestamp element, if present

- Any previous XAdESArchiveTimeStamp elements

The schema follows:

```
Schema Definition:


<xsd:element name="XAdESArchiveTimeStamp"
             type="TimeStampType"/>
```

**Note**

Some material in this chapter is reprinted from [XAdES] with permission. Such material is © ETSI 2002. Further use, redistribution, modification is strictly prohibited. ETSI standards are available from http://pda.etsi.org/pda/ and http://www.etsi.org/eds/.

# Part IV | Keying

Cryptographic security is based on keys. Both authentication (covered in Part III) and confidentiality (covered in Part V) depend on keying and use the KeyInfo XML element, which is described in depth in Chapter 13.

A wide variety of keys exist: some are shared, some come in private/public pairs, and some are dynamically agreed to by the communicating parties. For many systems, the task of locating the key needed and determining that it is currently valid and trusted can prove complex and difficult. To offload this task from lightweight clients, such as personal digital assistants (PDAs), an XML Key Management protocol is under development. Chapter 14 gives an overview of the state of that ongoing effort.

# 13 | The KeyInfo Element

Both XMLDSIG and XML Encryption use the KeyInfo element. It appears as the child of a SignedInfo, EncryptedData, or EncryptedKey element and provides information to a recipient about what keying material to use in validating a signature or decrypting encrypted data. (This element is also used in XKMS, as described in Chapter 14.)

In both signature and encryption, the KeyInfo element is optional, because the recipient may be able to determine the right key to use from the application context. For example, in a protocol application, the channel over which the recipient gets the message or some other name, index, or data in the message may signal the recipient about which key or keys to use.

Each KeyInfo element can have zero or more child elements that give the value of or refer in various ways to the keying material. A KeyInfo with no content is about as useful as no KeyInfo at all. Even so, the standards include this option, as it may be easier for applications that dynamically calculate the KeyInfo content. It might not be convenient, at the time that the application outputs the KeyInfo start tag, to know whether it will have content.

All child elements of a KeyInfo element must refer to the same key. You might want multiple child elements because different recipients understand different forms. You might even want multiple child elements for a single recipient, if you were not sure which form of key reference they could use.

**Soapbox**

In retrospect, because KeyInfo is a major shared element between XMLDSIG and XML Encryption that had to be substantially augmented for encryption, it would have been better if this element had its own namespace and was defined in a separate document.

## KeyInfo Element Syntax

In this chapter, the following namespace prefixes are used for the sake of brevity:

```
xmlns:ds='http://www.w3.org/2000/09/xmldsig#'
xmlns:enc='http://www.w3.org/2001/04/xmlenc#'
xmlns:dsm='http://www.w3.org/2001/04/xmldsig-more#'
```

The syntax for KeyInfo, as defined in XMLDSIG, follows:

```
<!-- XMLDSIG KeyInfo DTD -->


<!ELEMENT KeyInfo (#PCDATA|KeyName|KeyValue|RetrievalMethod|
                   X509Data|PGPData|SPKIData|MgmtData
                   %KeyInfo.ANY;)* >
<!ATTLIST KeyInfo
        Id  ID  #IMPLIED >
```

In schema notation, it has the following form:

```
<!-- KeyInfo schema -->


<element name="KeyInfo" type="ds:KeyInfoType"/>
<complexType name="KeyInfoType" mixed="true">
    <choice maxOccurs="unbounded">
        <element ref="ds:KeyName"/>
        <element ref="ds:KeyValue"/>
        <element ref="ds:RetrievalMethod"/>
        <element ref="ds:X509Data"/>
        <element ref="ds:PGPData"/>
        <element ref="ds:SPKIData"/>
        <element ref="ds:MgmtData"/>
        <any processContents="lax" namespace="##other"/>
        <!-- (1,1) elements from (0,unbounded) namespaces -->
    </choice>
    <attribute name="Id" type="ID" use="optional"/>
</complexType>
```

XML Encryption extends this definition to include the EncryptedKey and AgreementMethod optional children of KeyInfo. Although defined in connection with encryption, these elements can also be used for a signature if the sender and recipient support them.

As expanded by XML Encryption, the KeyInfo DTD would be something like the following:

```
<!-- Extended KeyInfo DTD -->


<!ELEMENT KeyInfo (#PCDATA|KeyName|KeyValue|RetrievalMethod|
                   X509Data|PGPData|SPKIData|MgmtData|
                   EncryptedKey|AgreementMethod|
                   %KeyInfo.ANY;)* >
<!ATTLIST KeyInfo
          Id  ID   #IMPLIED >
```

In schema notation, the extended KeyInfo looks like this:

```
<!-- Extended KeyInfo schema -->

<element name="KeyInfo" type="ds:KeyInfoType"/>
<complexType name="KeyInfoType" mixed="true">
    <choice maxOccurs="unbounded">
        <element ref="ds:KeyName"/>
        <element ref="ds:KeyValue"/>
        <element ref="ds:RetrievalMethod"/>
        <element ref="ds:X509Data"/>
        <element ref="ds:PGPData"/>
        <element ref="ds:SPKIData"/>
        <element ref="ds:MgmtData"/>
        <element ref="enc:AgreementMethod"/>
        <element ref="enc:EncryptedKey"/>
        <any processContents="lax" namespace="##other"/>
        <!-- (1,1) elements from (0,unbounded) namespaces -->
    </choice>
    <attribute name="Id" type="ID" use="optional"/>
</complexType>
```

## KeyInfo Child Elements

Table 13-1 summarizes the child elements of KeyInfo specified in XML Security. The URI given is intended for use in the Type attribute of a Retrieval-Method element (see Section 13.3) or of a Reference element (see Chapter 10).

You can extend the specifications of many of KeyInfo's children, including PGPData, SPKIData, and X509Data, with elements from another namespace.

**Table 13-1** | KeyInfo Child Elements

| Implementation | Element Name | Type URI |
|---|---|---|
| XMLDSIG: Required<br>XMLENC: Deprecated | KeyValue | http://www.w3.org/2001/04/xmldsig-more#KeyValue |
| XMLDSIG: Optional<br>XMLENC: Required | EncryptedKey | http://www.w3.org/2001/04/xmlenc#EncryptedKey |
| XMLDSIG: Recommended<br>XMLENC: Required[1] | RetrievalMethod | http://www.w3.org/2001/04/xmldsig-more#RetrievalMethod |
| XMLDSIG: Optional<br>XMLENC: Optional | AgreementMethod | http://www.w3.org/2001/04/xmlenc#AgreementMethod |
| XMLDSIG: Optional<br>XMLENC: Recommended[2] | KeyName | http://www.w3.org/2001/04/xmldsig-more#KeyName |
| XMLDSIG: Optional<br>XMLENC: Optional | X509Data | http://www.w3.org/2000/09/xmldsig#X509Data |
| XMLDSIG: Optional<br>XMLENC: Optional | PGPData | http://www.w3.org/2000/09/xmldsig#PGPData |
| XMLDSIG: Optional<br>XMLENC: Optional | SPKIData | http://www.w3.org/2000/09/xmldsig#SPKIData |
| XMLDSIG: Deprecated<br>XMLENC: Deprecated | MgmtData | http://www.w3.org/2000/09/xmldsig#MgmtData |

1. Required only for same-document retrieval of EncryptedKey.
2. Recommended for KeyName referral to the CarriedKeyName of an EncryptedKey.

This extension is possible only if it is safe to ignore these extension or complementary elements while claiming support for the types specified in the standards. If it is not safe to ignore these elements, then you must specify the alternative structures to those specified by the standard as children of Key-Info, not grandchildren. (Of course, new structures from external namespaces can incorporate elements from the XMLDSIG namespace via features of the schema type definition language, as described in Chapter 5. They can create a DTD that mixes their own and XMLDSIG qualified elements, or a schema that permits, includes, imports, or derives new types based on XMLDSIG elements.)

The XML Security recommendations do not define the type URIs containing "xmldsig-more" in their path component. Rather, these URIs appear in an in-progress draft. Some implementations may not recognize such URIs even if the corresponding element is mandatory or recommended to implement. Because the URI is used only in RetrievalMethod or Reference elements, the element can be supported as a KeyInfo child without the URI necessarily being recognized in a Type attribute. For example, KeyValue is mandatory to implement as an element, but recognition of the type URI "http://www.w3.org/2001/04/xmldsig-more#KeyValue" is optional. The "Implementation" column in Table 13-1 applies to the element used as a child of KeyInfo, not to recognizing it as a Type.

### Private Keys

XML digital signatures and encryption need only public and shared secret keys, so their specifications do not include a syntax for private keys. Such a syntax has been defined for RSA private keys in connection with XML key management, as described in Chapter 14.

## 13.1  The KeyValue Element

The KeyValue element contains the actual value of a single public key that may be useful in validating a signature, decrypting data, or agreeing on a key. See Table 13-1 for its identifier. The following sections specify structures for DSA, RSA, and DH keys. The KeyValue element can include application-defined keys as element content qualified by another namespace or as character content. Element content is the preferred method because namespaces provide a mechanism to avoid conflicts.

XMLDSIG defines the KeyValue element syntax as follows:

```
<!-- XMLDSIG KeyValue DTD -->
<!ELEMENT KeyValue (#PCDATA|DSAKeyValue|RSAKeyValue
                    %KeyValue.ANY;)* >
```

As expanded by XML Encryption, it would be something like this:

```
<!-- Extended KeyValue DTD -->
<!ELEMENT KeyValue (#PCDATA|DSAKeyValue|RSAKeyValue|DHKeyValue
                    %KeyValue.ANY;)* >
```

In schema notation, the extended syntax has the following form:

```
<!-- Extended KeyValue schema -->

<element name="KeyValue" type="ds:KeyValueType"/>
<complexType name="KeyValueType" mixed="true">
    <choice>
        <element ref="ds:DSAKeyValue"/>
        <element ref="ds:RSAKeyValue"/>
        <element ref="enc:DHKeyValue"/>
        <any namespace="##other" processContents="lax"/>
    </choice>
</complexType>
```

Table 13-2 lists the child elements of KeyValue (grandchild elements of Key-Info) specified by XML Security. You use the listed URI in the Type attribute of RetrievalMethod or Reference elements.

**History**

When XMLDSIG standardization was initiated, the RSA patent had not yet expired. IETF policy stated that DSA signatures were the preferred, mandatory-to-implement algorithm. (Having one or more mandatory-to-implement algorithms is necessary to ensure that different implementations can interoperate.) RSA, as encumbered technology, could only be recommended. Since then, the RSA patent has expired. Newer IETF standards frequently mandate RSA and make DSA only recommended or optional, although sometimes both are mandatory; however, particularly with XMLDSIG going jointly through both the IETF and W3C standards processes, it is bureaucratically difficult to go back and change such things. All known XMLDSIG implementations include RSA signature support, so you will be reasonably safe if you think of both as required.

**Table 13-2** KeyValue Child Elements

| Implementation | Element Name | Type URI |
|---|---|---|
| XMLDSIG:Required<br>XMLENC: N/A | DSAKeyValue | http://www.w3.org/2000/09/xmldsig#DSAKeyValue |
| XMLDSIG:Recommended<br>XMLENC:Required | RSAKeyValue | http://www.w3.org/2000/09/xmldsig#RSAKeyValue |
| XMLDSIG:Optional<br>XMLENC:Optional | DHKeyValue | http://www.w3.org/2001/04/xmlenc#DHKeyValue |

### 13.1.1   The DSAKeyValue Element

[FIPS 186-2] specifies Digital Signature Algorithm (DSA) keys and the DSA. DSA public key values can have the following fields:

- P = a prime modulus meeting the [FIPS 186-2] requirements
- Q = an integer in the range $2^{159} < Q < 2^{160}$, which is a prime divisor of P − 1
- G = an integer with certain properties with respect to P and Q
- J = (P − 1) / Q
- Y = $G^X$ mod P (where X is part of the private key and not made public)
- seed = a DSA prime generation seed
- pgenCounter = a DSA prime generation counter

Parameter J is available for inclusion solely for efficiency, as it is calculable from P and Q. Parameters seed and pgenCounter are used in the DSA prime number generation algorithm specified in [FIPS 186-2]. As such, they are optional; note, however, that either both must be present or both must be absent. This prime generation algorithm, which provides assurance that a weak prime is not being used, yields values for P and Q.

Parameters P, Q, and G can be public and common to a group of users. They might be known from the application context. As such, they are optional; note, however, that P and Q must either both appear or both be absent. If P, Q, seed, and pgenCounter are all present, implementations are not required to check whether they are consistent and are free to use either P and Q or seed and pgenCounter. All parameters are encoded as base-64 [RFC 2045] values.

Arbitrary-length integers (e.g., "bignums" such as RSA moduli) are represented in XML octet strings as defined by the XML digital signature CryptoBinary type (see Chapter 10).

The U.S. Digital Signature Algorithm [FIPS 186-2] uses DSA keys. The DTD for a DSAKeyValue is as follows:

```
<!-- DSAKeyValue DTD -->

<!ELEMENT DSAKeyValue (P, Q)?, J?, G?, Y,
                       (Seed, PgenCounter)?) >
<!ELEMENT P (#PCDATA) >
<!ELEMENT Q (#PCDATA) >
<!ELEMENT J (#PCDATA) >
<!ELEMENT G (#PCDATA) >
<!ELEMENT Y (#PCDATA) >
<!ELEMENT Seed (#PCDATA) >
<!ELEMENT PgenCounter (#PCDATA) >
```

In schema notation, it has the following form:

```
<!-- DSAKeyValue Schema -->

<element name="DSAKeyValue" type="ds:DSAKeyValueType"/>
<complexType name="DSAKeyValueType">
    <sequence>
        <sequence minOccurs="0">
            <element name="P" type="ds:CryptoBinary"/>
            <element name="Q" type="ds:CryptoBinary"/>
        </sequence>
        <element name="J" type="ds:CryptoBinary"
                minOccurs="0"/>
        <element name="G" type="ds:CryptoBinary"
                minOccurs="0"/>
        <element name="Y" type="ds:CryptoBinary"/>
        <sequence minOccurs="0">
            <element name="Seed" type="ds:CryptoBinary"/>
            <element name="PgenCounter"
                    type="ds:CryptoBinary"/>
        </sequence>
    </sequence>
</complexType>
```

## 13.1.2   The RSAKeyValue Element

RSA key values have two fields—Modulus and Exponent. Here is an example:

```
<RSAKeyValue>
<Modulus> xA7SEU+e0yQH5rm9kbCDN9o3aPIo7HbP7tX6WoocLZ
    AtNfyxSZDU16ksL6WjubafOqNEpcwR3RdFsT7bCqnXPBe5ELh5u4
    VEy19MzxkXRgrMvavzyBpVRgBUwUlV5foK5hhmbktQhyNdy/6LpQ
    RhDUDsTvK+g9Ucj47es9AQJ3U=
</Modulus>
<Exponent>AQAB</Exponent>
</RSAKeyValue>
```

XML Security arbitrary-length integers (e.g., "bignums" such as RSA moduli) are represented as octet strings as defined by the digital signature CryptoBinary type (see Chapter 10).

The Rivest-Shamir-Adelman algorithm [RSA] uses RSA keys. You can use this algorithm for both signing and encryption. The DTD for an RSAKeyValue element follows:

```
<!-- RSAKeyValue DTD -->

<!ELEMENT RSAKeyValue (Modulus, Exponent) >
<!ELEMENT Modulus (#PCDATA) >
<!ELEMENT Exponent (#PCDATA) >
```

In schema notation, it has the following form:

```
<!-- RSAKeyValue Schema -->

<element name="RSAKeyValue"
        type="ds:RSAKeyValueType"/>
<complexType name="RSAKeyValueType">
    <sequence>
        <element name="Modulus"
                type="ds:CryptoBinary"/>
        <element name="Exponent"
                type="ds:CryptoBinary"/>
    </sequence>
</complexType>
```

### 13.1.3   The DHKeyValue Element

A Diffie-Hellman (DH) public key, as specified in [RFC 2631], consists of a maximum of six quantities: two large primes ("P" and "Q"), a "Generator" (g), the public key ("Public"), and two validation parameters ("seed" and "pgenCounter"). These quantities are related as follows:

- Public = $(g^x \bmod p)$, where x is the corresponding private key

- P = $(j^x q + 1)$ where j >= 2

The "seed" and "pgenCounter" values are optional and can be used to determine whether the DH key has been generated in conformance with the algorithm specified in [RFC 2631]. Because the primes and Generator can be safely shared over many DH keys, they may be known from the application environment and are optional.

The DTD for a DHKeyValue follows:

```
<!-- DHKeyValue DTD -->

<!ELEMENT DHKeyValue (( P, Q, Generator)?, Public,
                       ( seed, pgenCounter)?) >
<!ELEMENT P (#PCDATA) >
<!ELEMENT Q (#PCDATA) >
<!ELEMENT Generator (#PCDATA) >
<!ELEMENT Public (#PCDATA) >
<!ELEMENT seed (#PCDATA) >
<!ELEMENT pgenCounter (#PCDATA) >
```

In schema notation, it has the following form:

```
<!-- DHKeyValue Schema -->

<element name="DHKeyValue"
         type="enc:DHKeyValueType"/>
   <complexType name="DHKeyValueType">
      <sequence>
         <sequence minOccurs="0">
            <element name="P"
                     type="ds:CryptoBinary"/>
            <element name="Q"
                     type="ds:CryptoBinary"/>
```

```
            <element name="Generator"
                        type="ds:CryptoBinary"/>
        </sequence>
        <element name="Public"
                    type="ds:CryptoBinary"/>
        <sequence minOccurs="0">
            <element name="seed"
                        type="ds:CryptoBinary"/>
            <element name="pgenCounter"
                        type="ds:CryptoBinary"/>
        </sequence>
      </sequence>
    </complexType>
</element>
```

## 13.2    The EncryptedKey Element

The EncryptedKey element provides a way to include a key that has been encrypted by another key. It is typically used in such cases as enveloped encryption (see Chapter 2). For the EncryptedKey URI identifier, see Table 13-1. The detailed specification of this element appears in Chapter 15 on XML Encryption.

## 13.3    The RetrievalMethod Element

The RetrievalMethod element appears as a child of KeyInfo. It conveys a reference to KeyInfo information that is stored at another location. For example, several signatures in a document might use a key supported by an X.509v3 certificate chain. With RetrievalMethod, that chain need appear only once in the document or remotely outside the document, and each signature's KeyInfo can then reference it. Use of RetrievalMethod is recommended for XMLDSIG implementations and, for same document retrievals only, required for XML Encryption implementations.

**Note**
The RetrievalMethod element is not an algorithm element, as are all other XML Security elements ending in "Method." That is, it does not have an Algorithm attribute.

RetrievalMethod uses the same syntax and retrieval behavior as the Reference element described in Chapter 10. It has a URI attribute and uses the Reference element processing model, with two exceptions:

- There are no DigestMethod or DigestValue child elements.

- Use of the URI attribute is mandatory.

The Type attribute to RetrievalMethod is an optional identifier for the type of data to be retrieved. Dereferencing a RetrievalMethod Reference for all KeyInfo types with a corresponding XML structure results in an XML element or document with that element as the root. The various "raw" key information types, such as rawX509Certificate (for which no XML structure exists), return a binary value and thus normally require a Type attribute. This result occurs because binary types are not unambiguously parseable. If the result of dereferencing and possibly transforming the specified URI is a node-set, it may need to be canonicalized.

The RetrievalMethod element DTD follows:

```
<!-- RetrievalMethod DTD -->


<!ELEMENT RetrievalMethod (Transforms?) >
<!ATTLIST RetrievalMethod
         URI    CDATA    #REQUIRED
         Type   CDATA    #IMPLIED >
```

In schema notation, it has the following form:

```
<!-- RetrievalMethod schema -->


<element name="RetrievalMethod"
        type="ds:RetrievalMethodType"/>
<complexType name="RetrievalMethodType">
    <sequence>
        <element name="Transforms"
                 type="ds:TransformsType"
                 minOccurs="0"/>
    </sequence>
    <attribute name="URI" type="anyURI"/>
    <attribute name="Type" type="anyURI" use="optional"/>
</complexType>
```

**Table 13-3** | Additional RetrievalMethod Type URIs

| Element Name | URI |
|---|---|
| DSAKeyValue | http://www.w3.org/2000/09/xmldsig#DSAKeyValue |
| RSAKeyValue | http://www.w3.org/2000/09/xmldsig#RSAKeyValue |
| DHKeyValue | http://www.w3.org/2001/04/xmlenc#DHKeyValue |
| – | http://www.w3.org/2000/09/xmldsig#rawX509Certificate |
| – | http://www.w3.org/2001/04/xmldsig-more#rawX509CRL |
| – | http://www.w3.org/2001/04/xmldsig-more#rawPGPKeyPacket |
| – | http://www.w3.org/2001/04/xmldsig-more#rawSPKISexp |
| PKCS7signedData | http://www.w3.org/2001/04/xmldsig-more#PKCS7signedData |
| – | http://www.w3.org/2001/04/xmldsig-more#rawPKCS7signedData |

The URIs in Table 13-3 can appear as the Type attribute of a Retrieval-Method, in addition to all of the URIs provided in Table 13-1.

## 13.4    The AgreementMethod Element

AgreementMethod, as you might be able to guess from its name, is actually an algorithm invocation. It calculates a shared key based on compatible keying information for the sender and recipient. Chapter 18, which discusses cryptographic algorithms, specifies AgreementMethod. See Table 13-1 for its identifier.

## 13.5    The KeyName Element

The KeyName element contains a character string that the signer or encrypter uses to identify the key to the recipient; see Table 13-1 for its identifier. This element need not be a "name" in the usual sense. For example, it could be a file name or a key index into a database. In particular, white space in the character content of KeyName may be significant, and unusual characters can occur.

In the XML Encryption context, KeyName may refer to the value of a CarriedKeyName attribute of an EncryptedKey element (see Chapter 15). Support of this ability is recommended for XML Encryption implementations.

The KeyName element syntax follows:

```
<!-- KeyName DTD -->


<!ELEMENT KeyName (#PCDATA) >
```

In schema notation, it has the following form:

```
<!-- KeyName schema -->


<element name="KeyName" type="string"/>
```

## 13.6    The X509Data Element

Like all other children of KeyInfo, an X509Data element contains information to help the recipient figure out which key to use, including information to link that key to an authenticating entity. It has the richest structure, in terms of alternate and parallel allowed element content, of any KeyInfo child element specified in the XML Security standards. For its identifier, see Table 13-1.

The X509Data element consists of one or more X509 key identifiers, X509 certificates, certificate identifiers, or revocation lists. (See [ISO 9594] and Chapter 2 for a discussion of X509 certificates and related identifiers.) Implementation of X509Data is optional.

The content of X509Data must include at least one element, from the following set of element types:

- The X509IssuerSerial element, which contains an X.509 issuer distinguished name/serial number pair that should comply with [RFC 2253], except for the representation of strings in names (as specified in Section 13.6.1)

- The X509SubjectName element, which contains an X.509 subject distinguished name that should comply with [RFC 2253], except for the representation of strings in names (as specified in Section 13.6.1)

- The X509SKI element, which contains the base-64 encoded plain (i.e., not DER-encoded) value of a X509 V.3–SubjectKeyIdentifier extension

- The X509Certificate element, which contains a base-64 encoded X509 V.3 certificate

- The X509CRL element, which contains a base-64 encoded certificate revocation list (CRL) [ISO 9594]

- Elements from an external namespace that accompanies, complements, or replaces any of the preceding elements, including the PKCS7signed-Data element found in the "http://www.w3.org/2001/04/xmldsig-more" namespace

Any X509IssuerSerial, X509SKI, and X509SubjectName elements that appear must refer to the certificate or certificates containing the validation key. All such elements that refer to a particular individual certificate must be grouped inside a single X509Data element; if the certificate to which they refer appears, it must also reside in that X509Data element.

Also, any X509IssuerSerial, X509SKI, and X509SubjectName elements that relate to the same key but different certificates may occur in multiple X509Data elements. They must occur within the same KeyInfo, but this requirement is not surprising because only one KeyInfo is allowed under any SignedInfo, EncryptedData, or EncryptedKey.

All certificates appearing in an X509Data element must relate to the validation key by either containing it or being part of a certification chain that terminates in a certificate containing the validation key.

These constraints are not intended to imply any ordering between X509Data or X509Data and other elements in a KeyInfo, or ordering between X509Data child elements within an X509Data.

The following is an example of an X509Data:

```
<KeyInfo>
  <X509Data> <!-- two pointers to certificate-A -->
    <X509IssuerSerial>
      <X509IssuerName>CN=TAMURA Kent, OU=TRL,
          O=IBM, L=Yamato-shi, ST=Kanagawa,
          C=JP</X509IssuerName>
      <X509SerialNumber>12345678</X509SerialNumber>
    </X509IssuerSerial>
    <X509SKI>31d97bd7</X509SKI>
  </X509Data>
  <X509Data><!-- single pointer to certificate-B -->
    <X509SubjectName>Subject of Certificate B</X509SubjectName>
  </X509Data>
```

```
    <X509Data> <!-- certificate chain -->
      <!--Signer cert,
         issuer CN=arbolCA,OU=FVT,O=IBM,C=US, serial 4-->
      <X509Certificate>MIICXTCCA..</X509Certificate>
      <!-- Intermediate cert subject CN=arbolCA,OU=FVT,O=IBM,C=US
           issuer CN=tootiseCA,OU=FVT,O=Bridgepoint,C=US -->
      <X509Certificate>MIICPzCCA...</X509Certificate>
      <!-- Root cert,
           subject CN=tootiseCA,OU=FVT,O=Bridgepoint,C=US -->
      <X509Certificate>MIICSTCCA...</X509Certificate>
    </X509Data>
  </KeyInfo>
```

The XMLDSIG standard does not make any direct provision for a PKCS#7 encoded "bag" of certificates or CRLs. However, a set of certificates or CRLs can occur within an X509Data element, and multiple X509Data elements can occur in a KeyInfo. Whenever multiple certificates appear in an X509Data element, at least one such certificate must contain the public key that verifies the signature. In addition, the PKCS7signedData element is defined outside the XML Security standards in a separate, in-progress draft.

### 13.6.1   Distinguished Name Encoding

X509 distinguished names can appear as content of the X509IssuerName, X509SubjectName, and KeyName elements. They should be encoded as follows:

1. Consider the string as consisting of Unicode characters.

2. Escape occurrences of the following special characters by prefixing each with the "\" character:

   - A "#" character occurring at the beginning of the string

   - One of the following characters: comma (","), plus sign ("+"), double quote ("""), back slash ("\"), less than ("<"), greater than (">"), or semicolon (";")

3. Escape all occurrences of ASCII control characters (Unicode range 0x00–0x1F) by replacing them with "\" followed by a two-digit hexadecimal number showing its Unicode number.

4. Because an XML document logically consists of characters, not octets, the resulting Unicode string is encoded according to the character encoding used for producing the physical representation of the XML document.

## 13.6.2 X509Data Syntax

The X509Data element syntax follows:

```
<!-- X509Data DTD -->


<!ELEMENT X509Data ( (X509IssuerSerial |
                      X509SKI |
                      X509SubjectName |
                      X509Certificate)+ |
                      X509CRL %X509.ANY;) >


<!ELEMENT X509IssuerSerial (X509IssuerName,
                            X509SerialNumber) >
<!ELEMENT X509IssuerName (#PCDATA) >
<!ELEMENT X509SerialNumber (#PCDATA) >


<!ELEMENT X509SKI (#PCDATA) >


<!ELEMENT X509SubjectName (#PCDATA) >


<!ELEMENT X509Certificate (#PCDATA) >


<!ELEMENT X509CRL (#PCDATA) >


<!--Note: This DTD and schema permit X509Data to be empty;
    this use is precluded by the standard stating that at
    least one element from the dsig namespace should be present
    in the PGP, SPKI, and X509 structures. This is easily
    expressed for the other key types, but not for X509Data
    because of its rich structure. -->
```

In schema notation, it has the following form:

```
<!-- X509Data schema -->

<element name="X509Data" type="ds:X509DataType"/>
<complexType name="X509DataType">
  <sequence maxOccurs="unbounded">
    <choice>
      <element name="X509IssuerSerial"
               type="ds:X509IssuerSerialType"/>
      <element name="X509SKI" type="base64Binary"/>
      <element name="X509SubjectName" type="string"/>
      <element name="X509Certificate"
               type="base64Binary"/>
      <element name="X509CRL" type="base64Binary"/>
      <any namespace="##other" processContents="lax"/>
    </choice>
  </sequence>
</complexType>


<complexType name="X509IssuerSerialType">
  <sequence>
    <element name="X509IssuerName" type="string"/>
    <element name="X509SerialNumber" type="integer"/>
  </sequence>
</complexType>
```

### 13.6.3  PKCS7signedData Element

A PKCS #7 [RFC 2315] "signedData" structure can be used as a bag of certificates, CRLs, or a mixture of the two. The PKCS7signedData element is specified to accommodate this structure within KeyInfo. The binary PKCS #7 structure is encoded in base-64 [RFC 2045]. Any signer information present is ignored. The following example elides the base-64 data:

```
<dsm:PKCS7signedData
 xmlns:dsm="http://www.w3.org/2001/04/xmldsig-more">
   ...
</dsm:PKCS7signedData>
```

Implementation of PKCS7signedData is optional. Its syntax follows:

```
<!-- PKCS7signedData DTD -->

<!ELEMENT PKCS7signedData (#PCDATA) >
```

In schema notation, it has the following form:

```
<!-- PKCS7signedData Schema -->

<element name="PKCS7signedData" type="base64Binary"/>
```

### 13.6.4  OCSP Tokens

Retrieving and examining all the CRLs for the certificates in a chain can take a lot of time and effort. To avoid this problem, some systems use an online server to obtain the status of certificates. Such servers return a secure token indicating the certificate status. It would be reasonable to use such a token as a child of X509Data in place of an X509CRL. No syntax for On-line Certificate Status Protocol (OCSP) tokens has been specified for XML Security as yet, but one is likely to be defined in connection with XKMS (see Chapter 14).

## 13.7    The PGPData Element

The PGPData element appears as a child of KeyInfo. It conveys information that relates to PGP public key pairs and signatures on such keys. See Table 13-1 for its identifier. The PGPKeyID and PGPKeyPacket are prespecified children of PGPData.

A PGPKeyID value is a base64Binary sequence containing a standard PGP public key identifier, as defined in [RFC 2440]. The PGPKeyPacket contains a base-64 encoded Key Material Packet, also as defined in [RFC 2440]. Siblings from an external namespace can complement or extend these child element types. Alternatively, a PGP XML structure in an external namespace might replace PGPData as a child of KeyInfo. PGPData must contain one PGP-KeyID and/or one PGPKeyPacket and may have zero or more elements from an external namespace.

Implementation of PGPData is optional. The PGPData element syntax follows:

```
<!    PGPData DTD  -->

<!ELEMENT PGPData ( (PGPKeyID, PGPKeyPacket?) |
                    (PGPKeyPacket)
                    %PGPData.ANY;) >

<!ELEMENT PGPKeyPacket  (#PCDATA)  >
<!ELEMENT PGPKeyID  (#PCDATA)  >
```

In schema notation, it has the following form:

```
<!-- PGPData schema -->
<element name="PGPData" type="ds:PGPDataType"/>
<complexType name="PGPDataType">
  <choice>
    <sequence>
      <element name="PGPKeyID" type="base64Binary"/>
      <element name="PGPKeyPacket" type="base64Binary"
              minOccurs="0"/>
      <any namespace="##other" processContents="lax"
          minOccurs="0" maxOccurs="unbounded"/>
    </sequence>
    <sequence>
      <element name="PGPKeyPacket" type="base64Binary"/>
      <any namespace="##other" processContents="lax"
          minOccurs="0" maxOccurs="unbounded"/>
    </sequence>
  </choice>
</complexType>
```

## 13.8   The SPKIData Element

The SPKIData element appears as a child of KeyInfo. It conveys information related to SPKI public key pairs, certificates, and other SPKI data. [RFC 2693] For its identifier, see Table 13-1.

SPKISexp is the only prespecified child element of SPKIData. It is the base-64 encoding of a SPKI canonical S-expression. SPKIData must have at least one SPKISexp; SPKISexp can be complemented or extended by siblings from an external namespace within SPKIData. Also, SPKIData can be entirely replaced with an alternative SPKI XML structure from an external namespace as a child of KeyInfo.

Implementation of SPKIData is optional. The SPKIData element syntax follows:

```
<!-- SPKIData DTD -->


<!ELEMENT SPKIData (SPKISexp %SPKIData.ANY;) >
       .

<!ELEMENT SPKISexp (#PCDATA) >
```

In schema notation, it has the following form:

```
<!-- SPKIData schema -->

<element name="SPKIData" type="ds:SPKIDataType"/>
<complexType name="SPKIDataType">
  <sequence maxOccurs="unbounded">
    <element name="SPKISexp" type="base64Binary"/>
    <any namespace="##other" processContents="lax"
        minOccurs="0"/>
  </sequence>
</complexType>
```

## 13.9    The MgmtData Element

The MgmtData element appears as a child of KeyInfo. It is defined as a string value used to convey in-band key distribution or agreement data as content.

**History**

The MgmtData element was included in the XML Digital Signature specification as a place holder. During the XML Encryption specification effort, two more precise and interoperable elements were defined for in-band key distribution or agreement: EncryptedKey and AgreementMethod. MgmtData would have been dropped from XMLDSIG except for one thing: W3C namespace stability rules would have required changing the XMLDSIG namespace because it would have been possible to produce XML that would have been valid under the original DTD/schema but would fail after MgmtData was removed (not that anyone was actually trying to use such XML). No one involved in implementation of this standard wanted a namespace change because it would eliminate interoperability with existing and, in some cases, deployed code. As a result, MgmtData remains as a deprecated wart on the XMLDSIG specification.

MgmtData is much too poorly defined to be interoperable and its use is not recommended. You should use EncryptedKey or AgreementMethod instead.

The MgmtData element syntax follows:

```
<!-- MgmtData DTD -->

<!ELEMENT MgmtData (#PCDATA)>
```

In schema notation, it has the following form:

```
<!-- MgmtData schema -->

<element name="MgmtData" type="string"/>
```

# 14 | XKMS: XML Key Management

The XKMS XML Key Management system has two goals:

- To minimize the effort required by clients to obtain keys and verify trust in them by providing a server or servers with which the client can have a trust relationship. This server or servers can then unload several tasks from the client: locating servers from which to obtain revocation information, obtaining and using revocation information, validating chains of certificates, and more.

- To provide, where appropriate, central control of policy among a group of clients by implementing that policy at the XKMS server or servers used by those clients.

The key management system consists of two parts:

- The Key Information Service, for obtaining keys and information about keys

- The Key Registration Service, for populating the database that a Key Information Service consults either directly, if queries are sent to the server hosting the database, or indirectly through queries from other servers

XKMS is an ongoing specification effort for which a working group was formed by the W3C in December 2001 [XKMS WG]. This chapter is based on the W3C Note by Verisign, Microsoft, and webMethods [XKMS]. Many details of the final recommendations of the new working group will undoubtedly differ from that Note, but the basic capabilities will likely include those described here. In a few cases, inconsistencies and undefined areas in the Note have already been resolved [XKMS 2]. You should interpret assertions made about XKMS in this chapter in light of this fact.

XKMS uses SOAP (see Chapter 8) for communications. An implementation could, however, use other transport wrappings and similar services or, in principle, even use encodings other than XML.

### Namespaces

This chapter uses the following namespace prefixes:

```
xmlns="http://www.w3.org/2000/10/XMLSchema"
xmlns:xkms="http://www.xkms.org/schema/xkms-2001-01-20"
xmlns:xmldsig="http://www.w3.org/2000/09/xmldsig#"
```

Elements without prefixes are usually those defined in XML Schema [Schema]. Those with the "xkms:" prefix refer to the protocol from the XKMS Note; those with the "xmldsig:" prefix come from the XML Digital Signature standard (see Chapter 10).

---

## 14.1   The Key Information Service

This section gives an overview of the Key Information Service Specification (X-KISS). See Figures 14-1 and 14-2.

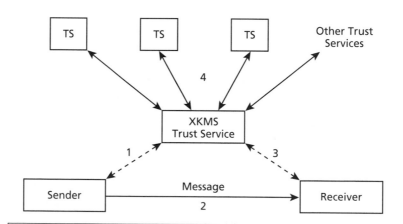

1. Sender securely registers his or her public signing key with an XKMS trust service.
2. Signed message is sent to the receiver.
3. Receiver retrieves the public key and verifies the signature.
4. In other cases, the trust service may obtain signing key information from other XKMS servers or other types of servers.

**Figure 14-1** | Signature key information service flow

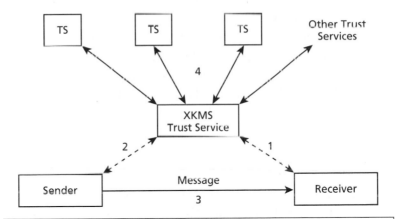

1. Receiver securely registers his or her encryption public key with an XKMS trust service.
2. Sender retrieves the public key and encrypts the message to the receiver.
3. Receiver receives and decrypts the message.
4. In other cases, the trust service may obtain encryption key information from other XKMS servers or other types of servers.

**Figure 14-2** | Encryption key information service flow

It is a particular goal of X-KISS to relieve clients of the need to do the following:

- Understand the complex non-XML syntax and semantics of various certificate types such as X.509v3

- Retrieve and understand information from various directory systems

- Perform revocation status determination

- Construct and understand trust chains

This specification will enable less capable devices, such as handheld personal digital assistants or cell phones, to more easily make use of XML Security based on complex public key infrastructures. In exchange, such devices generally surrender the ability to enforce their own trust policies. Instead, they get the trust policy of the key information service they elect to use.

## 14.1.1  X-KISS Services

XKMS defines three levels (tiers) of key information service. It mentions the possibility of higher-level services, such as those dealing with long-term trust relationships or the status of trust assertions, but leaves their specification to others.

### Retrieval Method

The lowest (Tier 0) is simply the ability to use the xmldsig:RetrievalMethod type of xmldsig:KeyInfo. This ability allows the application to retrieve the object pointed to by a URL. [XMLDSIG] recommends that implementation be able to at least handle "http:" scheme URLs. An XKMS service does not actually provide this level, so why the XKMS document lists this ability isn't completely clear.

### Locate Service

The next level of service (Tier 1) retrieves and provides information concerning keys. As described later in this chapter, a request message includes a query that uses xmldsig:KeyInfo to indicate what the client knows about the key and a section in which the client specifies the information it wants. For example, a client might know only the key name and want the key value. Alternatively, it might have an X.509v3 certificate but wish to use the XKMS service to parse this certificate and extract the key value and key name.

The Locate Service provides no trust assertion. It does not perform such trust actions as checking for revocation.

### Validate Service

The highest-level service (Tier 2) provides the same services of the Locate Service as well as assurance, within the service's trust policy, of the validity and binding between provided or returned data items and the identified key.

For example, a client could provide a key name and value and obtain a trusted assertion that the key value was bound to that key name. Alternatively, it could provide a certificate chain, including an end-user certificate, and receive in return the key name, key value, a trusted binding between them, and confidence that neither that certificate nor any higher-level certificates in the chain was revoked.

### 14.1.2  Locate Service

The Locate Service accepts an xmldsig:KeyInfo element to specify the public key for a particular query. It returns one or more xmldsig:KeyInfo elements that relate to the same key. The xkms:Respond element (see Section 14.2) specifies the elements to be returned.

```
Schema Definition:

<element name="Locate">
   <complexType>
      <sequence>
         <element name="Query" type="xmldsig:KeyInfo"/>
         <element name="Respond" >
            <complexType>
               <sequence>
                  <element name="string"
                           type="string"
                           minOccurs="0"
                           maxOccurs="unbounded"/>
               </sequence>
            </complexType>
         </element>
      </sequence>
   </complexType>
</element>
```

The schema for the response from an XKMS key information service follows:

```
Schema Definition:

<element name="LocateResult">
   <complexType>
      <sequence>
         <element name="Result" type="xkms:ResultCode"/>
         <element name="Answer" >
            <complexType>
               <all>
                  <element name="xmldsig:KeyInfo"
                           type="xmldsig:KeyInfo"
                           minOccurs="0"
                           maxOccurs="unbounded"/>
               </all>
            </complexType>
```

```
      </element>
    </sequence>
  </complexType>
</element>
```

When XKMS is wrapped in SOAP, all xkms:ResultCode values other than Success, Incomplete, and NoMatch are returned as SOAP Fault elements with a fault code of "Server" (changed in the current draft of SOAP to "Receiver"). The XKMS implementation defines the structure of the SOAP detail element.

## 14.1.3  Validate Service

Using the Validate Service, a client can request an assertion of the binding between an xmldsig:KeyInfo element and other data such as an identifier. The request includes an xkms:KeyBinding model for the assertion requested.

### xkms:ValidityInterval

This element specifies the time limits on the validity of the assertion. Its schema follows:

```
<complexType name="ValidityInterval">
  <sequence>
    <element name="NotBefore" type="timeInstant"/>
    <element name="NotAfter" type="timeInstant"/>
  </sequence>
</complexType>
```

- NotBefore is the time at which validity starts.

- NotAfter is the time just before which validity stops.

You can omit either or both values, in which case the end of the time interval remains unspecified. If you omit both, you are purporting to ask about an assertion for all time.

### xkms:KeyId

A KeyID specifies a URI identifier for the key. It differs from the KeyName, which need not be a URI. If the KeyID is a URL, a binding is asserted between the key and the address and protocol specified. For example, a KeyID in a Prototype or Query element specifying the "https:" or "mailto:" scheme indicates an intention to use the specified key with the given protocol.

The KeyID element has the following schema:

```
<element name="KeyID" type="string" minOccurs="0"/>
```

### xkms:KeyUsage

KeyUsage specifies the general types of usage for which the key is intended. If no KeyUsage is given, all uses are permitted. Its schema follows:

```
<simpleType name="KeyUsageValue" base="string">
    <enumeration value="Encryption"/>
    <enumeration value="Signature"/>
    <enumeration value="Exchange"/> <!-- key exchange -->
</simpleType>

<element name="KeyUsage">
    <complexType>
        <all>
            <element name="string" type="xkms:KeyUsageValue"
                    minOccurs="0" maxOccurs="unbounded"/>
        </all>
    </complexType>
</element>
```

### xkms:ProcessInfo

The ProcessInfo element can provide processing information associated with a key binding. It is optional, and clients should treat it as opaque. Its schema follows:

```
<element name="ProcessInfo" type="string" minOccurs="0"/>
```

### xkms:PassPhrase

The PassPhrase element contains a MAC (hash) function output value encoded in base-64. For further information, see Section 14.4.1.

### xkms:KeyBinding, xkms:Query, and xkmx:Prototype

The KeyBinding element asserts a binding between data elements that relate to a public key, including KeyName, KeyValue, and X509Data elements. The service asserts this binding by sending a KeyBinding to the client.

The Query and Prototype elements have the same schema as KeyBinding:

```
<complexType name="KeyBinding">
   <sequence>
      <element name="Status"
               type="xkms:BindingStatus"/>
      <element name="KeyID" type="string"
                            minOccurs="0"/>
      <element name="KeyInfo" type="xmldsig:KeyInfo"/>
      <element name="PassPhrase" type="string"
                                  minOccurs="0"/>
      <element name="ProcessInfo" type="string"
                                   minOccurs="0"/>
      <element name="ValidityInterval"
               type="xkms:ValidityInterval"/>
      <element name="KeyUsage" type="xkms:KeyUsage"
            minOccurs="0" maxOccurs="unbounded"/>
   </sequence>
</complexType>
```

## Request Message

A Request message consists of a Validate element, whose schema is as follows:

```
<element name="Validate">
  <complexType>
    <all>
      <element name="query" type="xkms:KeyBinding"/>
      <element name="respond">
        <complexType>
          <all>
            <element name="string" type="s:string"
                     minOccurs="0"
                     maxOccurs="unbounded"/>
          </all>
        </complexType>
      </element>
    </all>
  </complexType>
</element>
```

- "Query" is a single KeyBinding structure that is to be completed and validated.

- "Respond" is a sequence of identifiers that specifies data elements requested by the client; they are returned in the response as defined in Section 14.2.

### Response Message

A Response message consists of a ValidateResponse element, whose schema follows:

```
<element name="ValidateResult">
  <complexType>
    <all>
      <element name="Result" type="xkms:ResultCode"/>
      <element name="Answer" >
        <complexType>
          <sequence>
            <element name="KeyBinding"
                     type="xkms:KeyBinding"
                     minOccurs="0" maxOccurs="unbounded"/>
          </sequence>
        </complexType>
      </element>
    </all>
  </complexType>
</element>
```

"Answer" is a sequence of KeyBinding elements that contain the results of the validation. If no results are found, the sequence is empty and the ResultCode NoMatch is returned.

The response message includes a ResultCode, as defined in Section 14.2.

## 14.2   XKMS Common Data Elements

XKMS makes heavy use of a variety of elements from XML Digital Signature. For the additional structures it defines, all values are sent as element data.

Some common data elements are described in this section.

### xkms:ResultCode

You use ResultCode—an enumerated type—to return result codes.

```
<simpleType name="ResultCode">
   <restriction base="string">
      <enumeration value="Success"/>
      <enumeration value="NoMatch"/>
      <enumeration value="Incomplete"/>
      <enumeration value="Failure"/>
      <enumeration value="Refused"/>
      <enumeration value="Pending"/>
   </restriction>
</simpleType>
```

- "NoMatch" means the search prototype could not be found.

- "Incomplete" means that only part of the requested information could be provided.

- "Failure" does not specify a reason for failure.

- "Pending" means that operation was queued for future processing.

### xkms:AssertionStatus

You use the AssertionStatus element in responses to indicate the status of an assertion such as a key binding.

```
<simpleType name="AssertionStatus" base="string">
   <enumeration value="Valid"/>
   <enumeration value="Invalid"/>
   <enumeration value="Indeterminate"/>
</simpleType>
```

### xkms:Reason

The Reason element provides further details on the xkms:AssertionStatus. If the assertion status is "Valid" or "Indeterminate," this element lists those status aspects that have been determined to be "Valid" or "Indeterminate," respectively. If the assertion status was "Invalid," it lists the aspects that are either "Invalid" or "Indeterminate." Table 14-1 defines aspects of the XKMS Reason string.

**Table 14-1** | XKMS Reason Strings

| Aspect String | Definition |
|---|---|
| IssuerTrust | The trust service believes in the assertion issuer. |
| Status | The trust service has positively verified the status of the assertion with sources that it trusts, such as verified certificate revocation lists or an online certificate status server. |
| ValidityInterval | The validity interval of the assertion includes the request. |
| Signature | The signature (or signed data, such as a certificate) was verified. |

### xkms:Respond

The Respond element in a request specifies, through one or more strings, the elements desired in the response. They consist of XMLDSIG elements or the private key element specified in Section 14.4.2. An XKMS service may return additional data not requested. See Table 14-2.

The schema for the xkms:Respond element follows:

```
Schema Definition:
<element name="Respond" >
   <complexType>
      <sequence>
         <element name="string" type="string"
                  minOccurs="0"
                  maxOccurs="unbounded"/>
      </sequence>
   </complexType>
</element>
```

## 14.3    The Key Registration Service

This section gives an overview of the Key Registration Service Specification (X-KRSS). It is just as important as the key information service. Securely entering the proper information and bindings is obviously critical to providing correct information, although storing a key binding probably occurs less often than retrieving it.

**Table 14-2** XKMS Respond Strings

| String | Element(s) | Description |
|---|---|---|
| KeyName | xmldsig:KeyName | Key name |
| KeyValue | xmldsig:KeyValue | Public key parameters |
| X509Cert | xmldsig:X509Data | X.509v3 certificate authenticating the specified key |
| X509Chain | xmldsig:X509Data[1] | X.509v3 certificate chain authenticating the specified key |
| X509CRL | xmldsig:X509Data | X.509v2 certificate revocation list |
| OCSP | xmldsig:X509Data | OCSP token authenticating the X.509v3 certificate [RFC 2560] |
| RetrievalMethod | xmldsig:RetrievalMethod | Retrieval method information |
| MgmtData | xmldsig:MgmtData | (Use not recommended; see Chapter 13) |
| PGP | xmldsig:PGPData | PGP certificate |
| PGPWeb | xmldsig:PGPData[1] | Collection of PGP certificates |
| SPKI | xmldsig:SPKIData[1] | SPKI certificates |
| Multiple | | Requests multiple answers if available |
| Private | | Requests the encrypted private key |

1. This element may occur multiple times.

## 14.3.1   X-KRSS Service

The key registration service uses an all-purpose Register operation. A public key, possibly the corresponding private key, and information bound to are present in the xkms:KeyBinding element. The policies stating to whom information will be given, including such sensitive issues as to whom to release a private key for key recovery if the server generated the key pair and retained the private key, are implementation dependent. Also implementation dependent is which public key infrastructure or types of certificates a key registration service supports or to which it is linked.

### Key Revocation

A registration service may permit clients to revoke previously registered assertions. This task is accomplished by sending a registration request in which the status is specified as "Invalid." Service policy dictates what authentication is required with such a request.

### Key Recovery

A registration service that has generated a public/private key pair for a client must return the private key (encrypted) at that time. It may also permit the client to obtain the private key later by submitting a similar registration request. The service policy dictates what authentication is required for such a request and what, if any, additional steps (e.g., invalidating the key binding) the service might take.

## 14.3.2   X-KRSS Register Messages

This section summarizes key registration messages.

### Registration

The client specifies a prototype KeyBinding element as the heart of a registration request. The information in that element may be incomplete, in which case the server is asked to fill in missing information before registering the binding. For example, the server would generally generate a name if no key name is provided; it might also generate a public/private key pair if none is provided.

### xkms:AuthInfo

The AuthInfo element contains data that authenticate the request. Such data might include a proof that the client possesses the private key corresponding to the public key being registered. The exact content depends on the algorithms in use and the party generating the public/private key pair. You use the AuthUserInfo element if the client generates the key pair; you use the AuthServerInfo element if the server generates the key pair.

```
<element name="AuthInfo" minOccurs="0">
   <complexType>
     <choice>
         <element name="AuthUserInfo"
                   type="xkms:AuthUserInfoType"/>
         <element name="AuthServerInfo"
                   type="xkms:AuthServerInfoType"/>
     </choice>
   </complexType>
</element>
```

### Request Message

A request message consists of the Register element, which has the following schema:

```
<element name="Register">
  <complexType>
    <sequence>
      <element name="KeyBinding"
               type="xkms:KeyBindingType"/>
      <element name="AuthInfo" minOccurs="0">
        <complexType>
          <choice>
            <element name="AuthUserInfo"
                     type="xkms:AuthUserInfoType"/>
            <element name="AuthServerInfo"
                     type="xkms:AuthServerInfoType"/>
          </choice>
        </complexType>
      </element>
      <element name="Respond" minOccurs="0" >
        <complexType>
```

```
            <sequence>
              <element name="string" type="string"
                         minOccurs="0"
                         maxOccurs="unbounded"/>
            </sequence>
          </complexType>
        </element>
      </sequence>
    </complexType>
</element>
```

- The KeyBinding structure specifies elements that the client requests be registered.

- AuthInfo provides information that authenticates the request.

- Respond (see Section 14.2) provides a sequence of identifiers that specify data elements that the client requests be returned in the response.

### Response Message

A RegisterResult element constitutes a response message. It has the following schema:

```
<element name="RegisterResult">
  <complexType>
    <sequence>
      <element name="Result" type="xkms:ResultCode"/>
      <element name="Answer" >
        <complexType>
          <all>
            <element name="KeyBinding"
                       type="xkms:KeyBinding"
                       minOccurs="0"
                       maxOccurs="unbounded"/>
          </all>
        </complexType>
      </element>
      <element name="Private" type="string" />
    </sequence>
  </complexType>
</element>
```

- KeyBinding specifies the key binding that was registered by the service, if present.

- Private conveys additional information provided by the server, such as values for private key parameters generated by the registration service. (See Section 14.4.2.)

- Both KeyBinding and Private are optional.

### 14.3.3   Bulk Registration Services

Manufacturers of equipment with built-in keys or certificates, such as smart card or cable modem makers, need some way to register large amounts of key information efficiently. The X-KRSS protocol described previously does not handle this need efficiently. To satisfy this goal a bulk key registration protocol, currently called XBULK, is under development.

## 14.4   XKMS Cryptographic Algorithms

This section describes some of the cryptographic algorithms (or lack thereof) that are supported by XKMS and related XML elements.

Clearly, a client must be assured that any response it receives which appears to be from an XKMS service actually comes from that service, has not been altered in transit, and is sent in response to the actual request submitted by the client. XKMS leaves the method of achieving such assurances up to the application, but recommends that it be built on one of the following:

- An XML digital signature in the response (Chapter 10)

- Communication over a channel secured at the transport layer, such as using TLS [RFC 2246]

- Communication over a channel secure at the network layer, such as IPSEC [RFC 2411]

In general, to avoid circularity, all of these choices require some preinstalled keying information at the client or a shared secret between the client and server as described later in this section.

### 14.4.1   Shared Secret Data

As part of an initial, bootstrap, or recovery operation, it is frequently necessary to provide some limited-use, one-time pass phrase or the like for human input. In some cases, this pass phrase will be read over a telephone line. XKMS policy states that when such strings are used, they must be encoded as XML, all space and control characters must be removed, and all uppercase Latin-1 alphabetic ("A" to "Z") characters must be converted to lowercase characters [XKMS]. Other characters, included accented characters, are neither removed nor converted. Keying material is derived from shared secret data such as a pass phrase using HMAC with a one-byte key, as listed in Table 14-3.

**Table 14-3** | Shared Secret HMAC Keying

| Application | Value |
|---|---|
| Authentication | x01 |
| Encoding of pass phrase—pass 1 | x02 |
| Encoding of pass phrase—pass 2 | x03 |
| Encryption of private key | x04 |

#### xkms:PassPhraseAuth Element

The PassPhraseAuth element contains a plain text, limited-use, shared secret pass phrase to authenticate a request. It has the following schema:

```
<element name="PassPhraseAuth" type="string"
                      minOccurs="0"/>
```

#### xkms:KeyBindingAuth Element

You use the KeyBindingAuth element to authenticate a KeyBinding using a previously established key, possibly one based on a shared secret pass phrase. It provides a signature over the KeyBinding element for the public key being registered.

```
<element name="KeyBindingAuth" minOccurs="0">
   <complexType>
      <sequence>
         <element ref="xmldsig:Signature"
```

```
                        minOccurs="0"/>
        </sequence>
    </complexType>
</element>
```

## 14.4.2   Registration of User-Generated Keys

You use the AuthUserInfoType element type to prove that a client is authorized to register a key. Depending on the server policy, it may contain a KeyBindingAuth element and/or PassPhraseAuth element (both of which were defined earlier) and/or a ProofOfPossession element (defined in this section).

The schema for AuthUserInfo follows:

```
<complexType  name="AuthUserInfoType">
  <sequence>
    <element name="ProofOfPossession" minOccurs="0">
      <complexType>
        <sequence>
          <element ref="xmldsig:Signature"
                   minOccurs="0"/>
        </sequence>
      </complexType>
    </element>
    <element name="KeyBindingAuth" minOccurs="0">
      <complexType>
        <sequence>
          <element ref="xmldsig:Signature"
                   minOccurs="0"/>
        </sequence>
      </complexType>
    </element>
    <element name="PassPhraseAuth" type="string"
             minOccurs="0"/>
  </sequence>
</complexType>
```

### xkms:ProofOfPossession Element

The ProofOfPossession element contains an XML digital signature over a KeyBinding using the private key corresponding to the public key being registered by that KeyBinding. Thus it constitutes proof that someone with knowledge of that private key constructed the KeyBinding. The recipients can satisfy themselves on this point by verifying the ProofOfPossession signature using the public key in the signed KeyBinding.

The schema for ProofOfPossession follows:

```
<element name="ProofOfPossession" minOccurs="0">
   <complexType>
     <sequence>
         <element ref="xmldsig:Signature" minOccurs="0"/>
     </sequence>
   </complexType>
</element>
```

### 14.4.3  Registration of Server-Generated Keys

A client uses the AuthServerInfoType when the service generates the keys. Depending on the server policy, the client may be required to provide a KeyBindingAuth and/or PassPhraseAuth element (both of which were defined earlier). The service must return the generated private key to the client in the Private element. See the "RSA Key Pairs" section for information about structure and encryption considerations.

The schema for the AuthServerInfoType follows:

```
<complexType  name="AuthServerInfoType">
    <element name="KeyBindingAuth" minOccurs="0">
      <complexType>
         <sequence>
            <element ref="xmldsig:Signature"
                     minOccurs="0"/>
         </sequence>
      </complexType>
    </element>
```

```
      <element name="PassPhraseAuth" type="string"
              minOccurs="0"/>
</complexType>
```

### RSA Key Pairs

If the registration service generates a public/private key pair, it must be able to convey the private key to the client. The schema below is defined for this purpose. The XKMS Note [XKMS] also specifies a method for encrypting this structure for return to the client. This method is not given in this book, as it will likely be replaced by the XML Encryption Recommendation (see Chapter 15).

```
<element name='RSAKeyPair'>
   <complexType content='elementOnly'>
     <all>
       <element name='Modulus' type='xmldsig:CryptoBinary'
               minOccurs='1' maxOccurs='1'/>
       <element name='PublicExponent'
               type='xmldsig:CryptoBinary'
               minOccurs='1' maxOccurs='1'/>
       <element name='PrivateExponent'
               type='xmldsig:CryptoBinary'
               minOccurs='1' maxOccurs='1'/>
       <element name='P' type='xmldsig:CryptoBinary'
               minOccurs='0' maxOccurs='1'/>
       <element name='Q' type='xmldsig:CryptoBinary'
               minOccurs='0' maxOccurs='1'/>
       <element name='DP' type='xmldsig:CryptoBinary'
               minOccurs='0' maxOccurs='1'/>
       <element name='DQ' type='xmldsig:CryptoBinary'
               minOccurs='0' maxOccurs='1'/>
       <element name='QINV' type='xmldsig:CryptoBinary'
               minOccurs='0' maxOccurs='1'/>
     </all>
   </complexType>
</element>
```

## 14.5    Security Considerations

Many complex security considerations apply to operating or using an XML key management service with capabilities along the lines of those described in this chapter. Attention should be paid to the security considerations given in the other chapters of this book as well as the considerations raised in [XKMS].

Anyone seriously interested in these questions should at least monitor and perhaps become active in the W3C XKMS working group [XKMS WG].

# Part V | Encryption

Chapter 15 takes an in-depth look at XML Encryption. Although the encryption effort is not as mature as that associated with the XML Digital Signature standard, it seems unlikely that major changes from what is described here will occur in the XML Encryption standard.

Combining authentication and confidentiality presents a number of problems, which are discussed in Chapter 16.

# 15 | XML Encryption

After Section 15.1 introduces XML Encryption, Section 15.2 describes its detailed syntax and Section 15.3 gives some examples of this encryption scheme. You can read Sections 15.2 and 15.3 in either order, depending on whether you prefer to learn first from examples or from detailed specifications.

Section 15.4 provides the processing rules for cipher text generation and decryption.

Section 15.5 describes a number of warning and security considerations in the use of XML Encryption.

This chapter is based on the XML Encryption Syntax and Processing W3C Working Draft [XMLENC]. When this book went to press, that draft was in Last Call by the XML Encryption Working Group [XMLENC WG].

## 15.1 Introduction to XML Encryption

"XML Encryption" encompasses the encryption of any kind of data, including the encryption of XML [XMLENC]. What makes it XML Encryption is that an XML element (either an EncryptedData or EncryptedKey element) contains or refers to the cipher text, keying information, and algorithms.

### 15.1.1 Why Another Encryption Syntax?

As with XMLDSIG, the motivation for a new XML syntax, instead of using existing binary and text syntaxes, was the desire to have encryption information and cipher text as structures that could be created, manipulated, and analyzed with XML tools. You can conveniently encrypt parts of XML documents, thereby smoothly integrating them in XML-based Web services. In addition, you can easily use XML pointers into the structure, make assertions about it, and have it point into other XML structures. Even just displaying and looking at a structure normally in the XML world becomes much easier if the structure is XML.

By the time the XML Encryption effort got rolling, the KeyInfo element existed and a syntax for algorithms had been specified in connection with XMLDSIG. Thus a few of the steps needed to develop XML Encryption had already been taken.

### 15.1.2   Encryption Granularity

You can use XML Encryption for encrypting arbitrary data. When using it to encrypt XML in place, however, this standard is limited to encrypting an entire element or the entire content of an element. The resulting Encrypted-Data element then replaces the encrypted element or the encrypted content.

**History**

The XML Encryption Working Group [XMLENC WG] has given significant thought to providing some syntax for encrypting attributes or attribute values in place. While there has been interest and the presentation of some informal proposals, a fully specified syntax with processing rules has not been presented to the working group.

### 15.1.3   Enveloping and Detached Encryption

The EncryptedData element produced by XML Encryption envelopes or references the cipher text. With enveloping encryption (Figure 15-1), the raw encrypted data consists of the CipherValue element's content. With referencing encryption (Figure 15-2), the CipherReference element's URI attribute points to the location of the raw encrypted data.

Although "enveloped" signatures make sense (see Chapter 10), the concept of an "enveloped" encryption used in the same way does not work. If you encrypt all information about the encryption, including the algorithm and any keying or other information, that information would become useless— that is, you would need to decrypt it to get the information you need to decrypt it. The term "enveloped encryption" refers to something quite different: encrypting data with a symmetric key and then encrypting that key with one or more public keys, as described in Chapter 2.

**Soapbox**

It's funny how the many questions about "meaning" that plague signatures barely come up with encryption. If something is encrypted, implementers seems to know that it just means that some digital process used the encrypting key and algorithm and changed some plain text into cipher text.

Similarly, at the bit level, a digital signature just means that some digital process with access to the signing key calculated the "signature." If possession of the signing key is controlled, high-level applications can, and frequently do, impute some "meaning" to the signature. Many people go too far, however, equating a digital signature to the conscious approval of some individual person or the like. (In fact, humans are incapable of performing cryptographically strong encryption or signing. Digital hardware and software whose trustworthiness is usually much worse than the cryptographic algorithm employed must mediate such actions.)

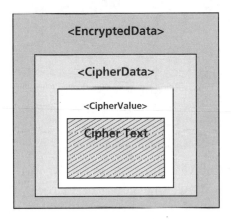

**Figure 15-1** | Enveloping encryption

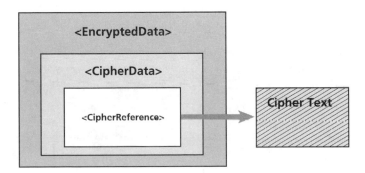

**Figure 15-2** | Detached encryption

## 15.2    XML Encryption Syntax

This section specifies the XML Encryption syntax. Using skeletal XML, the EncryptedData element has the following structure:

```
<EncryptedData Id? Type?>
  <EncryptionMethod/>?
  <ds:KeyInfo>
    <EncryptedKey>?
    <AgreementMethod>?
    <ds:KeyName>?
    <ds:RetrievalMethod>?
    <ds:*>?
  </ds:KeyInfo>?
  <CipherData>
    <CipherValue>?
    (CipherReference URI?)?
  </CipherData>
  <EncryptionProperties/>?
</EncryptedData>
```

The syntax of XML Encryption is described in detail in the rest of this section. Applications that conform to the XML Encryption standard must implement all elements noted here unless otherwise stated. The following XML preamble, including the declaration, internal entities, and import of the XMLDSIG namespace, is part of specifying the syntax using [Schema]:

```
<?xml version="1.0" encoding="utf-8"?>
<!-- XML Schema context -->

<!DOCTYPE schema PUBLIC "-//W3C//DTD XMLSchema 200102//EN"
  "http://www.w3.org/2001/XMLSchema.dtd"
[
<!ATTLIST schema
  xmlns:xenc CDATA #FIXED 'http://www.w3.org/2001/04/xmlenc#'
  xmlns:ds CDATA #FIXED 'http://www.w3.org/2000/09/xmldsig#'
>
<!ENTITY % p "">
<!ENTITY % s "">
]>
```

```
<schema xmlns='http://www.w3.org/2001/XMLSchema' version-'1.0'
        xmlns:ds='http://www.w3.org/2000/09/xmldsig#'
        xmlns:xenc='http://www.w3.org/2001/04/xmlenc#'
        targetNamespace='http://www.w3.org/2001/04/xmlenc#'
        elementFormDefault='qualified'>


<import namespace='http://www.w3.org/2000/09/xmldsig#'
        schemaLocation=
'http://www.w3.org/TR/2001/CR-xmldsig-core 20010419/xmldsig-
core-schema.xsd' <!-- wrapped due to line length limit! -->
/>
```

The funny "p" and "s" ENTITY attributes are artifacts of the way [Schema] is specified. They stand for prefix and suffix, respectively. XML Schema uses them in constructs such as "xmlns&s;='foo'" and "<&p;foo/>". They default to "xs:" and ":xs". These attributes are set to null in the preceding code to avoid having to use "xs" or some other namespace prefix on all schema constructs.

### Versioning

Unlike most encryption standards, XML Encryption does not have a version number field. Instead, XML Encryption uses the namespace [Names] for this purpose. XML Encryption currently uses the "http://www.w3.org/2001/04/xmlenc#" namespace, but a new XML Encryption version would use a new namespace.

### 15.2.1  The EncryptedType

EncryptedType is the abstract type from which EncryptedData and Encrypted-Key are derived. Its schema follows:

```
<!-- EncryptedType Schema -->


<complexType name='EncryptedType' abstract='true'>
  <sequence>
    <element name='EncryptionMethod'
             type='xenc:EncryptionMethodType'
             minOccurs='0'/>
    <element ref='ds:KeyInfo' minOccurs='0'/>
    <element ref='xenc:CipherData'/>
```

```
    <element ref='xenc:EncryptionProperties'
            minOccurs='0'/>
  </sequence>
  <attribute name='Id' type='ID' use='optional'/>
  <attribute name='Type' type='anyURI' use='optional'/>
  <attribute name='MimeType' type='string' use='optional'/>
  <attribute name='Encoding" type='string' use='optional'/>
</complexType>
```

The "abstract" schema attribute means that you cannot use EncryptedType directly. Instead, you can use it only to derive other types.

The ds:KeyInfo element is optional. [XMLDSIG] contains the original definition of this element, which carries information about the key used to encrypt the CipherData. (See Chapter 13.)

CipherData is a mandatory child of EncryptedType. It contains or points to the cipher text. (See Section 15.2.2.)

EncryptionProperties can contain information concerning the encryption such as the time it was performed. (See Section 15.2.3.)

The optional Id attribute of EncryptedType provides the usual method of referencing the element within a document.

The optional Type attribute provides information about the plain text and/or its processing before encryption. If the plain text is an element or element content that EncryptedData replaces, you should provide a Type so that decryption can restore the XML. A Type could also indicate, for example, compression of plain text before encryption that would need to be decompressed after decryption to ensure its recovery.

The optional MimeType attribute gives the MIME [RFC 2045] type of the encrypted data, and the optional Encoding attribute specifies how it has been encoded. For example, MimeType could be "image/jpeg" and Encoding could be "base64". Both attributes are purely advisory, so no validation is required. Note that this information is unnecessary when the application can deduce it from the Type attribute. For example, if Type indicates that an element or element content was encrypted, then it will always be encoded in UTF-8.

EncryptionMethod is an optional element that describes the encryption algorithm applied to the cipher data. If this element is absent, the recipient

must know, from the application context, the encryption algorithm. The
schema for the EncryptionMethod element follows.

```
<!-- EncryptionMethod schema -->

<element name="EncryptionMethod"
        type="xenc:EncryptionMethodType"/>
<complexType name="EncryptionMethodType" mixed="true">
   <sequence>
      <element name='KeySize' minOccurs='0'
              type='xenc:KeySizeType'/>


      <element name='OAEPparams' minOccurs='0'
              type='base64Binary'/>
      <any namespace='##other' minOccurs='0'
                            maxOccurs='unbounded'/>
      <!-- (0,unbounded) elements from
          (1,1) external namespace -->
   </sequence>
   <attribute name="Algorithm"
           type="anyURI" use="required"/>
</complexType>
```

Which child elements to EncryptionMethod are allowed or required depends
on the specific Algorithm attribute value; however, KeySize is always permitted.
([Schema] does not provide a facility for expressing child element allowability
based on attribute values.) The presence of any child element under EncryptionMethod that the algorithm does not permit, or the presence of a KeySize
child that is inconsistent with the algorithm, must be treated as an error.

Table 15-1 lists some types, the first two of which must be supported.

**Table 15-1** | Plain Text Types

| Name | Attribute Value |
|---|---|
| Element | Type='http://www.w3.org/2001/04/xmlenc#Element' |
| Content | Type='http://www.w3.org/2001/04/xmlenc#Content' |
| Media Type[1] | MimeType='*/*' |
| 1. Media Type is intended to be a MIME type [RFC 2045]. Implementation of all such types occurs through simple octet stream encryption. | |

### 15.2.2 The CipherData Element

The CipherData element is a mandatory child of the EncryptedData and EncryptedKey elements. It provides the encrypted data by either containing or pointing to it via a CipherValue or CipherReference child, respectively. CipherValue provides a base-64 [RFC 2045] encoded octet sequence of cipher text. CipherReference provides a reference to an external location containing cipher text information.

The schema for CipherData follows:

```
<!-- CipherData Schema -->

<element name='CipherData'
         type='xenc:CipherDataType'/>
<complexType name='CipherDataType'>
  <sequence>
    <choice>
      <element name='CipherValue'
               type='ds:CryptoBinary'/>
      <element ref='xenc:CipherReference'/>
    </choice>
  </sequence>
</complexType>
```

### The CipherReference Element

If you do not supply a CipherValue element, a CipherReference element identifies a source that, when processed, yields the cipher text octet sequence.

You obtain the actual value as follows: The CipherReference URI is dereferenced. If the CipherReference element contains a sequence of Transforms, the data resulting from the dereferenced URI is transformed to yield the intended cipher value. For example, if the value is encoded in base-64 within an XML document, the Transforms could specify an XPath expression to extract the base-64 text followed by a base-64 decoding.

The syntax of the URI and Transforms resembles that used for [XMLDSIG] reference validation. Signature and encryption processing do differ, however. In [XMLDSIG], both generation and validation processing start with the same source data and perform any Transforms in the same order. In encryption, the decrypter has only the cipher data. The specified Transforms are enumerated for the decrypter, in the order necessary to obtain the cipher text octets. The encrypter generally performed these steps in the reverse order. For this reason, the CipherReference Transforms element appears in the XML Encryption namespace.

**Soapbox**

While you follow different steps to create an EncryptedData element, for example, than to create a Signature element, a Transforms element need not exist during the preparation of such elements. Transforms must exist only for the receiver to use as a list of steps to perform in the appropriate order. Putting the CipherReference and Reference Transforms in different namespaces can prove confusing, particularly given that XML Encryption also uses the XMLDSIG namespace Transforms in the ReferenceList element and that in all cases the Transform element resides in the XMLDSIG namespace.

For example, if the relevant cipher value is captured within a CipherValue element in a different XML document, the CipherReference might look as follows:

```
<CipherReference
 URI="http://www.example.com/CipherValues.xml">
  <Transforms>
    <ds:Transform
Algorithm="http://www.w3.org/TR/1999/REC-xpath-19991116">
      <ds:XPath xmlns:rep="&repository;">
        self::text()[parent::CipherValue[@id="example1"]]
      </XPath>
    </Transform>
    <Transform
Algorithm="http://www.w3.org/2000/09/xmldsig#base64"/>
  </Transforms>
</CipherReference>
```

XML Encryption implementations must include the CipherReference feature and the same URI encoding, dereferencing, scheme, and HTTP response codes as are required of XMLDSIG implementations. Implementation of the

Transforms feature is optional. The schema definition for CipherReference
follows:

```
<!-- CipherReference Schema -->

<element name='CipherReference'
         type='xenc:CipherReferenceType'/>
<complexType name='CipherReferenceType'>
  <choice>
    <element name='Transforms' minOccurs='0'/>
  </choice>
  <attribute name='URI' type='anyURI' use='required'/>
</complexType>
<complexType name="TransformsType">
  <sequence>
    <element ref="ds:Transform"
             maxOccurs="unbounded"/>
  </sequence>
</complexType>
```

### 15.2.3   The EncryptionProperties Element

```
EncryptionProperties Identifier:
    http://www.w3.org/2001/04/xmlenc#EncryptionProperties
```

You can use the preceding identifier within a ds:Reference element to identify
the referent's type.

You can place additional information concerning the generation of an
EncryptedData or EncryptedKey in the optional EncryptionProperties element. For example, this information could include a date/time stamp created
when encryption occurred or the serial number of cryptographic hardware
in use during encryption. The Target attribute identifies the EncryptedData
or EncryptedKey structure being augmented.

```
<!-- EncryptionProperties Schema -->

<element name='EncryptionProperties'
         type='xenc:EncryptionPropertiesType'/>
<complexType name='EncryptionPropertiesType'>
```

```
 <sequence>
   <element ref='xenc:EncryptionProperty'
            maxOccurs='unbounded'/>
 </sequence>
 <attribute name='Id' type='ID' use='optional'/>
</complexType>


<element name='EncryptionProperty'
         type='xenc:EncryptionPropertyType'/>
<complexType name='EncryptionPropertyType' mixed='true'>
  <choice maxOccurs='unbounded'>
    <any namespace='##other' processContents='lax'/>
  </choice>
  <attribute name='Target' type='anyURI' use='optional'/>
  <attribute name='Id' type='ID' use='optional'/>
  <anyAttribute
   namespace="http://www.w3.org/XML/1998/namespace"/>
</complexType>
```

The anyAttribute element in the schema permits inclusion of any attribute or attributes in the XML namespace, such as xml:space, xml:lang, or xml:base.

## 15.2.4  The EncryptedData Element

The EncryptedData element is the core element of the syntax. Not only does its CipherData child contain the encrypted data, but this element also replaces the encrypted element or serves as the new document root. Its syntax follows:

```
<!-- EncryptedData schema -->

<element name='EncryptedData'
         type='xenc:EncryptedDataType'/>
<complexType name='EncryptedDataType'>
  <complexContent>
    <extension base='xenc:EncryptedType'/>
  </complexContent>
</complexType>
```

## 15.2.5   The EncryptedKey Element

```
Identifier:
   http://www.w3.org/2001/04/xmlenc#EncryptedKey
```

You can use the preceding identifier with a ds:RetrievalMethod element to identify the referent's type.

You use the EncryptedKey element to transport encryption keys encrypted with a key-encrypting key from the originator to a recipient. You can use it as a stand-alone XML document, place it within an application document, or include it inside an EncryptedData element as a child of a ds:KeyInfo element. The key value is encrypted to the recipient(s). See Figure 15-3.

The syntax for EncryptedKey follows:

```
<!-- EncryptedKey schema -->

<element name='EncryptedKey'
        type='xenc:EncryptedKeyType'/>
<complexType name='EncryptedKeyType'>
  <complexContent>
    <extension base='xenc:EncryptedType'>
      <sequence>
        <element ref='xenc:ReferenceList'
                minOccurs='0'/>
        <element name='CarriedKeyName' type='string'
                minOccurs='0'/>
      </sequence>
      <attribute name='Recipient' type='string'
                use='optional'/>
    </extension>
  </complexContent>
</complexType>
```

ReferenceList is an optional element containing pointers to data and keys encrypted using this key. The reference list may contain multiple references to EncryptedKey and EncryptedData elements. (See Section 15.2.6.)

CarriedKeyName is an optional element for associating a user-readable name with the key value. You can use it to reference the key using the ds:KeyName element within ds:KeyInfo. Unlike with an ID type attribute value, the same

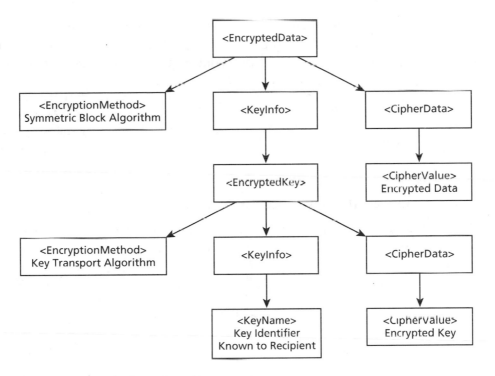

**Figure 15-3** Typical enveloped key structure

CarriedKeyName label may occur multiple times within a single document. The value of the key should remain the same in all EncryptedKey elements identified with the same CarriedKeyName label within a single XML document. Note, however, that the key may have been encrypted in different ways in different EncryptedKey elements.

Recipient is an optional attribute that contains a hint about the recipient for which this encrypted key value is intended. Its contents are application dependent.

The Type attribute inherited from EncryptedType can specify the type of the encrypted key if necessary.

### Reference by the ds:RetrievalMethod Element
Using ds:RetrievalMethod with a Type of "http://www.w3.org/2001/04/xmlenc#EncryptedKey" provides a way to link to an EncryptedKey element containing the key needed to decrypt the data. The ds:RetrievalMethod with this type is always a child of the ds:KeyInfo element and may appear multiple

times. If more than one instance of a ds:RetrievalMethod occurs in a ds:
KeyInfo of this type, then the EncryptedKey objects must contain the same
key value, possibly encrypted in different ways and/or for different recipients.

```
<!--

    <attribute name='Type' type='anyURI' use='optional'
    fixed='http://www.w3.org/2001/04/xmlenc#EncryptedKey' />
-->
```

## 15.2.6   The ReferenceList Element

ReferenceList is an element that contains pointers from an EncryptedKey to
items encrypted by that key. Its schema follows:

```
<!-- ReferenceList schema -->

<element name='ReferenceList'>
  <complexType>
    <sequence>
      <element name='DataReference'
               type='xenc:ReferenceType'
               minOccurs='0' maxOccurs='unbounded'/>
      <element name='KeyReference'
               type='xenc:ReferenceType'
               minOccurs='0' maxOccurs='unbounded'/>
    </sequence>
  </complexType>
</element>

<complexType name='ReferenceType'>
  <sequence>
    <any namespace='##other' minOccurs='0'
                             maxOccurs='unbounded'/>
  </sequence>
  <attribute name='URI' type='anyURI' use='optional'/>
</complexType>
```

You use DataReference elements to refer to EncryptedData elements encrypted
using the key defined in the enclosing EncryptedKey element. Multiple
DataReference elements can point to multiple EncryptedData elements
encrypted by the same key.

You use KeyReference elements to refer to EncryptedKey objects encrypted using the key defined in the enclosing EncryptedKey element. Multiple KeyReference elements can point to multiple EncryptedKey elements encrypted by the same key.

Both types of references may include a child Transforms element to aid the recipient in retrieving the pointed-to EncryptedKey and/or EncryptedData elements. These elements could include information such as XPath Transforms, decompression Transforms, or information on how to retrieve the objects from a document storage facility. For example:

```
<ReferenceList>
  <DataReference URI="#invoice34">
    <ds:Transforms>
      <ds:Transform
Algorithm="http://www.w3.org/TR/1999/REC-xpath-19991116">
        <ds:XPath
          xmlns:xenc="http://www.w3.org/2001/04/xmlenc#">
          self::xenc:EncryptedData[@Id="example1"]
        </ds:XPath>
      </ds:Transforms>
    </ds:Transform>
  </DataReference>
</ReferenceList>
```

## 15.2.7 Extensions to the ds:KeyInfo Element

You can obtain the keying material that decrypting needs in three ways:

1. The EncryptedData or EncryptedKey element you are trying to decrypt can specify the associated keying material through a child of ds:KeyInfo. You can use all of the child elements of ds:KeyInfo specified in [XMLDSIG] along with the EncryptedKey and AgreementMethod added in [XMLENC]. (See Chapter 13.) Note the following:

   a. Using the literal, unprotected ds:KeyValue to transport the encryption key is not recommended.

   b. Support of ds:KeyName to refer to an EncryptedKey CarriedKeyName is recommended.

c. Support for same-document ds:RetrievalMethod is required.

d. Encryption applications must support EncryptedKey.

2. A detached (not inside ds:KeyInfo) EncryptedKey element can specify the EncryptedData or EncryptedKey to which its decrypted key will apply via a DataReference or KeyReference (see Section 15.2.6).

3. The recipient may determine the keying material for the application based on context; in this case, the transmitted XML does not have to provide the keying material.

## 15.3    Encryption Examples

The following examples are based on a hypothetical medical patient record:

```
<MedInfo xmlns='http://x.example/medinfo'>
  <Identification>
    <Name>John Q. Doe, Jr<Name/>
    <Address>...</Address><SSN>000-00-0000</SSN>
  </Identification>
  <Medical>...</Medical>
  <Financial>
    <Insurance>...</Insurance>
    <Billing>...History...</Billing>
    <Payment>
      <Type>CreditCard</Type>
      <Number>0000 1111 2222 3333</Number>
      <Expires>04/02</Expires>
    </Payment>
  </Financial>
</MedInfo>
```

This XML contains information characterized by different levels of sensitivity and to which different people probably have different access permissions. For example, a person's name and address is usually considered less sensitive than his or her financial information, which in turn is usually considered less sensitive than information about the individual's medical problems and the prognosis for any chronic conditions. Some medical personnel, however, may have access to that medical information but not to the generally less sensitive financial information.

### 15.3.1 Encrypting XML Elements

The medical history and credit card number of our hypothetical patient John are sensitive information that should be controlled. To keep them confidential, you can encrypt them as shown in Example 15-1.

***Example 15-1*** *XML element encryption*

```
<MedInfo xmlns='http://x.example/medinfo'
         xmlns:xenc='http://www.w3.org/2001/04/xmlenc#'
         xmlns:ds='http://www.w3.org/2000/09/xmldsig#'>
  <Identification>
    <Name>John Q. Doe, Jr<Name/>
    <Address>...</Address><SSN>000-00-0000</SSN>
  </Identification>
  <xenc:EncryptedData
    Type='http://www.w3.org/2001/04/xmlenc#Element'>
    <ds:KeyInfo><ds:KeyName>Medical</ds:KeyName></ds:KeyValue>
    <xenc:CipherData><xenc:CipherValue>...
    </xenc:CipherValue></encx:CipherData>
  </xenc:EncryptedData>
  <Financial>
    <Insurance>...</Insurance>
    <Billing>...History...</Billing>
    <xenc:EncryptedData
      Type='http://www.w3.org/2001/04/xmlenc#Element'>
      <ds:KeyInfo><ds:KeyName>Pay</ds:KeyName></ds:KeyValue>
      <xenc:CipherData><xenc:CipherValue>...
      </xenc:CipherValue></xenc:CipherData>
    </xenc:EncryptedData>
  </Financial>
</MedInfo>
```

By encrypting the entire Payment and Medical elements from their start to end tags, you hide the identities of the elements (although this hiding would be of little importance if the schema is publicly known, for example). The CipherData elements contain the encrypted serialization of the Medical and Payment elements.

### 15.3.2   Encrypting XML Element Content

The mere fact that someone has a credit card or medical information probably isn't very sensitive, just as everyone in the file might have a Social Security number. On the other hand, the actual credit card number, medical records content, and Social Security number might be more sensitive. As an alternative strategy, you could use element content encryption, as shown in Example 15-2.

**Example 15-2**   *XML element content encryption*

```
<MedInfo xmlns='http://x.example/medinfo'
         xmlns:xenc='http://www.w3.org/2001/04/xmlenc#'
         xmlns:s='http://www.w3.org/2000/09/xmldsig#'>
  <Identification>
    <Name>John Q. Doe, Jr<Name/>
    <Address>...</Address>
    <SSN><xenc:EncryptedData
         Type='http://www.w3.org/2001/04/xmlenc#Content'>
      <ds:KeyInfo><ds:KeyName>SSN</ds:KeyName></ds:Keyinfo>
      <xenc:CipherValue><xenc:CipherData>...
      </xenc:CipherData></xencenc:CipherValue>
    </xenc:EncryptedData></SSN>
  </Identification>
  <Medical><xenc:EncryptedData
           Type='http://www.w3.org/2001/04/xmlenc#Content'>
    <ds:KeyInfo><ds:KeyName>Medical</ds:KeyName></ds:KeyValue>
    <xenc:CipherData><xenc:CipherValue>...
    </xenc:CipherValue></xenc:CipherData>
  </xenc:EncryptedData></Medical>
  <Financial>
    <Insurance>...</Insurance>
    <Billing>...History...</Billing>
    <Payment>
      <Type>CreditCard</Type>
      <Number><xenc:EncryptedData
              Type='http://www.w3.org/2001/04/xmlenc#Content'>
        <ds:KeyInfo><ds:KeyName>Pay</ds:KeyName></ds:KeyValue>
        <xenc:CipherData><xenc:CipherValue>...
        </xenc:CipherValue></xenc:CipherData>
```

```
      </xenc:EncryptedData></Number>
      <Expires>04/02</Expires>
    </Payment>
  </Financial>
</MedInfo>
```

In Example 15-2, the element names SSN, Medical, and Number are in the clear, but their character content is encrypted. Although Examples 15-1 and 15-2 each use a single strategy, there is no reason that you could not mix them, keeping some elements and some element contents encrypted. In both cases, a different key is shown for each field so that processes authorized for some, but not all, data can receive keys for just those data.

### 15.3.3   Encrypting Arbitrary Data

If an application requires encrypting some arbitrary, possibly binary data or the entirety of an XML document, then it can just treat all data involved as an octet stream. The resulting EncryptedData can act as the top-level element of a new document or can be embedded in a larger document. For example, for an encrypted XML document, you might have the following:

```
<?xml version='1.0'?>
<EncryptedData xmlns='http://www.w3.org/2001/04/xmlenc#'
               xmlns:ds='http://www.w3.org/2000/09/xmldsig#'
               MimeType='text/xml'>
  <ds:KeyInfo><ds:KeyName>docKey123</s:KeyName></ds:Keyinfo>
  <CipherData>
    <CipherValue>...1sYyMjiAgEfe3urH...</CipherValue>
  </CipherData>
</EncryptedData>
```

For an encrypted JPEG with the cipher text stored remotely, you might have this code:

```
...
  <EncryptedData xmlns='http://www.w3.org/2001/04/xmlenc#'
                 xmlns:ds='http://www.w3.org/2000/09/xmldsig#'
                 MimeType-'image/jpeg'
                 Encoding='base64'>
    <ds:KeyInfo><ds:KeyName>foo</ds:KeyName></ds:KeyInfo>
```

```
    <CipherData>
      <CipherReference URI='http://bar.example/file.jpg'/>
    </CipherData>
  </EncryptedData>
...
```

### 15.3.4  Super-Encryption

An XML document may contain zero or more EncryptedData elements. EncryptedData cannot be the parent or child of another EncryptedData element. However, the actual encrypted data can be anything, including EncryptedData and EncryptedKey elements.

Encrypting previously encrypted information is called super-encryption. During super-encryption of an EncryptedData or EncryptedKey element, you must encrypt the entire element. Encrypting only the content of these elements or encrypting selected child elements is an invalid instance under the XML Encryption schema.

As an example, consider the following:

```
<Foo>
  <EncryptedData Id='ED1'
                 xmlns='http://www.w3.org/2001/04/xmlenc#'
                 Type='http://www.w3.org/2001/04/xmlenc#Element'>
    <CipherData>
      <CipherValue>originalEncryptedData</CipherValue>
    </CipherData>
  </EncryptedData>
</Foo>
```

A valid super-encryption of the subdocument that would be found by the XPath Expression

```
//xenc:EncryptedData[@Id='ED1']
```

would be

```
<Foo>
  <EncryptedData Id='ED2'
                 xmlns='http://www.w3.org/2001/04/xmlenc#'
                 Type='http://www.w3.org/2001/04/xmlenc#Element'>
```

```
   <CipherData>
     <CipherValue>newLongerEncryptedData</CipherValue>
   </CipherData>
  </EncryptedData>
 </pay:PaymentInfo>
```

where *newLongerEncryptedData* is the base-64 encoding of the cipher text
octets resulting from encrypting the EncryptedData element with Id='ED1'.

### 15.3.5  Referenced EncryptedKey

The following EncryptedData structure is very similar to some of those given
previously. This time, however, the key is referenced using a ds:Retrieval-
Method:

```
[L01] <EncryptedData Id='ED'
        xmlns='http://www.w3.org/2001/04/xmlenc#'
        xmlns:ds='http://www.w3.org/2000/09/xmldsig#'>
[L02]   <EncryptionMethod
       Algorithm='http://www.w3.org/2001/04/xmlenc#aes128-cbc'/>
[L03]   <ds:KeyInfo>
[L04]     <ds:RetrievalMethod URI='#FK'
            Type="http://www.w3.org/2001/04/xmlenc#EncryptedKey"/>
[L05]     <ds:KeyName>FooKey</ds:KeyName>
[L06]   </ds:KeyInfo>
[L07]   <CipherData><CipherValue>DEADBEEF
          </CipherValue></CipherData>
[L08] </EncryptedData>
```

[L02] This "AES-128-CBC" is a symmetric key block cipher.

[L03] The "AES" key is located at "#EK".

[L04] ds:RetrievalMethod indicates the location of a key with type http://
www.w3.org/2001/04/xmlenc#EncryptedKey.

[L05] ds:KeyName provides an alternative method of identifying the key to
decrypt the CipherData. Both ds:KeyName and ds:KeyRetrievalMethod
should identify the same key value, and they could identify the same key.

Within the same XML document, there exists an EncryptedKey element that
is referenced from [L04]:

```
[L09] <EncryptedKey Id='EK'
                     xmlns='http://www.w3.org/2001/04/xmlenc#'
                     xmlns:ds='http://www.w3.org/2000/09/xmldsig#'>
[L10]    <EncryptionMethod
          Algorithm="http://www.w3.org/2001/04/xmlenc#rsa-1_5"/>
[L11]    <ds:KeyInfo >
[L12]      <ds:KeyName>John Smith</ds:KeyName>
[L13]    </ds:KeyInfo>
[L14]    <CipherData><CipherValue>...
          abf396q0tFyenuyEhL65uQ==</CipherValue></CipherData>
[L15]    <ReferenceList>
[L16]      <DataReference URI='#ED'/>
[L17]    </ReferenceList>
[L18]    <CarriedKeyName>FooKey</CarriedKeyName>
[L19]  </EncryptedKey>
```

[L09] The EncryptedKey element is similar to the EncryptedData element, except that the plain text is normally a key value.

[L10] The EncryptionMethod is a key transport algorithm based on the RSA public key algorithm.

[L12] The ds:KeyName of "John Smith" is a property of the key necessary for decrypting (using RSA) the CipherData of this EncryptedKey.

[L14] The CipherData's CipherValue is the base-64 encoding of an octet sequence that results from encrypting the plain text data for the Encrypted-Key. You use the EncryptedKey's EncryptionMethod algorithm to encrypt these octets. The algorithm does not imply the type of the octets.

[L15–17] A ReferenceList identifies the objects (DataReference and KeyReference) encrypted with this key. The DataReference contains a list of references to data encrypted by the symmetric key carried within this EncryptedKey element.

[L18] You use the CarriedKeyName element to identify the encrypted key value. You can reference it by the KeyName element in ds:KeyInfo elsewhere. Because ID attribute values must be unique within a document, Carried-KeyName can be identical in several EncryptedKey structures containing the same key value that has been encrypted for different recipients.

## 15.4    Processing Flow

This section describes the sequence of operations for XML encryption and decryption processing. The XML Encryption Recommendation [XMLENC] attempts to define the boundary between the application and an encrypter or decrypter, but it remains flexible because some steps may be carried out by either one. Discussion of cryptographic and directly related processing, where XMLDSIG is used as an analogy, appears in the subsections "Encryption Processing" and "Decryption Processing." Discussion of other "application" processing appears in the subsections "Pre-encryption Processing," "Post-encryption Processing," "Pre-decryption Processing," and "Post-decryption Processing."

### 15.4.1  Encryption

The following steps need to be performed for successful XML encryption.

**Pre-encryption Processing**

Obtain the data to be encrypted as an octet sequence. If the data to be directly encrypted is an XML element or XML element content, the octet sequence is a UTF-8 encoded string representation of the element or its content, respectively. To obtain this representation, you can use a standardized XML canonicalization algorithm (see Chapter 9). Consider using Canonical XML to serialize the data, especially if the XML will be decrypted in an environment where different namespace declaration or xml namespace attributes are in scope—this difference may change the meaning of the data in an undesirable way. For many purposes, almost any printing to parseable UTF-8 encoded XML will work well.

Other processing may be done, such as compressing the octet sequence. To assure interoperability, the Type attribute of the resulting EncryptedData or EncryptedKey must indicate that such processing has taken place; the processing can then be undone upon decryption. You also need to ensure that the recipient will implement your Type.

**Encryption Processing**

For each data item or key to be encrypted, do the following:

1. Select the algorithm (and parameters) to use in encrypting the item.

2. Obtain the encryption keying material.

    a. If the key will be encrypted, recursively apply this process to create an EncryptedKey element.

    b. If the key will be represented, construct the appropriate ds:KeyInfo element.

    c. If the key was encrypted, the ds:KeyInfo may have the EncryptedKey as a child or may point to it with a ds:RetrievalMethod or with a ds:KeyName referring to a CarriedKeyName in the EncryptedKey.

    d. If the key resulted from a key agreement algorithm, the ds:KeyInfo will have or point to an AgreementMethod child, which may itself have keying information children.

3. Obtain the octet sequence to encrypt.

4. Encrypt the sequence using the key and encryption algorithm. If the algorithm requires it, prefix the cipher text with the appropriate initialization vector (IV).

5. Construct the CipherData element.

    a. If the octet sequence produced in this step will be enveloped, it is encoded in base-64 and becomes the content of a CipherValue element.

    b. If you plan to store the octet sequence produced in this step elsewhere, construct a CipherReference element by which the recipient can retrieve it. (This step may require constructing a Transforms element.)

6. Build the EncryptedData or EncryptedKey element. This element will include the CipherData child element. It may also include Encryption-Method, KeyInfo, and/or EncryptionProperties child elements, as well as Type, Id, MimeType, and/or Encoding attributes. An EncryptedKey element may include ReferenceList and/or CarriedKeyName child elements and/or a Recipient attribute. (These items are not permitted with EncryptedData.)

### Post-encryption Processing

1. If the data being encrypted consists of an XML element or XML element content, the processing removes the unencrypted data and replaces it with the new XML structure using the same encoding as the parent XML document.

2. If the data being encrypted consists of an external octet sequence, you probably want to use the EncryptedData element by including or referencing the encrypted data as the top-level element in a new XML document or insert it into another XML document or database (this processing is application dependent).

### 15.4.2   Decryption

Perform the following steps for successful XML decryption.

**Pre-decryption Processing**

To decrypt each EncryptedData or EncryptedKey, parse the element and obtain the EncryptionMethod, KeyInfo, and CipherData elements from it or from the application.

**Decryption Processing**

1. Determine the encryption algorithm and parameters.

2. Obtain the decryption keying information.

   a. If an AgreementMethod represents this information, the encryption algorithm and parameters may affect the resulting key, particularly its size.

   b. If the decryption keying information is either represented by an EncryptedKey as the child of the KeyInfo element or pointed to by a RetrievalMethod or named by a KeyName, recursively apply this process to obtain the key.

3. Obtain the data to decrypt.

   a. If CipherData has a CipherValue child, base-64 decode its contents.

   b. If CipherData has a CipherReference child, either retrieve the data and apply any Transforms, or use an equivalent method for the application's purposes—for example, by retrieving a copy of the cipher text from a local cache.

4. If the encryption algorithm and parameters specify it, strip any IV from the data and provide it to the algorithm. Decrypt the cipher data with the encryption algorithm, parameters, and keying material.

### Post-decryption Processing

1. If the plain text is a key, save it for processing the associated Encrypted-Data or EncryptedKey.

2. When the data is XML, the resulting octets are interpreted as an UTF-8 encoded string of XML characters representing an element or element content. If the plain text comes from an EncryptedData structure and the Type is "Element" or "Content," use the resulting characters to replace the EncryptedData element. If the target document is not in UTF-8, re-encode the characters with the encoding of the parent XML document.

3. For other Type values (e.g., proprietary compressed data), handle them according to the Type. If the Type is unknown, the application should indicate an error.

### 15.4.3  XML Encryption

The preceding specification presumes that the data to be encrypted are processed as an octet sequence. When encrypting XML, the application is responsible, as part of pre-encryption processing, for serializing the XML into an octet sequence that will be useful subsequent to decryption. For instance, if the application wishes to encode/compress the data into some XML packaging format, it needs to marshal the XML accordingly and identify the resulting type with the optional Type attribute of the EncryptedData element. The likelihood of interoperable decryption and subsequent use will depend on the decrypting application's support for a given Type. In addition, if processing of the data will occur both before and after decryption (e.g., XML Signature [XMLDSIG] validation or XSLT Transform [XSLT]), the encrypter must be careful to preserve information necessary for that process's success.

## 15.5    Encryption Security Considerations

This section discusses some special security considerations in XML Encryption.

### 15.5.1  Combining XMLDSIG and XML Encryption

Special considerations apply when you use both authentication and confidentiality together. Refer to Chapter 16 for more details.

### 15.5.2   Information Revealed

As discussed in Chapter 2, when you share a symmetric key amongst multiple recipients, you can safely use that key only for data intended for all recipients. That is, any recipient not sent the data might intercept the information and decrypt it.

Application designers should not reveal any information in parameters or algorithm identifiers (e.g., in plain text URIs) that weakens the encryption or tends to compromise the plain text.

### 15.5.3   Care with Algorithms and Expressions

Take care when executing or interpreting algorithms, executable content such as XSLT stylesheets, or even XPath expressions. Such actions can consume unacceptable amounts of time, memory, or other resources, cause errors, or, in the worst case, release viruses or other malware. Some clients may be unable to decrypt even properly encrypted material that has been correctly encoded into XML because of algorithms or other optional capabilities they do not implement, URIs they cannot or will not dereference, insufficient resources, policy, or other reasons.

Stick to the simplest options, preferably those whose implementation is mandatory or at least recommended, to ensure the widest interoperability for your applications.

# 16 | Combining Encryption and Signature

It is common to have data that must be authenticated to one or more recipients, for which all or parts of the data must remain confidential. While it is difficult to formulate general rules that always apply to such cases, Section 16.1 gives some of the general considerations. Section 16.2 describes a special Decryption Transform that makes it easier to determine which cipher text to decrypt before verifying a signature.

## 16.1 General Considerations

Let's look at the simplest case, signing and encrypting a single block of data. Should we encrypt and then sign or should we sign and then encrypt? You need to examine each case individually to determine the best option. Even in the case of a single data block, multiple possibilities exist. The following sections describe three general possibilities along with their advantages and disadvantages.

**Note**

> In the absence of other considerations, signing and then encrypting is the best choice. Evidence indicates that, for certain secure symmetric encryption algorithms and secure symmetric authentication algorithms, either authenticating and then encrypting or encrypting and then authenticating can lead to compromise when subject to certain attacks [Krawczyk]. This weakness is not present if you use either CBC chained or stream encryption, so the types of encryption described in Chapter 18 are safe in this regard. Nevertheless, this point demonstrates that blindly combining secure cryptographic mechanisms can result in an insecure system.

### 16.1.1   Encryption of Signed Data and Signature

Suppose you have some signed data, and that data and the Signature element are all encrypted into a cipher text described by an EncryptedData element. Figure 16-1 shows a maximally detached case, and Figure 16-2 shows a maximally enveloping case. (Mixed detached and enveloped cases are also possible.)

**Advantages**

• This arrangement hides the maximum amount of data, making the encryption the most effective. When some forms of public key cryptography are in use, the signature key identifies the signer. In that case, the signature key must be encrypted, as it is here, to conceal the identity of the signer.

• This nesting hides the Signature element, preventing failed attempts to verify it while the data it signed as plain text remain cipher text.

• Because the signature covers the plain text, it is still verifiable after removing the encryption; it can also be kept with the data if desired. It is possible to reencrypt the signed data in the same or a different way after decrypting the signed data.

**Disadvantages**

• If the data has been damaged, you must go through the effort to decrypt it before you can check the signature and find that the data is damaged.

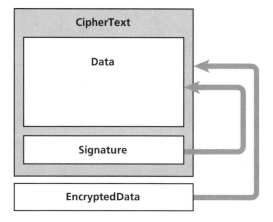

**Figure 16-1** | Encryption of signed data and Signature (detached)

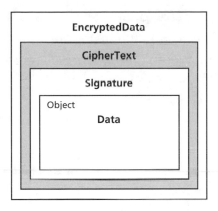

**Figure 16-2** | Encryption of signed data and Signature (enveloping)

- In many encryption systems based on public keys, anyone can encrypt a message to any recipient. Care should be taken in designing a system such that a naive recipient will not be misled into believing that, because data is encrypted to them, the data were originally sent to the recipient. For example, assume Alice creates the message "Let's elope," signs it, and then encrypts it for and sends it to Bob. For whatever reason, Bob decrypts the message, then reencrypts it for and sends it to Charlie. This transfer could cause confusion. As a solution to this specific problem, you might simply include intended recipient and date information in the signed data.

**Soapbox**

The second disadvantage cited here doesn't actually relate to the encryption or even to the existence of the data in digital form. If Alice manually signs a two-word message on a piece of paper and physically mails it to Bob, he could physically forward it to Charlie. Somehow, performing this transfer digitally seems to confuse people. Some [Davis] consider this issue to be a critical problem that should be fixed by changing basic formats. Most such complaints come from a document view, usually based on electronic mail examples (see Appendix E). As most of the data in electronic mail is intended for human interpretation without context, this perspective pushes your thinking in a document direction. From the secure protocol point of view, a basic secure design criterion calls for protection against the replay or forwarding of parts of messages, or similar actions, by malicious parties or through error. Unfortunately, human languages, such as English, were not designed with these criteria in mind.

### 16.1.2   Encryption of Signed Data But Not Signature

An intermediate possibility, if the signature is detached, is to encrypt only the data signed, but not the Signature element (see Figure 16-3). The encryption could be enveloped without changing the advantages and disadvantages associated with this strategy.

**Advantages**

- Because the signature covers the plain text, it remains verifiable after removing the encryption; it can also be kept with the data if desired. It is possible to reencrypt the signed data in the same or a different way after decrypting it.

**Disadvantages**

- Placing the Signature element outside the encryption makes the Reference DigestMethod and DigestValue information accessible in plain text. This approach may reveal information that the encryption is intended to hide.

- If the data has been damaged, you must go through the effort to decrypt it before you can check the signature and find that it fails.

- The Signature key may reveal signer identity information that should have remained concealed.

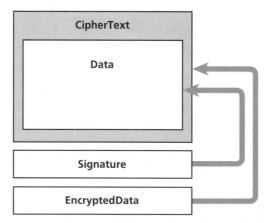

**Figure 16-3** | Encryption of signed data but not of Signature (detached)

### 16.1.3   Signing Encrypted Data

In this situation, the cipher text and EncryptedData element are signed. Figure 16-4 shows a maximally detached example. As described in Section 16.1.1, maximally enveloped and mixed versions are possible.

### Advantages

- If someone has tampered with the data, you will find out at an early stage—when the signature fails—without having to go through the effort of decrypting it.

### Disadvantages

- The signature covers the cipher text and is invalidated when the data is decrypted. Thus, the cipher text and decryption key must be remembered or rederived to be able to store the data with a verifiable signature. Furthermore, to demonstrate the signature to a third party requires revealing the decryption key. This approach might compromise other data encrypted with the same or a related key.

- The Signature key may reveal signer identity information that should have remained concealed.

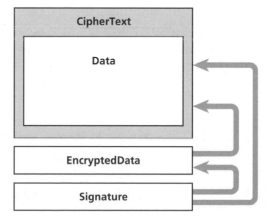

**Figure 16-4**   Signature of cipher text and EncryptedData (detached)

## 16.2     The Decryption Transform

The Decryption Transform makes it easier to verify XML signatures over data when some of the data has been encrypted before and some after the signature was applied. The signature verifier needs to know which parts to decrypt and which parts to leave encrypted when trying to verify the signature. (This section is based on a W3C Working Draft [Decrypt] but subsequent recommendations will likely have similar characteristics and limitations.)

### 16.2.1   Introduction to the Decryption Transform

The Decryption Transform works as follows: A Transform is added to appropriate Reference elements in a SignedInfo or Manifest element (see Chapter 10). The Transform takes a list of encrypted parts of the data as parameters. When validating the signature, any other encrypted data encountered within the digested data are decrypted; those listed in the Transform are left encrypted. The concept is simple, but to precisely describe the processing and limitations becomes more complicated.

In protocol applications (see Appendix E), the protocol syntax typically specifies how, in what order, and over which parts of the protocol message signature and/or encryption operations are applied. Therefore, the general mechanism of the Decryption Transform is not essential, although it could be used in certain circumstances. Even in cases where the protocol is very flexible, it would normally be designed to be self-documenting. That is, some indicators would be securely included that enable recipients participating in the protocol to know which decryptions and signature verifications they should perform in what order. Where data of an unknown security structure are forwarded within a protocol message, the data can normally be treated as opaque without further analysis.

For document applications (see Appendix E), the data is usually more free form, and it is desirable for the status of data to be apparent outside of any protocol context. Furthermore, later, independent processes might choose to encrypt parts of the signed data so that the signature no longer verifies. Thus the Decryption Transform is clearly applicable in some document cases.

### 16.2.2  Decryption Transform Syntax

The algorithm identifier for the Decryption Transform is

```
http://www.w3.org/2001/04/decrypt#
```

which is also the namespace for parameter elements to the Transform. This identifier serves as the value of the Algorithm attribute of a Transform element. It takes, as explicit parameters, an arbitrary number of Except elements, each of which has a URI attribute that points to data that were encrypted during calculation of the signature. These URIs are limited to same-document URIs that point at EncryptedData elements. Example 16-1 shows a Reference element with a Decryption Transform.

**Example 16-1**  *Decryption Transform*

```
<Reference URI="" xmlns="http://www.w3.org/2000/09/xmldsig#">
  <Transforms>
    <Transform Algorithm=
"http://www.w3.org/2000/09/xmldsig#enveloped-signature"/>
    <Transform Algorithm="http://www.w3.org/2001/04/decrypt#"
              xmlns:dct="http://www.w3.org/2001/04/decrypt#">
      <dct:Except URI="#foo"><dct:Except URI="#bar">
    </Transform>
  </Transforms>
  <DigestMethod Algorithm=
"http://www.w3.org/2001/04/xmldsig-more#md5"/>
  <DigestValue>qZk+NkcGgWq6PiVxeFDCbJ==</DigestValue>
</ds:Reference>
```

Following is the schema for the Except element of the Decryption Transform:

```
Schema Definition:
<?xml version="1.0" encoding="utf-8"?>
<!DOCTYPE schema  PUBLIC "-//W3C//DTD XMLSchema 200102//EN"
         "http://www.w3.org/2001/XMLSchema.dtd"
[ <!ENTITY % p ''>
  <!ENTITY % s ''>
]>
<schema xmlns='http://www.w3.org/2001/XMLSchema' version='0.1'
        xmlns:dt='http://www.w3.org/2001/04/decrypt#'
```

```
        targetNamespace='http://www.w3.org/2001/04/decrypt#'
        elementFormDefault='qualified'>


<element name="Except" type="dt:ExceptType"/>
<complexType name='ExceptType'>
  <attribute name='Id' type='ID' use='optional'/>
  <attribute name='URI' type='anyURI' use='required'/>
</complexType>
```

### 16.2.3  Decryption Transform Processing

Now we get to the tricky part—how to rigorously specify decrypting parts of XML in the XPath data model while minimally changing its serialization in other ways.

The Decryption Transform requires an XPath node-set as input. If the previous Transform or the Reference URI yields an octet stream, it must be parsed. This requirement is only reasonable, as the Transform will look for the EncryptedData elements within the input data. Those that are referenced by the Except parameters are left alone; the others are decrypted and the results plugged in. The XPath data model, on which XML Encryption and Signature are based, does not provide any mechanism for performing "transplant surgery" on an XPath node–set, however. As a consequence, much of the processing is defined in terms of substitutions within and augmentations of an octet sequence. In fact, an implementation is merely required to get the same result as it would obtain by following the specified steps. As long as it meets this requirement, it may implement processing in a different fashion.

1. Serialize the input node-set as specified in the data pipeline discussion in Chapter 10. Remember what part of the resulting octet string came from each EncryptedData that is to be decrypted. If the first element serialized is an EncryptedData, it must be of type "http://www.w3.org/2001/04/xmlenc#Element."

2. Replace the serializations of the EncryptedData elements to be decrypted with the serializations of their decryption.

3. Preserve the namespace context of the input node-set by surrounding the octet string with a dummy element. Include in that element all ancestor namespace declarations in scope for the top element of the

node set. (This effort requires that the node-set have a single root; that is, one node must be the ancestor of every other node and every attribute and namespace declaration in the node set.) For example, prefix the octet string with "<dummy . . .>" where ". . ." is the namespace declarations, and suffix it with "</dummy>".

4. Preserve the entity context of the input node, if any, by prefixing the octet string with a Document Type Definition having those entity declarations.

5. Parse the resulting octet string and output the resulting XPath node-set.

## 16.2.4  Decryption Transform Limitations

The concept of a way to protect signed data such that later modifications can be undone and the signature still verified is quite audacious. Even when it is limited to encryption of XML in the same document as the signature, it cannot be done perfectly.

The processing description given in Section 16.2.3 listed a number of caveats. In addition, the following limitations exist:

- The Decryption Transform succeeds only if it has access to the keys and algorithms needed to decrypt the data in question.

- EncryptedKey elements are not handled.

- Cases of super-encryption of data already encrypted when the Signature element was formed are not handled. (Super-encryption of data unencrypted at signature time can be handled by multiple decryption Transform elements.)

# Part VI | Algorithms

Throughout both XML Digital Signatures, covered in Part III, and XML Encryption, covered in Part V, we have noted provisions for referring to algorithms using URIs as well-known names. These include both cryptographic algorithms, which actually do the bit scrambling and unscrambling of cryptography, and algorithms operating at the XML or text level. For most types of algorithms, one or a few algorithms are mandatory to implement—their use maximizes the possibility of interoperability. Other algorithms are optional. The URI naming convention is so general that proprietary or nonstandard user-specified algorithms are easily accommodated though their use decreases the chances for interoperability.

Chapter 17 provides an overview of the types of algorithms found in XML Security; Chapter 18 offers specifications for each cryptographic algorithms used, and Chapter 19 does the same for non-cryptographic algorithms.

# 17 | Overview of Algorithms

XML Security elements require the specification of a variety of algorithms to fill various roles, such as signature generation and data encryption. Section 17.1 describes the uniform syntax used for this specification. Section 17.2 presents an overview of the various algorithmic roles and the elements that fill them, together with tables of some summary information on the algorithms.

Chapters 18 and 19 provide additional details on specific cryptographic and non-cryptographic algorithms, respectively.

## 17.1    Algorithm Syntax

XML Security represents algorithms that it uses via an element with an Algorithm attribute. This attribute's value is a URI (see Chapter 7) that indicates the particular algorithm to use, whereas the element name indicates the role played by the algorithm.

Each algorithm has some implicit inputs or parameters, depending on its role. A list of such roles and their implicit inputs appears in Section 17.2.

Some algorithms also take explicit parameters provided by the element or text content of the algorithm role element, as specified for the particular algorithm. When using element content, parameter elements have algorithm- or role-specific names. These element content names must appear in the main namespace of the XML Digital Signature or XML Encryption standards, that is

```
http://www.w3.org/2000/09/xmldsig#
http://www.w3.org/2001/04/xmlenc#
```

or in an algorithm-specific namespace. (See Figure 17-1.) The order of such input parameter elements, if more than one exist, need not be significant. The algorithm role elements are defined with mixed content to allow text content input.

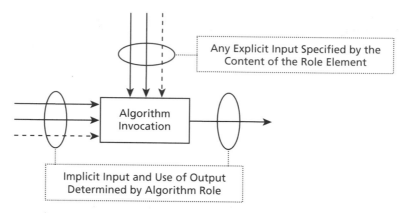

**Figure 17-1** | XML Security algorithm model

As an example, consider the arithmetic algorithm division. We will show it taking two explicit parameters, the dividend and the divisor, but no implicit parameters. In XML Security syntax, filling the role of "ExampleMethod" would be something like

```
<ExampleMethod Algorithm="http://arithmetic.example/division">
    <Dividend>60</Dividend>
    <Divisor>5</Divisor>
</ExampleMethod>
```

which would produce an output of "12". This example is not typical of XML Security, as all of its algorithms take implicit parameters and most of its algorithms don't take any explicit parameters.

**History**

The exact syntax for algorithm-specifying elements was one of the more contentious items in early XMLDSIG design. Because no native or preexisting standard for XML functional notation existed, lengthy arguments were put forth both for and against providing explicit attributes giving the encoding of parameters, element names versus attribute values for algorithm selection, position-dependent child element parameters, element content versus text content for explicit inputs, and more. Once these issues were settled for XMLDSIG, XML Encryption—reasonably enough—just copied the results and used the same syntax.

**Note**

Applications must exercise care when executing the various algorithms that might be specified and when processing any "executable content" that might be provided to such algorithms as parameters, such as XSL Transforms [XSLT]. The algorithms specified in the standards will usually be implemented in a trusted library. Even there, however, perverse parameters might cause unacceptable processing or memory demand. Even more care might be warranted with application-defined algorithms.

## 17.2   Algorithmic Roles

This section lists all of the algorithmic elements/roles in the XML Security specifications in alphabetic order. Table 17-1 summarizes the roles.

Next, for each role, a subsection briefly describes that role and provides an enumeration of its implicit parameters. The subsections also include a table of algorithms that can be used in that role.

**History**

In this chapter, you will notice a difference between XMLDSIG and XML Encryption in the style of URIs for algorithms that can be considered composed of other algorithms.

The XMLDSIG Working Group chose to create single URIs that incorporate all algorithmic elements such as a public key signature algorithm, padding method, and message digest algorithm. Thus we have one URI for RSA SHA1, another URI for RSA-SHA256, and so on. This format could have been expressed as a single RSA algorithm with an explicit parameter that could be SHA1, SHA256, or other message digest algorithm. Using a single URI is less verbose and encourages the use of compatible "cipher suites."

The XML Encryption Working Group chose to move more toward the orthogonal specification of algorithm components that make up an encryption method. For example, AgreementMethod algorithms and OAEP encryption algorithms take an explicit DigestMethod as a parameter rather than encoding this parameter into the AgreementMethod or OAEP-based EncryptionMethod URI. This method is more verbose but more flexible and avoids a combinatorial explosion in the number of URIs if many different combinations might be used.

**Table 17-1** | Algorithm Role Elements

| Role Element/Role Section | Function Section(s) | Possible Parent Elements of the Role Element | Security Service in Which Role Is Used |
|---|---|---|---|
| AgreementMethod Section 17.2.1 | Key Agreement—18.2 | KeyInfo | XMLDSIG XMLENC |
| CanonicalizationMethod Section 17.2.2 | Canonicalization—19.1 | SignedInfo | XMLDSIG |
| DigestMethod Section 17.2.3 | Message Digests—18.1 | AgreementMethod EncryptionMethod[1] Reference | XMLDSIG XMLENC |
| EncryptionMethod Section 17.2.4 | Block Encryption—18.5 Stream Encryption—18.6 Key Transport—18.7 Symmetric Key Wrap—18.8 | EncryptedData EncryptedKey | XMLENC |
| Retrieval Method Chapter 14 | None[2] | KeyInfo | XMLDSIG XMLENC |
| SignatureMethod Section 17.2.5 | Message Authentication—18.3 Signature—18.4 | SignedInfo | XMLDSIG |
| Transform Section 17.2.6 | Canonicalization—19.1 Transform—19.2 | Transforms | XMLDSIG XMLENC |

1. For algorithms specified in this book, DigestMethod appears as a child of Encryption Method only for the RSA-OAEP algorithm, where it is an explicit parameter.
2. RetrievalMethod is not an algorithmic role, even though its name makes it look like it should be one.

Both philosophies are commonly seen and seem to work. This difference probably reflects the different balance of opinions among the members of the two working groups.

## 17.2.1   AgreementMethod

An AgreementMethod algorithm element appears as the child of KeyInfo. It takes as implicit input the type of key to be agreed upon, as described in Section 18.2. As explicit input, it takes a DigestMethod, an optional Nonce, and possibly other explicit inputs. As optional explicit input, it takes compatible sender and recipient keying information. From these inputs, it calculates a shared secret key.

Table 17-2 lists AgreementMethod algorithms.

**Table 17-2** | Key Agreement Algorithms

| Implementation | Name | URI |
|---|---|---|
| XMLDSIG: Optional XMLENC: Optional | Diffie-Hellman | http://www.w3.org/2001/04/xmlenc#dh |

## 17.2.2   CanonicalizationMethod

The CanonicalizationMethod role performs the canonicalizing of the SignedInfo element in a Signature element. It takes the SignedInfo element as an implicit input.

You can also use the canonicalization algorithms with the Transform role element (see Section 17.2.6). Because you can use Transform in both signatures and encryption, implementation requirements for both are listed here. Table 17-3 lists canonicalization algorithms.

## 17.2.3   DigestMethod

The DigestMethod appears as the child of a Reference. As an implicit input, it takes the data referred to by the Reference URI attribute, after processing by any Transform elements specified.

**Table 17-3** | Canonicalization Algorithms

| Implementation | Name/URI |
|---|---|
| XMLDSIG: Required<br>XMLENC: Recommended | Canonical XML<br>http://www.w3.org/TR/2001/REC-xml-c14n-20010315 |
| XMLDSIG: Recommended<br>XMLENC: Required | Canonical XML with Comments<br>http://www.w3.org/TR/2001/REC-xml-c14n-20010315#WithComments |
| XMLDSIG: Required[1]<br>XMLENC: Optional | Exclusive XML Canonicalization<br>http://www.w3.org/TR/xml-exc-c14n# |
| XMLDSIG: Recommended[1]<br>XMLENC: Optional | Exclusive XML Canonicalization with Comments<br>http://www.w3.org/TR/xml-exc-c14n#WithComments |
| XMLDSIG: Not Recommended[2]<br>XMLENC: Not Recommended | Minimal Canonicalization<br>http://www.w3.org/2000/09/xmldsig#minimal |

1. Exclusive XML Canonicalization does not actually appear in the XMLDSIG Recommendation. As explained in Chapter 9, it is the most appropriate canonicalization for signatures where the context of the signed XML may change. Its listing here as "Required" should therefore be considered editorial.

2. As explained in Section 19.1, minimal canonicalization is a text-based canonicalization, not an XML-based algorithm.

The DigestMethod can also appear as the child of EncryptionMethod, if the encryption algorithm specified is RSA-OAEP, or as a child of Agreement-Method. In these cases, its use and implicit inputs are complex, as described in Sections 18.7.2 and 18.2.

Table 17-4 lists DigestMethod algorithms.

**History**

> SHA384 was not popular with XML Security working groups. It does the same work as SHA512, albeit using different constants, and then truncates the output from 512 to 384 bits. For XML applications, where terseness is not a goal, there is little reason not to just use SHA512 instead of SHA384.
>
> Some argument focused on the inclusion of RIPEMD-160. The XML Encryption Working Group decided that without it the list would be too "U.S.-centric" and that Europeans were bound to use it anyway, so a standard URI for it might as well be specified. (While RIPEMD-256 produces a 256-bit message digest, it was not included because it has only 160 bits of strength.)

### 17.2.4  EncryptionMethod

EncryptionMethod appears as a child of either the EncryptedData or EncryptedKey element. In the first case, its role is specified for the encryption and decryption of data. In the second case, its role is normally specified for the encryption and decryption of a key. In both cases, it takes, as implicit inputs, keying information and the plain text to encrypt or cipher text to decrypt. Table 17-5 lists encryption algorithms.

**History**

> The XML Encryption Working Group's logic in setting the implementation requirements of the various key lengths in AES was as follows: For almost all uses, 128 bits is probably adequate. Paranoid developers will want to use 256 bits. Thus, these two lengths are required. A length of 192 bits is stronger than most anyone needs but not strong enough for the paranoid, so who would want to use it? As a result, it is optional to implement.

### 17.2.5  SignatureMethod

SignatureMethod appears as the child of a SignedInfo element. This algorithmic role is applied to the result from CanonicalizationMethod and the keying material, which are its implicit inputs, to yield the SignatureValue. Table 17-6 lists authentication algorithms.

**Table 17-4** | Message Digest Algorithms

| Implementation | Name | URI |
|---|---|---|
| XMLDSIG: Required<br>XMLENC: Required | SHA1 | http://www.w3.org/2000/09/xmldsig#sha1 |
| XMLDSIG: Recommended<br>XMLENC: Recommended | SHA256 | http://www.w3.org/2001/04/xmlenc#sha256 |
| XMLDSIG: Optional<br>XMLENC: Optional | SHA384 | http://www.w3.org/2001/04/xmldsig-more#sha384 |
| XMLDSIG: Optional<br>XMLENC: Optional | SHA512 | http://www.w3.org/2001/04/xmlenc#sha512 |
| XMLDSIG: Optional<br>XMLENC: Optional | RIPEMD160 | http://www.w3.org/2001/04/xmlenc#ripemd160 |
| XMLDSIG: Optional<br>XMLENC: Optional | MD5 | http://www.w3.org/2001/04/xmldsig-more#md5 |

**Table 17-5** | Encryption Algorithms

| Implementation (XMLENC Only) | Name | URI |
| --- | --- | --- |
| Required | TRIPLEDES | http://www.w3.org/2001/04/xmlenc#tripledes-cbc |
| Required | AES-128 | http://www.w3.org/2001/04/xmlenc#aes128-cbc |
| Required | AES-256 | http://www.w3.org/2001/04/xmlenc#aes256-cbc |
| Required | RSA-v1.5 | http://www.w3.org/2001/04/xmlenc#rsa-1_5 |
| Required | RSA-OAEP | http://www.w3.org/2001/04/xmlenc#rsa-oaep-mbg1p |
| Required | Triple DES Key Wrap | http://www.w3.org/2001/04/xmlenc#kw-tripledes |
| Required | AES-128 Key Wrap | http://www.w3.org/2001/04/xmlenc#kw-aes128 |
| Required | AES-256 Key Wrap | http://www.w3.org/2001/04/xmlenc#kw-aes256 |
| Optional | AES-192 | http://www.w3.org/2001/04/xmlenc#aes192-cbc |
| Optional | ARCFOUR | http://www.w3.org/2001/04/xmldsig-more#arcfour |
| Optional | AES-192 Key Wrap | http://www.w3.org/2001/04/xmlenc#kw-aes192 |

**Table 17-6** | Signature Algorithms

| Implementation (XMLDSIG Only) | Name | URI |
|---|---|---|
| Required | DSAwithSHA1 | http://www.w3.org/2000/09/xmldsig#dsa-sha1 |
| Required | HMAC-SHA1 | http://www.w3.org/2000/09/xmldsig#hmac-sha1 |
| Recommended | RSAwithSHA1 | http://www.w3.org/2000/09/xmldsig#rsa-sha1 |
| Optional | HMAC-MD5 | http://www.w3.org/2001/04/xmldsig-more#hmac-md5 |
| Optional | HMAC-SHA256 | http://www.w3.org/2001/04/xmldsig-more#hmac-sha256 |
| Optional | HMAC-SHA384 | http://www.w3.org/2001/04/xmldsig-more#hmac-sha384 |
| Optional | HMAC-SHA512 | http://www.w3.org/2001/04/xmldsig-more#hmac-sha512 |
| Optional | HMAC-RIPEMD160 | http://www.w3.org/2001/04/xmldsig-more#hmac-ripemd160 |
| Optional | RSAwithSHA256 | http://www.w3.org/2001/04/xmldsig-more#rsa-sha256 |
| Optional | RSAwithSHA384 | http://www.w3.org/2001/04/xmldsig-more#rsa-sha384 |
| Optional | RSAwithSHA512 | http://www.w3.org/2001/04/xmldsig-more#rsa-sha512 |
| Optional | RSAwithRIPEMD160 | http://www.w3.org/2001/04/xmldsig-more#rsa-ripemd160 |
| Not Recommended | RSAwithMD5 | http://www.w3.org/2001/04/xmldsig-more#rsa-md5 |

## 17.2.6  Transform

Transform algorithms appear in a Transforms element, which in turn is the child of a Reference, RetrievalMethod, or CipherReference element. These algorithms take one implicit input, which can be either an XPath node-set or an octet sequence. This input comes from the previous Transform, if one exists. Otherwise, it consists of the data to which the Reference, Retrieval-Method, or CipherReference ancestor of the Transform refers. See Chapter 10 for more information on the Transforms data pipeline model. Table 17-7 lists Transform algorithms, other than canonicalization algorithms.

**Note**

> You can also use all CanonicalizationMethod algorithms described in Section 17.2.1 as Transform algorithms.

**Table 17-7** | Transform Algorithms

| Implementation | Name | URI |
|---|---|---|
| XMLDSIG: Required<br>XMLENC: N/A | Enveloped Signature | http://www.w3.org/2000/09/xmldsig#enveloped-signature |
| XMLDSIG: Required<br>XMLENC: Required | Base64 | http://www.w3.org/2000/09/xmldsig#base64 |
| XMLDSIG: Recommended<br>XMLENC: Recommended | XPath | http://www.w3.org/TR/1999/REC-xpath-19991116 |
| XMLDSIG: Recommended<br>XMLENC: N/A | Decryption Transform | http://www.w3.org/2001/04/decrypt# |
| XMLDSIG: Optional<br>XMLENC: Optional | XSLT | http://www.w3.org/TR/1999/REC-xslt-19991116 |
| XMLDSIG: Recommended[1]<br>XMLENC: Optional | XPointer | http://www.w3.org/2001/04/xmldsig-more/xptr |
| XMLDSIG: Experimental<br>XMLENC: Experimental | Schema | http://www.w3.org/TR/2001/REC-xmlschema-1-20010502/ |

1. This Recommended status applies only to a very limited number of XPointer facilities. The rest of XPointer is Optional. (See Chapter 10.)

# 18 | Cryptographic Algorithms

This chapter describes cryptographic algorithms that can be specified in XML Security by a well-known URI. These algorithms are characterized by complex logical and arithmetic manipulation of binary octet strings. See Chapter 17 for an overview of algorithms and Chapter 19 for descriptions of non-cryptographic algorithms that are XML or text oriented.

## 18.1    Message Digests

You use message digest algorithms in the following contexts:

- DigestMethod, to digest referenced data in a Reference element.

- SignatureMethod, as part of the signature or message authentication code algorithm, although in the cases listed here, the message digest algorithm is indicated by part of the SignatureMethod algorithm URI.

- EncryptionMethod, as part of the encryption algorithm. In the cases given in this chapter, it appears as an explicit parameter in the form of a DigestMethod element.

- AgreementMethod, as part of the key agreement algorithm. In the cases given in this chapter, it appears as an explicit parameter in the form of a DigestMethod element.

See Chapter 2 for a discussion of message digests. See also Figure 18-1.

### 18.1.1  MD5

```
MD5 Identifier:
    http://www.w3.org/2001/04/xmldsig-more#md5
```

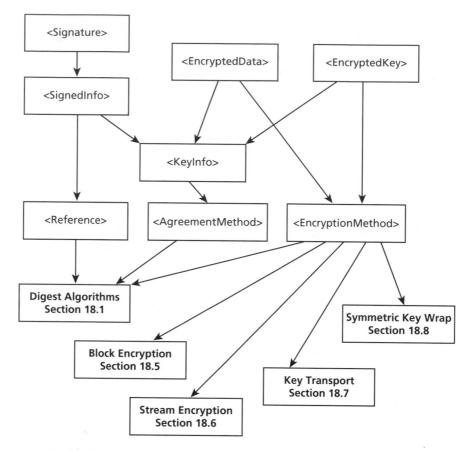

**Figure 18-1** | Digest and encryption algorithm element ancestors

The MD5 algorithm [RFC 1321] takes no explicit parameters. An example of an MD5 DigestAlgorithm element is

```
<DigestMethod
  Algorithm="http://www.w3.org/2001/04/xmldsig-more#md5"/>
```

An MD5 digest is a 128-bit string. In a Reference element, the content of the DigestValue element is the base-64 [RFC 2045] encoding of this bit string viewed as a 16-byte stream. For example, the MD5 of "abc" is the following in hexadecimal format:

```
90015098 3cd24fb0 d6963f7d 28e17f72
```

**Soapbox**

> MD5 is not considered to be very strong by current cryptographic standards. That is, 128 bits of hash is not much and collisions have been found in MD5 outputs.

### 18.1.2 SHA-1

```
SHA-1 Identifier:
    http://www.w3.org/2000/09/xmldsig#sha1
```

The SHA-1 algorithm [FIPS 180-1] takes no explicit parameters. Implementation of SHA-1 is mandatory for conformant implementations of the XML Digital Signature standard. An example of a SHA-1 algorithm element is

```
<DigestMethod
  Algorithm="http://www.w3.org/2000/09/xmldsig#sha1"/>
```

A SHA-1 digest is a 160-bit string. When it is used as a DigestMethod, the content of the DigestValue element will be the base-64 encoding of this bit string viewed as a 20-byte stream. For example, the DigestValue element for the message digest

```
A9993E36 4706816A BA3E2571 7850C26C 9CD0D89D
```

from Appendix A of the SHA-1 standard would be

```
<DigestValue>qZk+NkcGgWq6PiVxeFDCbJzQ2J0=</DigestValue>
```

### 18.1.3 Additional SHA Versions

```
Additional SHA Version Identifiers:
    http://www.w3.org/2001/04/xmlenc#sha256
    http://www.w3.org/2001/04/xmldsig-more#sha384
    http://www.w3.org/2001/04/xmlenc#sha512
```

These additional SHA versions take no explicit parameters. Implementation is optional under the XML Digital Signature standard. Under the XML Encryption standard, SHA-256 is recommended while SHA-384 and SHA-512 are optional [FIPS 180-2]. An example of an algorithm element for one of these is

```
<DigestMethod
  Algorithm="http://www.w3.org/2001/04/xmldsig-more#sha512"/>
```

SHA-256, SHA-384, and SHA-512 produce digest strings of 256, 384, and 512 bits, respectively. When used as a DigestMethod, the content of the DigestValue element is the base-64 encoding of this bit string viewed as a 32-, 48-, or 64-byte stream.

### 18.1.4  RIPEMD-160

```
RIPEMD-160 Identifier:
    http://www.w3.org/2001/04/xmlenc#ripemd160
```

The implementation of RIPEMD-160 is optional; it takes no explicit parameters [RIPEMD-160]. An example of an algorithm element is

```
<DigestMethod
  Algorithm="http://www.w3.org/2001/04/xmlenc#ripemd160"/>
```

A RIPEMD-160 digest is a 160-bit string. When it is used as a DigestMethod, the content of the DigestValue element is the base-64 encoding of this bit string viewed as a 20-byte stream.

The RIPEMD-160 hash of the 14-byte string

```
message digest
```

is

```
5d0689ef 49d2fae5 72b881b1 23a85ffa 21595f36
```

## 18.2    Key Agreement Algorithms

A key agreement algorithm provides a secret quantity shared between the sender and the recipient based on certain types of compatible public keys from both parties. An optional OriginatorKeyInfo parameter child of an AgreementMethod element indicates the information associated with the originator used to determine the key. An optional RecipientKeyInfo child indicates that associated with the recipient.

**Note**

The AgreementMethod element appears as the content of a KeyInfo element because, like other KeyInfo children, it yields a key. This KeyInfo is, in turn, a child of an EncryptedData, EncryptedKey, or Signature element. The Algorithm attribute (and KeySize child, if any) of the EncryptionMethod element under this EncryptedData or EncryptedKey element or the Algorithm attribute of the SignatureMethod under this Signature element is an implicit parameter to the key agreement computation. That sounds—and is—a bit complex, but look at Figure 18 2. Trace up from AgreementMethod to Key Info. Notice that KeyInfo has three possible ancestors: Signature, EncryptedData, and EncryptedKey. Each of these ancestors has a child that is a keyed cryptographic algorithm, either SignatureMethod or EncryptionMethod. The encryption or signature algorithm used determines how many bits of key are extracted from the shared secret. A KeySize element must be provided under EncryptionMethod if the encryption algorithm does not itself specify the key size. In addition, the sender may include a KA-Nonce element under AgreementMethod to ensure that a different shared secret, and thus different keying material, is generated, even for repeated agreements using the same sender and recipient public keys. For example:

```
<EncryptedData xmlns="http://www.w3.org/2001/04/xmlenc#">
  <EncryptionMethod Algorithm="Example:Block/Alg">
    <KeySize>80</KeySize>
  </EncryptionMethod>
  <ds:KeyInfo xmlns:ds="http://www.w3.org/2000/09/xmldsig#">
    <AgreementMethod Algorithm="Example:Agreement/Algorithm">
      <KA-Nonce> Zm9v </KA-Nonce>
      <DigestMethod
Algorithm="http://www.w3.org/2001/04/xmlenc#sha1">
      <OriginatorKeyInfo>
        <ds:KeyValue>...originator...</ds:KeyValue>
```

```
      </OriginatorKeyInfo>
      <RecipientKeyInfo>
        <ds:KeyValue>...recipient...</ds:KeyValue>
      </RecipientKeyInfo>
    </AgreementMethod>
  </ds:KeyInfo>
  <CipherData>...</CipherData>
</EncryptedData>
```

If the agreed-upon key is used to encrypt a key, rather than encrypting data, then AgreementMethod would appear inside a KeyInfo inside an Encrypted-Key element. If it were used for an authentication code, it would appear inside a KeyInfo inside a Signature element.

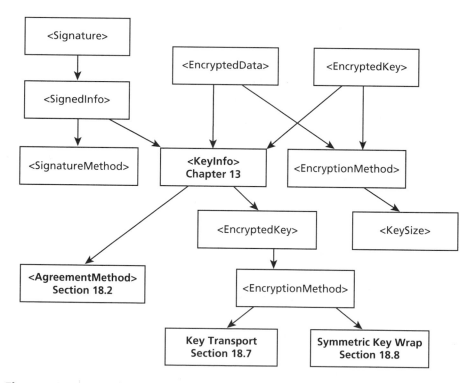

**Figure 18-2** | KeyInfo descendant algorithms

Implementation of AgreementMethod is optional. Its syntax follows:

```
<!-- AgreementMethod DTD -->

<!ELEMENT AgreementMethod
          (#PCDATA|KA-Nonce|DigestMethod|OriginatorKeyInfo|
          RecipientKeyInfo %Method.ANY;)* >
<!ATTLIST AgreementMethod
          Algorithm    CDATA     #REQUIRED >

<!ELEMENT KA-Nonce (#PCDATA) >
```

In schema syntax, it has the following form:

```
<!-- AgreementMethod Schema -->

<element name="AgreementMethod"
         type="xenc:AgreementMethodType"/>
<complexType name="AgreementMethodType" mixed="true">
  <sequence>
    <element name="KA-Nonce" minOccurs="0"
             type="base64Binary"/>
    <element ref="ds:DigestMethodType"
             minOccurs="0">
    <element name="OriginatorKeyInfo" minOccurs="0"
             type="ds:KeyInfoType">
    <element name="RecipientKeyInfo" minOccurs="0"
             type="ds:KeyInfoType">
    <any namespace="##other" minOccurs="0"
                             maxOccurs="unbounded"/>
    <!-- (0,unbounded) elements from (1,1) external namespace -->
  </sequence>
  <attribute name="Algorithm" type="anyURI" use="required"/>
</complexType>
```

## 18.2.1  Diffie-Hellman Key Agreement

```
Diffie-Hellman Identifier:
    http://www.w3.org/2001/04/xmlenc#dh
```

A Diffie-Hellman (DH) key agreement involves the derivation of shared secret information based on compatible DH keys from the sender and recipient. As described in Chapter 13, a DH public key includes three quantities: a prime (p), a generator (g), and a quantity (Public) such that

Public = $g^x$ mod p.

The corresponding private key is x.

Two DH public keys are compatible if they have the same prime and generator. If, for the second one,

Y = $g^y$ mod p

then the two parties can calculate the shared secret

ZZ = ( $g^{x*y}$ mod p )

even though each knows only its own private key and the other party's public key. Leading zero octets must be maintained in ZZ, so it will be the same length, in octets, as p. The standards require that p be at least 512 bits and g at least 160 bits. To obtain strong security, numerous other complex considerations apply in the generation of DH keys [RFC 2631].

The DH key agreement algorithm is optional to implement. An example of a DH AgreementMethod element follows:

```
<AgreementMethod Algorithm="http://www.w3.org/2001/04/xmlenc#dh"
                 xmlns:s="http://www.w3.org/2000/09/xmldsig#" >
    <KA-Nonce> Zm9v </KA-Nonce>
    <DigestMethod
        Algorithm="http://www.w3.org/2000/09/xmldsig#sha1"/>
    <OriginatorKeyInfo>
        <s:X509Data><s:X509Certificate>
            ...
        </s:X509Certificate></s:X509Data>
    </OriginatorKeyInfo>
    <RecipientKeyInfo>
        <s:KeyValue>...</s:KeyValue>
    </RecipientKeyInfo>
</AgreementMethod>
```

The AgreementMethod derives some shared secret octet sequence ZZ. The amount of actual keying material needed is calculated as follows:

Keying Material = KM(1) | KM(2) | . . .

where "|" is byte stream concatenation and

KM(counter) = DigestAlg(ZZ | counter | EncryptionAlg | KA-Nonce | KeySize)

DigestAlg is the message digest algorithm specified by the DigestMethod child of AgreementMethod.

EncryptionAlg is the URI of the encryption or signature algorithm, including possible key wrap algorithms, where the derived keying material will be used ("Example:Block/Alg" in the EncryptedData example above), not the URI of the agreement algorithm.

KA-Nonce is the base-64 decoding of the text child of the KA-Nonce child of AgreementMethod, if present. As specified in base-64 decoding, white space is ignored. If the KA-Nonce element is absent, it is null.

Counter is a one-byte counter starting at 1 and being incremented by 1. It is expressed as two hexadecimal digits with uppercase letters.

KeySize is the size in bits of the key to be derived from the shared secret represented as the UTF-8 string for the corresponding decimal integer with only digits in the string and no leading zeros. For some algorithms, the key size is inherent in the URI. For others, such as ARCFOUR, it may be explicitly provided.

For example, the initial KM(1) calculation for the EncryptedData example would be as follows, where the two-character UTF-8 sequence "01" represents the byte counter value of 1, ZZ is the shared secret, and "foo" is the base-64 decoding of "Zm9v":

SHA-1 ( ZZ01Example:Block/Algfoo80 )

Assuming that ZZ is 0xDEADBEEF, that would be

```
SHA-1 (0xDEADBEEF30314578616D706C653A426C6F636B2F416C67666F6F3830)
```

whose value is

```
0x534C9B8C4ABDCB50038B42015A181711068B08C1
```

Each application of DigestAlg with a successive counter value produces some potential keying material. From the concatenated string of one or more KMs, enough leading octets are taken to meet the need for an actual key and the remainder discarded. For example, if DigestAlg is SHA1, which produces 20 octets of hash, then for 128-bit AES the first 16 octets from KM(1) would be taken and the remaining 4 octets would be discarded. For 256-bit AES, all of KM(1) suffixed with the first 12 octets of KM(2) would be taken and the remaining 8 octets of KM(2) would be discarded.

## 18.3    Message Authentication Codes

A Message Authentication Code (MAC) is calculated from the data to be authenticated and a secret quantity. The HMAC algorithm [RFC 2104] is the basis of all MACs that XML Security specifies, although other strong MAC techniques exist as well [Schneier]. You can use the HMAC algorithm with any hash code.

MAC algorithm identifiers appear as the value of the Algorithm attribute of SignatureMethod elements, as shown in Figure 18-3. Their implicit inputs consist of their keying material and the octet stream output by the signature's CanonicalizationMethod. MACs are syntactically identical to signatures but imply a shared secret key.

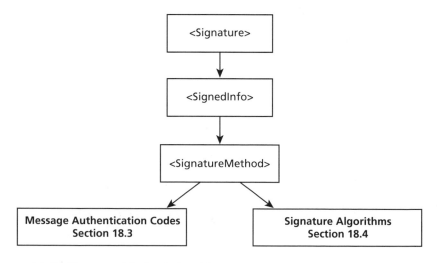

**Figure 18-3** | SignatureMethod algorithms

### 18.3.1 HMAC SHA-1

```
HMAC SHA-1 Identifier:
    http://www.w3.org/2000/09/xmldsig#hmac-sha1
```

Implementation of HMAC SHA-1 is mandatory for applications that conform to the XML Digital Signature standard. The HMAC algorithm [RFC 2104] takes the truncation length in bits as an explicit parameter; if the application does not specify the parameter, then all bits of the hash are output. An example of an HMAC SignatureMethod element follows:

```
<SignatureMethod Algorithm=
"http://www.w3.org/2000/09/xmldsig#hmac-sha1">
    <HMACOutputLength>128</HMACOutputLength>
</SignatureMethod>
```

The output of the HMAC algorithm is ultimately the output (possibly truncated) of the chosen digest algorithm. This value is encoded in base-64 in the SignatureValue element. For example, the SignatureValue element for the HMAC-SHA1 digest

```
9294727A 3638BB1C 13F48EF8 158BFC9D
```

from the test vectors in [RFC 2104] would be

```
<SignatureValue>kpRyejY4uxwT9I74FYv8nQ==</SignatureValue>
```

The DTD for the HMACOutputLength element follows:

```
<!-- HMACOutputLength DTD -->

<!ELEMENT HMACOutputLength (#PCDATA)>
```

In schema notation, it has the following form:

```
<!-- HMACOutputLength Schema Definition -->

<simpleType name="HMACOutputLengthType">
    <restriction base="integer"/>
</simpleType>
```

### 18.3.2  Additional HMAC Variations

```
Additional HMAC Variation Identifiers:
    http://www.w3.org/2001/04/xmldsig-more#hmac-md5
    http://www.w3.org/2001/04/xmldsig-more#hmac-sha256
    http://www.w3.org/2001/04/xmldsig-more#hmac-sha512
    http://www.w3.org/2001/04/xmldsig-more#hmac-ripemd160
```

Implementation of these HMAC variations is optional. All variations use the technique described in [RFC 2104] and have an optional HMACOutput-Length explicit parameter as described in Section 18.3.1. The only difference involves the message digest algorithm used.

## 18.4    Signature Algorithms

Signature algorithm identifiers appear as the Algorithm attribute of SignatureMethod elements, as shown in Figure 18-3. They take two implicit parameters: their keying material and the octet stream output by CanonicalizationMethod. MAC and signature algorithms are syntactically identical, but a signature implies public key cryptography.

### 18.4.1  DSA

```
DSA Identifier:
    http://www.w3.org/2000/09/xmldsig#dsa-sha1
```

The DSA algorithm [DSS] is mandatory to implement for XML Digital Signature applications. It takes no explicit parameters. An example of a DSA SignatureMethod element follows:

```
<SignatureMethod
  Algorithm="http://www.w3.org/2000/09/xmldsig#dsa-sha1"/>
```

The output of the DSA algorithm is a pair of integers usually referred by the pair (r, s). The signature value consists of the base-64 encoding of the concatenation of two octet streams for the values r and s. Integer-to-octet steam conversion must be performed according to the I2OSP operation defined in the PKCS#1 specification [RFC 2437] with an "L" parameter equal to 20. For example, the SignatureValue element for a DSA signature (r, s) with values specified in hexadecimal as

```
r = 8BAC1AB6 6410435C B7181F95 B16AB97C 92B341C0
s = 41E2345F 1F56DF24 58F426D1 55B4BA2D B6DCD8C8
```

from the example in Appendix 5 of the DSS standard would be

```
<SignatureValue>
    i6watmQQQ1y3GB+VsWq5fJKzQcBB4jRfH1bfJFj0JtFVtLotttzYyA==
</SignatureValue>
```

---

## 18.4.2  RSA-SHA1

```
RSA-SHA1 Identifier:
   http://www.w3.org/2000/09/xmldsig#rsa-sha1
```

RSA-SHA1 refers to the RSASSA-PKCS1-v1_5 encoding/padding algorithm
[RFC 2437] used with the SHA-1 algorithm (see Section 18.1.2). It is recommended that this algorithm be implemented in XML Digital Signature applications. The RSA algorithm takes no explicit parameters. An example of an
RSA SignatureMethod element follows:

```
<SignatureMethod
 Algorithm="http://www.w3.org/2000/09/xmldsig#rsa-sha1"/>
```

The SignatureValue content for an RSA signature is the base-64 [RFC 2045]
encoding of the octet string computed as per [RFC 2437, Section 8.1.1:
signature generation operation for the RSASSA-PKCS1-v1_5 signature
scheme]. The EMSA-PKCS1-V1_5-ENCODE function [RFC 2437, Section
9.2.1] specifies that the value input to the signature function must contain
a prepended algorithm object identifier for the hash function. However, the
availability of an ASN.1 parser and recognition of OIDs are not required of
a signature verifier. The PKCS#1 v1.5 representation appears as follows:

ENCRYPT (PAD (ASN.1 (OID, DIGEST ( data ) ) ) )

Note that the padded ASN.1 will have the following form:

01 | FF* | 00 | prefix | message digest

Here "|" is concatenation; "01", "FF", and "00" are the fixed x01, xFF, and x00
octets, respectively; "message digest" is the SHA1 digest of the data; and "prefix" is the ASN.1 BER SHA1 algorithm designator prefix required in PKCS#1
[RFC 2437], that is,

```
hex 30 21 30 09 06 05 2B 0E 03 02 1A 05 00 04 14
```

This prefix makes it easier to use standard cryptographic libraries. The <u>xFF</u> octet must be repeated the maximum number of times such that the quantity being encrypted is one octet shorter than the RSA modulus.

The resulting base-64 string is the value of the child text node of the SignatureValue element:

```
<SignatureValue>IWijxQjUrcXBYoCei4QxjWo9Kg8D3p9tlWoT4
    t0/gyTE96639In0FZFY2/rvP+/bMJ01EArmKZsR5VW3rwoPxw=
</SignatureValue>
```

### 18.4.3    Additional RSA Variations

```
Additional RSA Identifiers:
    http://www.w3.org/2001/04/xmldsig-more#rsa-md5
    http://www.w3.org/2001/04/xmldsig-more#rsa-sha256
    http://www.w3.org/2001/04/xmldsig-more#rsa-sha512
    http://www.w3.org/2001/04/xmldsig-more#rsa-ripems160
```

These algorithms all use the same encoding/padding method as RSA-SHA1 but with different message digest functions and a different prefix to indicate the different message digest function. The prefix to use for MD5 follows:

```
MD5 Prefix
    hex 30 20 30 0C 06 08 2A 86 48 86 F7 0D 02 05 05 00 04 10
```

**Note**

> Recent cryptographic advances have indicated some signs of weakness in MD5. While these frailties do not affect its use with HMAC, use of RSA-MD5 is not recommended.

## 18.5    Block Encryption Algorithms

Block encryption algorithms are designed for encrypting and decrypting data. Their identifiers normally appear as the value of the Algorithm attributes of EncryptionMethod elements that are children of EncryptedData (see Figure 18-1).

Block encryption algorithms take, as implicit arguments, the data to encrypt or decrypt, the keying material, and their direction of operation. All of the algorithms specified in this section require an initialization vector (IV). This IV is encoded with the cipher text. For user-specified block encryption algorithms, the IV, if any, could be specified as being with the cipher data, as the content of an algorithm element, or elsewhere.

The IV is prefixed to and encoded with the data for the block encryption algorithms for ease of availability to the decryption code and to emphasize its association with the cipher text. Good cryptographic practice requires that you use a different IV for every encryption.

### Padding

Because the data being encrypted consists of an arbitrary number of octets, the data size may not be a multiple of the block size. Padding the plain text up to the block size before encryption and unpadding after decryption resolves this discrepancy. The padding algorithm is to calculate the smallest nonzero number of octets—say, N—that must be suffixed to the plain text to bring it up to a multiple of the block size. We will assume the block size is B octets, so N is in the range of 1 to B. Pad by suffixing the plain text with N – 1 arbitrary pad bytes and a final byte whose value is N. On decryption, take the last byte and, after "sanity checking" it, strip that many bytes from the end of the decrypted cipher text.

For example, assume an eight-byte block size and plain text of 0x616263. The padded plain text would then be 0x616263???????05, where the "??" bytes can be any value. Similarly, plain text of 0x2122232425262728 would be padded to 0x2122232425262728?????????????08.

### 18.5.1  Triple DES

```
TRIPLEDES Identifier:
    http://www.w3.org/2001/04/xmlenc#tripledes-cbc
```

The triple DES algorithm is described in [FIPS 46-3] and ANSI X9.52 [3DES]. It is composed of three sequential DES operations. Encryption applications must implement triple DES for data encryption.

Triple DES consists of a DES encrypt, a DES decrypt, and a DES encrypt used in Cipher Block Chaining (CBC) mode [FIPS 81] with 192 bits of key and a 64-bit IV. Of the key bits, the first 64 bits are used in the first DES operation, the second 64 bits in the middle DES operation, and the third 64 bits in the last DES operation.

Each 64 key bits contain 56 effective bits and 8 parity bits. Thus the 192 bits being transported for a triple DES key contain only 168 operational bits. (Depending on the criterion used for analysis, the effective key strength may be thought to be 112, due to "meet in the middle" attacks, or even slightly less.)

The IV prefixes the resulting cipher text before being encoded in base-64 for inclusion in XML output. An example triple DES EncryptionMethod follows:

```
<EncryptionMethod
  Algorithm="http://www.w3.org/2001/04/xmlenc#tripledes-cbc"/>
```

### 18.5.2   AES

```
AES Identifiers:
    http://www.w3.org/2001/04/xmlenc#aes128-cbc
    http://www.w3.org/2001/04/xmlenc#aes192-cbc
    http://www.w3.org/2001/04/xmlenc#aes256-cbc
```

The Advanced Encryption Standard (AES) algorithm is described in [FIPS 197]. XML Encryption implementations must support AES with 128-bit and 256-bit keys. AES may also optionally be implemented for 192-bit keys. It has a 128-bit block size and is used in CBC mode with a 128-bit IV. The IV prefixes the resulting cipher text before being encoded in base-64 for inclusion in XML output. An example AES EncryptionMethod follows:

```
<EncryptionMethod
  Algorithm="http://www.w3.org/2001/04/xmlenc#aes128-cbc"/>
```

## 18.6   Stream Encryption Algorithms

Simple stream encryption algorithms generate, based on the key, a stream of octets that are XORed with the plain text octets to produce the cipher text on encryption and with the cipher text octets to produce plain text on decryption. They are normally used for the encryption of data. Thus they are specified by the value of the Algorithm attribute of the EncryptionMethod child of an EncryptedData element. See Figure 18-1.

**Note**

It is critical that you use each simple stream encryption key (or key and initialization vector, if an IV is also used) once only. If the same key (or key and IV) is ever used on two messages, then, by XORing the two cipher texts, you obtain the XOR of the two plain texts. This result is usually very compromising.

> The XOR nature of stream ciphers makes it trivial to change specific bits in the plain text. Changing a bit in the cipher text changes the corresponding bit of plain text without changing any other plain text bits. This case illustrates the common need, beyond encryption, for integrity or authentication, if the plain text should be trusted after decryption.

Stream algorithms typically use the optional KeySize explicit parameter. In cases where the key size is not apparent from the algorithm URI or key source, as with key agreement methods, this parameter sets the key size. If the size of the key is apparent and disagrees with the KeySize parameter, the application must return an error. Implementation of any stream algorithms is optional. The schema for the KeySize parameter follows:

```
<!-- KeySize DTD -->

<!ELEMENT KeySize (#PCDATA) >
```

In schema syntax, it has the following form:

```
<!-- KeySize Schema -->

<simpleType name='KeySizeType'>
    <restriction base="integer"/>
</simpleType>
```

## 18.6.1  ARCFOUR

```
ARCFOUR Identifier
    http://www.w3.org/2001/04/xmldsig-more#arcfour
```

ARCFOUR is a fast, simple stream encryption algorithm that interoperates with RSA Security's RC4 algorithm. Implementation of ARCFOUR is optional. An example of an ARCFOUR EncryptionMethod follows:

```
<EncryptionMethod
  Algorithm="http://www.w3.org/2001/04/xmldsig-more#arcfour">
  <KeySize>40</KeySize>
</EncryptionMethod>
```

## 18.7    Key Transport Algorithms

Key transport algorithms are public key encryption algorithms specified for encrypting and decrypting keys. As implicit input, they take their keying material and the key to encrypt (transport). Their identifiers normally appear as Algorithm attributes to EncryptionMethod elements that are children of EncryptedKey, which is in turn a child of KeyInfo (see Figure 18-1). The type of key being transported—that is, the algorithm in which the transported key will be used—is given by the Algorithm attribute of the EncryptionMethod child of the EncryptedData or Encrypted/Key parent of this KeyInfo (see Figure 18-2).

Key transport algorithms may optionally be used to encrypt data. In that case, they appear directly as the Algorithm attribute of an Encryption-Method child of an EncryptedData element. Because they use public key algorithms directly, these algorithms do not work efficiently in the transport of any amounts of data significantly larger than symmetric keys.

The key transport algorithms given in this section are used in conjunction with the Cryptographic Message Syntax (CMS) of S/MIME [RFC 2630].

### 18.7.1   RSA Version 1.5

```
RSA Version 1.5 Identifier:
    http://www.w3.org/2001/04/xmlenc#rsa-1_5
```

RSA version 1.5 is the RSAES-PKCS1-v1_5 algorithm described in [RFC 2437]. It takes no explicit parameters. An example of an RSA Version 1.5 EncryptionMethod element follows:

```
<EncryptionMethod
  Algorithm="http://www.w3.org/2001/04/xmlenc#rsa-1_5"/>
```

The CipherValue for such an encrypted key is the base-64 [RFC 2045] encoding of the byte string computed as per PKCS#1 [RFC 2437, Section 7.2.1: encryption operation]. As specified in the EME-PKCS1-v1_5 function [RFC 2437, Section 9.1.2.1], the value input to the key transport function is as follows:

ENCRYPT ( PAD ( KEY ))

Here the padding has the following special form:

02 | PS* | 00 | key

where "|" is concatenation; "02" and "00" are the fixed octets x02 and x00; "PS" is a string of strong pseudo-random octets [RFC 1750] at least eight octets long, containing no zero octets, and long enough that the value of the quantity being encrypted is one byte shorter than the RSA modulus; and "key" is the key being transported. The key is 192 bits for triple DES and 128, 192, or 256 bits for AES. Support of this key transport algorithm for triple DES keys is mandatory under XML Encryption. Support of this algorithm for AES or other keys is optional. RSA-OAEP is recommended for the transport of AES keys.

The resulting base-64 [RFC 2045] string is the value of the child text node of the CipherValue element. For example:

```
<CipherValue>IWijxQjUrcXBYoCei4QxjWo9Kg8D3p9tlWoT4
            t0/gyTE96639In0FZFY2/rvP+/bMJ01EarmK∠
            sR5VW3rwoPxw=
</CipherValue>
```

## 18.7.2   RSA-OAEP

```
RSA OAEP Identifier:
    http://www.w3.org/2001/04/xmlenc#rsa-oaep-mgf1p
```

The RSAES-OAEP-ENCRYPT algorithm is described in [RFC 2437]. (OAEP stands for Optimal Asymmetric Encryption Padding. The next-to-last character of the URI is the digit 1, and "mgf" stands for "mask-generating function.") As explicit parameters, the RSA-OAEP algorithm takes a message digest function and an optional octet string OAEPparams. The OAEP message digest function is indicated by the Algorithm attribute of a child Digest-Method element, and the octet string is the base-64 decoding of the text child of an optional OAEPparams element. (The SHA-1 digest function is always used inside the mask generator function when this identifier specifies the key transport algorithm.) An example of an RSA-OAEP element follows:

```
<EncryptionMethod
 Algorithm="http://www.w3.org/2001/04/xmlenc#rsa-oaep-mgf1p">
  <DigestMethod
```

```
Algorithm="http://www.w3.org/2000/09/xmldsig#sha1"/>
  <OAEPparams>Zm9v</OAEPparams>
<EncryptionMethod>
```

The CipherData for an RSA-OAEP encrypted key is the base-64 [RFC 2045] encoding of the byte string computed as per PKCS#1 [RFC 2437, Section 7.1.1: encryption operation]. As described in the EME-OAEP-ENCODE function [RFC 2437, Section 9.1.1.1], the value input to the key transport function is calculated by using the message digest function and the string specified in the DigestMethod and OAEPparams element and by using the mask generator function MGF1 specified in [RFC 2437]. The desired output length for EME-OAEP-ENCODE is one byte shorter than the RSA modulus.

Standards-conformant XML Encryption applications must implement RSA-OAEP for the transport of 128- and 256-bit AES keys. They may optionally implement RSA-OAEP for the transport of 192-bit AES keys, triple DES keys, and other keys.

## 18.8    Symmetric Key Wrap Algorithms

Symmetric key wrap algorithms are shared secret key encryption algorithms designed for encrypting and decrypting symmetric keys and providing an integrity check. They take, as implicit parameters, their keying material and the key to encrypt or decrypt. Their identifiers appear as Algorithm attributes to EncryptionMethod elements that are children of EncryptedKey, which is in turn a child of KeyInfo (see Figure 18-1). The type of key being wrapped is indicated by the Algorithm attribute of the EncryptionMethod child of the parent of the KeyInfo grandparent of the EncryptionMethod specifying the symmetric key wrap algorithm (see Figure 18-2).

### 18.8.1  CMS Key Checksum

Some key wrap algorithms use the Key Checksum defined in CMS [RFC 2630]. It provides an integrity check value for the key being wrapped. The algorithm follows:

1. Compute the 20-octet SHA-1 hash of the key being wrapped [FIPS 180-1].

2. Use the first 8 octets of this hash as the checksum value.

## 18.8.2  Triple DES Key Wrap

```
Triple DES Key Wrap Identifiers:
    http://www.w3.org/2001/04/xmlenc#kw-tripledes
```

Standards-conformant XML Encryption applications must support triple DES wrapping of triple DES keys and may optionally support triple DES wrapping of AES or other keys. An example of a Triple DES Key Wrap EncryptionMethod element follows:

```
<EncryptionMethod
  Algorithm="http://www.w3.org/2001/04/xmlenc#kw-tripledes"/>
```

The following algorithm wraps (encrypts) a key (the wrapped key, WK) under a triple DES key-encrypting key (KEK):

1. Represent the key being wrapped as a byte sequence. If it is a triple DES key, this byte sequence is 24 octets (192 bits) produced by inserting an odd parity bit as the bottom bit of each octet.

2. Compute the key checksum defined in Section 19.12.1; call it CKS.

3. Let WKCKS = WK || CKS, where || means concatenation.

4. Generate eight random octets; call it IV [RFC 1750].

5. Encrypt WKCKS in CBC mode using KEK as the key and IV as the initialization vector. Call the result TEMP1.

6. Let TEMP2 = IV || TEMP1.

7. Reverse the order of the octets in TEMP2; call the result TEMP3.

8. Encrypt TEMP3 in CBC mode using the KEK and an initialization vector of 0x4ADDA22C79E82105. The resulting cipher text is the desired result. It is 40 octets long if a triple DES key is being wrapped.

The following algorithm unwraps (decrypts) a key:

1. Check whether the length of the cipher text is reasonable given the key type. It must be 40 bytes for a triple DES key and either 32, 40, or 48 bytes for an AES key. If the length is wrong, return an error.

2. Decrypt the cipher text with triple DES in CBC mode using the KEK and an IV of 0x4ADDA22C79E82105. Call the output TEMP3.

3. Reverse the order of the octets in TEMP3; call the result TEMP2.

4. Decompose TEMP2 into IV, the first eight octets, and TEMP1, the remaining bytes.

5. Decrypt TEMP1 using triple DES in CBC mode using the KEK and the IV found in Step 4. Call the result WKCKS.

6. Decompose WKCKS. CKS is the last eight octets and WK, the wrapped key, consists of those octets before the CKS.

7. Calculate a CMS Key Checksum over the WK, and compare it with the CKS extracted in Step 6. If they are not equal, return an error.

8. WK is the wrapped key, now extracted for use in data decryption.

This specification matches that given in [RFC 2630].

### 18.8.3   AES Key Wrap

```
AES Key Wrap Identifiers:
    http://www.w3.org/2001/04/xmlenc#kw-aes128
    http://www.w3.org/2001/04/xmlenc#kw-aes192
    http://www.w3.org/2001/04/xmlenc#kw-aes256
```

Implementation of AES key wrap is mandatory under XML Encryption only for 128- and 256-bit key-encrypting keys. None of the versions of AES key wrap takes any explicit parameters; all of them take the usual implicit parameters of encryption algorithms with no initialization vector.

The AES key wrap algorithm described below, as suggested by NIST [AES, AES KMS], provides for confidentiality and integrity. It is defined only for

**Table 18-1** | AES Key Wrap Implementation Requirements

| Key-Encrypting Key Size | Wrapped Key Size | Requirement |
|---|---|---|
| 128 | 128 | Required |
| 128 | Other than 128 | Optional |
| 192 | Any | Optional |
| 256 | 256 | Required |
| 256 | Other than 256 | Optional |

parameters that are multiples of 64 bits. The information wrapped need not actually be a key. The algorithm is the same whatever the size of the AES key used in wrapping, called the key-encrypting key (KEK). Table 18-1 shows the detailed implementation requirements for various key-encrypting key sizes and wrapped data sizes.

### AES Key Wrap Algorithm

Assume that the data to be wrapped consist of N 64-bit data blocks.

If N is 1, then 64 bits are appended, consisting of the repeated octet xA6, and a single AES operation is performed for wrap. Unwrap is also a single AES operation, followed by checking the 64-bit integrity constant and extracting the initial 64 bits of the wrapped quantity.

If N > 1, then 6 * N AES operations are performed for wrap or unwrap. Definitions used in the pseudocode given below are as follows:

- The key to be wrapped is denoted as P(1), P(2), P(3), . . . , P(N).

- The result of wrapping will be N + 1 64-bit blocks denoted as C(0), C(1), C(2), . . . , C(N).

- K represents the key-encrypting key.

- Assume integer variables i, j, and t, an intermediate 64-bit register A, a 128-bit register B, and an array of 64-bit quantities R(1) through R(N).

- "|" represents concatenation, so "x | y", where x and y are 64-bit quantities, is the 128-bit quantity with x in the most significant bit positions and y in the least significant bit positions.

- "AES(K)enc(x)" is the operation of AES encrypting the 128-bit quantity x under the key K.

- "AES(K)dec(x)" is the corresponding decryption operation.

- "XOR(x, y)" is the bitwise exclusive OR of x and y.

- "MSB(x)" and "LSB(y)" are the most significant 64 bits and least significant 64 bits of x and y, respectively.

**Soapbox**

One of NIST's explicit design criteria for key wrapping was that every cipher text bit had to be a complex function of every plain text bit after encryption and every plain text bit had to be a complex function of every cipher text bit after decryption. As this is true of single-block AES encryption and decryption, it is obviously true for N = 1. For larger N, the wrap algorithm uses AES to combine adjacent 64-bit blocks so that each of the six iterations of the main loop spread data from a block farther along the data array (wrapping around when it reaches the end). Because the largest AES key is 256 bits (i.e., four 64-bit blocks), you might guess that the main loop count of 6 was chosen so that those four blocks and the one block of integrity check code would be thoroughly mixed. With a fixed count, however, this complete mixing may not occur for larger N. It would seem there is wasted computation for smaller N in the range $1 < N < 4$.

### Wrap

The key wrap algorithm is as follows:

1. If N is 1:

   $$B = AES(K)enc(0xA6A6A6A6A6A6A6A6 \mid P(1))$$

   $$C(0) = MSB(B)$$

   $$C(1) = LSB(B)$$

   If $N > 1$, perform the following steps:

2. Initialize variables:

   Set A to 0xA6A6A6A6A6A6A6A6

   For $i = 1$ to N,

   $$R(i) = P(i)$$

3. Calculate intermediate values:

   For $j = 0$ to 5,

   For $i = 1$ to N,

   $$t = i + j * N$$

   $$B = AES(K)enc(A \mid R(i))$$

   $$A = XOR(t, MSB(B))$$

   $$R(i) = LSB(B)$$

4. Output the results:

    Set $C(0) = A$

    For $i = 1$ to N,

    $C(i) = R(i)$

**Unwrap**

The key unwrap algorithm is as follows:

1. If N is 1:

    $B = AES(K)dec(C(0) \,|\, C(1))$

    $P(1) = LSB(B)$

    If MSB(B) is 0xA6A6A6A6A6A6A6A6, return success. Otherwise, return an integrity check failure error.

    If $N > 1$, perform the following steps:

2. Initialize the variables:

    $A = C(0)$

    For $i - 1$ to N,

        $R(i) = C(i)$

3. Calculate intermediate values:

    For $j = 5$ to 0,

        For $i = N$ to 1,

            $t = i + j * N$

            $B = AES(K)dec(XOR(t, A) \,|\, R(i))$

            $A = MSB(B)$

            $R(i) = LSB(B)$

4. Output the results:

    For $i - 1$ to N, $P(i) = R(i)$

    If A is 0xA6A6A6A6A6A6A6A6, return success. Otherwise, return an integrity check failure error.

## Example

For example, wrapping the data

```
0x00112233445566778899AABBCCDDEEFF
```

with the KEK

```
0x000102030405060708090A0B0C0D0E0F
```

produces the cipher text of

```
0x1FA68B0A8112B447, 0xAEF34BD8FB5A7B82, 0x9D3E862371D2CFE5
```

# 19 | Non-cryptographic Algorithms

This chapter describes non-cryptographic XML or text-oriented algorithms that you can specify in XML Security by a well-known URI. See Chapter 17 for an overview of algorithms in XML Security and Chapter 18 for a description of cryptographic algorithms.

## 19.1    Canonicalization Algorithms

Chapter 9 discusses in detail the topic of XML canonicalization and the standard methods for canonicalizing XML. The identifiers for Canonical XML and Exclusive XML Canonicalization are given in Sections 19.1.1and 19.1.2, respectively. The identifier for Minimal Canonicalization, along with a discussion of that algorithm, appears in Section 19.1.3. Both Canonicalization-Method and Transform elements can use Canonicalization algorithms. See Figure 19-1.

**Soapbox**

Chapters 9, 10, and 15 provide detailed discussions of the use of canonicalization for signatures and encryption. You need to use the appropriate canonicalization for your application but, in the absence of other information, you probably want to use Exclusive XML Canonicalization for signatures and Canonical XML if you choose to canonicalize XML before encrypting. This advice is contrary to the signature recommendation, which specifies Canonical XML. That recommendation was written before developers recognized the problem of signature robustness in the face of changed XML context and before the specification of Exclusive XML Canonicalization.

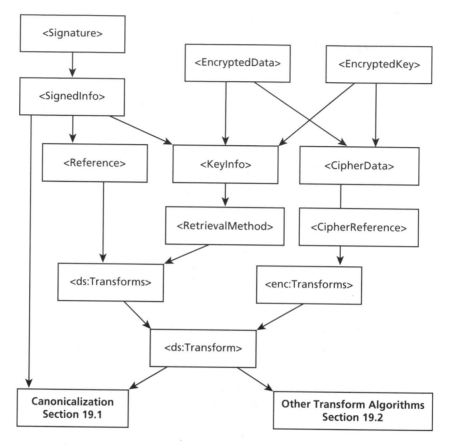

**Figure 19-1** | Canonicalization and other Transform algorithm element ancestors

## 19.1.1   Canonical XML

```
Canonical XML Identifiers:
   http://www.w3.org/TR/2001/REC-xml-c14n-20010315
   http://www.w3.org/TR/2001/REC-xml-c14n-20010315#WithComments
```

Implementation of Canonical XML without comments, represented by the first identifier in the preceding code, is mandatory for applications that conform to the XML Digital Signature standard. Implementation of Canonical XML with comments is recommended.

In conjunction with XML Encryption applications, implementation of either form of Canonical XML is optional.

An example element follows:

```
<CannonicalizationMethod
  Algorithm="http://www.w3.org/TR/2001/REC-xml-c14n-20010315"/>
```

### 19.1.2  Exclusive XML Canonicalization

```
Exclusive XML Canonicalization Identifiers:
   http://www.w3.org/TR/2001/06/xmldsig-excl-c14n#
   http://www.w3.org/TR/2001/06/xmldsig-excl-c14n#WithComments
```

Implementation of Exclusive XML Canonicalization is optional.

An example element follows:

```
<CannonicalizationMethod
  Algorithm="http://www.w3.org/TR/2001/06/xmldsig-excl-c14n#"/>
```

### 19.1.3  Minimal Canonicalization

```
Minimal Canonicalization Identifier:
   http://www.w3.org/2000/09/xmldsig#minimal
```

Implementation of Minimal Canonicalization is optional. An example of a minimal canonicalization element follows:

```
<Transform
  Algorithm="http://www.w3.org/2000/09/xmldsig#minimal"/>
```

**History**

> Minimal Canonicalization was not implemented by any of those parties involved in the XML canonicalization or signature interoperation testing. Its specification is included only because some participants in the XML Security standardization process insisted that they planned to implement it.

The minimal canonicalization algorithm has two steps:

1. Convert the character encoding to UTF-8 (without any byte order mark). If an encoding appears in an XML declaration, remove it. Implementations of Minimal Canonicalization must understand both UTF-8

[RFC 2279] and UTF-16 [RFC 2781] as input encodings. If a non-Unicode input is understood and translated to Unicode, then and only then must you perform text normalization to Normal Form C [NFC].

2. Normalize line endings, as provided by the XML Recommendation [XML] and described in Chapter 9.

This algorithm processes the input octet stream into an output octet stream. If the application has a node-set for the implicit input, then it must convert that node-set into octets. However, Minimal Canonicalization is not particularly appropriate for processing XPath node-sets, the results of same-document URI references, or the output of other types of XML-based Transforms. It is most appropriate for simple character normalization of plain text or possibly well-formed XML that has no namespace or external entity complications.

## 19.2    Transformation Algorithms

A Transform element appears as the child of the Transform element, which in turn can appear as the child of a Reference, RetrievalMethod, or Cipher-Reference. (See Figure 19-1.) As implicit input, these elements take the output of their previous Transform sibling or, if none exists, the data obtained by dereferencing the URI attribute of their parent.

**Note**

> The Transform element, while identical in structure in XML Signature and XML Encryption, is considered, for those recommendations, different and to reside in their respective different namespaces. The Transform element, however, is always found in the XML Signature namespace.

### 19.2.1  Canonicalization

You can also use any algorithm listed in Section 19.1 as a transform algorithm. The identifier is the same regardless of the role filled by the algorithm.

### 19.2.2  Base-64 Decoding

```
Base64 Identifier:
    http://www.w3.org/2000/09/xmldsig#base64
```

The normative specification for base-64 decoding transforms is [RFC 2045]. The base-64 Transform element takes no explicit parameter content; rather, the algorithm decodes the implicit input. This transform is useful if an application needs to access the raw data associated with the encoded content of an element. Its implementation is mandatory.

This transform requires an octet stream for input. If an XPath node-set (or sufficiently functional alternative) is given as input, then it is converted to an octet stream by performing operations logically equivalent to the following steps:

1. Apply an XPath transform with the expression

```
self::text()
```

2. Take the string value of the node-set.

Thus, if an XML element is identified by a bare name XPointer (see Chapter 7) in the Reference URI, and its content consists of character data encoded in base-64, this transform automatically does the following:

- Strips away the start and end tags of the identified element and any of its descendant elements

- Strips away any descendant comments and processing instructions

The output is an octet stream.

### 19.2.3  XPath Filtering

```
XPath Identifier:
    http://www.w3.org/TR/1999/REC-xpath-19991116
```

The normative specification for XPath expression evaluation is [XPath]. The XPath expression to be evaluated appears as the character content of a transform parameter child element named XPath in the XMLDSIG namespace. Implementation of this transform is recommended. The DTD for the XPath element follows:

```
<!-- XPath DTD -->

<!ELEMENT XPath (#PCDATA) >
```

In schema notation, it has the following form:

```
<!-- XPath Schema -->

<element name="XPath" type="string"/>
```

### XPath Transform Input

The input required by this transform is an XPath node-set. If the actual input is an XPath node-set resulting from a null URI or bare name XPointer deref-erence, then comment nodes will have been omitted. If the actual input is an octet stream, then the application must convert the octet stream to an XPath node-set suitable for use by Canonical XML with comments. (A subsequent application of the required Canonical XML algorithm would strip away these comments.) In other words, the input node-set should be equivalent to the one created by the following process:

1. Initialize an XPath evaluation context by setting the initial node equal to the input XML document's root node, and set the context position and size to 1.

2. Evaluate the following XPath expression:

```
(//. | //@* | //namespace::*)
```

The evaluation of this expression includes all of the document's nodes (includ-ing comments) in the node-set.

### XPath Transform Output

The transform output is also an XPath node-set. The XPath expression appearing in the XPath parameter is evaluated once for each node in the input node-set. The result is converted to a Boolean value. If the Boolean value is true, then the node is included in the output node-set. If the Boolean value is false, then the node is omitted from the output node-set. In effect, the XPath expression is an XPath predicate except that the usual surrounding square brackets are omitted.

This transform ensures that only specifically defined changes to the input XML document are permitted after the signature is affixed. To do so, omit those nodes that are allowed to change, and include all other input nodes in the out-put. The XPath expression author is responsible for including all nodes whose changes should affect the validity of signatures in their application context.

An example would be a document requiring two enveloped signatures. Each signature must omit itself from its own digest calculations. It is also necessary to exclude the second signature element from the digest calculations of the first signature to ensure that adding the second signature does not break the first signature. Thus the EnvelopedSignature transform (see Section 19.2.4) is inadequate for the second signature, but probably adequate for the first signature.

### XPath Transform Evaluation

The XPath transform establishes the following evaluation context for each node of the input node-set:

- A context node equal to a node of the input node-set.

- A context position, initialized to 1.

- A context size, initialized to 1.

- A library of functions equal to the function set that XPath defines plus a function named "here( )" (see the XPath Function "here()" later in this chapter).

- A set of variable bindings. No means for initializing these bindings is defined, so the set of variable bindings used when evaluating the XPath expression is empty. Use of a variable reference in the XPath expression, therefore, results in an error.

- The set of namespace declarations in scope for the XPath expression.

As a result of the context node setting, the XPath expressions appearing in this transform will be quite similar to those used by XSLT. The only difference is that the size and position are always 1, reflecting the fact that the transform automatically visits every node. (In XSLT, you recursively call the command "apply-templates" to visit the nodes of the input tree.)

Even if comments were removed from the input node-set, the comment nodes still exist in the underlying parse tree and can separate text nodes. For example, the markup

```
<e>Hello, <!-- comment --> world!</e>
```

contains two text nodes. Therefore, the expression

```
self::text()[string()="Hello, world!"]
```

would fail. Should this problem arise in an application, you can solve it in one of two ways:

- By converting the document to Canonical XML before the XPath transform, to physically remove the comments and concatenate resulting adjacent text

- By matching the node based on the parent element's string value

For example, using the expression

```
self::text()[string(parent::e)="Hello, world!"]
```

would work.

### XPath Function "here( )"

The function "here( )" is defined as follows:

```
node-set here( )
```

The "here( )" function returns a node-set containing the attribute or processing instruction node or the parent element of the text node that directly bears the XPath expression. This expression results in an error if the containing XPath expression does not appear in the same XML document against which the XPath expression is being evaluated. It works in the same way as the "here( )" function added by XPointer (see Chapter 7).

### XPath Transform Example

As an example, consider the creation of an enveloped signature (a Signature element that is a descendant of an element being signed). Although the signed content should not change after signing, the elements within the Signature element do change (e.g., the digest value must be put inside the DigestValue and the SignatureValue must be subsequently calculated). One way to prevent these changes from invalidating the digest value in Digest-Value is to add an XPath transform that omits all Signature elements and their descendants. For example:

```
<Document>
  ...
  <Signature xmlns="http://www.w3.org/2000/09/xmldsig#">
    <SignedInfo>
      ...
```

```
        <Reference URI="">
          <Transforms>
            <Transform
Algorithm="http://www.w3.org/TR/1999/REC xpath-19991116">
              <XPath
                xmlns:dsig="http://www.w3.org/2000/09/xmldsig#">
                not(ancestor-or-self::dsig:Signature)
              </XPath>
            </Transform>
          </Transforms>
          <DigestMethod
            Algorithm="http://www.w3.org/2000/09/xmldsig#sha1"/>
          <DigestValue>...</DigestValue>
        </Reference>
      </SignedInfo>
      <SignatureValue>...</SignatureValue>
    </Signature>
    ...
</Document>
```

Due to the null Reference URI in this example, the XPath transform input node-set contains all nodes in the entire parse tree, starting at the root node, except the comment nodes. Each node in this node-set is included in the output node-set except if the node or one of its ancestors has a tag of "Signature" in the XMLDSIG namespace.

A more elegant solution uses the "here( )" function to omit only the Signature containing the XPath transform, thereby allowing enveloped signatures to sign other signatures. In the preceding example, you would use the following XPath element:

```
<XPath xmlns:dsig="http://www.w3.org/2000/09/xmldsig#">
    count(ancestor-or-self::dsig:Signature |
          here()/ancestor::dsig:Signature[1]) >
    count(ancestor-or-self::dsig:Signature)
</XPath>
```

Because the XPath equality operator converts node-sets to string values before comparison, we must instead use the XPath union operator ("|").

For each node of the document, the predicate expression is true if and only if the node-set containing the node and its Signature element ancestors does not include the enveloped Signature element containing the XPath expression. That is, the union must not produce a larger set if the enveloped Signature element is in the node-set given by ancestor-or-self::Signature.

### 19.2.4   Enveloped Signature Transform

```
Enveloped Signature Identifier:
    http://www.w3.org/2000/09/xmldsig#enveloped-signature
```

An enveloped signature transform removes the entire Signature element containing the transform from the data being transformed. If it appears in a Reference, then that Signature element would generally not be included in the digest calculated. In such a case, the digest calculation removes the entire string of characters that an XML processor uses to match the subdocument of which the Signature element is the apex. The output of the transform is equivalent to the output that would result from replacing this transform with an XPath transform containing the following XPath parameter element:

```
<XPath xmlns:dsig="http://www.w3.org/2000/09/xmldsig ">
    count(ancestor-or-self::dsig:Signature |
        here()/ancestor::dsig:Signature[1]) >
    count(ancestor-or-self::dsig:Signature)
</XPath>
```

The input and output requirements of this transform are identical to those of the XPath transform. You do not have to use an XPath expression evaluator to create this transform. However, this transform must produce the same output as the XPath transform parameterized by the XPath expression above. See also Section 19.2.3 on XPath filtering.

### 19.2.5   XSLT Transform

```
XSLT Identifier:
    http://www.w3.org/TR/1999/REC-xslt-19991116
```

The normative specification for the XSL transform is [XSLT]. The XSL transformation is encoded within an XSLT namespace-qualified stylesheet element that must be the sole child of the Transform element. Implementation of this transform is optional. The XSLT processing model determines whether it causes in-line processing of XSLT declarations embedded in the input. Applying multiple stylesheets successively may require multiple Transform elements. You can invoke a remote stylesheet by using the XSLT "include" or "import" feature within the stylesheet child of the Transform element.

The DTD for the stylesheet element follows:

```
<!-- stylesheet DTD -->

<!ELEMENT stylesheet (#PCDATA) >
```

In schema notation, it has the following form:

```
<!-- stylesheet Schema -->

<element name="stylesheet" type="string"/>
```

This transform requires an octet stream as input. If the actual input is an XPath node-set, then the signature application should attempt to convert it to octets (i.e., apply Canonical XML), as described in the Transform pipeline model detailed in Chapter 10.

The output of this transform is an octet stream. The [XSLT] specification states the processing rules for the XSL stylesheet or Transform element. We recommend that XSLT transform authors use an output method of "xml" for XML and HTML. XSLT implementations do not produce consistent serializations of their output; for signature purposes, then, you must usually insert a transform after the XSLT transform to canonicalize the output. These steps will help to ensure interoperability of the resulting signatures among applications that support the XSLT transform. Note that if the output is actually HTML, then the result of these steps is logically equivalent to [XHTML].

### 19.2.6  XPointer

```
XPointer Identifier:
    http://www.w3.org/2001/04/xmldsig-more/xptr
```

This transform algorithm takes an [XPointer] as an explicit parameter. It provides a more powerful way to extract parts of an XML document to sign, including fail-over provisions. Full implementation of XPointer is optional, however. An example of its use follows, where failure to find a node with an ID of "foo" would fail over to the second search, that for an element named "Zab" in the "urn:baz" namespace with an attribute named "Tag" having the value "foo".

```
<Transform
  Algorithm="http://www.w3.org/2001/04/xmldsig-more/xptr">
  <Xpointer
   xmlns="http://www.w3.org/2001/04/xmldsig-more/xptr">
    xpointer(id("foo"))
    xmlns(bar=urn:baz)
    xpointer(//bar:Zab[@Tag="foo"])
  </XPointer>
</Transform>
```

The DTD for the XPointer element follows:

```
<!-- XPointer DTD -->

<!ELEMENT XPointer (#PCDATA)>
```

In schema notation, it has the following form:

```
<!-- XPointer Schema -->

<element name="XPointer" type="string"/>
```

Input to this transform consists of an octet stream (which is then parsed into XML). Output from this transform is a node-set; the results of the XPointer are processed as defined in Chapter 6 for a same-document XPointer.

### 19.2.7   XML Schema Validation

```
Schema Validation Identifier:
    http://www.w3.org/TR/2001/09/Validate#
```

**History**

The XML schema validation transform was temporarily included in an intermediate draft of XMLDSIG but currently has its own separate informal document.

This transform provides control over schema validation [Schema]. If no explicit parameters are provided, it indicates that the schema validation must be applied to the implicit input data according to the schema information within that data. If the Transform element has as its sole child a namespace-qualified "schema" element, that element contains the schema to use for validation. The [Schema] processing model determines whether it causes in-line processing of local schema declarations in the input. Applying multiple schemas successively may require multiple Transform elements. You can invoke a remote schema by using the [Schema] "include" or "import" features within the schema child element of the Transform element.

While most of the changes made by [Schema] are additions that are outside the XPath data model, schema validation can affect default attribute values and element content. When this possibility can occur, both the signer and the verifier must do the same schema validation for a signature to be meaningful.

## 19.2.8   Decryption Transform

Refer back to Chapter 16 for information on the decryption transform.

# Appendixes

Supplemental information is provided in the six appendixes for this book.

First, Appendix A lists some implementations, software development kits, sets of test vectors, and the like for the various XML Security standards, although this will no doubt be out of date by the time this book is published. Nevertheless, it should provide a useful starting point.

Appendixes B, C, and D describe three of the several organizations involved in issuing XML Security or cryptographic standards, in particular, the W3C, IETF, and NIST.

Appendix E goes into greater depth on the difference between the paper or document point of view and the protocol or message point of view, a difference that is alluded to many times in the body of this book.

Finally, Appendix F provides the full schema for SOAP encoding.

# Appendix A | XML Security Implementations

The existence of numerous independent, interoperable implementations shows the vitality of a protocol. In fact, the existence of such implementations is a key criterion for advancing beyond the first rung of the IETF standardization ladder.

Explicit interoperability testing has been performed for Canonical XML, XMLDSIG, XML Encryption, and Exclusive XML Canonicalization. Furthermore, several sources have indicated the availability of toolkits, software development kits (SDKs), source code, or test vectors for these standards and XKMS.

The latest Canonical XML interoperability matrix is found at

```
http://www.w3.org/Signature/2000/10/10-c14n-interop.html
```

and is linked off the XMLDSIG Working Group site [XMLDSIG WG]. Note that, at the time this book goes to press, it has not been updated since July 2001. Participation in that interoperability primarily indicates early involvement. The XMLDSIG interoperability matrix also details the interoperability of Canonical XML features. For this reason, it is not important if a current XMLDSIG interoperability participant was not included in the old Canonical XML interoperability matrix.

The latest XMLDSIG interoperability matrix is found at

```
http://www.w3.org/Signature/2001/04/05-xmldsig-interop.html
```

and is linked off the XMLDSIG Working Group site [XMLDSIG WG]. Notwithstanding its file name, it was updated in April 2002. It is a reasonable place to look for information on XMLDSIG and Canonical XML implementations.

The latest XML Encryption interoperability matrix is found at

```
http://www.w3.org/Encryption/2002/02-xenc-interop.html
```

and is linked off the XML Encryption Working Group site [XMLENC WG]. As this book goes to press, information is being added to this matrix. In the future, it should be a reasonable place to look for information on XML Encryption implementations.

The latest Exclusive XML Canonicalization interoperability matrix is found at

```
http://www.w3.org/Signature/2002/02/01-exc-c14n-interop.html
```

and is linked off the XMLDSIG Working Group site [XMLDSIG WG]. As this book goes to press, information is being added to this matrix. In the future, it should be a reasonable place to look for information on Exclusive XML Canonicalization implementations.

No interoperability-testing matrix has been created for XKMS as yet, but one will likely appear at some point in the future.

> The information in this appendix is taken from the [XMLDSIG WG], [XMLENC WG], and [XKMS WG] Working Group Web sites, the Web sites of the participating companies and persons, and other sources. No attempt has been made to confirm the information, and its accuracy is not guaranteed. Licenses or payment may be required to use some of the resources listed here. **The information presented here continues to evolve rapidly and will change.**

Table A-1 provides a general implementation overview. The following sections give some information on the implementation or other resources available from each company or person listed in Table A-1.

---

## A.1    Apache

**URL**

```
http://www.apache.org
```

> Reports indicate that, at this time, the Apache Xalan package does not properly implement the XPath data model for namespaces. It does **not** distribute namespace declarations over all descendant elements that are in scope.

> Namespace prefixes work correctly, but explicit checks for the existence of a declaration may fail where they should succeed. Code that depends on the correct implementation of this distribution is not common.

### XMLDSIG

An implementation of Canonical XML and XML Signature for Java by Christian Geuer-Pollmann is available. See

```
http://xml.apache.org/security/index.html
```

There is also a collection of test vectors that includes those from Merlin Hughes of Baltimore and Gregor Karlinger of IAIK. See

```
http://cvs.apache.org/viewcvs.cgi/xml-security/data/
```

## A.2    Baltimore Technologies

### URL

```
http://www.baltimore.com
```

Baltimore Technologies participated fully in the early Canonical XML interoperability testing as well as the later XMLDSIG, Exclusive XML Canonicalization, and XML Encryption interoperability testing. Its product interoperated successfully on all points in the XMLDSIG testing (except Minimal Canonicalization, which no one else implemented either).

### XMLDSIG and Exclusive XML Canonicalization

For information about the Baltimore Technologies XMLDSIG product, see

```
http://www.baltimore.com/keytools/xml/index.html
```

A set of signature test vectors produced by Merlin Hughes of Baltimore is maintained at the following site (Warning: The URL is line wrapped due to insufficient print width):

```
http://cvs.apache.org/viewcvs.cgi/xml-security/data/ie/
baltimore/merlin-examples/
```

The Baltimore Technologies product also interoperated successfully on all points in the Exclusive XML Canonicalization testing and a set of Exclusive

**Table A-1** | Implementations on Working Group Web Sites

| Company/Person | Section | XMLDSIG | Exclusive XML Canonicalization | (Canonical XML) | XMLENC | XKMS |
|---|---|---|---|---|---|---|
| Apache | A.1 | I S V | | I S | | |
| Baltimore Technologies | A.2 | IV | IV | I | IV | |
| Capslock | A.3 | I | | | | |
| Done Information (Done 360) | A.4 | | | I | | |
| DSTC | A.5 | I | | I | | |
| Entrust | A.6 | T | | T | | T |
| Fujitsu | A.7 | I | | | | |
| GapXse | A.8 | I S | | | | |
| HP Web Services | A.9 | T | | | | |
| IAIK | A.10 | I T V | IV | I T | | |
| IBM | A.11 | I T | I | I | I T | |
| Infomosaic | A.12 | T V | T | | | |
| JDSS II | A.13 | T | | | | |
| Mather | A.14 | | | S | | |
| Microsoft | A.15 | I T | | | | |
| NEC | A.16 | I T | | T | | |

**Table A-1** (continued)

| | | IT | IV | |
|---|---|---|---|---|
| Phaos Technology | A.17 | I T | | T |
| Poupou | A.18 | | | T |
| RSA Security | A.19 | I T | | T |
| Siggen | A.20 | | I | |
| Verisign | A.21 | T | | T |
| W3C | A.22 | V | S | |
| WebSig | A.23 | I | | |
| Wedgetail | A.24 | I T | | |
| XML Sec | A.25 | I S | I | |

I = Successful Interoperability, S = Source Code, T = Toolkit/SDK  V = Test Vectors.

Note: The XMLENC and Exclusive XML Canonicalization columns are sparse because their interoperability testing has not been done for very long. A number of other implementations of XMLENC and Exclusive XML Canonicalization exist.

XML Canonicalization test vectors linked off the Exclusive XML Canonicalization interoperability page at

```
http://www.w3.org/Signature/2002/02/01-exc-c14n-interop.html
```

### XML Encryption

The Baltimore Technologies product interoperated successfully on all points in the XML Encryption testing. Merlin Hughes also maintains a set of XML Encryption test vectors linked off the XML Encryption interoperability page at

```
http://www.w3.org/Encryption/2002/02-xenc-interop.html
```

## A.3    Capslock

### URL

```
http://www.capslocksecurity.com
```

Capslock was a successful participant in the XMLDSIG interoperability testing, missing only a few points relating to optional XPath and XSLT features.

### XMLDSIG

For information on the Capslock "Ubisecure Signature" XMLDSIG product, see

```
http://www.capslocksecurity.com/products/Ubisecure.htm#Signature
```

## A.4    Done Information

Done Information (also known as "Done 360") participated in the early Canonical XML interoperability testing. Its product was then transferred to Capslock.

## A.5    DSTC

### URL

```
http://www.dstc.edu.au
```

DSTC (Distributed Systems Technology Centre) was a successful participant in the XMLDSIG interoperability testing, missing only a few points relating to optional RetrievalMethod, XPath, and XSLT features.

### XMLDSIG

For information on DSTC's XMLDSIG product, which is free for noncommercial use, see

```
http://security.dstc.com/products/xmldsig/
```

It appears that the company's Java Crypto and Security Implementation is now being marketed for commercial use by Wedgetail.

## A.6    Entrust

### URL

```
http://www.entrust.com
```

### XMLDSIG

Entrust/Toolkit for Java supports XMLDSIG. See

```
http://www.entrust.com/developer/java/index.htm
```

### XKMS

Entrust maintains a Java XKMS reference implementation as a service on the Web with which you can interact. See

```
http://xkms.entrust.com/xkms/index.htm
```

## A.7    Fujitsu

### URL

```
http://www.fujitsu.com
```

Fujitsu was a successful participant in the XMLDSIG interoperability testing, missing a few points relating to optional RetrievalMethod, XPointer, XPath, and XSLT features.

Its Java-based implementation supports three key stores: the Java Security API, Microsoft Crypto API (including smart card), and Fujitsu's security library. You can choose whether to include Fujistu's XSLT processor, required for XPath filtering. If it is not included, you can use the JAXP parser in place of Fujitsu's XML parser. The signature processor (xmldsig.jar) is 146 KB. The XML parser (xmlpro.jar) is about 300 KB and the XSLT processor (xml-trans.jar) is about 400 KB.

### XMLDSIG

For current information on Fujitsu's XMLDSIG products, see

```
http://xml.fujitsu.com/en/index.html
```

## A.8    GapXse

### URL

```
http://www.di.unipi.it/~claudio/gapxse/
```

### XMLDSIG

GapXse has a downloadable Java implementation of XMLDSIG implemented by students at "Dipartimento di Informatica dell 'Universita' di Pisa." It has successfully interoperated for all tested features except for Minimal Canonicalization (which no one else implemented either), the XPath here( ) function, and XSLT.

## A.9    HP Web Services

### URL

```
http://www.hp.com
```

HP has successfully interoperated for all XMLDSIG features except for Minimal Canonicalization (which no one else has implemented either).

### XMLDSIG

HP Web Services Platform 2.0 can be downloaded from

```
http://www.hpmiddleware.com/webservices
```

## A.10   IAIK

### URL

```
http://www.iaik.at
```

IAIK (Institute for Applied Information Processing and Communications) participated fully and with complete success in the early Canonical XML interoperability testing. It was a successful participant in the XMLDSIG interoperability testing as well, missing only a few points relating to optional XSLT features and Minimal Canonicalization (which no one else implemented either). It successfully interoperated for all Exclusive XML Canonicalization features tested.

### XMLDSIG and Exclusive XML Canonicalization

The IAIK XML Signature Library (IXSIL) is available at

```
http://jcewww.iaik.at/products/ixsil/index.php
```

A set of signature test vectors produced by Gregor Karlinger of IAIK is maintained at

```
http://cvs.apache.org/viewcvs.cgi/xml-security/data/at/iaik/
```

and Exclusive XML Canonicalization test vectors are linked off that standards interoperability page at

```
http://www.w3.org/Signature/2002/02/01-exc-c14n-interop.html
```

## A.11   IBM

### URL

```
http://www.ibm.com
```

IBM participated fully and with complete success in the early Canonical XML interoperability testing. The company participated and interoperated successfully on all points in the XMLDSIG testing (except Minimal Canonicalization, which no one else implemented either). For XML Encryption, it implemented all mandatory aspects; however, the company has not implemented the recommended normalized form C generation or optional Diffie-Hellman key values or key agreement, SHA-256, SHA-512, RIPEMD-160, or XPointer support in the Decryption Transform "Except" URI value.

### XMLDSIG, XMLENC, and XKMS

The IBM security suite, implemented in Java, includes XMLDSIG, XML Encryption, and XKMS. It also includes XACL, the XML Access Control Language.

```
http://www.alphaworks.ibm.com/tech/xmlsecuritysuite
```

See also the article at

```
http://www.ibm.com/developerworks/library/s-xmlsec.html
```

## A.12    Infomosaic

### URL

```
https://www.infomosaic.net/
```

Infomosaic successfully interoperated for all XMLDSIG features except for the optional XSLT transform and Minimal Canonicalization (which no one else implemented either).

### XMLDSIG

Infomosaic has an XMLDSIG and Canonical XML product available in C and C++ source code and other forms. See

```
https://www.infomosaic.net/XMLSign/
```

The company also operated a "Secure XML Verify( )" Web service at

```
http://www.infomosaic.net/XMLSign/SecureXMLVerifyWS.htm
```

## A.13    JDSS II

### XMLDSIG

A Java implementation of XMLDSIG is available from

```
http://www.digitalkey.com/
```

## A.14 Mather

### URL

```
http://tjmather.com
```

### Canonical XML

Canonical XML for Perl by T. J. Mather is available from

```
http://tjmather.com/xml-canonical/
```

## A.15 Microsoft

### URL

```
http://www.microsoft.com
```

Microsoft was a successful participant in the XMLDSIG interoperability testing, missing only a few features relating to RetrievalMethod and XPath features that are optional in the standard.

### XMLDSIG

The Microsoft XMLDSIG implementation is documented in the ".NET" Framework SDK—see System.Security.Cryptography.Xml. It is available for download from MSDN. Microsoft expects to add XML Encryption support soon.

### XKMS

Microsoft maintains client and server sample code (ASP .NET) at

```
http://msdn.microsoft.com/library/en-
us/dnaspp/html/implementingxkms.asp
```

## A.16 NEC

### URL

```
http://www.nec.com
```

NEC participated fully and interoperated successfully on all features in the XMLDSIG testing (except Minimal Canonicalization, which no one else implemented either).

### XMLDSIG

NEC has an XML Digital Signature Software Library available at

```
http://www.sw.nec.co.jp/soft/xml_s/appform_e.html
```

## A.17 Phaos Technology

### URL

```
http://www.phaos.com
```

Phaos participated fully and interoperated successfully on all features in the XMLDSIG testing (except Minimal Canonicalization, which no one else implemented either). It also participated in XML Encryption interoperability and implemented all required and recommended features being tested except for the recommended normalized form C generation. Of optional XML Encryption features being tested for interoperability, the company implemented all except RIPEMD-160.

### XMLDSIG and XMLENC

For information on products from Phaos for XMLDSIG, XML Canonicalization, and XML Encryption, see

```
http://www.phaos.com/e_security/prod_xml.html
```

Phaos also maintains a set of XML Encryption test vectors linked off the XML Encryption interoperability page at

```
http://www.w3.org/Encryption/2002/02-xenc-interop.html
```

## A.18 Poupou

### XKMS Interoperability Web Service (.NET)

Sébastien Pouliot maintains a site from which you can download an XKMS client. The site also provides a service with which you can interact. These services are all oriented to the Microsoft .NET system. See

```
http://www24.brinkster.com/xkms/
```

## A.19    RSA Security

### URL

```
http://www.rsasecurity.com
```

RSA Security was a successful participant in the XMLDSIG interoperability testing, missing only a few points relating to optional RetrievalMethod, XPointer, XSLT features, and Minimal Canonicalization (which no one else implemented either).

### XMLDSIG and XKMS

RSA's BSAFE Cert-J SDK supports XMLDSIG and XKMS. See

```
http://www.rsasecurity.com/products/bsafe/certj.html
```

## A.20    Siggen

### URL

```
http://www.xmlsecurity.org
```

Although listed separately in the Canonical XML interoperability matrix, this product appears to be part of the current Apache XML Project. See Section A.1 on Apache.

## A.21    Verisign

### URL

```
http://www.verisign.com
```

Verisign sponsors the "http://www.xmltrustcenter.org" site.

### XMLDSIG

The Verisign XML Signature Java SDK is available from

```
http://www.xmltrustcenter.org/xmlsig/developer/verisign/index.htm
```

### XKMS

The Verisign XKMS Java toolkit/SDK is available from

```
http://www.xmltrustcenter.org/xkms/index.htm
```

Verisign is one of the original authors of XKMS.

## A.22   W3C

### URL

```
http://www.w3.org
```

W3C is the World Wide Web Consortium.

### Canonicalization

Canonical XML and Exclusive Canonical XML for Python, by Joseph Reagle and Richard Salz, are available at

```
http://dev.w3.org/cvsweb/2001/xmlsec-python/
```

### XMLDSIG

A small set of test vectors for XMLDSIG is maintained that can be accessed through a link on the interoperability page at

```
http://www.w3.org/Signature/2001/04/05-xmldsig-interop.html
```

## A.23   WebSig

### URL

```
http://xml.apache.org/security/index.html
```

Although listed separately in the XMLDSIG interoperability matrix, this product appears to be part of the current Apache XML Project. It successfully participated in the XMDSIG interoperability tests for all features except Minimal Canonicalization (which no one else implemented either). See Section A.1 on Apache.

## A.24   Wedgetail

### URL

```
http://www.wedgetail.com/
```

Wedgetail markets the DSTC product for commercial use. See Section A.5 on DSTC.

### XMLDSIG

For further information on the Wedgetail product, see

```
http://www.wedgetail.com/xmlsecurity/
```

---

## A.25    XML Sec

### URL

```
http://www.aleksey.com/xmlsec/index.html
```

This library of cryptographic code includes an XML Security Library by Aleksey Sanin.

### XMLDSIG

XML Sec successfully participated in the XMLDSIG interoperability tests for all features (except Minimal Canonicalization, which no one else implemented either).

### XML Encryption

XML Sec participated in the XML Encryption interoperability testing successfully for all required and recommended features. It also interoperated successfully for almost optional features tested, except for the Decryption Transform.

# Appendix B | The W3C and W3C Documents

The World Wide Web Consortium (W3C) is the primary organization for official World Wide Web recommendations.

Tim Berners-Lee formed the W3C in 1994 and continues to act as its director. The consortium is now jointly hosted by the Massachusetts Institute of Technology's Laboratory for Computer Science (MIT/LCS), INRIA (Institut National de Recherche en Informatique et Automatique), and Keio University of Japan (Shonan Fujisawa Campus). The members of the W3C, which constitute the W3C Advisory Committee, are dues-paying organizations that, along with the U.S. Defense Advanced Research Projects Agency and the European Commission, fund the organization.

The W3C has change control over various Web content standards, including HTML, XML, and PNG (Portable Network Graphics), and a variety of content built on those standards. It also controls other Web standards such as P3P (Platform for Personal Privacy Protection) and PICS (Platform or Internet Content Selection). The W3C also standardizes application program interfaces (APIs) related to its standards and produces reference code that it makes available.

The W3C technical reports are all available on the Web. Each contains links to the previous version of the technical report, unless it is the first posted version, and a link with a URL to whatever is the latest version. Each publicly released version is given a particular status (see Section B.2) and a specific URL at the W3C site. That document version is then guaranteed by the W3C to be maintained at that URL forever.

See [W3C] to learn more about the W3C.

## B.1     Access to W3C Documents

The primary source for W3C documents is the W3C Web site Technical Reports page at

```
http://www.w3.org/TR/
```

This Web page provides access to the official and publicly released W3C documents. Some organizations may keep a local repository of W3C documents, so you might check locally first.

## B.2     W3C Document Status

All public W3C documents have one of five possible statuses:

- **Note:** A Note is a dated exposition of an idea, comment, or document. It does not represent commitment by W3C to pursue work related to the Note.

- **Working Draft:** A Working Draft represents work in progress and a commitment by W3C to pursue work in this area. It does not imply consensus by a group or W3C.

- **Candidate Recommendation:** A Candidate Recommendation is work that has received significant review from its immediate technical community within the W3C. It is an explicit call to those outside of the related Working Groups or the W3C itself for implementation and technical feedback.

- **Proposed Recommendation:** A Proposed Recommendation is work that

  - Represents consensus within the group that produced it, and

  - Has been proposed by the director to the advisory committee for review.

- **Recommendation:** A Recommendation is work that represents consensus within the W3C and has the director's approval. The W3C considers that the ideas or technology specified by a Recommendation are appropriate for widespread deployment and promote the W3C's objectives.

W3C documents contain their status prominently on the first page, so any change in status requires issuance of a new version.

**Soapbox**

> Although the W3C uses the term "Recommendation," its Recommendations are just as much standards as IETF standards, and IETF standards are just as much recommendations as W3C Recommendations. (See Appendix C.)

## B.3    W3C Document Format

W3C technical reports are, of course, available in Web formats—traditionally, HTML. However, they are now evolving through XHTML and some are available in an XML format. It is also common for the documents to be available in additional formats, mostly page oriented, such as Postscript, PDF, and even plain text.

## B.4    W3C Document Disclaimer

The W3C requires the following disclaimer with its documents:

### W3C® DOCUMENT NOTICE AND LICENSE

Copyright © 1994–2002 World Wide Web Consortium (Massachusetts Institute of Technology, Institut National de Recherche en Informatique et en Automatique, Keio University). All Rights Reserved. http://www.w3.org/Consortium/Legal/

Public documents on the W3C site are provided by the copyright holders under the following license. The software or Document Type Definitions (DTDs) associated with W3C specifications are governed by the Software Notice. By using and/or copying this document, or the W3C document from which this statement is linked, you (the licensee) agree that you have read, understood, and will comply with the following terms and conditions:

Permission to use, copy, and distribute the contents of this document, or the W3C document from which this statement is linked, in any medium for any purpose and without fee or royalty is hereby granted, provided that you include the following on ALL copies of the document, or portions thereof, that you use:

1. A link or URL to the original W3C document.

2. The preexisting copyright notice of the original author, or if it doesn't exist, a notice of the form: "Copyright © [$date-of-document] World Wide Web Consortium (Massachusetts Institute

of Technology, Institut National de Recherche en Informatique et en Automatique, Keio University). All Rights Reserved. http://www.w3.org/Consortium/Legal/" (Hypertext is preferred, but a textual representation is permitted.)

3. If it exists, the STATUS of the W3C document.

When space permits, inclusion of the full text of this NOTICE should be provided. We request that authorship attribution be provided in any software, documents, or other items or products that you create pursuant to the implementation of the contents of this document, or any portion thereof.

No right to create modifications or derivatives of W3C documents is granted pursuant to this license. However, if additional requirements (documented in the Copyright FAQ) are satisfied, the right to create modifications or derivatives is sometimes granted by the W3C to individuals complying with those requirements.

THIS DOCUMENT IS PROVIDED "AS IS," AND COPYRIGHT HOLDERS MAKE NO REPRESENTATIONS OR WARRANTIES, EXPRESS OR IMPLIED, INCLUDING, BUT NOT LIMITED TO, WARRANTIES OF MERCHANTABILITY, FITNESS FOR A PARTICULAR PURPOSE, NON-INFRINGEMENT, OR TITLE; THAT THE CONTENTS OF THE DOCUMENT ARE SUITABLE FOR ANY PURPOSE; NOR THAT THE IMPLEMENTATION OF SUCH CONTENTS WILL NOT INFRINGE ANY THIRD-PARTY PATENTS, COPYRIGHTS, TRADEMARKS, OR OTHER RIGHTS.

COPYRIGHT HOLDERS WILL NOT BE LIABLE FOR ANY DIRECT, INDIRECT, SPECIAL, OR CONSEQUENTIAL DAMAGES ARISING OUT OF ANY USE OF THE DOCUMENT OR THE PERFORMANCE OR IMPLEMENTATION OF THE CONTENTS THEREOF.

The name and trademarks of copyright holders may NOT be used in advertising or publicity pertaining to this document or its contents without specific, written prior permission. Title to copyright in this document will at all times remain with copyright holders.

## B.5    W3C Software Disclaimer

The W3C requires the following disclaimer with its software and it interprets DTDs and schemas to be software:

### W3C® SOFTWARE NOTICE AND LICENSE

Copyright © 1994–2002 World Wide Web Consortium (Massachusetts Institute of Technology, Institut National de Recherche en Informatique et en Automatique, Keio University). All Rights Reserved. http://www.w3.org/Consortium/Legal/

This W3C work (including software, documents, or other related items) is being provided by the copyright holders under the following license. By obtaining, using, and/or copying this work, you (the licensee) agree that you have read, understood, and will comply with the following terms and conditions:

Permission to use, copy, modify, and distribute this software and its documentation, with or without modification, for any purpose and without fee or royalty, is hereby granted, provided that you include the following on ALL copies of the software and documentation or portions thereof, including modifications, that you make:

1. The full text of this NOTICE in a location viewable to users of the redistributed or derivative work.

2. Any preexisting intellectual property disclaimers, notices, or terms and conditions. If none exists, a short notice of the following form (hypertext is preferred, text is permitted) should be used within the body of any redistributed or derivative code: "Copyright © [$date-of-software] World Wide Web Consortium (Massachusetts Institute of Technology, Institut National de Recherche en Informatique et en Automatique, Keio University). All Rights Reserved. http://www.w3.org/Consortium/Legal/"

3. Notice of any changes or modifications to the W3C files, including the date changes were made. (We recommend you provide URIs to the location from which the code is derived.)

THIS SOFTWARE AND DOCUMENTATION IS PROVIDED "AS IS," AND COPYRIGHT HOLDERS MAKE NO REPRESENTATIONS OR WARRANTIES, EXPRESS OR IMPLIED, INCLUDING,

# Appendix C | The IETF and IETF Documents

The Internet Engineering Task Force (IETF) is the primary organization for Internet protocol standards. The IETF is an open organization that has evolved over many years and is currently under the general supervision of the Internet Architecture Board (IAB) and the Internet Engineering Steering Group (IESG). The first general IETF meeting was held in July 1986. IETF participants are volunteers, and the group has no defined membership. Funding comes from meeting attendance fees, contributions, and the Internet Society [ISOC]. You can learn more about the IETF from its Web site; see [IETF] for more information.

The IETF series of permanent documents is most analogous to a series of numbered books on a shelf. Once an RFC is issued, it is not changed. For historical reasons, these documents are called "Requests for Comments" (RFCs), a name that reflects the spirit of early IETF RFC documents but is somewhat misleading these days. The first RFC was issued in 1969, when RFCs were paper documents. While the IETF generally welcomes comments, the main purpose of most RFCs is to inform the community rather than to solicit comments. The Internet Draft series of transient, versioned drafts now supports the IETF comment solicitation function. This book references few Internet Drafts, due to their temporary nature, and then only as "works in progress." Such Drafts normally expire after six months.

The IETF specifies all central network layer, transport layer, and routing protocols in the Internet, which operate between the lower physical layers and the higher application layers. These protocols include TCP/IP, the global domain name system (DNS), and numerous routing protocols. The IETF also handles standards for some important applications, such as e-mail (SMTP [RFC 2821, 2822], MIME [RFC 2045]) and NFS (network file system), and it has expanded to a few standards below the Internet layer, including MPLS [RFC 3031].

The IETF considers the bits on the wire between interoperating systems to be the most important aspect of networking standards. It almost never standardizes application program interfaces (APIs), although it sometimes provides an API in an Informational RFC.

In general, standards for the World Wide Web have protocol and transport aspects as well as content aspects. The IETF handles the protocol and transport standards, particularly HTTP [RFC 2616]. The W3C handles content-type standards, particularly [HTML] and [XML] (see Appendix B).

**History**

Some contentious moments arose between the IETF and the W3C over XML Security. The IETF has a larger number of active participants and a stronger track record in the security and cryptographic area. The W3C has change control over XML and owns basic XML standards. The result of the two groups' interaction was a series of compromises.

- XMLDSIG was standardized by the first-ever joint IETF/W3C working group, with documents progressing along the standards tracks of, and being published by, both organizations.

- Canonicalization of XML was worked on in the XMLDSIG working group but advanced only along the W3C standards track, with the final version also being published as an Informational IETF document.

- XML Encryption is a W3C working group effort with the understanding that final versions of its documents would also be published as Informational IETF documents.

## C.1    RFC Status

An RFC can have one of seven statuses:

- **Informational:** Intended to provide information for the Internet community. It does not state an IETF standard of any type, although other organizations' standards are sometimes republished as Informational RFCs for convenience.

- **Experimental:** A specification for use within a limited-scope experiment.

- **Best Current Practice (BCP):** An IETF recommendation as to the best practice in some area or the best practice that some part of the IETF complex should follow.

- **Proposed Standard:** The first step on the standardization ladder. It indicates that the IETF is likely to standardize something in the particular area and it should not have any obvious flaws in it. Not considered to have any assurance of stability.

- **Draft Standard:** The second step on the standardization ladder. It indicates a reasonably stable specification. There must be at least two independent interoperable implementations of any standard to reach this level. An emphasis on interoperability is a hallmark of the IETF process.

- **Internet Standard:** The third and highest step on the standardization ladder. It indicates substantial successful deployment and widespread interoperability.

- **Historic:** The graveyard state for documents that are no longer valid.

In addition, RFCs contain information at the top of their title page indicating whether they modify or make obsolete an earlier RFC.

## C.2   Access to RFCs

RFCs are relatively easy to find on the Internet. Many companies and educational institutions maintain complete local repositories of RFCs, so you should check for such a local repository that may be convenient to you.

When the IETF announces an RFC, primary English RFC repositories already have the RFC. The following URLs are paths to primary repository directories. The English versions are authoritative. Their directories have a file for each RFC with a file name of the form "rfcnnnn.txt: without leading zeros—for example, rfc2821.txt or rfc792.txt. If the file is also available in Postscript or PDF, a version of the file will exist with a ".ps" or ".pdf" suffix.

```
English:
  ftp://nis.nsf.net/documents/rfc/
  ftp://ftp.rfc-editor.org/in-notes/
  ftp://wuarchive.wustl.edu/doc/rfc/
  http://sunsite.org.uk/rfc/
```

```
ftp://ftp.ncren.net/rfc/
ftp://ftp.nic.it/rfc/
ftp://ftp.imag.fr/pub/archive/IETF/
ftp://ftp.normos.org/ietf/rfc/
ftp://ftp.ietf.rnp.br/rfc/
ftp://ftp.gigabell.net/pub/rfc/
ftp://ftp.fccn.pt/pub/IETF/RFCs/
ftp://oasisstudios.com/pub/RFC/
ftp://sunsite.dk/mirrors/rfc/
French:
http://abcdrfc.free.fr
Spanish:
http://lucas.hispalinux.es/htmls/estandares.html
```

The documents for "standards-track" RFCs—that is, those in the Proposed, Draft, or Internet Standard state (or later in the Historic state)— do not contain any indication of their state. Rather, they just say that they specify a standard. As a consequence, their state can be changed without reissuing the RFC: RFCs are never changed or reissued, although they are sometimes made obsolete by a subsequent RFC. You can consult the "rfc-index.txt" file for the status of any RFC, including whether it has been modified or made obsolete by a subsequent RFC. This file is found in the same directories as the RFCs.

Some search facilities and pointers to other RFC sites are also available on the RFC Editor Web site [RFC Editor].

## C.3   RFC Format

To correspond with the model of RFCs as books, RFCs are mostly paginated documents. For historical reasons, they are usually in ASCII and appear in a fixed-width font. Pages have a line of header and a line of footer. A form feed (x0C) character separates pages, and figures are drawn by "ASCII art." RFCs can also be in Postscript (.ps) or PDF (.pdf); for standards-track RFCs, an authoritative ASCII (.txt) version must exist.

**History**

This ASCII format is fairly archaic but it has stood the test of time in being readable, authorable, and searchable on almost any platform for several decades and appears likely to continue to work as well for the foreseeable future. Numerous proposals for other formats have been made over the years, as fads have come and gone, including Postscript, PDF, HTML, and XMl These options have all been plagued by various problems, including at least some of the following: lack of searchability, font incompatibilities, proprietary software requirements, and the problem that the suggested "best" format keeps changing. For these reasons, plain text ASCII will likely remain the format of choice for the IETF.

# Appendix D | The NIST and NIST Documents

The U.S. National Institute of Science and Technology (NIST) has been in existence for more than 100 years under a variety of names. For some time now, it has been part of the U.S. Department of Commerce and, until recently, was called the National Bureau of Standards (NBS). NIST's purpose is "to develop and promote measurement, standards, and technology to enhance productivity, facilitate trade, and improve the quality of life" [NIST].

The aspect of NIST of interest to us is its publication of Federal Information Processing Standards (FIPS). In principle, FIPS are binding only on agencies and other parts of the U.S. government. In practice, they are very influential and commonly become the definitive description of an algorithm or security practice. At the same time, NIST is mandated to work with private industry in the development of national and international voluntary standards, some of which then become FIPS.

**Soapbox**

Amazingly, the rules of some international standards bodies prohibit them from making normative references to NIST documents but permit them to make normative references to IETF RFCs. This situation arises because NIST FIPS are "national" documents describing U.S. standards but these international bodies have recognized the IETF as a competent "international" organization. (This restriction may apply even where the IETF document is an Informational RFC that effectively restates a NIST FIPS!) This stance seems curious but makes political sense, even though NIST documents tend to be more solid, polished and formal than the average IETF RFC.

Note the following:

- NIST and other parts of the U.S. government chose and refined the Data Encryption Standard, DES [FIPS 46-3, 81], from industry proposals.

- The government generated the Digital Signature Algorithm/Standard, DSA/DSS [FIPS 186-2] and related Secure Hash Standard, SHA-1 [FIPS 180-1] and upcoming extensions [FIPS 180-2].

- NIST chose the Advanced Encryption Standard [AES] in a contest generally recognized as fair, open, and international.

You can find more general information at [NIST].

## D.1    Access to NIST FIPS Documents

The current online home page for FIPS is

```
http://www.itl.nist.gov/fipspubs/
```

The government's level of commitment to the stability of this URL or those of particular FIPS documents remains unclear. On occasion we have found broken links within the NIST Web site. If you run into this problem, just try other paths through the Web page hierarchy to get what you want.

FIPS are also generally publicly available as printed documents through the U.S. Government Printing Office [GPO].

## D.2    Status of NIST Documents

The process of becoming a fully approved FIPS is fairly arduous and time-consuming, so it is often useful to reference draft FIPS or draft revisions of FIPS. Further information on the approval process for FIPS is available through

```
http://www.itl.nist.gov/fipspubs/
```

FIPS are numbered. A revision causes the addition of a hyphen and revision number. For example, FIPS 186 is the Digital Signature Standard; after two revisions, its latest version is [FIPS 186-2], which replaces all previous versions. (DSS/DSA is still commonly used to refer to the original U.S. government-devised signature algorithm, although later versions of FIPS 186 have added other signature algorithms, thus permitting their use by U.S. government agencies without a waiver or exception.)

Because of the legal effect of FIPS on U.S. government agencies, FIPS that no longer warrant presumptive government adherence are "withdrawn." Such FIPS may still provide useful information and may still be available from NIST.

## D.3   Format of FIPS

FIPS documents that relate to computer security are available online from NIST. They are provided, in a seemingly random choice, in HTML, PDF, WordPerfect, Microsoft Word, Postscript, or, less commonly, text or in multiple alternative forms from this list.

# Appendix E | The Paper and Protocol Points of View

This appendix contrasts two points of view:

- The "paper" point of view, where digital objects of interest are like pieces of paper written and viewed by people

- The "protocol" point of view, where objects of interest are dynamic composite protocol messages

XML is a very flexible technology. You can use it effectively for purposes that fit either of these points of view, even though its origin was in the paper (i.e., document) world. However, people accustomed to taking one point of view sometimes experience great difficulty in grasping the other. Even after they understand the other viewpoint, they tend to initially consider things from their accustomed point of view and assume that most of the universe of interest is best viewed from that perspective.

Much of the IETF's traditional work has concerned low-level binary protocol constructs. These constructs are almost always viewed from the protocol point of view. The W3C, in contrast, has concentrated on human presentation syntaxes and higher-level application constructs that tend more toward the paper point of view. Protocol design by those who take the paper point of view can be problematical.

This appendix defines and contrasts these two points of view. Each viewpoint is exaggerated for effect. The exaggerated paper point of view is given in paragraphs headed **PAPER**. The exaggerated protocol point of view is given in paragraphs headed **PROTOCOL**.

This entire appendix can be considered a soapbox.

**Soapbox**

## E.1    The Basic Points of View

**PAPER:** The important objects are complete digital documents, analogous to pieces of paper, viewed in isolation by people. See Figure E-1.

A major concern is to be able to present such objects as directly as possible to a court or other third party. Because what is presented to the person is all that is important, anything that can affect it, such as a stylesheet, must be considered an intrinsic part of the paper. Sometimes proponents of the paper orientation forget that the "paper" originates in a computer; may travel over, be processed in, and stored in computer systems; and is viewed on a computer. such operations may involve transcoding, enveloping, composition of messages from pieces of other messages, or data reconstruction.

**PROTOCOL:** What is important are bits on the wire generated and consumed by computer protocol processes. These bits are marshaled into composite messages that can have rich, multilevel structure. See Figure E-2. No person ever sees the full message as such; rather, it is viewed as a whole only by a "geek" when debugging—even then he or she sees some translated visible form. If you ever have to demonstrate something about such a message in a court or to a third party, there isn't any way to avoid having experts interpret it. Sometimes proponents of the protocol orientation forget that pieces of such messages are actually included in or influence data displayed to a person.

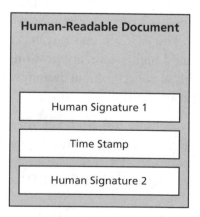

**Figure E-1** | Example paper point of view object

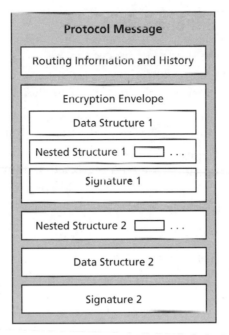

**Figure E-2** | Example protocol point of view object

## E.2 Questions of Meaning

Human "meaning" is something that the paper-oriented person considers extraordinarily important but the protocol-oriented person rarely thinks about.

### E.2.1 Core Meaning

**PAPER:** The "meaning" of a document is a deep and interesting human question related to volition. The document should typically include or reference human language policy, warranty, or disclaimer information. At an absolute minimum, it must satisfy a requirement for some sort of semantic labeling. The assumed situation is always a person interpreting the whole "paper" without other context. Thus it is reasonable to consult attorneys during message design so that the documents will hold up in court, require human-readable statements "within the four corners" of the paper, and take other similar steps during document creation.

**PROTOCOL:** The "meaning" of a protocol message is clear from the protocol specification. This specification frequently defines a protocol message in terms of the state machines of the sender and recipient processes; it may have no significant connection with human volition. Such processes have additional context and the message usually appears meaningful only with that additional context. Adding any human-readable text that is not functionally required is silly. Consulting attorneys in design is a bad idea that complicates the protocol and could tie a design effort in knots. Entities communicating with a protocol have already agreed to that protocol specification. Verbiage to support legal action, if any, should appear in that specification, rather than cluttering up messages.

### E.2.2 Adjunct Meaning

Adjuncts are things that can be added or are logically addenda.

**PAPER:** From a paper point of view, at the top level we have the equivalent of a person looking at a document. As a consequence, adjunct items such as digital signatures, person's names, dates, and so on must be self-documenting as to semantics. Thus a digital signature needs to include, in human-readable form, what that signature means; for example, is the signer a witness, an author, a guarantor, or something else? Similarly, a person's name or a date needs to be accompanied, in human-readable form, by an identification of that person's role or the meaning of the date—for example, editor, author, or contributor or date of creation, modification, revocation, or distribution. Furthermore, given the unrestrained scope of what can be documented, during the design process, the programmer faces the risk of trying to enumerate and standardize all possible "semantic tags" for each type of adjunct data. This effort can be a difficult, complex, and essentially infinite task (a rat hole).

**PROTOCOL:** From a protocol point of view, the protocol specification defines the semantics of the message and every adjunct in it. Thus, if the protocol includes a slot for a digital signature, person's name, a date, or whatever, the party that is to enter that data, the party or parties that are to read it, and its meaning are all predefined. Even if several meanings are possible, a separate enumerated type field can specify which particular meaning applies. There is no reason for such a type field to be human-readable. Only the "meanings" directly relevant to the particular protocol need be considered.

Another way to look at this issue is that the "meaning" of each adjunct is promoted to the level of the protocol specification, resulting in simpler adjunct data. The paper-oriented point of view encourages pushing the "meaning" of each adjunct into, and coupling it with, the adjunct.

## E.3   Processing Models

The paper-oriented and protocol-oriented perspectives have very different views on what is likely to happen to an object.

### E.3.1   Amount of Processing

**PAPER:** The model involves a quasi-static object similar to a piece of paper. With pieces of paper, you simply transfer them as a whole, from one storage area to another, or add signatures, date stamps, or similar adjuncts. (Possibly, you might want an extract from a document or seek to combine multiple documents into a summary, but that isn't the common case.)

**PROTOCOL:** The standard model of a protocol message is as an ephemeral, composite, multilevel object that a source process creates and that a destination process consumes. The source process constructs such a message from information contained in previously received messages, information stored locally, local calculations, and so on. It is normal for complex processing to take place.

### E.3.2   Granularity of Processing

**PAPER:** The paper point of view generally focuses on uniform processing or evaluation of the entire object being specified. There may be an allowance for attachments; if so, they would probably take the form of simple, one-level, self-documenting attachments.

**PROTOCOL:** Processing is complex and almost always affects different pieces of the message differently. Some pieces may be intended for use only by the destination process and be extensively processed there. Others may be present so that the destination process can, at some point, do minimal processing and forward them in other messages to yet other processes. The object's structure can be computationally rich and have multilevel or recursive aspects.

Because messages are processed in context, you can have things like a single signature that covers the combination of some data in the message, some received in previous messages and stored, and some locally calculated data.

### E.3.3    Extensibility of Processing

**PAPER:** Individuals with a paper point of view rarely think of extensibility as a complex problem. They assume that their design, perhaps aided with a simple version scheme, will meet requirements. If they come from an SGML/DTD or similar world of closed private document preparation systems, they may assume that detailed knowledge of new versions or extensions can be easily and synchronously distributed to all participating sites.

**PROTOCOL:** Individuals with a protocol point of view assume that all protocols will need extension and that it will not be possible to update all implementations at the same time when deploying and/or retiring such extensions, if ever. This problem can prove difficult, but those taking the protocol perspective try to provide the tools needed, such as the following:

- Carefully defined versioning and extension/feature labeling

- The ability to negotiate version and features, where practical, and at least a specification of how parties running different levels or features should interact

- Providing length/delimiting information for all data so that the data can at least be skipped if not understood

- Destination labeling so that a process can tell when it should ignore data except for passing it through to a later player

## E.4    Security and Canonicalization

Security is a subtle area. Some problems can be solved in a general way, and those solutions are typically incorporated into standard security syntaxes such as those for ASN.1 [RFC 2630] and XML [XMLDSIG, XMLENC]. With application-specific questions, and particularly questions of exactly what information you need to authenticate or encrypt, more complex solutions are needed.

Questions of exactly what needs to be secured and how to do so robustly are deeply entwined with canonicalization. They are somewhat different for authentication and encryption.

## E.4.1    Canonicalization

Chapter 9 describes canonicalization as the transformation of the "significant" information in a message into a "standard" form, discarding "insignificant" information. For example, it might involve encoding into a standard character set or changing line endings into a standard encoding and discarding the information about the original character set or line ending encodings. Obviously, what is "standard" and what is "significant" vary with the application or protocol and can be tricky to determine. For a particular syntax, such as ASCII [ASCII], ASN.1 [ASN.1], or XML [XML], a standard canonicalization is often specified or developed through practice. This effort leads to the design of applications that assume such standard canonicalization and, in turn, reduces the need for customized, application-specific canonicalization.

**PAPER:** From the paper point of view, canonicalization is suspect, if not outright evil. After all, if you have a piece of paper with writing on it, you can view any modification to "standardize" its format as an unauthorized change in the original message as created by the "author." With this perspective, digital signatures are viewed as authenticating signatures or seals or time stamps on the bottom of the "piece of paper." They do not justify and should not depend on changes in the message appearing above them. Similarly, encryption is seen as just putting the "piece of paper" in a vault that only certain people can open, and does not justify any standardization or canonicalization of the message.

**PROTOCOL:** From the protocol point of view, a pattern of bits is calculated; processed, stored, and communicated; and finally parsed and acted on. Most of these bits have never been seen and never will be seen by a person. In fact, many of the parts of the message will be artifacts of encoding, protocol structure, and computer representation, rather than anything intended for a person to see. In theory, it might be possible to convey unchanged the "original" idiosyncratic form of any digitally signed part through the computer process, storage, and communications channels that implement the protocol and usefully signed in that form. In practical systems of any complexity, however, achieving this goal is unreasonably difficult for most parts of messages. Even if it were possible, the result would be virtually useless, as you would still have to repeatedly test the equivalence of the local message form with the preserved original form. Thus signed data must be canonicalized as part of signing and verification to compensate for insignificant changes made in processing, storage, and communication. Even if, miraculously, an initial system design avoids all cases of signed message reconstruction based on processed data or reencoding based on the character set, line ending, capitalization, numeric representation, time zones, or whatever, later protocol revisions and extensions are certain to eventually require such reconstruction and/or reencoding. As a consequence, canonicalization is clearly a necessity for protocol applications. It is just a question of which canonicalization or canonicalizations to use.

## E.4.2   Digital Authentication

**PAPER:** The paper-oriented view on authentication tends to focus on "digital signatures" and "forms." Because they are always worried about human third parties and viewing the document in isolation, individuals taking this perspective want the "digital signature" characteristics of "non-repudiability" and similar characteristics. (See any standard reference on the subject for the special meaning of these terms in this context.) According to this point of view, you have a piece of paper or form that a person signs. Sometimes a signature covers only part of a form, but that's usually because a signature can cover only data that are already there. Normally, at least one signature covers the "whole" document/form. Thus the goal is to insert digital signatures into documents without changing the document type and even "inside" the data being signed (which requires a mechanism to skip the signature so that it does not try to sign itself). This view was well represented in the standardization of XML digital signatures resulting in provisions for enveloped signatures and the enveloped signature transform algorithm.

**PROTOCOL:** From a protocol-oriented view, the right kind of authentication to use—whether a "digital signature" or symmetric keyed authentication code—is just another engineering decision affected by questions of efficiency, desired security model, and so on. Furthermore, the concept of signing a "whole" message seems bizarre (unless it is a copy being saved for archival purposes, in which case you might be signing an entire archive at once anyway). Typical messages consist of various pieces with various destinations, sources, and security requirements. Additionally, you can't sign certain fields because they change as the message is communicated and processed, such as hop counts, routing history, or local forwarding tags. One protocol message commonly contains a mix of different kinds of authentication.

### E.4.3    Canonicalization and Digital Authentication

For authenticating protocol system messages of practical complexity, you have three choices

1. Doing too little canonicalization and having brittle authentication, useless due to insignificant failures to verify

2. Doing the sometimes difficult and tricky work of selecting or designing an appropriate canonicalization or canonicalizations to be used as part of authentication generation

3. Doing too much canonicalization and having insecure authentication, which is useless because it still verifies even when the signed data change significantly

The only useful option is the second choice.

### E.4.4    Encryption

In terms of processing, transmission, and storage, encryption turns out to be much easier than signatures to implement. Why? The output of encryption is essentially arbitrary binary information, and it is clear from the very beginning that those bits need to be transferred to the destination in some absolutely clean way that does not change even one bit. Because the encrypted bits are, by definition, meaningless to humans, the paper-oriented person has no incentive to change them to make them more "readable." For this reason, appropriate techniques of encoding at the source, such as base-64 [RFC 2045], and decoding at the destination are always incorporated to protect or "armor" the encrypted data.

While the application of canonicalization is more obvious with digital signatures, it may also apply to encryption, particularly the encryption of parts of a message. Sometimes elements of the environment containing the plain text data affect its interpretation. Consider the effects of the character encoding or bindings of dummy symbols. When the data is decrypted, the decryption may take place in an environment with different character encoding and dummy symbol bindings. With a plain text message part, it is usually clear which of these environmental elements should be incorporated in or conveyed with the message. An encrypted message part, however, is opaque. Thus you may need some canonical representation that incorporates such environmental factors.

**PAPER:** From the paper perspective, you think about encryption of the entire document. Because signatures are always envisioned as human assent, people with this point of view vehemently assert that encrypted data should never be signed unless you know what the plain text means.

**PROTOCOL:** With the protocol perspective, messages are complex, composite, multilevel structures. Some pieces of them are forwarded multiple hops. Thus the design question becomes which fields should be encrypted by which techniques to which destinations and with which canonicalization scheme. It sometimes makes perfect sense to sign encrypted data you don't understand; for example, the signature could just be for integrity protection or a time stamp, as the protocol specifies.

## E.5    Unique Internal Labels

It is desirable to be able to reference parts of structured messages or objects by some sort of "label," "ID," or "tag." The idea is that this label forms a fixed "anchor" that can be used "globally," at least within an application domain, to reference the tagged part.

**PAPER:** From the paper point of view, it seems logical to just provide for a text tag, so that users or applications could easily come up with short, readable tags. These tags would probably be meaningful to a person if generated by humans (i.e., "Susan") and at least fairly short and systematic if generated automatically (i.e., "A123"). The ID attribute type in XML [XML] appears to have been thought of this way, although it can be used in other ways.

**PROTOCOL:** From a protocol point of view, unique internal labels look very different than they do from a paper point of view. You should assume that pieces of different protocol messages will later be combined in a variety of ways, so that previously unique labels can conflict. Only three possibilities exist if you need such tags:

1. Have a system for dynamically rewriting such tags to maintain uniqueness. This tactic is usually a disaster, for two reasons:

   a. It invalidates any stored copies of the tags that are not rewritten. It is usually impossible to ensure that more copies aren't lurking somewhere that you failed to update.

   b. It invalidates digital signatures that cover a changed tag.

2. Use some form of hierarchical qualified tags. With this approach the total tag can remain unique even if a part is moved, because its qualification changes. This strategy avoids the digital signature problems of the first approach, but it damages the concept of a globally unique anchor embedded in and moving with the data. Also, stored tags may still be invalidated by data moves. Nevertheless, within a particular carefully designed protocol, such as IOTP [RFC 2801], this tactic can work.

3. Construct a lengthy, globally unique tag string. This can be done successfully in one of two ways:

   a. By using a good-enough random number generator and big-enough random tags

   b. More sequentially, similar to the way e-mail message IDs are created [RFC 2822]

From a protocol point of view, such tags are difficult. If you really need them, however, the third choice works best.

## E.6   Examples

IETF protocols are replete with examples of the protocol viewpoint, such as TCP [RFC 793], IPSEC [RFC 2411], SMTP [RFC 2821], and IOTP [RFC 2801, 2802].

The Extensible Markup Language [XML] provides an example of something that can be viewed both ways and where the best results frequently result from paying attention to both the paper and protocol points of view.

Computerized court documents, human to human email, and the policy portions of the X.509v3 Certificate [ISO 9594] standard are examples designed, to a significant extent, from the paper point of view.

## E.7    Resolution of the Points of View

Each point of view has its own merits. Certainly the paper point of view has intuitive simplicity and is acceptable for applications where it meets the needs.

The protocol point of view can come close to encompassing the paper point of view as a limiting case. In particular, it does so in the following circumstances:

- As the complexity of messages declines to a single payload (perhaps with a few attachments)

- As the mutability of the payload declines to some standard format that needs little or no canonicalization

- As the number of parties and amount of processing during message transfers declines

- As the portion of the message intended for more or less direct human consumption increases

In these cases, the protocol point of view would be narrowed to something close to the paper point of view. Even when the paper point of view is questionable, the extension of a protocol, such as adding optional lack of canonicalization and/or optional policy statement/pointer/semantic label inclusion, will usually satisfy the perceived needs of individuals holding a paper point of view.

On the other hand, the paper point of view is difficult to stretch to encompass the protocol case. From a strict paper perspective, canonicalization is wrong; inclusion of human-language policy text within every document and a semantic tag with every adjunct would be mandatory; and so on. Objects designed in this way are rarely suitable for protocol use, as they tend to be improperly structured to accommodate hierarchy and complexity, inefficient (due to unnecessary text and self-documenting inclusions), and insecure (due to brittle signatures).

Thus, to produce usable protocols, it is best to start with the protocol point of view and add such paper-perspective items as are necessary to gain acceptance.

# Appendix F | SOAP Encoding Schema

This appendix provides the schema for the encoding defined in the SOAP specification. It is long but quite repetitive as much of the typing is cloned from XML Schema [Schema].

```
<!-- Schema defined in the SOAP Version 1.2 Part 2 specification
     17 December 2001 Working Draft:
     http://www.w3.org/TR/2001/WD-soap12-part2-20011217/

  $Id: soap-encoding.xsd,v 1.1 2001/12/14 13:35:22 ylafon Exp $
     Copyright 2001 W3C (Massachusetts Institute of Technology,
     Institut National de Recherche en Informatique et en
     Automatique, Keio University). All Rights Reserved.
     http://www.w3.org/Consortium/Legal/

     This document is governed by the W3C Software License [1]
     as described in the FAQ [2].
[1]
 http://www.w3.org/Consortium/Legal/copyright-software-19980720
[2]
 http://www.w3.org/Consortium/Legal/IPR-FAQ-20000620.html#DTD
-->

<xs:schema
  xmlns:xs="http://www.w3.org/2001/XMLSchema"
  xmlns:tns="http://www.w3.org/2001/12/soap-encoding"
  targetNamespace="http://www.w3.org/2001/12/soap-encoding" >

<xs:attribute name="root" type="xs:boolean" default="0" >
  <xs:annotation>
    <xs:documentation>
```

```
'root' can be used to distinguish serialization roots from other
elements that are present in a serialization but are not roots
of a serialized value graph
      </xs:documentation>
   </xs:annotation>
</xs:attribute>


<xs:attributeGroup name="commonAttributes" >
   <xs:annotation>
     <xs:documentation>
Attributes common to all elements that function as accessors or
represent independent (multi-ref) values.  The href attribute is
intended to be used in a manner like CONREF.  That is, the
element content should be empty if the href attribute appears
      </xs:documentation>
   </xs:annotation>
   <xs:attribute name="id" type="xs:ID" />
   <xs:attribute name="href" type="xs:anyUR"" />
   <xs:anyAttribute namespace="##other" processContents="lax" />
</xs:attributeGroup>


<!-- Global Attributes.  The following attributes are intended
to be usable via qualified attribute names on any complex type
referencing them. -->
<!-- Array attributes. Needed to give the type and dimensions of
an array's contents, and the offset for partially-transmitted
arrays. -->
<xs:simpleType name="arrayCoordinate" >
   <xs:restriction base="xs:string" />
</xs:simpleType>
<xs:attribute name="arrayType" type="xs:string" />
<xs:attribute name="offset" type="tns:arrayCoordinate" />
<xs:attributeGroup name="arrayAttributes" >
   <xs:attribute ref="tns:arrayType" />
   <xs:attribute ref="tns:offset" />
</xs:attributeGroup>
<xs:attribute name="position" type="tns:arrayCoordinate" />
<xs:attributeGroup name="arrayMemberAttributes" >
  <xs:attribute ref="tns:position" />
```

```
</xs:attributeGroup>
<xs:group name="Array" >
  <xs:sequence>
    <xs:any namespace="##any" minOccurs="0"
                              maxOccurs="unbounded"
          processContents="lax" />
  </xs:sequence>
</xs:group>

<xs:element name="Array" type="tns:Array" />
<xs:complexType name="Array" >
  <xs:annotation>
    <xs:documentation>
'Array' is a complex type for accessors identified by position
    </xs:documentation>
  </xs:annotation>
  <xs:group ref="tns:Array" minOccurs="0" />
  <xs:attributeGroup ref="tns:arrayAttributes" />
  <xs:attributeGroup ref="tns:commonAttributes" />
</xs:complexType>

<!-- 'Struct' is a complex type for accessors identified by
     name.
Constraint: No element may be have the same name as any other,
nor may any element have a maxOccurs > 1. -->

<xs:element name="Struct" type="tns:Struct" />

<xs:group name="Struct" >
  <xs:sequence>
    <xs:any namespace="##any" minOccurs="0"
                              maxOccurs="unbounded"
          processContents="lax" />
  </xs:sequence>
</xs:group>

<xs:complexType name="Struct" >
  <xs:group ref="tns:Struct" minOccurs="0" />
  <xs:attributeGroup ref="tns:commonAttributes"/>
</xs:complexType>
```

```xml
<!-- 'Base64' can be used to serialize binary data using base64
encoding as defined in RFC2045 but without the MIME line length
limitation.
-->

<xs:simpleType name="base64" >
  <xs:restriction base="xs:base64Binary" />
</xs:simpleType>

<!-- Element declarations corresponding to each of the simple
types in the XML Schemas Specification. -->

<xs:element name="duration" type="tns:duration" />
<xs:complexType name="duration" >
  <xs:simpleContent>
    <xs:extension base="xs:duration" >
      <xs:attributeGroup ref="tns:commonAttributes" />
    </xs:extension>
  </xs:simpleContent>
</xs:complexType>

<xs:element name="dateTime" type="tns:dateTime" />
<xs:complexType name="dateTime" >
  <xs:simpleContent>
    <xs:extension base="xs:dateTime" >
      <xs:attributeGroup ref="tns:commonAttributes" />
    </xs:extension>
  </xs:simpleContent>
</xs:complexType>

<xs:element name="time" type="tns:time" />
<xs:complexType name="time" >
  <xs:simpleContent>
    <xs:extension base="xs:time" >
      <xs:attributeGroup ref="tns:commonAttributes" />
    </xs:extension>
  </xs:simpleContent>
</xs:complexType>
```

```xml
<xs:element name="date" type="tns:date" />
<xs:complexType name="date" >
  <xs:simpleContent>
    <xs:extension base="xs:date" >
      <xs:attributeGroup ref="tns:commonAttributes" />
    </xs:extension>
  </xs:simpleContent>
</xs:complexType>

<xs:element name="gYearMonth" type="tns:gYearMonth" />
<xs:complexType name="gYearMonth" >
  <xs:simpleContent>
    <xs:extension base="xs:gYearMonth" >
      <xs:attributeGroup ref="tns:commonAttributes" />
    </xs:extension>
  </xs:simpleContent>
</xs:complexType>

<xs:element name="gYear" type="tns:gYear" />
<xs:complexType name="gYear" >
  <xs:simpleContent>
    <xs:extension base="xs:gYear" >
      <xs:attributeGroup ref="tns:commonAttributes" />
    </xs:extension>
  </xs:simpleContent>
</xs:complexType>

<xs:element name="gMonthDay" type="tns:gMonthDay" />
<xs:complexType name="gMonthDay" >
  <xs:simpleContent>
    <xs:extension base="xs:gMonthDay" >
      <xs:attributeGroup ref="tns:commonAttributes" />
    </xs:extension>
  </xs:simpleContent>
</xs:complexType>

<xs:element name="gDay" type="tns:gDay" />
<xs:complexType name="gDay" >
  <xs:simpleContent>
```

```xml
      <xs:extension base="xs:gDay" >
        <xs:attributeGroup ref="tns:commonAttributes" />
      </xs:extension>
    </xs:simpleContent>
  </xs:complexType>

<xs:element name="gMonth" type="tns:gMonth" />
<xs:complexType name="gMonth" >
  <xs:simpleContent>
    <xs:extension base="xs:gMonth" >
      <xs:attributeGroup ref="tns:commonAttributes" />
    </xs:extension>
  </xs:simpleContent>
</xs:complexType>

<xs:element name="boolean" type="tns:boolean" />
<xs:complexType name="boolean" >
  <xs:simpleContent>
    <xs:extension base="xs:boolean" >
      <xs:attributeGroup ref="tns:commonAttributes" />
    </xs:extension>
  </xs:simpleContent>
</xs:complexType>

<xs:element name="base64Binary" type="tns:base64Binary" />
<xs:complexType name="base64Binary" >
  <xs:simpleContent>
    <xs:extension base="xs:base64Binary" >
      <xs:attributeGroup ref="tns:commonAttributes" />
    </xs:extension>
  </xs:simpleContent>
</xs:complexType>

<xs:element name="hexBinary" type="tns:hexBinary" />
<xs:complexType name="hexBinary" >
  <xs:simpleContent>
    <xs:extension base="xs:hexBinary" >
      <xs:attributeGroup ref="tns:commonAttributes" />
```

```
       </xs:extension>
     </xs:simpleContent>
  </xs:complexType>


  <xs:element name="float" type="tns:float" />
  <xs:complexType name="float" >
    <xs:simpleContent>
      <xs:extension base="xs:float" >
        <xs:attributeGroup ref="tns:commonAttributes" />
      </xs:extension>
    </xs:simpleContent>
  </xs:complexType>


  <xs:element name="double" type="tns:double" />
  <xs:complexType name="double" >
    <xs:simpleContent>
      <xs:extension base="xs:double" >
        <xs:attributeGroup ref="tns:commonAttributes" />
      </xs:extension>
    </xs:simpleContent>
  </xs:complexType>


  <xs:element name="anyURI" type="tns:anyURI" />
  <xs:complexType name="anyURI" >
    <xs:simpleContent>
      <xs:extension base="xs:anyURI" >
        <xs:attributeGroup ref="tns:commonAttributes" />
      </xs:extension>
    </xs:simpleContent>
  </xs:complexType>


  <xs:element name="QName" type="tns:QName" />
  <xs:complexType name="QName" >
    <xs:simpleContent>
      <xs:extension base="xs:QName" >
        <xs:attributeGroup ref="tns:commonAttributes" />
      </xs:extension>
    </xs:simpleContent>
  </xs:complexType>
```

```xml
<xs:attribute name="NOTATION" type="tns:NOTATION" />
<xs:complexType name="NOTATION" >
  <xs:simpleContent>
    <xs:extension base="xs:NOTATION" >
      <xs:attributeGroup ref="tns:commonAttributes" />
    </xs:extension>
  </xs:simpleContent>
</xs:complexType>

<xs:element name="string" type="tns:string" />
<xs:complexType name="string" >
  <xs:simpleContent>
    <xs:extension base="xs:string" >
      <xs:attributeGroup ref="tns:commonAttributes" />
    </xs:extension>
  </xs:simpleContent>
</xs:complexType>

<xs:element name="normalizedString"
            type="tns:normalizedString" />
<xs:complexType name="normalizedString" >
  <xs:simpleContent>
    <xs:extension base="xs:normalizedString" >
      <xs:attributeGroup ref="tns:commonAttributes" />
    </xs:extension>
  </xs:simpleContent>
</xs:complexType>

<xs:element name="token" type="tns:token" />
<xs:complexType name="token" >
  <xs:simpleContent>
    <xs:extension base="xs:token" >
      <xs:attributeGroup ref="tns:commonAttributes" />
    </xs:extension>
  </xs:simpleContent>
</xs:complexType>

<xs:element name="language" type="tns:language" />
<xs:complexType name="language" >
```

```
  <xs:simpleContent>
    <xs:extension base="xs:language" >
      <xs:attributeGroup ref="tns:commonAttributes" />
    </xs:extension>
  </xs:simpleContent>
</xs:complexType>

<xs:element name="Name" type="tns:Name" />
<xs:complexType name="Name" >
  <xs:simpleContent>
    <xs:extension base="xs:Name" >
      <xs:attributeGroup ref="tns:commonAttributes" />
    </xs:extension>
  </xs:simpleContent>
</xs:complexType>

<xs:element name="NMTOKEN" type="tns:NMTOKEN" />
<xs:complexType name="NMTOKEN" >
  <xs:simpleContent>
    <xs:extension base="xs:NMTOKEN" >
      <xs:attributeGroup ref="tns:commonAttributes" />
    </xs:extension>
  </xs:simpleContent>
</xs:complexType>

<xs:element name="NCName" type="tns:NCName" />
<xs:complexType name="NCName" >
  <xs:simpleContent>
    <xs:extension base="xs:NCName" >
      <xs:attributeGroup ref="tns:commonAttributes" />
    </xs:extension>
  </xs:simpleContent>
</xs:complexType>

<xs:element name="NMTOKENS" type="tns:NMTOKENS" />
<xs:complexType name="NMTOKENS" >
  <xs:simpleContent>
    <xs:extension base="xs:NMTOKENS" >
      <xs:attributeGroup ref="tns:commonAttributes" />
```

```
        </xs:extension>
      </xs:simpleContent>
  </xs:complexType>


  <xs:element name="ID" type="tns:ID" />
  <xs:complexType name="ID" >
    <xs:simpleContent>
      <xs:extension base="xs:ID" >
        <xs:attributeGroup ref="tns:commonAttributes" />
      </xs:extension>
    </xs:simpleContent>
  </xs:complexType>


  <xs:element name="IDREF" type="tns:IDREF" />
  <xs:complexType name="IDREF" >
    <xs:simpleContent>
      <xs:extension base="xs:IDREF" >
        <xs:attributeGroup ref="tns:commonAttributes" />
      </xs:extension>
    </xs:simpleContent>
  </xs:complexType>


  <xs:element name="ENTITY" type="tns:ENTITY" />
  <xs:complexType name="ENTITY" >
    <xs:simpleContent>
      <xs:extension base="xs:ENTITY" >
        <xs:attributeGroup ref="tns:commonAttributes" />
      </xs:extension>
    </xs:simpleContent>
  </xs:complexType>


  <xs:element name="IDREFS" type="tns:IDREFS" />
  <xs:complexType name="IDREFS" >
    <xs:simpleContent>
      <xs:extension base="xs:IDREFS" >
        <xs:attributeGroup ref="tns:commonAttributes" />
      </xs:extension>
    </xs:simpleContent>
  </xs:complexType>
```

```
<xs:element name="ENTITIES" type="tns:ENTITIES" />
<xs:complexType name="ENTITIES" >
  <xs:simpleContent>
    <xs:extension base="xs:ENTITIES" >
      <xs:attributeGroup ref="tns:commonAttributes" />
    </xs:extension>
  </xs:simpleContent>
</xs:complexType>

<xs:element name="decimal" type="tns:decimal" />
<xs:complexType name="decimal" >
  <xs:simpleContent>
    <xs:extension base="xs:decimal" >
      <xs:attributeGroup ref="tns:commonAttributes" />
    </xs:extension>
  </xs:simpleContent>
</xs:complexType>

<xs:element name="integer" type="tns:integer" />
<xs:complexType name="integer" >
  <xs:simpleContent>
    <xs:extension base="xs:integer" >
      <xs:attributeGroup ref="tns:commonAttributes" />
    </xs:extension>
  </xs:simpleContent>
</xs:complexType>

<xs:element name="nonPositiveInteger"
            type="tns:nonPositiveInteger" />
<xs:complexType name="nonPositiveInteger" >
  <xs:simpleContent>
    <xs:extension base="xs:nonPositiveInteger" >
      <xs:attributeGroup ref="tns:commonAttributes" />
    </xs:extension>
  </xs:simpleContent>
</xs:complexType>

<xs:element name="negativeInteger" type="tns:negativeInteger" />
<xs:complexType name="negativeInteger" >
```

```xml
      <xs:simpleContent>
        <xs:extension base="xs:negativeInteger" >
          <xs:attributeGroup ref="tns:commonAttributes" />
        </xs:extension>
      </xs:simpleContent>
  </xs:complexType>


<xs:element name="long" type="tns:long" />
<xs:complexType name="long" >
  <xs:simpleContent>
    <xs:extension base="xs:long" >
      <xs:attributeGroup ref="tns:commonAttributes" />
    </xs:extension>
  </xs:simpleContent>
</xs:complexType>


<xs:element name="int" type="tns:int" />
<xs:complexType name="int" >
  <xs:simpleContent>
    <xs:extension base="xs:int" >
      <xs:attributeGroup ref="tns:commonAttributes" />
    </xs:extension>
  </xs:simpleContent>
</xs:complexType>


<xs:element name="short" type="tns:short" />
<xs:complexType name="short" >
  <xs:simpleContent>
    <xs:extension base="xs:short" >
      <xs:attributeGroup ref="tns:commonAttributes" />
    </xs:extension>
  </xs:simpleContent>
</xs:complexType>


<xs:element name="byte" type="tns:byte" />
<xs:complexType name="byte" >
  <xs:simpleContent>
    <xs:extension base="xs:byte" >
      <xs:attributeGroup ref="tns:commonAttributes" />
```

```
      </xs:extension>
    </xs:simpleContent>
</xs:complexType>


<xs:element name="nonNegativeInteger"
            type="tns:nonNegativeInteger" />
<xs:complexType name="nonNegativeInteger" >
  <xs:simpleContent>
    <xs:extension base="xs:nonNegativeInteger" >
      <xs:attributeGroup ref="tns:commonAttributes" />
    </xs:extension>
  </xs:simpleContent>
</xs:complexType>


<xs:element name="unsignedLong" type="tns:unsignedLong" />
<xs:complexType name="unsignedLong" >
  <xs:simpleContent>
    <xs:extension base="xs:unsignedLong" >
      <xs:attributeGroup ref="tns:commonAttributes" />
    </xs:extension>
  </xs:simpleContent>
</xs:complexType>


<xs:element name="unsignedInt" type="tns:unsignedInt" />
<xs:complexType name="unsignedInt" >
  <xs:simpleContent>
    <xs:extension base="xs:unsignedInt" >
      <xs:attributeGroup ref="tns:commonAttributes" />
    </xs:extension>
  </xs:simpleContent>
</xs:complexType>


<xs:element name="unsignedShort" type="tns:unsignedShort" />
<xs:complexType name="unsignedShort" >
  <xs:simpleContent>
    <xs:extension base="xs:unsignedShort" >
      <xs:attributeGroup ref="tns:commonAttributes" />
    </xs:extension>
```

```
    </xs:simpleContent>
  </xs:complexType>

  <xs:element name="unsignedByte" type="tns:unsignedByte" />
  <xs:complexType name="unsignedByte" >
    <xs:simpleContent>
      <xs:extension base="xs:unsignedByte" >
        <xs:attributeGroup ref="tns:commonAttributes" />
      </xs:extension>
    </xs:simpleContent>
  </xs:complexType>

  <xs:element name="positiveInteger" type="tns:positiveInteger" />
  <xs:complexType name="positiveInteger" >
    <xs:simpleContent>
      <xs:extension base="xs:positiveInteger" >
        <xs:attributeGroup ref="tns:commonAttributes" />
      </xs:extension>
    </xs:simpleContent>
  </xs:complexType>
  <xs:element name="anyType" />
</xs:schema>
```

# References and Acronyms

This section provides a merged alphabetic listing of references and acronyms.

**Note**

> For W3C documents, the date and W3C status (Recommendation, Note, and so on) of the version mentioned in this book is listed but the URL given is sometimes that for the most recent version. As a result, the status and date may disagree if you go to that URL because you will see a more recent version. You can find the exact version referenced by looking back through previous versions, all of which should be available on the W3C Web site.

[3DES]—Triple DES. See [FIPS 46-3] and ANSI X9.52.

[AES]—Advanced Encryption Standard. See [FIPS 197].

[AES KMS]—AES Key Management. See <http://csrc.nist.gov/encryption/kms/> for pointers to AES key wrap specification.

[ASCII]— *USA Standard Code for Information Interchange*, X3.4. American National Standards Institute: New York, 1968.

[ASN.1]—Abstract Syntax Notation 1. See [ISO 8824].

[BEEP]—Blocks Extensible Exchange Protocol. See [RFC 3080].

[BER]—Basic Encoding Rules. See [ISO 8825-1].

[Bourret]— *XML Namespaces FAQ*, Ronald Bourret, <http://www.rpbourret.com/xml/NamespacesFAQ.thm#q1_1>, March 2001. *Namespace Myths Exploded*, Ronald Bourret, <http://www.xml.com/pub/a/2000/03/08/namespaces/index.html>, March 8, 2000.

[C14N-20000119]—Early draft: *Canonical XML Version 1.0*, W3C Working Draft, T. Bray, J. Clark, J. Tauber, and J. Cowan, <http://www.w3.org/TR/2000/WD-xml-c14n-20000119.html>, January 19, 2000.

[Canon]—*Canonical XML Version 1.0*, W3C Recommendation, John Boyer, <http://www.w3.org/TR/2001/REC-xml-c14n-20010315>, March 15, 2001.

[CMS]—Cryptographic Message Syntax. See [RFC 2630].

[CSS1]—*Cascading Style Sheets, Level 1*, W3C Recommendation, Håkon Wium Lie and Bert Bos, <http://www.w3.org/TR/REC-CSS1>, December 17, 1996, revised January 11, 1999.

[CSS2]—*Cascading Style Sheets, Level 2*, W3C Recommendation, Bert Bos et al., <http://www.w3.org/TR/REC-CSS2>, May 12, 1998.

[Davis]—*Defective Sign and Encrypt in S/MIME, PKCS#7, MOSS, PEM, PGP, and XML*, D. Davis, USENIX Annual Technical Conference, 2001.

[Decrypt]—*Decryption Transform for XML Signature*, W3C Working Draft, T. Imamura and H. Maruyama, <http://www.w3.org/TR/2001/WD-xmlenc-decrypt-20011018>, October 2001.

[DER]—Distinguished Encoding Rules. See [ISO 8825-1].

[Directive]—*Directive 1999/93/EC of the European Parliament and of the Council of 13 December 1999 on a Community Framework for Electronic Signatures*, <http://europa.eu.int/eur-lex/en/lif/dat/1999/en_399L0093.html>.

[DOM]—*Document Object Model (DOM) Level 1 Specification*, W3C Recommendation, <http://www.w3.org/TR/1998/REC-DOM-Level1-19981001/>, October 1998.

[ETSI]—European Telecommunications Standards Institute, <http://www.etsi.org>.

[Exclusive]—*Exclusive XML Canonicalization Version 1.0*, W3C Working Draft, D. Eastlake and J. Reagle, <http://www.w3.org/TR/2001/WD-xmlenc-core-20011018/>, October 18, 2001. See also latest version linked off [XMLENC WG].

[FIPS]—Federal Information Processing Standard. See Appendix D.

[FIPS 46-3]—*Data Encryption Standard (DES)*, U.S. Federal Information Processing Standard, <http://csrc.ncsl.nist.gov/publications/fips/fips46-3/fips46-3.pdf>, October 25, 1999.

[FIPS 81]—*DES Modes of Operation*, U.S. Federal Information Processing Standard, <http://www.itl.nist.gov/fipspubs/fip81.htm>, December 2, 1980.

[FIPS 180-1]—*Secure Hash Standard* (SHA-1), U.S. Federal Information Processing Standard, <http://csrc.ncsl.nist.gov/cryptval/shs.html>, April 17, 1995.

[FIPS 180-2]—*Secure Hash Standard*, Draft (SHA-256/384/512), U.S. Federal Information Processing Standard, not yet issued. See Appendix D.

[FIPS 186-2]—*Digital Signature Standard (DSS)*, U.S. Federal Information Processing Standard, <http://csrc.ncsl.nist.gov/publications/fips/fips186-2/fips186-2-change1.pdf>, January 27, 2000.

[FIPS 197]—*Specification of the Advanced Encryption Standard (AES)*, U.S. Federal Information Processing Standard, <http://csrc.nist.gov/publications/fips/fips197/fips-197.pdf>, November 26, 2001.

[Foo]—See [RFC 3092].

[Georgia]—*Web Currents, A Publication of the Administrative Office of the Georgia Courts*, vol. 1, no. 2, <http://www.georgiacourts.org/aoc/publications/WC_April_2000.pdf>, April 2000.

[GPO] —U.S. Government Printing Office; see <http://www.gpo.gov/>.

[Harold]—*XML Bible*, Elliotte R. Harold, Hungry Minds, Inc., 1999, ISBN: 0764532367.

[HTML]—*HTML 4.0 Specification*, W3C Recommendation, D. Raggett, <http://www.w3.org/TR/html401>, December 24, 1999.

[HTTP]—Hypertext Transfer Protocol. See [RFC 2616].

[IANA-LANGCODES]—*Registry of Language Tags*, Internet Assigned Numbers Authority, <http://www.iana.org/in-notes/iana/assignments/languages/>.

[IEEE 754]—*IEEE Standard for Binary Floating-Point Arithmetic*, Institute of Electrical and Electronics Engineers, ANSI/IEEE 754-1985.

[IETF]—Internet Engineering Task Force, <http://www.ietf.org>. See Appendix B.

[Infoset]—*XML Information Set,* W3C Proposed Recommendation, J. Cowan, <http://www.w3.org/TR/2001/PR-xml-20010810>, August 2001.

[IOTP]—Internet Open Trading Protocol. See [RFC 2801, 2802, 2803].

[IPSEC]—Internet Protocol Security. See [RFC 2411].

[ISO]—International Standards Organization, Geneva, Switzerland, <http://www.iso.ch>.

[ISO 639]—ISO 639:1988, *Code for the Representation of Names of Languages,* International Organization for Standardization, 1988.

[ISO 3166]—ISO 3166-1:1997, *Codes for the Representation of Names of Countries and Their Subdivisions—Part 1: Country Codes,* International Organization for Standardization, 1997.

[ISO 8824]—ITU-T Recommendation X.680 (1997) | ISO/IEC 8824-1: 1998, *Information Technology—Abstract Syntax Notation One (ASN.1): Specification of Basic Notation,* ITU-T Recommendation X.681 (1997) | ISO/IEC 8824-2:1998, *Information Technology—Abstract Syntax Notation One (ASN.1): Information Object Specification,* ITU-T Recommendation X.682 (1997) | ISO/IEC 8824-3:1998, *Information Technology—Abstract Syntax Notation One (ASN.1): Constraint Specification,* ITU-T Recommendation X.683 (1997) | ISO/IEC 8824-4:1998, *Information Technology—Abstract Syntax Notation One (ASN.1): Parameterization of ASN.1 Specifications,*<http://www.itu.int/ITU-T/studygroups/com17/languages/index.html>.

[ISO 8825-1]—ITU-T Recommendation X.690 (1997) | ISO/IEC 8825-1: 1998, *Information Technology—ASN.1 Encoding Rules: Specification of Basic Encoding Rules (BER), Canonical Encoding Rules (CER) and Distinguished Encoding Rules (DER),* <http://www.itu.int/ITU-T/studygroups/com17/languages/index.html>.

[ISO 8879]—ISO 8879:1986(E), *Standard Generalized Markup Language,* International Organization for Standardization, 1986.

[ISO 9594]—*Information Technology—Open Systems Interconnection— The Directory Authentication Framework,* ITU-T Recommendation X.509 version 3 (1997), ISO/IEC 9594-8:1997.

[ISO 10118]—ISO/IEC 10118 3:1998, *Information Technology—Security Techniques—Hash-Functions—Part 3: Dedicated Hash-Functions,* International Organization for Standardization, 1998.

[ISO 10179]—ISO/IEC 10179:1996, *Document Style Semantics and Specification Language (DSSSL),* International Standard, International Organization for Standardization, International Electrotechnical Commission.

[ISO 10646]—ISO/IEC 10646-1:2000, *Information Technology—Universal Multiple-Octet Coded Character Set (UCS)—Part 1: Architecture and Basic Multilingual Plane,* International Organization for Standardization, 2000.

[ISOC]—The Internet Society, <http://www.isoc.org>.

[ITU]—International Telecommunications Union, <http://www.itu.int>.

[JIS]—Personal conversation, Jeff Schiller.

[Kerberos]—See [RFC 1510].

[Krawczyk ]—*The Order of Encryption and Authentication for Protecting Communications (Or: How Secure Is SSL?),* Hugo Krawczyk Crypto, 2001.

[MAC]—Message Authentication Code. See Chapter 2.

[MPLS]—Multi-Protocol Label Switching. See [RFC 3031].

[Microsoft]—Microsoft Corporation, <http://www.microsoft.com>.

[Names]—*Namespaces in XML W3C Recommendation,* W3C Recommendation, <http://www.w3.org/TR/1999/REC-xml-names-19990114>, T. Bray, D. Hollander, and A. Layman, January 1999.

[Netscape]—Netscape, Inc., <http://www.netscape.com>.

[NetSec]—*Network Security: Private Communications in a Public World,* Charlie Kaufman, Radia Perlman, and Mike Speciner, Prentice-Hall Series in Computer Networking and Distributed Communications, 1995.

[New Mexico]—XCI (XML Court Interface) HOME PAGE, <http://www.nmcourt.fed.us/xci/xcihome.htm>, July 2000.

[NFC]—Normalized Form C. *Unicode Normalization Forms,* TR15, Revision 18, M. Davis and M. Dürst, <http://www.unicode.org/unicode/reports/tr15/tr15-18.html >, November 1999. *Normalization Corrigendum,* The

Unicode Consortium, <http://www.unicode.org/unicode/uni2errata/Normalization_Corrigendum.htm>.

[NIST]—National Institute of Science and Technology, <http://www.nist.gov>.

[OAEP]—Optimal Asymmetric Encryption Padding. See [RFC 2437].

[OASIS]—Organization for the Advancement of Structured Information Standards, <http://www.oasis-open.org>. See also OASIS's security committee, <http://www.oasis-open.org/committees/security/index.shtml>.

[OCSP]—Online Certificate Status Protocol. See [RFC 2560].

[Opera]—Opera Software ASA, <http://www.opera.com>.

[Orman]—Work in progress, including comparisons of strength of public and symmetric keys, Hilarie Orman and Paul Hoffman, 2001.

[P3P]—*The Platform for Privacy Preferences 1.0 (P3P1.0) Specification,* W3C Working Draft, <http://www.w3.org/TR/P3P/>, September 28, 2001.

[P3P-Sec]—*A P3P Assurance Signature Profile,* W3C Note, J. Reagle, <http://www.w3.org/TR/2001/NOTE-xmldsig-p3p-profile-20010202/>, February 2, 2001.

[PKCS#1]—Public Key Cryptographic Standard #1. See [RFC 2437].

[RFC]—Request for Comments. See Appendix B.

[RFC Editor]—See <http://www.rfc-editor.org/>.

[RFC 791]—*Internet Protocol,* J. Postel, <ftp://ftp.rfc-editor.org/in-notes/rfc791.txt>, September 1, 1981.

[RFC 793]—Transmission Control Protocol, J. Postel, <ftp://ftp.rfc-editor.org/in-notes/rfc793.txt>, September 1, 1981.

[RFC 1034]—*Domain Names—Concepts and Facilities,* P. Mockapetris, <ftp://ftp.rfc-editor.org/in-notes/rfc1034.txt>, November 1, 1987.

[RFC 1035]—*Domain Names—Implementation and Specification,* P. Mockapetris, <ftp://ftp.rfc-editor.org/in-notes/rfc1035.txt>, November 1, 1987.

[RFC 1321]—*The MD5 Message-Digest Algorithm*, R. Rivest, <ftp://ftp.rfc-editor.org/in-notes/rfc1321.txt>, April 1992.

[RFC 1510]—*The Kerberos Network Authentication Service (V5)*, J. Kohl and C. Neuman, <ftp://ftp.rfc-editor.org/in-notes/rfc1510.txt>, September 1993.

[RFC 1738]—*Uniform Resource Locators (URL)*, T. Berners-Lee, L. Masinter, and R. McCahill, <ftp://ftp.rfc-editor.org/in-notes/rfc1738.txt>, December 1994; see also [RFC 2396].

[RFC 1750]—*Randomness Recommendations for Security*, D. Eastlake 3rd, S. Crocker, and J. Schiller, <ftp://ftp.rfc-editor.org/in-notes/rfc1750.txt>, December 1994.

[RFC 1766]—*Tags for the Identification of Languages*, H. Alvestrand, <ftp://ftp.rfc-editor.org/in-notes/rfc1766.txt>, 1995.

[RFC 2045]—*Multipurpose Internet Mail Extensions (MIME) Part One: Format of Internet Message Bodies*, N. Freed and N. Borenstein, <ftp://ftp.rfc-editor.org/in-notes/rfc2045.txt>, November 1996.

[RFC 2104]—*HMAC: Keyed-Hashing for Message Authentication*, H. Krawczyk, M. Bellare, and R. Canetti, <ftp://ftp.rfc-editor.org/in-notes/rfc2104.txt>, February 1997.

[RFC 2141]—*URN Syntax*, R. Moats, <ftp://ftp.rfc-editor.org/in-notes/rfc2141.txt>, May 1997.

[RFC 2246]—*The TLS Protocol Version 1.0*, T. Dierks and C. Allen, <ftp://ftp.rfc-editor.org/in-notes/rfc2246.txt>, January 1999.

[RFC 2253]—*Lightweight Directory Access Protocol (v3): UTF-8 String Representation of Distinguished Names*, M. Wahl, S. Kille, and T. Howes, <ftp://ftp.rfc-editor.org/in-notes/rfc2253.txt>, December 1997.

[RFC 2279]—*UTF-8, a Transformation Format of ISO 10646*, F. Yergeau, <ftp://ftp.rfc-editor.org/in-notes/rfc2279.txt>, January 1998.

[RFC 2315]—*PKCS 7: Cryptographic Message Syntax Version 1.5*, B. Kaliski, <ftp://ftp.rfc-editor.org/in-notes/rfc2315.txt>, March 1998.

[RFC 2368]—*The Mailto URL Scheme*, P. Hoffman, L. Masinter, and J. Zawinski, <ftp://ftp.rfc-editor.org/in-notes/rfc2368.txt>, July 1998.

[RFC 2376]—*XML Media Types,* E. Whitehead and M. Murata, <ftp://ftp.rfc-editor.org/in-notes/rfc2376.txt>, July 1998.

[RFC 2396]—*Uniform Resource Identifiers (URI): Generic Syntax,* T. Berners-Lee, R. Fielding, and L. Masinter, <ftp://ftp.rfc-editor.org/in-notes/rfc2396.txt>, August 1998.

[RFC 2401]—*Security Architecture for the Internet Protocol,* S. Kent and R. Atkinson, <ftp://ftp.rfc-editor.org/in-notes/rfc2401.txt>, November 1998.

[RFC 2411]—*IP Security Document Roadmap,* R. Thayer, N. Doraswamy, and R. Glenn, <ftp://ftp.rfc-editor.org/in-notes/rfc2411.txt>, November 1998.

[RFC 2437]—*PKCS #1: RSA Cryptography Specifications Version 2.0,* B. Kaliski and J. Staddon, <ftp://ftp.rfc-editor.org/in-notes/rfc2437.txt>, October 1998.

[RFC 2440]—*OpenPGP Message Format,* J. Callas, L. Donnerhacke, H. Finney, and R. Thayer, <ftp://ftp.rfc-editor.org/in-notes/rfc2440.txt>, November 1998.

[RFC 2459]—*Internet X.509 Public Key Infrastructure Certificate and CRL Profile,* R. Housley, W. Ford, W. Polk, and D. Solo, <ftp://ftp.rfc-editor.org/in-notes/rfc2459.txt>, January 1999.

[RFC 2460]—*Internet Protocol, Version 6 (IPv6) Specification,* S. Deering and R. Hinden, <ftp://ftp.rfc-editor.org/in-notes/rfc2460.txt>, December 1998.

[RFC 2560]—*X.509 Internet Public Key Infrastructure Online Certificate Status Protocol—OCSP,* M. Myers, R. Ankney, A. Malpani, S. Galperin, and C. Adams, <ftp://ftp.rfc-editor.org/in-notes/rfc2560.txt>, June 1999.

[RFC 2616]—*Hypertext Transfer Protocol—HTTP/1.1,* R. Fielding, J. Gettys, J. Mougul, H. Frystyk, and T. Berners-Lee, <ftp://ftp.rfc-editor.org/in-notes/rfc2616.txt>, January 1997.

[RFC 2630]—*Cryptographic Message Syntax,* R. Housley, <ftp://ftp.rfc-editor.org/in-notes/rfc2630.txt>, June 1999.

[RFC 2631]—*Diffie-Hellman Key Agreement Method,* E. Rescorla, <ftp://ftp.rfc-editor.org/in-notes/rfc2631.txt>, June 1999.

[RFC 2633] *S/MIME Version 3 Message Specification*, B. Ramsdell, ed., <ftp://ftp.rfc-editor.org/in-notes/rfc2633.txt>, June 1999.

[RFC 2693]—*SPKI Certificate Theory*, C. Ellison, B. Frantz, B. Lampson, R. Rivest, B. Thomas, and T. Ylonen, <ftp://ftp.rfc-editor.org/in-notes/rfc2693.txt>, September 1999.

[RFC 2732]—*Format for Literal IPv6 Addresses in URL's*, R. Hinden, B. Carpenter, and L. Masinter, <ftp://ftp.rfc-editor.org/in-notes/rfc2732.txt>, December 1999.

[RFC 2781]—*UTF-16, an Encoding of ISO 10646*, P. Hoffman and F. Yergeau, <ftp://ftp.rfc-editor.org/in-notes/rfc2781.txt>, February 2000.

[RFC 2801]—*Internet Open Trading Protocol—IOTP Version 1.0*, D. Burdett, <ftp://ftp.rfc-editor.org/in-notes/rfc2801.txt>, April 2000.

**History**

RFC 2801 is the largest RFC issued by the IETF to date. (Its size is partly related to the writing style used, which leans toward completeness.)

[RFC 2802]—*Digital Signatures for the v1.0 Internet Open Trading Protocol (IOTP)*, K. Davidson and Y. Kawatsura, <ftp://ftp.rfc-editor.org/in-notes/rfc2802.txt>, April 2000.

[RFC 2803]—*Digest Values for DOM (DOMHASH)*, H. Maruyama, K. Tamura, and N. Uramoto, <ftp://ftp.rfc-editor.org/in-notes/rfc2803.txt>, April 2000.

[RFC 2821]—*Simple Mail Transfer Protocol*, J. Klensin, <ftp://ftp.rfc-editor.org/in-notes/rfc2821.txt>, April 2001.

[RFC 2822]—*Internet Message Format*, P. Resnick, <ftp://ftp.rfc-editor.org/in-notes/rfc2822.txt>, April 2001.

[RFC 3031]—*Multiprotocol Label Switching Architecture*, E. Rosen, A. Viswanathan, and R. Callon, <ftp://ftp.rfc-editor.org/in-notes/rfc3031.txt>, January 2001.

[RFC 3075]—See [XMLDSIG], <ftp://ftp.rfc-editor.org/in-notes/rfc3075.txt>.

[RFC 3076]—See [Canon], <ftp://ftp.rfc-editor.org/in-notes/rfc3076.txt>.

[RFC 3080]—*The Blocks Extensible Exchange Protocol Core,* M. Rose, <ftp://ftp.rfc-editor.org/in-notes/rfc3080.txt>, March 2001.

[RFC 3092]—*Etymology of "Foo,"* D. Eastlake 3rd, C. Manros, and E. Raymond, <ftp://ftp.rfc-editor.org/in-notes/rfc3092.txt>, April 1, 2001.

[RIPEMD-160]—See [ISO 10118]. Also <ftp://ftp.rsasecurity.com/pub/cryptobytes/crypto3n2.pdf> or <http://www.esat.kuleuven.ac.be/~cosicart/pdf/AB-9601/AB-9601.pdf>.

[RSA]—Rivest-Shamir-Adelman. See "A Method for Obtaining Digital Signatures and Public-Key Cryptosystems," R. Rivest, A. Shamir, and L. Adleman, *Communications of the ACM,* 21(2):120–126, February 1978.

[Schema]—*XML Schema Part 0: Primer,* W3C Recommendation, D. Fallside, <http://www.w3.org/TR/2001/REC-xmlschema-0-20010502/>, May 2001. *XML Schema Part 1: Structures,* W3C Recommendation, D. Beech, M. Maloney, and N. Mendelsohn, <http://www.w3.org/TR/2001/REC-xmlschema-1-20010502/>, May 2001. *XML Schema Part 2: Datatypes,* W3C Recommendation, P. Biron and A. Malhotra, <http://www.w3.org/TR/2001/REC-xmlschema-2-20010502/>, May 2001.

[Schneier]—*Applied Cryptography, Second Edition: Protocols, Algorithms, and Source Code in C,* Bruce Schneier, John Wiley and Sons, 1996, ISBN: 0-471-11709-9.

[SGML]—Standard General Markup Language. See [ISO 8879].

[SHA-1]—Secure Hash Algorithm 1. See [FIPS 180-1].

[SMTP]—Simple Mail Transport Protocol. See [RFC 2821, 2822].

[SOAP]—Simple Object Access Protocol. See Chapter 7 and *SOAP Version 1.2 Part 0: Primer,* W3C Working Draft, <http://www.w3.org/TR/soap12-part0/>, December 17, 2001. *SOAP Version 1.2 Part 1: Messaging Framework,* W3C Working Draft, <http://www.w3.org/TR/soap12-part1/>, December 17, 2001. *SOAP Version 1.2 Part 2: Adjuncts,* W3C Working Draft, <http://www.w3.org/TR/soap12-part2/>, December 17, 2001.

[SOAP-Sec]—*SOAP Security Extensions: Digital Signature,* W3C Note, J. Reagle, <http://www.w3.org/TR/2001/NOTE-SOAP-dsig-20010206/>, 6 February 2001.

[TLS]—Transport Layer Security. See [RFC 2246].

[Unicode]—*The Unicode Standard, Version 3.0,* The Unicode Consortium, Addison-Wesley Developers Press, Reading, MA, 2000, ISBN 0-201-61633-5.

[URI]—Uniform Resource Identifier. See Chapter 6.

[VTrust]—The Verisign XML trust site, <www.xmltrustcenter.org>.

[VXML]—*Voice Extensible Markup Language (VoiceXML) Version 2.0,* W3C Working Draft, S. McGlashan et al., <http://www.w3.org/TR/voicexml20>, October 23, 2001.

[W3C]—World Wide Web Consortium, <http://www.w3.org>.

[X509v3]—See [ISO 9594].

[XAdES]—*XML Advanced Electronic Signatures (XAdES),* European Telecommunications Standards Institute, ETSI TS 101 903 draft V1.1.1 (2000-02), February 2002.

[XBase]—*XML Base,* W3C Recommendation, J. Marsh, June 27, 2001.

[XHTML]—*XHTML Basic,* W3C Recommendation, M. Baker, M. Ishikawa, S. Matsui, P. Stark, T. Wugofski, and T. Yamakami, <http://www.w3.org/TR/xhtml-basic>, December 19, 2000.

[XInclude]—*XML Inclusions (XInclude) Version 1.0,* W3C Working Draft, Jonathan Marsh and David Orchard, <http://www.w3.org/TR/xinclude/>, May 16, 2001.

[XKMS]—*XML Key Management Specification (XKMS),* W3C Note, Warwick Ford, Phillip Hallam-Baker, Barbara Fox, Blair Dillaway, Brian LaMacchia, Jeremy Epstein, and Joe Lapp, <http://www.w3.org/TR/xkms/>, March 30, 2001. See Chapter 14.

[XKMS 2]— *XML Key Management Specification (XKMS 2.0),* W3C Working Draft, Phillip Hallam-Baker, <http://www.w3.org/TR/2002/WD-xkms2-20020318/>, March 18, 2002.

[XKMS WG]—XKMS Working Group. See [XKMS] and <http://www.w3.org/2001/XKMS/>.

[XLink]—*XML Linking Language (XLink) Version 1.0,* W3C Recommendation, Steve DeRose, Eve Maler, and David Orchard, <http://www.w3.org/TR/xlink/#intro>, June 27, 2001.

[XML]—*Extensible Markup Language (XML) 1.0 (Second Edition)*, W3C Recommendation, T. Bray, J. Paoli, C. M. Sperberg-McQueen, and E. Maler, <http://www.w3.org/TR/REC-xml>, February 1998.

[XML A]—*Extensible Markup Language (XML) 1.0 Annotated Version*, <http://www.xml.com/axml/testaxml.htm>, February 10, 1998.

[XMLDSIG]—*XML—Signature Syntax and Processing*, W3C Proposed Recommendation, D. Eastlake, J. Reagle, and D. Solo, <http://www.w3.org/TR/2001/PR-xmldsig-core-20010820/>, August 2001. See Chapter 10.

[XMLDSIG WG]—XML Digital Signature Working Group. See [XMLDSIG] and <http://www.w3.org/Signature/>.

[XMLENC]—*XML Encryption Syntax and Processing*, W3C Working Draft, <http://www.w3.org/TR/2001/WD-xmlenc-core-20011018/>, October 2001. See Chapter 15.

[XMLENC WG]—XML Encryption Working Group. See [XMLENC] and <http://www.w3.org/Encrytion/2001/>.

[XPath]—*XML Path Language (XPath) Version 1.0*, W3C Recommendation, J. Clark and S. DeRose, <http://www.w3.org/TR/1999/REC-xpath-19991116>, October 1999.

[XPointer]—*XML Pointer Language (XPointer) Version 1.0*, W3C Working Draft, Steve DeRose, Eve Maler, and Ron Daniel Jr., <http://www.w3.org/TR/2001/WD-xptr-20010108>, January 8, 2001.

[XSL]—*Extensible Stylesheet Language (XSL) Version 1.0*, W3C Candidate Recommendation, Sharon Adler et al., <http://www.w3.org/TR/xsl/>, August 28, 2001.

[XSLT]—*XSL Transforms (XSLT) Version 1.0*, W3C Recommendation, J. Clark, <http://www.w3.org/TR/1999/REC-xslt-19991116.html>, November 1999.

# Index

# Also Available from Addison-Wesley

0-201-74852-5

0-201-73063-4

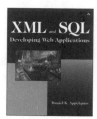

0-201-65796-1

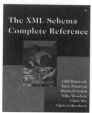

0-672-32374-5

0-201-70914-7

0-201-67487-4

0-201-77059-8

0-201-70915-5

0-201-77641-3

0-201-77006-7

0-201-75605-6

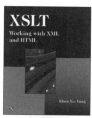

0-201-71103-6

0-201-72920-2

0-672-32354-0

0-201-77004-0

0-201-75081-3

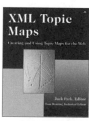

0-201-74960-2

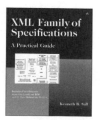

0-201-70359-9

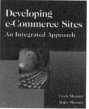

0-201-65764-3

0-201-74095-8

0-201-70344-0

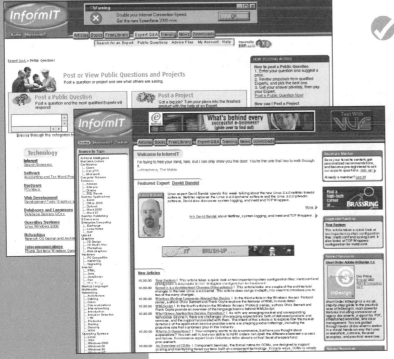

# Register
## Your Book

at www.awprofessional.com/register

You may be eligible to receive:

- Advance notice of forthcoming editions of the book
- Related book recommendations
- Chapter excerpts and supplements of forthcoming titles
- Information about special contests and promotions throughout the year
- Notices and reminders about author appearances, tradeshows, and online chats with special guests

## Contact us

If you are interested in writing a book or reviewing manuscripts prior to publication, please write to us at:

Editorial Department
Addison-Wesley Professional
75 Arlington Street, Suite 300
Boston, MA 02116 USA
Email: AWPro@aw.com

Visit us on the Web: http://www.awprofessional.com